WRIGLEY FIELD

WRIGLEY FIELD

The Unauthorized Biography

STUART SHEA

with
George Castle

Potomac Books, Inc.
Washington, D.C.

First paperback edition published 2006

Copyright © 2004 by Potomac Books, Inc.

Library of Congress Cataloging-in-Publication Data

Shea, Stuart.
Wrigley Field : the unauthorized biography / Stuart Shea.—1st ed.
p.   cm.
Includes bibliographical references and index.
ISBN 1-57488-586-3 (alk. paper)
1. Wrigley Field (Chicago, Ill.)—History.   2. Chicago Cubs (Baseball team)—History.
I. Castle, George.   II. Title.
GV416.C372S54   2004
796.357'06'877311—dc22   2004007043

ISBN 1-57488-941-9 (paperback)

Printed in Canada on acid-free paper that meets the American National Standards Institute Z39-48 Standard.

Potomac Books, Inc.
22841 Quicksilver Drive
Dulles, Virginia 20166

First Edition

10   9   8   7   6   5   4   3   2   1

This book is for all baseball fans.

Contents

Acknowledgments

Chris Kahrl of Brassey's, Inc., is responsible for this book. Her simple faith that I could write it was a bigger inspiration than she knows. I'm proud to call her a friend as well as a colleague. Don McKeon is a terrific publisher, and I thank him for his trust and friendship. Julie Kimmel provided yeoman production work.

George Castle wrote the chapter on non-baseball events at Wrigley and provided several photographs. In addition, he conducted interviews and lent me articles from his collection that helped improve my understanding of Lake View and the fans in the right-field bleachers during the 1970s.

My friend Chris Bluhm of Blue Vine Photography took the cover and title page photos.

Raymond D. Kush wrote, in the mid-1970s, the first serious work about the construction of Wrigley Field. Published in the 1981 SABR *Baseball Research Journal*, his piece has formed a basis for much ensuing Wrigley Field research. Meeting Ray and sharing in his knowledge has been a pleasure, and he selflessly provided notes, edits, photographs, and reminiscences to make this book much better than it would have been.

When I was about 60 percent through this project, unofficial (but indispensable) Cubs historian Ed Hartig lent me his well-researched Wrigley Field chronology. This information helped me to verify dates and pointed me in some new directions. Ed also gave me feedback that allowed me to present a more accurate work.

I am lucky to have good friends. Gary Gillette, a treasured working colleague, is always more than generous with his time and his feedback, to say nothing of his constant friendship. For his great qualities, his endless wisdom about baseball, and the pizzas he and Vicki Gillette make, I will be forever grateful. Thanks, guys.

Pete Palmer and Greg Spira helped in major ways. I am proud to call them friends, and I thank them for their counsel. Cecilia Garibay, Tom Shea, John Shea II, Mark Caro, and Frank Kras, irreplaceable every one, contributed valuable feedback, and Dave Smith and David Vincent deserve kudos.

Society for American Baseball Research members Reed Howard, Bob McConnell, and Stew Thornley shared information and research. If you love baseball, you might want to become part of this organization—if you aren't already.

Thanks also to Sharon Pannozzo, Chuck Wasserstrom, and Samantha Newby of the Chicago Cubs' media relations department for their ongoing kindness and professional courtesy.

The staff of the Chicago Public Library was helpful. Gloria Price made the archives of the Lake View Historical Society available to me. I also benefited from the resources of the St. Louis Public Library, the Library of Congress in Washington, D.C., the Loyola University Library, the St. Paul Public Library, and the *Sporting News* Research Center in St. Louis (special thanks to Steve Gietschier and Jim Maier).

Karen Chasteen of the Richmond County School District in Richmond, Indiana, contributed information about Charles Weeghman. Denise Young of the William Wrigley Company deserves thanks for sharing articles from the company's files.

Thanks also to George Castle's interviewees: the late Martin "Red" Mottlow, the late Carmella Hartigan, Tim Cronin, Arlene Gill, John McDonough, Mike North, and, above all, E. R. "Salty" Saltwell.

My family and friends are always appreciated for many things, including their encouragement of my work. My mother, Marion Claire Smith, still encourages my baseball fanaticism; she even accompanied my brothers and me to Opening Day 1977 at Wrigley Field. My dad, John Shea II, took me to my first game at Wrigley Field in 1971. We have returned many times since, though not enough. My brothers John III and Tom have shared countless baseball experiences with me.

I have also had great times at the ballpark with Sheila Spica, Toby Dye, Jack O'Regan, and Agustin, Adrian, Liz, and Marco Antonio Garibay.

Credit should also go to Sam Dorrance, Norman Humphrey, and the rest of the sales and marketing departments of Brassey's. They, in large part, are responsible for any success this book may enjoy.

My biggest thanks, however, go to Cecilia Garibay. Our second date, in 1982, was at Wrigley Field. I spent most of the game watching her.

Introduction
Myths In Concrete

It's a hazy, hot summer Saturday afternoon. The Chicago Cubs have just finished off an opponent—or, just as likely, been finished off by one. As the
sun shines from the west, its beams slanting eastward down Addison Street,
fans spill out of the venerable ballpark on the city's North Side and scatter
around the neighborhood for the next stop on their ride through Wrigleyville.

Some fans, of course, simply head home. Many board the crowded elevated Chicago Transit Authority train a block away to head north toward
Evanston or south toward downtown. Some take the Clark Street bus north
or south (although on game days, that bus can take an hour to move a few
blocks). Others will hop the Addison bus going west.

Still others head to their cars, docked all around the park both legally
and illegally, for twenty dollars here and fifteen dollars there, or for a few
quarters if you are lucky enough to find a metered space. Many fans, especially kids from schools or Park District programs, congregate outside the
park's left-field wall on Waveland Avenue, playing in groups or looking cool
just standing there, waiting to get into the yellow buses that will return them
home.

Fans sticking around the ballpark have plenty of options. Some of them
will head to one of the many nearby bars for a few more libations. Some fans
will repair to one of the myriad Japanese, Mexican, Thai, or Italian restaurants in the neighborhood, while others head for theater, films, dancing, or
shopping. Groups of fans with pictures, programs, baseballs, and baseball
cards spend hours waiting near the Cubs' parking lot, just across from the
firehouse on Waveland, in hopes of snaring an autograph. Others hang
around the gate near the right-field corner, near Addison and Sheffield, hoping to get a signature and a "hello" from a visiting player ready to step onto
the team bus.

It's an almost perfect scene—the local baseball park serving as a meeting
place for fans of all stripes, for locals and visitors from far-flung towns.

For those unfamiliar with the geography of Chicago, it's helpful to note that the Lake View neighborhood extends roughly from Belmont Avenue (3200 north) on the south up to Irving Park Road (4000 north) and from Lake Michigan west to Ashland Avenue.

Lake View has only in the last twenty years become a swinging area, a tourist haven, the "in" place to be during a Chicago summer. And the area around Wrigley Field has been called "Wrigleyville" only since the 1970s.

Fewer than a hundred years ago, there was no ballpark, no nightlife, no trains or buses, no ball club, and no fans. No Wrigleyville. No Wrigley *anything*, except for a chewing gum company.

Until 1916, Major League Baseball was never played north of downtown in Chicago, and the beloved "North Siders" actually played on the near West Side.

Over the last century, Wrigley Field and its neighborhood have gone through all sorts of changes, some good, some not. As recently as the mid-1980s, there were whispers that Wrigley was obsolete and that the Cubs would have to build a spanking new facility in order to be fiscally competitive.

The relatively recent history of Wrigley Field, and Lake View, as a play area for sports-minded yuppies, kids, Northwestern University students, and tourists is only part of the story.

There are plenty of tales about the evolution of the seemingly ageless ballpark, the athletic teams that have inhabited it, and the neighborhood that has supported it, tolerated it, profited from it, complained about it, and—most of all—grown up with it.

But ninety years of ball at Wrigley Field have given birth to myriad legends of the place, legends that overrun the truth like ivy on a brick wall. Viewpoints of the neighborhood of Lake View, of Wrigley Field, and of the Chicago Cubs are sometimes so thick and murky that the truth is almost impossible to find.

Wrigley Field was built for the Cubs.
There has never been advertising on the walls at Wrigley Field.
Wrigley Field has always been nothing but an open-air bar.
In the old days, Wrigley Field didn't have music blaring.
William Wrigley invented Ladies Day in the 1920s.
P. K. Wrigley would never have permitted lights in his park.
Wrigley Field never had a night game until 1988.
P. K. Wrigley never disturbed his neighbors at night.
Fans have always sat on the rooftops across from Wrigley Field.
P. K. Wrigley left others in charge of baseball and concentrated on the ballpark.
P. K. Wrigley never came to see the Cubs play.
P. K. Wrigley hated artificial turf.
Bill Veeck planted the ivy at Wrigley Field overnight.
Wrigleyville has always been a yuppie haven.

Wrigley Field stands alone against the grim forces of modern baseball, resisting the money-driven changes of the modern era.

Myths all of them, demonstrably wrong. And, in each case, the myth is covering up a far more interesting reality.

What this book hopes to do is lay bare the myths and get to something far more interesting: the real story. If this book is successful, readers will know much more than they did previously about Wrigley Field and its surrounding neighborhood of Lake View.

This book outlines how the ballpark was built, why it was constructed at Clark and Addison, and who built it. In addition, it's an attempt to convey what it might have been like to be there at various times in the past, and how the park and the neighborhood have influenced one another over the passing decades.

Perhaps most important, it's intended to be a fun read. The passing parade of Wrigley Field's people, events, changes, comedies, and, yes, tragedies has been as interesting as that of any other sports arena in the history of this country, including Yankee Stadium, Churchill Downs, Fenway Park, the Rose Bowl, Ebbets Field, or the Boston Garden. Wrigley Field has seen it all: baseball, football, basketball, boxing, wrestling, women's pro baseball, and even vaudeville. But mostly Wrigley has seen baseball, good and bad, glorious and embarrassing.

Come on in and grab a seat. The peanut vendor is coming up the aisle, and someone is yelling "Beer here!" Pete Alexander and Gabby Hartnett are warming up . . . Ernie Banks is tossing the ball around from first . . . Ryne Sandberg's at second . . . Billy Jurges is manning shortstop, with Ron Santo at third . . . Billy Williams is in left . . . that's gotta be Hack Wilson in center. Sammy Sosa's charging out to right field as the fans come to their feet. . . .

CHAPTER 1

The Construction of a Shrine

LAKE VIEW

Before there was Wrigleyville, there was Lake View.

In the 1870s and 1880s, Chicago was far smaller in area (as well as in population, of course) than now. In fact, many neighborhoods of today's Chicago weren't even part of the city back then. One such area is a town then called Lake View. A smaller part of present-day Chicago that includes Wrigleyville still bears the name. The independent town of Lake View stretched from Fullerton (2400 north) on the south all the way to Devon (6400 north) on the north, from Lake Michigan on the east to what is now known as Western Avenue (2400 west).

Joseph Sheffield, founder of the Chicago, Rock Island, and Pacific Railroad, was also the founder of Lake View. The Illinois General Assembly certified the area as a town in 1837. Sheffield, a very successful businessman in the middle of the nineteenth century, envisioned Lake View as a quiet community removed from the cities in which he made much of his money. In a sense, he was an early version of the high-class suburbanite who doesn't want to live near his customers and can afford not to.

However, the first white resident of Lake View was actually Conrad Sulzer, who showed up in 1837 and purchased one hundred acres of land. The regional library in Chicago's Lincoln Square neighborhood bears his name. Prior to Sulzer, Sheffield, and the rest, Lake View had been home to mostly Illinois and Pottawatomie Indians, although Sac, Algonquin, Fox, and Kickapoo also were resident. Even into the late nineteenth century, good numbers of Native Americans were still in the area, but most of them appear to have been driven out forcibly.

According to Steven Bedell Clark's *The Lakeview Saga 1837–1985*, the Lake View town hall was built at Addison and Halsted, where now stands a police station from which officers occasionally come to haul away a drunk Cubs fan or three.

CEMETERY GATES

In the 1850s, Wunder's and Graceland cemeteries opened in Lake View, several blocks north of where Wrigley Field now stands. Both still serve the community—their grounds and walls are visible from the elevated (or "el") trains traveling south toward Wrigley, and both cemeteries border Clark Street just a few blocks north of the park.

The Lake View House hotel was constructed in 1853. The hotel apparently possessed a grand view of Lake Michigan. The hotel, and several restaurants, served cemetery visitors at the time when it usually took half a day by wagon to reach Lake View from Chicago. Following the Civil War, some of Chicago's richest citizens began to follow Joseph Sheffield's lead and build homes in the area.

Local politicians noticed Lake View's progress, which also increased after dispossessed citizens headed north from downtown after the 1871 fire. In 1874, Lake View High School, the first township high school in the state, was constructed; it's still there, a few blocks northwest of Wrigley at Irving Park and Ashland.

THE LEARNING ANNEX

During the 1880s, Chicago instituted an effort to annex the town. Annexation increased the city's population and, therefore, its tax base. With more dollars, the city could provide better services for its citizens. A cholera epidemic in the 1880s led a large number of Lake View citizens to demand improved hygienic conditions and plumbing.

By 1900, Chicago would be the second-largest city in the country in population and the largest in area due in no small part to aggressive annexation of surrounding communities. "It is a locality peculiarly fitted for the homes of the working classes. Cable cars and steam roads, and fresh clean property at low prices invite such people here," said David Goodwillie, an advocate for the annexation of Lake View, at the time.

By the late 1800s, the change had already begun from farm to city. In 1883, the first phones were wired up in the formerly rural burg. By 1905, the number of telephones in the area had grown tenfold to thirty-three hundred. That year, the Lake View Central Telephone Company erected a building at 3522 N. Sheffield. Located just a half block south of what is now Wrigley, this building later housed Illinois Bell and remains in use today by SBC.

Members of the independent-minded Lake View government—who knew that their power would disappear if Chicago swallowed their town—didn't submit to the 1889 annexation without a fight. Lake View mayor William Boldenweck got permission from his board of advisors to seize thirty-two-hundred dollars of the town's assets in an attempt to legally fight the annexation order.

"About the only people who were against annexation were public officials," said Richard C. Bjorklund, a onetime president of the Ravenswood–Lake View Historical Association, in a 1989 article published in *The Good News Weekly*. Eventually, Judge John Peter Altgeld (later governor of Illinois) ruled that the City of Chicago had the right to take over the community, most of whose members supported the annexation.

However, many Lake View residents still bristled at what they felt was unnecessary city control. A September 1912 *Ravenswood News* item noted, "The residents of North Lincoln Street are decidedly opposed to the new name, 'Pulaski,' adopted by the City Council Wednesday night. The new name, although it is that of Count Casimir Pulaski, the Polish patriot who served in America and was killed at Savannah in 1779, savors too much of a nationality which has few representatives in Ravenswood. The local residents resent the suggestion or implication that they are 'Pollocks' [sic] and are wrathful as a result of the Council's action."

The city eventually chose to name another street "Pulaski" and left Lincoln Avenue unchanged.

ITS OWN THING

Lake View's character was already established before the town was annexed. It was a freewheeling, growing, exciting place where families, businessmen, fun seekers, and even rich folks, building summer homes on the lake, gathered cheek-by-jowl. By the late 1800s, the neighborhood's two prime shopping areas—Lincoln and Belmont and Clark and Diversey—were already established. These corners remain among the busiest in the city.

Lake View had its own unique way of collecting revenue as well: during the nineteenth century, several street corners, including the one at Clark and Waveland, featured toll gates where pedestrians and drivers of horse carriages had to pay to get through.

And the residents didn't shy from a drink. According to nineteenth-century Lake View resident Edward Walsh, John Berringer ("Beer John") owned a beer garden at Clark and Diversey back in the 1860s. Foremost among the imbibers were the Germans settling in the neighborhood, although other ethnic groups liked their alcohol as well.

Although it has decreased somewhat, a German presence survives in Lincoln Square and Lake View to the present. For many years, Zum Deutschen Eck was an extremely popular restaurant; it finally shut down in the 1990s. The Huettenbar and Laschet's Inn remain well-attended German-themed bars, and the Merz Apothecary has served the area for more than a hundred years.

GETTING AROUND

While putting up a North Side ballpark might have been folly even five years prior to 1913, new forms of public transportation—the electric streetcar and the elevated trains—were by then serving the north side of the city. Cable cars had stopped running in 1906, replaced by more efficient streetcars. In addition, commuter train lines, which had run downtown and on the South and West Sides since 1893, had been improved with elevated tracks built all the way up the North Side close to Lake Michigan.

According to Harold Mayer and Richard Wade's *Chicago: Growth of a Metropolis*, Wilson Avenue (ten blocks north of Addison) was the northernmost stop, until 1908, on what was called the Northwest Line. At this time, with many well-off folks moving north of Uptown, the elevated line was expanded all the way to Evanston, a prosperous suburb immediately north of Chicago along the lakefront.

What would later become the Chicago Transit Authority built a series of train lines around the areas it served, some above ground, some beneath, and some even traversing alleyways. Today, some trains on the Douglas and Ravenswood lines still run at street level, cutting through alleys and close to backyards. However, the train stations of the north-south line and Ravenswood lines in the Lake View/Wrigley areas are entirely above ground.

In the late 1800s and early 1900s, the power of the city lay in the South Side, and some North Siders felt like second-class citizens. An article in the *Chicago Daily Tribune* on December 1, 1913, stated, "Complaints had been made to the *Tribune* that while the south side trains are making better time than before through routing, the Northwestern [service toward Evanston] service is slower. This was denied by Mr. [Bratten] Budd [of the Chicago Elevated Railways system], who insisted the same running time from terminus to loop of each line is being made today, although more trains are run."

The North Side, though, was beginning to feel its oats. People were moving north to build homes on inexpensive land, and companies were constructing factories on this unplowed and undeveloped real estate. In addition, the lakeside area around Wilson Avenue, the Uptown neighborhood, had become a hopping entertainment district.

Mayer and Wade write, "The preeminence of the South Side began to diminish after the [1893 World's] Fair. The supremacy of that area had stemmed largely from the excellence of its transit facilities. But the completion of elevated transit lines into other sections of the city, coupled with the electrification and expansion of street railways, substantially reduced this advantage in the decades after 1893. The North and West sides now enjoyed the stimulus of good connections with downtown, and both witnessed spectacular growth."

During those years, the Chicago elevated line services built play lots and parks underneath their dusty and noisy tracks, with these civic improvements apparently intended as a public relations measure.

PEACEFUL CONTEMPLATION AT CLARK AND ADDISON

The land on which Wrigley Field sits today was earmarked for a theological seminary 130 years ago.

One of the most famous and successful Lutheran missionaries in American history was William Alfred Passavant (1821–94). Born in Zelienople, Pennsylvania, Passavant was a natural leader, according to his mother: "When the boys play soldier, Willie always wants to be captain."

Interested in the spiritual from a very young age, Passavant directed his efforts toward public service and spent much of his life founding benevolent institutions. In college at fifteen, he soon earned a medical degree. He was married in 1845 and eventually fathered ten children. The year after his nuptials, Passavant founded the Pittsburgh Infirmary, which would later become Passavant Hospital, the first Protestant hospital in the country.

Passavant then moved west to Chicago. In 1865, he founded Passavant Hospital of Chicago, which was destroyed six years later in the Great Fire. However, Passavant reopened its doors in 1884 and immediately became one of the city's top hospitals due to its excellent staff and facilities. Eventually, Passavant Hospital of Chicago merged with Wesley Hospital and became Northwestern Memorial, still one of the area's premier health centers.

Not content with founding hospitals, Passavant also edited religious journals and established orphanages. When Passavant inherited a parcel of land in Lake View (which at that time was still a prairie and not part of Chicago), he turned the bucolic, tree-lined area into a theological seminary where young men could study and contemplate in quiet—though it is difficult to imagine anyone getting any studying done around Wrigley Field today.

Steven Bedell Clark notes that churches were a huge part of the building of Lake View. The German residents of the area were mostly Roman Catholic and Lutheran, while Polish Catholics also moved in starting in the 1880s. Belgians were also part of the neighborhood's makeup.

According to the records of the Evangelical Lutheran Church of America, the ground for the seminary at Chicago was presented by Passavant for development in 1868, though the Theological Seminary of the Evangelical Lutheran Church did not open until 1891. George Castle found in

1989 that four seminary buildings were constructed on the site: a main dormitory, two residential homes for professors, and a home for the seminary president.

TOO DARNED LOUD

The German character of the Lake View neighborhood included music halls and beer gardens, and the presence of the seminary did not appear to change the locals' habits much. One important gathering spot was the Bismarck Garden at Halsted and Grace, just a few blocks from the seminary.

In addition, the Milwaukee Road Railroad line, used both for freight and commuter travel, ran along what is now Clark Street (the west side of the park). The railway transported gravel, coal, and sand to local builders, while ice and milk were brought in for local residents. The increasing numbers of streetcars and elevated trains made things even louder.

Within only a few years after the seminary opened, everyone concerned decided that the area had become too busy to provide an adequate setting for contemplative study. As Marjory R. Wing, representing the school, noted at the time, students were constantly bothered by "smoke, dust, grime, soot, dirt, [and] foul gases; railroading by night and day; whistles, ding-donging of bells late and early and in between times, and the ceaselessness of undesirable traffic incidental thereto that is growing more unbearable every week."

The 1908 opening of the Ravenswood elevated line made it even easier to get to Lake View, and construction continued unabated. The next year, the Lutheran church finally got an opportunity to address the problem. Charles Havenor of Milwaukee offered to buy the land, and the church accepted in a heartbeat. The July 8, 1909, issue of *Leslie's Weekly* gives the details.

> Charles S. Havenor, of the Milwaukee Baseball Club of the American Association, has bought for $175,000 the eight-acre tract in North Clark Street, Chicago. This property is considered the best vacant location in Chicago for a baseball park, and the purchase on its face appears to portend the entrance of an American Association club into that city, with a big baseball war as the result. It has been known that the American Association at various times in the last few years has cast covetous eyes on Chicago territory, and at one time last fall plans were all set for an invasion, but later abandoned. It looks as if the sports pages will be full of "baseball war" talk again this winter as in the past.

This does not mean that the Lutherans deserted the area. The seminary moved to west suburban Maywood but returned to Chicago (this time on the South Side) in 1967. In addition, the Holy Trinity Lutheran Church, which moved to Lake View in 1914, stands just two blocks west of Wrigley Field.

Despite the seminary's departure, the religious character of the neighborhood increased. Chicago is often called the City of Churches, and Lake View built more than its share. The Germans, Swedes, and Irish constructed houses of worship around the area, many of which still function today.

Strangely, some sources erroneously report that the land went directly from the church to the Chicago Cubs. Some others opine that the land wasn't sold to the Cubs, but to the Federal League's Chicago Whales, who first inhabited the park. In fact, however, there was a three-year period after the Lutheran Church sold the land before Whales owner Charley Weeghman built his park.

What happened during that 1910–13 gap? Who was Charley Weeghman? Who was Charles Havenor? Who really owned the land, and why did they want it?

THE FREE MINORS AND CHICAGO

In 1909, the American Association (AA), baseball's top minor league, had clubs in eight large Midwestern cities: Columbus, Indianapolis, Kansas City, Louisville, Milwaukee, Minneapolis, St. Paul, and Toledo. The 1910 census put all of these cities thirty-first or higher in population, with Milwaukee ranking the highest at tenth.

The Association was no scrub league, either; the Milwaukee, Minneapolis, and Indianapolis entries all drew more fans in 1909 than the American League's Washington Senators or the National League's Boston "Rustlers." The minor leagues were still free of affiliations with big league organizations, which meant that American Association clubs could compete to win on their own terms.

Some of the league's more ambitious owners thought that the time was right to expand to Chicago, and that the Windy City could support three professional teams. Chicago in the 1910 census was the second-largest city in the country, having grown nearly 30 percent over the previous decade.

So a few enterprising businessmen began exploring Chicago as a site for a future club. At this time, the White Sox owned the South Side, playing at 39th and Wentworth while readying a new park at 35th and Shields. The Cubs were playing at the West Side Grounds, located at Polk and Wolcott Streets on the near southwest side.

Therefore, the burgeoning North Side—with Lake View's single-family homes and its taste for beer and song, with Uptown's swinging nightlife nearby, and with new public transportation systems—was a potentially excellent location.

Charles Havenor's first wife, Agnes Havenor, owned the AA Milwaukee Brewers. The Havenors and the Cantillons, Joe and Mike (owners of the rival Minneapolis Millers), had much to gain by scoping out a location for a club and selling the ballpark land to a new American Association franchise.

However, despite the purchase of the land, the American Association couldn't break into Chicago. Organized leagues were prohibited from moving into already represented territory without 60 percent approval from the league already represented in the market. The Cubs and White Sox worked in concert to block the AA's efforts, so the plan to expand was set aside.

Piece by piece, Havenor divested himself of his share of the land to a three-man partnership composed of real estate investor Edmund Archambault and the Cantillon brothers. Mike was business manager of the club, while Joe served as field manager. Havenor passed away after selling the property, before the land was leased to the Federal League.

Looking back, in 1913, on the history of the Clark and Addison site, Irv Sanborn of the *Tribune* noted that "control of the site was originally obtained by the late Charles Havenor of Milwaukee and the Cantillon brothers, owners of the Minneapolis club, with a view to invading Chicago with an Association team. When that move was abandoned some years ago, the Havenor interest in the lot was taken over by a relative by marriage of the Cantillons [Edmund Archambault]."

So even though the American Association never made it into Chicago, the league's ambition to do so was part of the process that helped bring Wrigley Field into existence.

BIRTH OF THE FEDS

David Pietrusza, in his book *Major Leagues,* noted that several entrepreneurs founded new associations to challenge the American and National Leagues between 1910 and 1912. One such loop, the United States League, had a franchise in Chicago in 1912. The team, known as the Chicago Green Sox, played at Gunther Park at Clark Street and Leland Avenue, about eleven blocks north of Wrigley Field. Burt Keeley, a native of Wilmington, Illinois, who had pitched for the Washington Senators in 1908 and 1909, signed on as skipper.

Despite high hopes, the league's financial footing quickly slid, and on June 24, the United States League disbanded. The Green Sox' brief history ended with a 17–15 record, according to Lloyd Johnson and Miles Wolff's *Encyclopedia of Minor League Baseball.*

A city park at Clark and Leland still exists, now known as Chase Park.

Despite sporting several baseball/softball diamonds, there is no marker at Chase Park indicating that a professional baseball team ever played there.

During the years from 1906 to 1913, local clubs, under the unswerving guidance of semipro gadfly Billy Niesen, also played at Gunther Park, a nice-looking if small field that had a remarkably well-built grandstand.

Despite their heavy losses, however, the club owners' dreams died hard. Several of the old United States League owners tried again in 1913, forming a new organization. Headed by John T. Powers, the owners initially named their loop the Columbian League, then settled on the Federal League. They opened for business in six cities, including Cleveland, Indianapolis, Pittsburgh, St. Louis, Chicago, and Covington, Kentucky, which quickly relocated to Kansas City.

The Chifeds, as the Chicago entry was named, played games in 1913 at the athletic fields of DePaul University, located at this time about twelve blocks south of Addison Street. With Keeley again at the helm, the Chifeds finished fourth in the six-club loop at 57–62.

Meanwhile, a reorganized United States League opened for business on May 10, 1913, with eight East Coast clubs: Baltimore, Brooklyn, Lynchburg, Virginia, Newark, New York, Philadelphia, Reading, and Washington. Just three days later, amid financial ruin, with players striking after not having been paid guaranteed Opening Day salaries of seventy-five dollars per game, the United States League capitulated after only seven games had been played. The May 31, 1913, *Sporting Life* noted the loop's passing in an article headlined "WORST FAILURE in the History of Base Ball Now Recorded," that derided the league as "the quickest and most ridiculous failure in the long history of base ball, a history teeming with ill-advised club and league ventures and with failures of small and great degree."

Researcher and writer Marc Okkonen described the North Side, in SABR's *The Federal League of 1914–15*, as "baseball-hungry." Though attendance records for the 1913 Feds are not available, the league did survive.

During the 1913 season, John Powers, who harbored dreams of elevating the Federal League to first-class minor league status, perhaps even to the Double-A level of the American Association, was pushed out of both club ownership and the presidency of the FL. The end of Powers' reign came after a markedly small-time stunt. During the 1913 season, he tried to get a Pittsburgh–Chicago game transferred from DePaul's field to his hometown of Sheffield, Illinois, but the Chifed players refused to travel. At that embarrassing point, the other owners saw to it that Powers was eased out of his command. *Sporting Life* reported on August 30, 1913, that Powers "had much to do with the launching of the new league, but with the infusion of new life he was not the man to carry it along."

James Gilmore, a tall, wealthy Chicago coal baron and manufacturer of ventilating engines, became one of two principals of the Chicago franchise and shortly thereafter was named interim president of the Federal League.

Powers's dreams of profitable minor league status were far less ambitious than those of some other owners in the league, who felt they could take on the majors. Gilmore was their man. After first agreeing to take on the league presidency on an interim basis, he quickly became besotted with the idea of growing the league. Gilmore transferred the league into ritzy new offices at Chicago's Old Colony Building.

The Sporting News [or *TSN*] ran an interview with Powers on October 13 in which the deposed prexy presented his candidacy for the Sour Grapes League. "I can't see where the Federal League has a chance as constituted at present . . . they can't hope to buck the major leagues and get away with it . . . they have a hopeless cause, as I see it, and I don't think they will start next season."

THE GILMORE GUY

Gilmore was more than ready for the challenge. Born in 1876, he grew up playing sandlot ball on the near southwest side of Chicago. While fighting in the war against Spain, he took ill and spent thirteen months recovering. He became a financial success in his thirties, rising from coal salesman to iron mogul in just two years.

An article entitled "The Genius of the Federal League," printed in the February 7, 1914, edition of *Literary Digest*, noted, "The real growth of the Federal League began last July, when James A. Gilmore assumed charge . . . the Chicago team was in financial difficulties. The club owners in desperation called on their friend, Jimmy Gilmore, president of a Chicago iron company, and who already had a big reputation as an organizer, for advice . . . Gilmore startled his callers by saying he would take charge of their club and league . . . he first mapped out a campaign against organized ball, the supreme body in baseball."

The upstart loop's aggressive plans included picking the pockets of the American League and National League of their established players. Gilmore and his lawyers believed that the so-called "reserve clause," binding one player to his team in perpetuity at the whim of the club, was invalid. Nevertheless, it was more than sixty years before arbitrator Peter Seitz would void baseball's reserve clause.

Others weren't even sure the Feds could start play in 1914. George "White Wings" Tebeau, a nineteenth-century outfielder who by 1913 was president of Kansas City's American Association club, believed that the Feds had lost significant money. He noted in the November 13 *Sporting News*, "The clubs lost something like $15,000 each during the 1913 season and I suppose for this reason people are chary about investing in the league . . . if

I were to offer $100,000 for the league—lock, stock, and barrel—my money would be gobbled up in an instant."

Gilmore, whose traits included not only big plans but also the ability to find big money to finance them, brought "new money" into the struggling league. Wealthy, somewhat raffish figures who fancied the dough presumably to be made in baseball, they also enjoyed the idea of battling with established club owners. Not all the owners were legitimate; some were cast aside when their talk proved thicker than their wallets. However, the Federal League did expand to eight clubs with new ownership taking over most of them.

The FL owners certainly were ambitious. St. Louis and Chicago were already served by *two* major league franchises, while Pittsburgh and Brooklyn would compete with National League clubs. The other four FL locations—Indianapolis, Baltimore, Buffalo, and Kansas City—already fielded successful minor league franchises, three from the International League and one from the American Association.

As an independent "outlaw" entity, the Federal League did not need to worry about securing approval from organized baseball before moving into these markets.

On December 1, 1913, the *Tribune* printed a rumor that the Chifeds would move to Milwaukee for 1914. E. C. Racey, an officer of the Chicago club, denied this scurrilous hearsay. Considering the tall tales Gilmore and his FL associates were spreading to throw organized baseball and the press off their trail, however, they may well have planted this rumor themselves. The league's Brooklyn franchise, for instance, was said to be headed toward Toronto until the day the agreement was put in place to house them in Flatbush; Gilmore's spirited campaign of disinformation kept the press completely in the dark.

"President Gilmore threw local reporters clear off the trail," the *Literary Digest* noted, "and he introduced a very apt tongue for telling fibs about his Toronto club." In fact, the press was told that the Toronto club was to be headed by Bernard Hepburn, a member of the Canadian parliament. Gilmore almost certainly led Hepburn and his Toronto cohorts to believe they were to obtain a franchise as well, the better to carry off the deception.

What was in it for Gilmore? Ambition and power, certainly; it probably wasn't the money. The Chicago *Inter-Ocean* reported on March 25, 1914, that the president's salary for the season would be fifteen thousand dollars.

DISTURBANCE AT THE HERON HOUSE

The Feds' campaign of deceit infuriated *The Sporting News*, the self-proclaimed "Bible of Baseball." As the virtual house organ for organized baseball, *TSN* was loath to give the new league a fair shake. Witness this from April 2, 1914: "The Federals have played the hypocrite in their declarations that they were not seeking players and would not sign players already under contract. . . . *The Sporting News* is still honestly of the opinion that there is no demand for the Federal League in the territory it expects to occupy."

Of course the Feds weren't always telling the truth; this was, after all, an outlaw league. The AL and the NL lied just as much about their internal matters, but this didn't seem to bother *TSN*.

The Sporting News was good at spreading rumors for its own purposes as well. In their January 8, 1914, issue, *TSN* ran an unattributed story claiming that Gilmore was to be deposed from the FL presidency. No Chicago paper bothered to comment on the rumor, and the story quickly shriveled up and blew away.

Criticism from the papers aside, the Feds brazenly solicited players already under contract, offering far better deals than they could get from their current clubs. Noted the *Literary Digest*, "I talked with a player who had been approached, and the proposition put up to him, he says, was that half of the three years' salary was to be paid in advance in cash and the rest was to be put in escrow . . . to do that, the promoters of the Federal League, necessarily, must have a standing in the banks." The process of advancing money to players would eventually put the Feds in tough financial straits.

Meanwhile, again showing his gift for fibbing, Gilmore stated to the *Chicago Daily News* in December 1913, presumably with a straight face, "The players signed for 1914 have all made application upon their initiative, without the slightest solicitation from any club in the new league."

The headlines were just beginning for the Federal League that winter, and one of the most uproarious chapters in Chicago sports history was about to begin. And the Feds got their boost from a rival.

MURPHY'S LAW

Chicago Cubs owner Charles W. Murphy was, by all accounts, an odd duck with a big mouth. Murphy bought the franchise with Charles Taft (half-brother of future president William Howard Taft) prior to the 1906 season. A meddlesome blowhard whose pronouncements and interference make George Steinbrenner look like a quiet schoolboy, Murphy annoyed Cubs fans, his players, other owners, and the press with his constant name-calling, chest thumping, rule breaking, lying, bullying, and self-promotion.

To give an idea of just how unpopular Murphy was, here is a representative quote of the day from the *Chicago American*'s sports column, "Dav's Day Dreams," on February 13, 1914: "Charles Webb Murphy's latest interview, written by himself, will be given to the public next week. Charles Webb, who has become his own best little interviewer, has chosen for his subject, 'Popularizing Baseball,' a subject concerning which he knows little but will say much.''

Not only was Murphy a creep, but he was also a double-dealer. Aided by the benign neglect of the National League office, which had been cowed by his bragging and threats, Murphy and Taft were allowed to serve as background owners of the Philadelphia Phillies, with Horace Fogel putting his name on the front door while serving as a cover for the carpetbaggers.

During the 1912 campaign, Fogel complained that his Phillies were being rooked out of the NL title by umpiring biased toward the New York Giants. Wrote W. S. Forman of the *Chicago Post* on February 28, 1914, "Fogel had been kicking all during the playing season about the umpiring, and he was right. The politics of the National League seemed to require a pennant for the Giants. Fogel was handed package after package in Philadelphia, when his men looked like pennant contenders.''

Murphy admitted to the *Post* that he was pushing Fogel to say this, both to tweak the league and to get under the skin of Giants manager Roger Bresnahan. Late in the 1912 season, the *Post* published another story, written by Fogel and vetted by Murphy, accusing the league of dirty dealing.

Then, when the matter hit the fan, and league officials were forced into taking at least cosmetic action, both Fogel and Murphy denied making any such statements and actually accused the *Post* of faking the story.

In November 1912, Fogel—rather than Murphy, the man behind it all—was bounced from the league for his muckraking, which was proving a public relations disaster for the senior circuit. Fogel would later attempt to hook up with the Feds, but his questionable character and lack of adequate funds meant he was soon out of the picture.

Murphy had been aided by the *Post* in his earlier publicity campaigns but, in the wake of the Fogel affair, the paper—hung out to dry and accused of fabricating a story—understandably turned against the Cubs owner.

Later, the *Post* would become a willing booster of the Feds, serving almost as a press liaison for the fledgling league. This was not unusual for the 1910s, just as it is not unusual today for newspapers to ally themselves with a corporation or sports franchise for political purposes. *The Sporting News* was, of course, the unofficial publicist for the dancing monkeys running the organized white major and minor leagues.

Those dancing monkeys, according to the 1914 W. S. Forman piece in the *Post*, were almost entirely to blame for the very existence of the Feds. Their tolerance of such a cad as Murphy, and their machinations allowing him to stay in the game, were to Forman the reasons that a rival league could steal so much attention: "The 'reason why' of the Federal League dates back to Nov. 25, 1912, when the directors of the National league held a special meeting in New York City, ostensibly to investigate the authorship of an article that had been published in the *Post* over the signature of Horace Fogel, the president of the Phillies. In reality, they met for the purpose of smearing a coat of carefully prepared whitewash over a mess that had developed in the 1912 pennant race."

Forman goes on to say that the obvious three-pronged fraud of bouncing Fogel, allowing Murphy to stay, and reelecting Tom Lynch as NL president undermined the public's confidence in the majors and allowed the Feds to gain hold of the public imagination.

> To have given the public a square deal on that occasion would have been a simple task. For Murphy stood out in the open, stripped at last of all hypocrisy and pretense. They had the goods on him in the Fogel case, riveted clean thru him and clinched on the other side. And THEY LET HIM GO. They took him back into the game he had dishonored, and they did it as part of a political deal that was about the rottenest thing of its kind ever pulled in baseball . . . The Federal League is founded on the stupidity shown by the board of directors of the National league when they broke faith with the fans in November of 1912.

What kind of a guy was Murphy? In 1912, he fired Cubs manager Frank Chance *during a game* as the crosstown White Sox were thrashing his club in the annual postseason City Series.

Paying his players poorly, failing to keep West Side Grounds in good shape, and constantly deriding his team to whoever would listen, Murphy tore apart the club before the 1913 season by ridding himself of Joe Tinker, Ed Ruelbach, and Mordecai Brown. He dumped new manager Johnny Evers the next season after another poor showing in the postseason Cubs–Sox series.

Peter Golenbock's *Wrigleyville* notes that "Murphy always viewed the intercity series with the White Sox as having the importance of the World Series. To the players, the series was merely an exhibition." Murphy's impulsive behavior began to draw fire from other owners, and the last straw was his cavalier mistreatment of Tinker the previous year.

TINKER, TAILOR . . .

Unhappy after one year in Cincinnati and refusing to report when traded to Brooklyn, shortstop Joe Tinker decided to go for broke. Desiring a salary of more than ten thousand dollars (rather than the seven thousand dollars the Dodgers wanted to pay), he lashed out. Reported John Seys in the December 22, 1913, *Daily News*: "It is not a certainty that Joe Tinker will wear a Brooklyn uniform next season . . . [Dodgers] president Charles Ebbets . . . has made up his mind as to the sum he intents [*sic*] to pay Tinker, and it is not near to the mark the shortstop is to demand."

Showing considerable guts for a player with little leverage, Tinker said, "I will not sign unless my demands are met. Ebbets can trade me to some other club which will give me what I want, or he can keep me out of organized ball. My mind is made up, the same as Ebbets', regarding salary."

Not that Charlie Murphy took the threat seriously. Showing both remarkable spleen and extremely bad judgment about local restaurant owner Charles Weeghman, he railed in the December 24, 1913, *Daily News*, "This Federal League is a joke from start to finish. The report has been going around that Charles Weeghman is going to finance the local club. He is not, for he told me so himself just the other day . . . I do not think Tinker will sign with the Federal League. All this talk of offering him $40,000 is nothing but a bluff . . . there is no one in the league who knows anything about baseball. Besides, they have no money and it takes money to be in the game today."

Murphy's blustering aside, Tinker and the Feds *both* ran a pretty good bluff. Knowing that the Chicago Federal club needed and wanted a marquee player with hometown connections, Tinker let it be known that he could be had for a price.

Therefore, on December 27, 1913, the star shortstop became the first big name to sign with the Federal League, garnering thirty-six thousand dollars as player-manager for the Chifeds in a three-year deal with at least ten thousand dollars advanced up front. The *Literary Digest* noted at the time, "I am reliably informed that Tinker received $15,000 in cash before he put his name to a contract."

The arrogance of organized baseball, personified by Charlie Murphy, came back to bite it. Murphy's big mouth and his decisions to dump contracts helped get the Federal League's foot in the door. And it forced the established AL and NL to act with their wallets and raise salaries to keep their biggest stars, such as Ty Cobb and Walter Johnson, from defecting.

The *Post* noted on April 13, 1914, "The real turning point in the fortunes of the Federals was the signing of Joe Tinker . . . as a result of [Charles Ebbets'] decision to refuse Joe a few hundred dollars more a season, the Feds grabbed him and made baseball a war which has cost the American and National leagues more than half a million dollars. Baseball salaries have been boosted to unheard-of levels as a result of the Fed invasion."

For instance, in order to keep Johnny Evers in the fold, the NL paid him twenty-five thousand dollars *not* to defect to the Feds. It was money well spent; in the 1914 season, Evers led the "Miracle" Boston Braves to a stunning NL pennant and an even more amazing World Series win over Connie Mack's Philadelphia A's. The Feds had offered Evers a then-astounding forty-thousand-dollar deal for three seasons.

Noted the *Chicago American* on February 13, 1914, "If Charley Weeghman is real wise he will sign Jawn Evers for his Feds. It would require but a year's receipts from one of Charley's restaurants to pay Jawn's salary."

The Feds wanted Walter Johnson, too. Bill Veeck Sr., working under the pen name of Bill Bailey, wrote in the April 3, 1914, *American*, "The Federal Leaguers figure that Walter Johnson, the Washington twirler, is the most valuable man in organized baseball."

He asked Joe Tinker what he would have paid Johnson to pitch for the Chifeds. "'I think Mr. Weeghman would have told him to insert his own figures in the contract,' answered Tinker." Persisting for a figure, Veeck was told, "'Well, I think Mr. Weeghman would have given him between $25,000 and $30,000 a year.'" That wrangling would wait another year.

The same day that Tinker signed, Charles Weeghman was announced as new president of the Chicago Federal League Baseball Club. Just six weeks later, the National League forced out Charlie Murphy as owner of the Cubs, with his shares being transferred to Charles Taft. Ring Lardner waxed poetic for the departed Murphy in the *Tribune*:

> Charlie, my darling, your sweet voice is hushed,
> And pale is the cheek that excitement once flushed.
> And silent the tongue that once uttered so much,
> The tongue that so frequently got you in Dutch.
> I'll miss you down here at the desk where I write,
> For you were the column conductor's delight;
> I'm wondering now wotinell I will do
> When I can no longer spring stuff about you.
> Fare thee well! And if forever,
> then forever, FARE THEE WELL!
> In my hopelessness, I never
> Dreamed that they could make thee sell.
> Would the boss would let me write it,
> All I really think of thee;
> Did I 'gainst his will indite it,
> He would tie a can to me.

CHARLEY WEEGHMAN

If one man could represent the big dreams, glorious successes, and hard falls that have characterized Chicago throughout its history, that man would be Charley Weeghman. Born in Richmond, Indiana, on March 7, 1874 (some reports in the 1910s claimed he was born in 1875), Charles Weeghman came to Chicago in 1892, following his graduation from high school, to chase dreams engendered by the announcement of the upcoming World's Fair. Charles Weeghman had ambitions that only the Chicago of the time could hope to fulfill; Richmond had just 16,608 people at the time and was far too small for Weeghman.

The opening paragraph of Theodore Dreiser's classic novel about Chicago in the 1890s, *Sister Carrie*, serves to illustrate the atmosphere of dreams and dread into which Weeghman came: "When Caroline Meeber boarded the afternoon train for Chicago, her total outfit consisted of a small trunk, a cheap imitation alligator-skin satchel, a small lunch in a paper box, and a yellow leather snap purse, containing her ticket, a scrap of paper with her sister's address in Van Buren Street, and four dollars in money. It was in August, 1889. She was eighteen years of age, bright, timid, and full of the illusions of ignorance and youth."

Arriving in Chicago with little but his dreams, Weeghman soon got a job as a coffee-pourer at a South Loop restaurant called Charlie King's on Fifth Avenue (now Wells Street). Good at his job, officious, and blessed with the gift of gab, Weeghman rose quickly in the ranks. His motto was, "I aim to please."

After receiving an appointment to headwaiter by Mr. King himself, Weeghman was soon made night manager, then floor manager. He learned the ins and outs of the restaurant racket and developed his own theories of successful customer service and how to increase traffic.

As head man, Weeghman was sitting in the catbird seat. Charlie King's was frequented by the politicians, mob figures, actors, popular singers, high-flying tourists, gamblers, and sports personalities of the day—and, perhaps most important, by the newspapermen. He met a cashier, also working at King's, named Bessie Webb.

This was heady company for an ambitious and cagey yet still wet-behind-the-ears rube such as Weeghman, but he learned quickly. And he had a dream: a polished-tile dream.

EATING ON THE RUN

One can generally get anything for a price in Chicago. Always on the go, on the make, and on the take, Chicago seemingly never sleeps, and its inhabitants are always seeking the next score, the next big deal. Both petty grifters and top-hatted bankers were attracted to the city in the early 1900s due to its seemingly unlimited potential for financial growth.

The 1893 World's Fair led more businesses to set up shop in Chicago. Banks, the livestock trade, manufacturers, and wholesalers needed qualified help, and hundreds of thousands came to Chicago.

Entire industries were growing to serve the growing working class. It was in the big cities of the 1890s and early 1900s that what we now know as America's middle class began to ascend. And the go-go pace of the time, defined by cable cars and newfangled commuter trains, meant that an increasingly large number people traveled to downtown Chicago to work.

And since these working people needed somewhere to eat, local entrepreneurs pushed a new phenomenon: fast food. In the excellent book *Challenging Chicago*, Perry Duis explains the eating habits of Chicagoans during the late 1800s. Duis noted that most working men went to bars, where the "free lunch" was in style, while the ladies traveled to such membership restaurants as the Woman's Exchange, on Wabash near Madison, and the Ogontz Club of Printer's Row, cited as the nation's first self-serve cafeteria. Duis says that the motives for the invention of the cafeteria were both financial and political: "Its dining members decided to reduce the overhead and eliminate what they regarded as a demeaning task of waitressing by lining up to serve themselves as they passed a table laden with platters and dishes."

The success of the Ogontz did not go unnoticed, and others in the early part of the decade soon followed with commercial versions of the self-serve format. In 1909, a lady named Mary Dutton began the Ontra Cafeteria chain. She had two stores downtown as well as a huge one in Uptown, then bustling with late-night entertainment and *nouveau riche* lakefront residents.

By 1910, the "free saloon lunch," as a longtime inducement to business in local bars, was under attack from religious groups. In 1933, the *Tribune* published a fond remembrance of the free lunch: "Every beer emporium furnished iced radishes, green onions, pickled beets, sliced tomatoes—and where could one go without having a pretzel bowl within reach? Caviar sandwiches abounded in the more pretentious places. Piping hot fried oysters were ready in season in many places. Crisp potato pancakes that melted in the mouth were free with a glass of beer. Cheese straws and French fried potatoes were munched between beer sips."

The public flaying of the free lunch led to the increased popularity of the non-alcohol-based mobile "sandwich wagons" and, eventually, to increased public acceptance of lunch counters. The most successful of the early lunch counter restaurateurs was John R. Thompson, who was on the ball by the mid-1890s. Duis noted, "Using one-arm chairs for easy access to counters, standard menus, and large-scale supply purchases to maximize profit, his chain grew to eight outlets in 1900 and thirty-nine in Chicago by 1914, all but seven of them in the loop." A competing chain called Raklios' had nineteen locations, and a third chain, Messenger's, was also very popular.

Charley Weeghman dreamed of opening his own restaurant.

CHARLEY'S WORLD

Raymond Kush wrote, in the 1981 SABR *Baseball Research Journal*, that over the years, Weeghman had saved twenty-eight hundred dollars in salary and tips. After Charlie King passed away, Weeghman and his wife, Bessie, opened up their own place at Fifth and Adams (not far from King's itself).

Bessie Webb and Charley Weeghman married in 1899 in Janesville, Wisconsin, and produced a daughter, Dorothy. Charley was the public presence and a popular man, but Bessie was said to provide the gravity in the operation, the keen business sense and attention to detail that her husband—a big talker and a dreamer—lacked.

Wells Street had for many years been one of the seedier areas of the city, dotted by beer halls and brothels. The city fathers had renamed it Fifth Avenue in the 1870s in an attempt to improve the street's character, but the new title had little effect. In 1918, the name "Wells Street" was reestablished.

One reason for Charlie King's popularity was its proximity to the high life, cheap beer, and cheaper women of Wells Street. The newsmen of the time liked that lifestyle and lauded Charlie King's in their papers.

But Charley Weeghman's restaurant was classier than the typical Wells joint. Writes Perry Duis, "The Weeghman chain featured a white tile décor to emphasize cleanliness, a punched-check bill to minimize confusion, and coffee served in special mugs to reduce both spilling and the number of dishes to wash."

These innovative touches certainly made things smoother for personnel and gave diners a more predictable experience. However, eating at your local fast-food joint, or "dairy-lunch counter," was often far from pleasant.

"You sit on a low stool, hat on, people waiting for your seat, no napkin, but quick service," groused a local guidebook of the time about the novel dairy-lunch phenomenon. Serving rows and rows of customers who ate quickly off tables that looked very much like old-style school desks, these lunch chains did plenty of business and made loads of money in the Chicago of the 1890s and early 1900s.

In this favorable environment, Weeghman's restaurant became a chain of two, then three, then five . . .

HOW DID HE DO IT?

Charley Weeghman's restaurants struck a chord. At his peak, the Weeghmans owned fifteen of them downtown, serving around thirty-five thousand patrons a day. Ultimately, Charley would be referred to as "the king of the one-armed dairy lunch" (sometimes called the "Baltimore lunch") and Chicago's "first fast-food tycoon."

Weeghman not only ran popular restaurants but also opened up several busy bakeries. He was celebrated for the size and quality of his sandwiches and rolls and, in fact, references to the chain's baked goods dot the contemporary reportage of Weeghman's doings. One of his nicknames was "Doughnut Charley," although most called him "Lucky Charley" for his seemingly instant rise to success, which came nearly as fast as fermenting dough.

But it wasn't easy. Weeghman had to put in a lot of time and elbow grease to get his chance. After he did that, he was determined to be successful, come hell or high water. And if that meant he had to follow the money down dark alleys, he would.

Weeghman quickly made friendships with characters best referred to as "shady." He made himself available to gamblers, showbiz types, writers, and politicians and soaked up what he could of the high life.

At the time, politicians were probably the least honorable people in the group. During the early 1900s, mobsters helped buy the election of Mayor "Big Bill" Thompson, probably the Windy City's most corrupt leader and one of the most mercenary mayors in the history of the country.

The mob had its hands in gambling, drugs, and prostitution, the three vices that never seem to go out of style. Whether Charley Weeghman got some of his working capital from this population, we are unlikely to ever know. But it would be no stretch to say that the young Weeghman had a well-known ability to give his customers at King's whatever they wanted.

During this time Chicago was a land both of amazing filth and spectacular ambition, growth, and beauty. It was the scene of both the desolation of the trapped factory girls in *Sister Carrie* and the hard-fought optimism of Carl Sandburg. It was the beautiful architecture and design work of Louis Sullivan and Frank Lloyd Wright as well as the exploitative ugliness of the meatpacking industry, heartbreakingly exposed by Upton Sinclair in *The Jungle*.

It was the scarcely believable poverty of the South Side and West Side slums, the quick-as-a-wink rebuilding of a city scorched by the terrible 1871 fire, and the shady character of its policemen and elected officials. Chicago had an often scurrilous press despite a group of amazingly talented newspaper writers.

Rudyard Kipling expressed his desire to see Chicago wiped off the face of the earth. Kaiser Wilhelm announced, "I should very much like to see Chicago."

It was H. L. Mencken in the October 28, 1917, *Tribune*: "In Chicago, there is the mysterious *something*. In Chicago, a spirit broods upon the face of the water. Find me a writer who is American and who has something new to say, and nine times out of ten I will show that he has some sort of connection with the abattoir by the lake—that he was bred there, got his start there, or passed through there during the days when he was tender."

In order for Weeghman to make his dreams come true, he needed money, notoriety, and a reputation for quality. He obtained all three in abundance, though he may have had to sell his soul in order to do it.

THE RAKE'S PROGRESS

"His restaurants, which offered food at low prices with rapid service, thrived and he became a millionaire," recorded the *Daily News* in 1938.

Charley Weeghman was around at the birth of what is now called "fast food," and it is impossible now to imagine any part of America—whether it be a big city, a suburban strip mall, or a country roadside exit—surviving without it. Weeghman's restaurant chain, and especially its innovation, standardization, and predictable product amid the chaos of the workday of the early twentieth century, serves as a delightful metaphor for the hot, swinging, innovative society Chicago was at that time.

Weeghman found the key to making a lot of money off the growing middle class and lower middle class by giving them dependable, quick lunch food, which fit with the population's fast-working, fast-living lifestyle.

His restaurants "were jammed, especially at noon when the ribbon clerks and the Rover boys dashed out for a slight snack," wrote Harry Neily. "Weeghman was going to town in a big way, but still was big-hearted Charley to all who knew him."

What Charley really wanted was to continue his move up the social ladder and become a gentleman of society, a sportsman. Handsome, rakish, and sporting dandified outfits, gardenias in his lapel, and bowler hats, Weeghman was enthusiastic enough to win over even the most cynical local reporters.

As the money rolled in from his restaurants, Weeghman began to diversify. He owned a theater at 58 West Madison Street in downtown Chicago and also invested in a pool hall, motion picture houses, and even a film production company. Baseball would be next.

WHEN JIMMY MET CHARLEY

When James Gilmore called on Lucky Charley, he got at least as much as he bargained for. Weeghman was ambitious, calculating, hardworking, friendly, proud, and fit for battle. As a *Literary Digest* article noted, "Mr. Weeghman for some time had wanted to buy a baseball club. In 1911 he tried to purchase the St. Louis Nationals."

Rebuffed in his efforts to join the old-money boys, Weeghman grew a chip on his shoulder the size of one of his sandwiches. "He takes some pride in saying that he made his wealth in his business," noted Sam Weller in the January 4, 1914, *Tribune*.

The December 27, 1913, Federal League reorganization, which named Weeghman Chicago club president and, according to the *Tribune*, its "principal backer," meant that the new loop had acquired a serious money man who was already a darling of the Chicago media. For many years after, Weeghman was known as the "angel" of the Federal League. Given his public persona and his huge bankroll, no other title would have fit.

A willing participant in the twists and turns of industry and a man who knew how to play the press, Weeghman would be joined in the executive suite by William Walker, a fishmonger with a successful business in the (still-extant) South Water Street market district.

While both Weeghman and Walker threw in buckets of money, the latter seemed content to remain a silent partner. Weeghman, described as "a live wire willing to risk his money in the fight" by Sox owner Charles Comiskey, was excellent copy.

Enthusiastic about any coverage, positive or mocking, Weeghman was one of the most well-known names and well-liked people in the city during the early part of the century. And he worked his buddies at the newspapers to get the coverage he needed.

"THE NAME GAME . . . CHIFEDS!"

In those less formal days, before the existence of marketing firms or PR consultancies, the Chicago Feds (much like the other clubs in the upstart league) didn't even have official names. The local sportswriters, therefore, took matters into their own ink-stained hands. While the *American* referred to Chicago's upstart nine as the Feds, or the local Feds, and at least once as the "tots," the *Post*—bald-faced supporters of the club—dubbed them, in a none-too-obtuse reference to Charley Weeghman's restaurants, the Buns. This name apparently was quite popular among fans and the press and stuck through the 1914 season. The *Post* also referred to them punningly as the "Feeds," while their manager's fame led to them being called the "Tinx" as well.

Ring Lardner of the *Tribune* took note of this and even proposed a reader contest to name the new club. However, he noted sadly on April 23 that "though more than a hundred fans have entered the competition and suggested nicknames for Joe Tinker's new club, not one has come across with an appellation that hit us right between the eyes." Lardner reported suggestions of food-oriented names such as the Sinkers, Doughnuts, Buns, Chefs, Feeds, Pies, Figs, and Bakers but commented that "none of these can be called convincing."

Weeghman and his Buns certainly had all the publicity and attention they could handle in those heady days of winter 1913–14. Lardner joked about the confluence of Weeghman's two businesses in the January 1, 1914,

Tribune: "We have it on good authority that coffee and two rolls will be served free to each patron of the local Federal League club next summer."

In the aftermath of Joe Tinker's shocking signing, more players defected to the upstart Federals. Otto Knabe, Mordecai Brown, Howie Camnitz, Cy Falkenborg, Russell Ford, Solly Hofman, and Al Bridwell, among others, inked with the new loop. The addition of known players to each league's team, a clause that Weeghman insisted each owner agree to, gave the new league some respectability and led a few early press dissenters closer to the Feds' corner.

CHARLES IN CHARGE

The extent to which the Chicago club was toting the Federal League's barge is clear from the reporting from the winter of 1913–14. As Charlie Comiskey noted about Weeghman and the Chifeds, "One club cannot make a league, and I don't believe his associates are in the same class with him as a sportsman."

Shortly after Weeghman took over the franchise, he was summed up thusly in the *Daily News*. "Mr. Weeghman, immensely popular among the sporting element of Chicago, says *he will make the Federal League just as important* a cog in the baseball machine as the National or American league." [Italics added.]

An article written by Harvey Woodruff in the February 15, 1914, *Tribune* noted that Weeghman and Walker would be in the hole for $125,000 each before the season was to open and that "Chicago probably will have the heaviest single investment of any club in the league." It was certain and would always remain known that Weeghman was the leading light in what was already being called "The Flap-Jack League."

Two months into his job, Weeghman was not certain that his fellow FL owners had the money needed to run the league. "Lucky Charley" was also clearly interested in bigger fish. "If six of the eight teams in the Federal League can show me the goods, I am in to stay," he averred in the January 17, 1914, *Daily News*.

"Would you buy the St. Louis Browns?" a reporter then asked.

"How much do they want?"

WHY LAKE VIEW?

It was important that Weeghman, Walker, and Gilmore find a large plot of land that could be quickly cleared. There was theoretically little to do but buy off the businesses and homes currently occupying the lot, clear the land, and build.

Later, the outlaws would find that tearing down some of the houses on the lot, getting required signatures from several hundred area residents, whistling past the objections of community groups, and fighting off the dogged efforts of organized ball to keep them out of the game would take big bites out of their wallets.

Weeghman, Walker, and Gilmore saw themselves as forward-thinking, groundbreaking fellows, dedicated to creating a new order for themselves outside of what they saw as a stodgy and irrelevant establishment—which is not to say that Weeghman didn't wish he had been "old money" himself.

Putting a new park on the north side of town was clearly their vision of progress. It was cheaper, far enough away from the White Sox and Cubs to help the Feds build their own identity, and would not suffer in comparison to the parks of established big league clubs. In addition, it made plenty of sense to claim this expanding part of the city for the newcomers.

In December, stories made the rounds that the Feds would acquire the site on what *Sporting Life,* on December 27, 1913, called "the famous open lot at Addison and Clark Streets." Gilmore refused to confirm or deny the reports.

Several years later, in January 1918, when Weeghman had bought the Cubs, *The Sporting News* gave its opinion as to why the park was built in Lake View: "The millionaires who own the Cubs love scenery of the North Shore, where their homes are located. They are eager to build up a baseball following there. The game, for them, is a hobby and a diversion. They care little for a few paltry hundred thousand dollars. They want to satisfy their pride and win glory for their section. They are not in the game for money alone."

At the time, the ultra-establishment *Sporting News* was angry with Weeghman for the Cubs' free spending on players, which the paper believed would lead to peril. This feeling clearly colors the paper's viewpoint of the team's owners. However, many of the people involved with the stadium at the time (and in the days of the Federal League) *were* North Siders, resolutely trendy and interested in trailblazing.

Bill Veeck Jr. raised two other possible reasons for the park's location. His father, Bill Veeck Sr., at the time writing under the name "Bill Bailey" for the *Chicago American,* would later work for the Cubs (as would the son). Veeck the younger felt that the decision to build a park in Lake View came down to money, specifically front-end cost and possible business.

Veeck *fils* opined that Weeghman wanted the land at Clark and Addison "to get a piece of land he could afford. Bear in mind, one wouldn't put up a ballpark next to a coal yard by choice." He also noted that since motorcars were not yet affordable for most, the park needed to be close to public transportation. "Clark and Addison was an ideal location because the streetcar and elevated lines were nearby."

ELSIE DABEL'S DIARY

The 1914 diary of Elsie Dabel, a teenage girl living in Lake View, is available as part of the Chicago Public Library's collection of documents from the Lake View Historical Society. Among Ms. Dabel's notes of going to Lake View High School, dusting the family's dining room, and heading to local theaters to see the moving picture shows of stars like Mary Pickford, she writes on January 30: "We are going to have a grand new ball park right here on Sheffield and Addison. The Federal League ball park. It's going to be a *pippin*. Oh, you Johnnies!"

MAKING A FEDERAL CASE OF IT

Some of the Fed owners were just out to line their pockets. Some of them had grander designs in mind, at least for public consumption. President James Gilmore and Brooklyn owner Robert Ward stood out as the most revolutionary.

The March 14, 1914, *Post* started an interview with Gilmore this way: "One glance at James A. Gilmore, big chief of the Federal League, and you are immediately stuck with the idea that he is quite a busy cup of tea . . . Three minutes' talk with him made the old dyed-in-the-wool, blown-in-the-bottle baseball scribes rub their eyes and wonder how a yelping baseball public ever got along without a third big league."

What made Gilmore such a firecracker? His manner, his bearing, and, above all, his radical ideas about the reserve clause. "Mr. Johnson of the American League criticizes us bitterly for not respecting the reserve clause of major league contracts," Gilmore said in the *Post*.

> Now, in my own defense, I want to say that *no* man should respect that clause. I don't think it is equitable to the ball player, because it is a clause that binds him practically for life without stipulating any salary after the first year.
>
> Personally, I think baseball players, with regard in their box-office worth, are the most miserably paid performers in the world . . . we intend that the men who bring fame to our fold shall be paid accordingly. We realize before we start that it is up to the players whether we shall draw the "gates" or not. When we see that it is one player or a set of players, we won't crawl behind the safe and tighten the strings on the "dough bag," as the boys affectionately term it, but rather will we share with them.

Meanwhile, Brooklyn owner Robert Ward told the press in late March that Fed players would share in the team's profits. "The plan is unique in baseball annals," reported the *Post*, "and seems to indicate that the Brooklyn Feds have a wealth of financial backing."

This is not to imply that either Gilmore or Ward were wild-eyed Bolsheviks. Their strategy of positive player–club relations was certainly slanted toward tempting talent from other clubs. The *New York Times* noted on April 6, 1914, that "President Ward of the Brooklyn Club stated yesterday that he believed his scheme of profit sharing with the ball players would be the means of attracting many players to his team."

Ward, a wealthy baker, was actually an old-fashioned fellow who disapproved of Sunday baseball, which by the early 1900s had become customary in organized leagues. This anti-Sabbath-ball stance brought great ridicule from *The Sporting News*. Ward's power, however, carried the day, and the Brookfeds remained idle each Sunday during the 1914 FL season.

SEALING THE DEAL

A great deal of intrigue and skullduggery shrouded the Feds' attempt to lease the land from the Cantillons and Archambault. The Feds were under a time crunch to get the land ready to build a ballpark in time for the 1914 season, but the deal to turn over the land went right down to the wire. Reported the *Tribune*'s Irv Sanborn on December 30, 1913: "Negotiations for the location, which at one time was to have housed an American Association team, have been on for a quite a spell and the deal was not consummated until the Federal people brought considerable pressure to bear on the owners of the north side property."

What kind of pressure? And why wouldn't the Cantillons, presumably with no other plans for the land, just sign the lease agreement? Because the major leagues were already up to their hips in this one, pressuring the Cantillons into refusing to sell. In his *Tribune* story, Sanborn continued, "The forces of organized baseball are said to have been working to block the scheme to locate a Federal League club on the Addison street site with some prospect of success."

They did this in many ways: threatening, pleading, cajoling, and, finally, trying to buy out the Feds. But it was too late. The power base of the Federal League was not interested in anything but equal footing. Weeghman, Walker, and Gilmore, who had earlier acquired a one-month, five-hundred-dollar option to lease the property on December 2, 1913, were more than ready with their own brand of hardball to combat the majors. Sanborn continues: "As a countermove, the Federal backers obtained an option on the old White Sox park at Thirty-ninth Street and Wentworth Avenue, occupied by the [Negro League] American Giants since the erection of Comiskey Park."

Faced with the resolve of Weeghman, Walker, and Gilmore, and contemplating the frightening possibility of the new Federal League club intending to compete just *four blocks* from the White Sox' current location, the major leagues had to give in. The Feds would be able to lease the Clark and Addison property, a property that eventually became one of Major League Baseball's great showplaces.

In a sharp last piece of strategy, Weeghman said he was holding on to his option on the 39th Street ball yard in case of emergency. (The emergency, presumably, would involve not getting his new North Side park built on time.) While the American Giants' owner, J. M. Schorling, denied that Weeghman had any such agreement, the point soon became moot. The *Tribune* reported the very next day, December 31, 1913, that Mike Cantillon was on his way down from St. Paul to sign the papers leasing the property to the Chicago Federal League club. The North Side would finally get its ballpark.

Reported the *Tribune* in February 1914, "the rental is $16,000 for the first year. In addition to the lease, Weeghman and Walker were compelled to buy a little piece of land [for $15,000] [that] was not included. It was only 15 [actually six] by 100 feet, but its possession was necessary before work on the park could be started."

The complete lease terms were sixteen thousand dollars for the first ten years, eighteen thousand dollars for the second ten, and twenty thousand dollars for each of the remaining seventy-nine years of the lease. Weeghman told the local papers in January 1914 that he had already obtained consent of local property owners to construct the park; he needed such permission in order to obtain a building permit.

Weeghman immediately violated two pieces of the agreement. The first was a stipulation that the renters spend no more than seventy thousand dollars on upkeep and construction on the grounds; the second was that they tamper with no members of the Minneapolis Millers.

First, he announced that his new stadium would cost $250,000, more than three times the amount for construction allowed by the contract. Then, in early March, Ring Lardner reported in the *Tribune* that the Whales had offered Joe Cantillon, player-manager of the Millers, a fifteen-thousand-dollar contract to come south. Cantillon stayed put.

In a very short time, events had transpired that would lead to the building of arguably the most beloved sports venue in America.

IF THEY BUILD IT, WHO WILL COME?

Building a new ballpark for a team just getting around to declaring itself major league was certainly an act of faith. Committing to doing so just four months before opening the season was both brave and foolhardy. But Weeghman wouldn't have it any other way. Even before getting the legal documents giving him a lease on the land at Clark and Addison, he was ready. On December 28, he told John Seys of the *Tribune*, "I propose to build a grand stand of steel or concrete to cost about $100,000 or $125,000 if necessary. I have asked for bids and within the next forty-eight hours the contract will be let."

The timing of the construction and the location of the park were perfect for several reasons. First, the humming Lake View area was easily accessible by elevated train and trolley car and, increasingly, by automobile. In addition, with population and attention moving to the north side of town, the Feds were unknowingly sowing seeds for a ballpark that would bind itself to its community.

A CITY OF BASEBALL

How could Chicago have been expected to support more than the two major league teams? Easy: the city was baseball-crazy. In addition to the baseball played by the Sox, Cubs, and local Negro League clubs, there was semipro ball, too.

As Robert G. Spinney wrote in *City of Big Shoulders: A History of Chicago*, baseball was a critical factor in the "Americanization" of immigrants, and Chicago has always been a city of immigrants: "In Chicago and other large cities, baseball became the first popular professional sport. It is especially important to consider baseball's social impact on ethnically diverse cities like Chicago. The baseball park was a place (and perhaps the only place) where all Chicagoans—Anglo-Americans, Germans, the Irish, Italians, Jews, the wealthy and the poor, the educated and the illiterate—met on equal terms. Chicagoans who had little in common shared a common experience: they could root for the home team."

An indoor baseball league began in Chicago in 1910 and prospered through the decade as clubs from all over the city competed during the winter. Independent clubs, park teams, and church clubs formed leagues. The 1914 indoor league title game was played between Marquette and Columbus before 967 fans at the St. Alphonsus gymnasium.

Other local semipro leagues had worked their way into Chicago's consciousness around the same time. The March 27, 1914, *Post* reported, "The Craftsman Baseball league clubs expect to play at the Washington Park field this season. The board of directors of the league have petitioned the board of park commissioners, asking the privilege of using the park grounds and no trouble is anticipated."

Back in February, the *American* had noted the birth of yet another league. In early April, the *Post* gave its readers all the dope.

> Another baseball league has blossomed forth, which is expected to prove a hummer. The new organization will be composed of teams residing back of the yards and will be called the Stock Yards league. There are so many boys anxious to join the new league that [organizer J.] Sokol was obliged to make it an eight-club circuit. Each club will be allowed to carry but eighteen players, and each player will have to sign a contract to play throughout the whole year—major league stuff. The clubs entered in this new organization are Jolly Boys, Woods, Silvery Bells, Willows, Waunettas, Seeley Colts, Starlights, and Deltas.

Clearly, with numerous semipro clubs and multiple major league franchises, Chicago was mad for the national game. But another key reason that all these clubs were able to support themselves is that each club identified with a very specific part of the city. In those days before radio or television allowed fans to "follow" their clubs on a minute-by-minute basis, physical proximity was far more important to being a rooter than it is now. And despite 1914's rapidly improving public transportation, Chicago was still a sprawling mix of diverse neighborhoods, each with its own personality. To this day, it still means something in the Windy City to say that you hail from Bridgeport, Logan Square, Bronzeville, Hegewisch, Edgebrook, Beverly, Pullman, or Rogers Park.

The idea of the North Side getting its own team was a big, big deal back in 1914. It showed many in the town that the power base of Chicago was indeed moving north; with a sparkling new park opening at Clark and Addison, the dirty old West Side Grounds became even less attractive, and fabled Comiskey suddenly seemed far away.

Having a team close to one's own neighborhood—just a good walk or a trolley or a bicycle ride from home—could now be a source of pride for residents of the North Side just as it already was for South and West Siders.

NUTS (AND BOLTS) TO YOU

Weeghman and his cohorts acquired a lease for the land bordered on the south by Addison Street, on the east by Sheffield Avenue, on the north by Waveland Avenue, and on the west by Clark Street. The official address of the property would be 1052 West Addison Street. (For many years, the park's official address has been 1060 West Addison.)

Weeghman noted in late December 1913 that the lot he would build on was 600 by 598 feet, but city hall measured the land leased by the Chifeds at 532 4/10 by 540 feet. The difference in sizes was due to Weeghman's premature belief that he would be able to easily acquire a small piece of land "connecting the property at Addison and North Clark streets," according to the *Daily News* of January 19. "[Weeghman] said it is owned by a friend of his who was offered $25,000 by an unknown party."

The over-the-top, last-minute offer was, of course, another attempt to throw the Feds off course. "I knew that organized ball was behind that offer," Weeghman told the *Tribune* on January 18. However, that option to sell the land to the third party expired, nobody showed up to buy the land on the agreed-upon date, and Weeghman eventually acquired the extra strip of real estate.

As the *Tribune* stated on January 20, 1914, "Organized ball made another effort yesterday morning to grab that little strip of ground on the Federal's site, thus blocking the chance to put a ball park there, but when the agent of the majors appeared he was informed that Charles Weeghman . . . had been ahead of him and had obtained the property. In desperation organized ball offered $40,000, but the much-coveted piece of real estate was already in the hands of the independent body and the agent retired crestfallen."

Comical as is the image of the major leagues offering forty thousand dollars for a piece of land six feet wide and a hundred feet long, it also shows just how desperate organized ball was to keep the Federal League out of the picture by thwarting its strongest franchise. Organized ball tried once more to hamstring the Feds in late January, putting up money to have local residents file an injunction to stop Weeghman and his men from building on the Clark and Addison property. The engineered protest did not work, but the story did get into the papers for a few days.

SHOW ME THE MONEY

By this time, the small strip of real estate was among the Feds' smallest worries. On Saturday, January 17, the league held a raucous and tense meeting in Chicago; during the meeting, it became clear that the new amalgamation was in something resembling deep trouble. Several writers voiced doubts that the league would even stay alive through the weekend.

Weeghman, apparently tired of pulling the train himself, was demanding that other club owners follow his lead and fork over the dough to make their clubs competitive—and quickly. Weeghman had options; organized baseball was, checkbook in hand, pleading with him to pull out of the Feds. "At four o'clock in the afternoon, it looked as if the Federal League was in great distress," penned the *Tribune*'s Sam Weller. "There was an air of nervous disorder about the meeting room in the Hotel LaSalle that seemed to forecast a collapse."

Sporting Life's April 4, 1914, issue quoted Weeghman's friend H. J. Murphy of Hyde Park, who noted that Charley "quit the fold at that meeting only to be brought in again by Otto Stifel, of St. Louis, who put up the necessary argument in the form of hard cash, and who, it is said, saved the Federal ship."

"Sloufed" owner Stifel responded to Weeghman's threat by committing a huge sum to player acquisition, urging other FL magnates to follow. They called Charley's bluff, and the league—for the moment—was saved.

Weeghman was contrite and gracious in the January 19 *Tribune*. "I wanted the other fellows who were going into this thing with me to show me some money and players," he noted, "and they showed me so much money right up in that meeting room Saturday afternoon that I felt ashamed for having asked it of them."

THE MAJORS DON'T GIVE UP

Even after Weeghman had signed the lease, farmed out plans for his ballpark, and stated publicly that he was behind the Feds 100 percent, the American League and National League bigwigs continued their ridiculous efforts to snuff out the new league, by hook or by crook. H. J. Murphy, Lucky Charley's South Side pal, told *Sporting Life* that, just before the January 17 meeting, Weeghman had been offered five hundred thousand dollars—*in cash*—to quit the Feds immediately. No go. According to Murphy, "I know that he is wrapped up body and soul in the new organization, and he has told me repeatedly that he fully expected the initial season to pay 100 cents on every dollar's worth of stock."

The *Inter-Ocean* reported in March that Weeghman "seemed hurt that whoever started the story—and [Weeghman] expressed the opinion that it was organized baseball—was so stingy with the figures in naming the cash consideration of the imaginary transaction."

Why would the major leagues try so hard to get rid of the Feds? The most important reason was to fend off an unwelcome competitor that was driving player salaries higher than any owner could have imagined in his worst nightmares a year before. Payouts for all good players rose every time the Feds threatened to steal one of them away. Even top-level minor leaguers, many of them very attractive to the new league, were obtaining top dollar from their clubs.

In addition, the majors wanted badly to fend off what they saw as the strongest organization in the new league, a well-publicized and well-financed club that would cut into White Sox and Cubs attendance. In mid-January 1914, someone in baseball came up with the idea of merging two of the top minor leagues, the International League and the American

Association, to freeze out the Feds, with the St. Paul club of the AA moving to Chicago. This idea went nowhere.

At one point, according to Bill Bailey (i.e., Veeck) of the *American*, organized baseball was even trying to buy Weeghman away from the Feds and into the American Association itself. On February 10, 1914, Bailey reported:

> Charles W. Murphy, president of the Cubs, to-day was on his way to New York, and he was hopping mad . . . the thing which has riled him is the fact that they [AL & NL] are trying to place a third league team in Chicago without his consent. This third league team is to be of the organized brand. Here is the scheme which the West Side magnate is of the opinion that they are trying to put through: They would tempt Charles Weeghman to ditch the Federals and grab the St. Paul franchise of the American Association. This team would be placed on the north side.

The defiant Murphy raged that "there isn't a chance for the American Association to place a team in Chicago. They have been trying to do it for years. They won't succeed." One would have thought this was right, because agreements were already in place to keep minor league organizations out of big league cities. However, these agreements were clearly not worth the parchment they were scratched on, because escape clauses were built in. And in this case, the AL and NL would try anything to peel Weeghman and his dollars away from Gilmore and the Feds.

As Bailey further explained, "In order to [allow a new organized ball league into a major league territory], it is necessary for five of the National League club owners and five of the American League fellows to vote their consent. It's a rule in organized baseball that the territory of the majors is sacred unless a majority of the club owners of both leagues vote their consent."

Ultimately, Weeghman didn't end up in the American Association. On February 17, the *Chicago Daily Journal* reported that Ban Johnson, president of the American League, shot down the plan to allow Lucky Charley to take either the St. Paul or Toledo AA club and bring it to Chicago. Maybe Johnson did nix the plan, but whether or not the AL approved, it would have made no sense for Weeghman to be in the AA, a successful minor league but a minor league nonetheless. Charley had his own self-proclaimed major league franchise riding a wave of popular press and about to open its own new ballpark. If Doughnut Charley couldn't have the Cubs, he wanted to beat them at their game. Why would he defect?

Indeed, Bailey noted, "Mr. Weeghman says that he will do nothing of the sort. He declares that he is in the Federal League to stick." It's hard to tell who was doing more denying that they wanted to be in business together—Weeghman or the major leagues—but a couple of years later, they would be sharing the same bed.

On March 5, after Charlie Murphy had been dumped from his throne atop the Cubs empire, the *Post* ran a story in which they noted that fans might get "a chance to see (possibly) Charley Weeghman become owner of the Cubs." He went to New York that week to meet with officials from the AL and NL, but it is not clear whether he was actually offered a chance to buy in. Whatever the content of those meetings, Weeghman stuck with the Feds, and the leagues finally had to swallow the idea that this merry band of rebels was determined to see this crazy thing through.

The Association, at the behest of various anti-Fed factions in the major leagues, considered the idea of putting a team in Chicago to cut into the Feds anyway, but this plan was quickly abandoned before anything came of it.

All sorts of operators were looking to cut in. In early January, it was reported that Weeghman had been offered ten thousand dollars cash in exchange for his Opening Day gate. Weeghman turned that proposition down flat.

GETTING IN TUNE

With property in hand, plus assurance that theirs wasn't the only franchise laying out the bucks, Weeghman and Walker went ahead with the next step: building their ballpark. The plans were laid out very quickly but were hardly haphazard.

Despite now having an option for a comparatively large parcel of land, the Federals did not plan to bulldoze the entire property for the ballpark. "Some of the buildings on the north end of the lot will be allowed to stand, as they bring in a rental of $6,000 a year," Weeghman noted. The park's left-field fence would creep up close to the rental properties but, for now, would not force their destruction.

However, some businesses and homes were marked for bulldozing. Most homeowners settled quickly with the Chifeds, but one business, American Sand and Gravel, liked its location and had to be "convinced" to leave. "We would like to accommodate the baseball men," said the company's manager, a Mr. Lewis, but "our lease still has a year and a half to run. It is not a question of money with us, but a question of whether we want to desert that location, which is one of the best we have."

Eventually, Mr. Lewis took the money and ran.

PLANS

On January 8, forty-two-year-old architect Zachary T. Davis, who had built "The Base Ball Palace of the World" (Comiskey Park) just four years earlier on the south side of town, submitted plans to Weeghman for the Federal League ballpark—or "plant," as it was referred to at the time. This use of "plant," with its subtext of ballpark as factory, is rather charming. Weeghman intended for his expensive new creation to serve not only as a baseball stadium but also as a shopping mall.

Irv Sanborn, in the January 8, 1914, *Tribune*, noted that the lot would have "space enough outside the stands on the corner of Addison and Clark streets for stores which would bring good rents." When Ring Lardner heard of this, he quipped, "Space is to be left on the Addison-Clark corner for several stores. What will you bet us that one of them won't be a restaurant?"

The Feds clearly had a strategy of keeping some land for rent. Weeghman himself told Harvey Woodruff of the *Tribune*, "The terms of our lease require an outlay of $125,000 in improvements, of which $75,000 must be within the first two years. This latter amount will be more than covered by the grand stand . . . When we place store buildings on part of the property and rent ground which we do not need, we figure that the revenue received will pay the rental and taxes on the whole tract and give us the space occupied by the park without one cent of expense."

While Davis's original plan had 125 feet of sidewalk space at the corner of Clark and Addison, it was decided that seventy-five feet of space would do it and that the extra room should be added to the dimensions of the playing field. The *Tribune* article noted that the buffed-up diamond (initially proposed as 325 feet to each foul line and 400 feet to center) would be "more spacious than the average major league park."

Weeghman said that he wanted the park to be more like the Polo Grounds than any other edifice but, when finished, the new Chicago baseball playpen bore little resemblance to the quadrilateral-shaped New York stadium. It was actually more like Comiskey Park, the diamond-shaped edifice Davis had built on the South Side. However, the skeleton of the grandstand itself *was* very much like that of the Polo Grounds.

In a 1989 *Cubs Magazine* article, Vickie Pietryga quoted Kurt Rim of Osborn Engineering, a company that had just helped renovate Wrigley Field: "Certainly Davis knew about baseball sight lines and the layout of a ballpark. From the steel work and column structure that was designed to hold an upper deck to the way he sized the ramps that can now hold 38,000 people, his knowledge of building a ballpark was more than adequate."

With the plans for Chicago's stadium finished, Davis—a native of Aurora, Illinois, west of South Side Chicago—went on to aid C. B. Comstock in designing Washington Park, new home of the Brooklyn Feds. Zachary Davis, with his brother Charles, also designed several other important buildings in Chicago, including the Naval Armory on Lake Shore Drive, Quigley Preparatory Seminary in Streeterville, and St. Ambrose Church on 47th Street. Zachary Davis died in 1946.

A FEW MORE PLANS

Davis's economical but attractive design was incredibly prescient. The park was planned to include a large single "grand stand" (at the time, the words were separated, with "grand" then meaning "great") rather than the double-decked stands Davis built for the South Side park. However, expansion was in Weeghman's mind from the beginning. He said at the time, "It will be so constructed that we can add wings to it at any time when patronage demands it." Irv Sanborn wrote in the January 8, 1914, *Tribune*, "The structure will have foundations and uprights designed to permit a second deck if desired at some future time."

The initial seating plan called for a total capacity of twenty thousand, including thirteen thousand in the grandstand (with eight thousand box seats), four thousand in pavilion seats at each end of the grandstand, and approximately three thousand ten-cent bleacher seats for the hardiest of "bugs."

In order to facilitate usage of the Addison Street elevated station, Davis designed an exit at Addison and Sheffield, close to the right-field corner. The corner of Clark and Addison was earmarked both for the park's main entrance and for access to the ballpark's proposed shopping complex.

The contractor hired to build what would be known as Weeghman Park was the Blome-Sinek Company, specializing in cement paving, asphalt floors, and concrete construction. The contractor, with its offices located near City Hall, estimated the construction and labor costs at $250,000. When the park was finished, both Blome-Sinek and Zachary and Charles Davis were allowed to post signs advertising their services on the ballpark wall facing Addison Street.

Building a park was a huge expense for Weeghman, but he pressed on. "When this thing started," Weeghman said in February, "we sat down and figured it out where we could sign a ball team and have a nice, modest little park for an expenditure of $50,000. We're in $125,000 and haven't started work on our grand stand."

Weeghman was already concerned about his image in the community. M. J. Wathey of the *Herald* reported on March 5 that "Weeghman promises that it will be an edifice of beauty, which will benefit the property around it rather than be a detriment."

TURN INTO EARTH

On February 23, the actual work began. The *Tribune* reported that "the first work fell to a wrecking crew, which began to tear down the frame buildings at the corner of Clark and Addison . . . Until the weather moderates it will be hardly possible to start the construction of the grand stand."

Four buildings on the seminary grounds were ripped down on February 24, but most observers didn't believe that the park could be thrown up in time. "It looks like a matter of difficulty to secure anything like a suitable plant by the time the season opens," noted the *Daily Journal* on February 28. Weeghman, however, remained confident, telling the papers that he expected everything to be ready for the club's first game in late April.

BREAKIN' THE GROUND

Weeghman and his men rushed to set up a flashy groundbreaking ceremony for the new ballpark. The photo-op was originally scheduled for March 3, with Mayor Carter Harrison to turn the first shovelful of dirt into a gaping hole at the corner of Sheffield and Addison (not, curiously, at Clark and Addison, where the main entrance was built). Sam Weller from the *Tribune* noted that "the moving picture camera man, officials of the local club, and the mayor are to be present, and all the fans are invited."

However, Mayor Harrison was ill and, despite the presence of thirty-five hundred fans at the site, the ceremony was pushed back to March 4 at 10:00 a.m. Two thousand Fed followers showed up on that frosty morning. In between speeches from city and club officials, a band performed patriotic songs (although an earlier report in the *Herald* had promised a tango orchestra). Harrison was still unable to attend, but Chicago's building commissioner, Henry Ericsson, turned the first spade of dirt. William Walker's young son J. W., nicknamed "Buster," smashed a bottle of bubbly over the shovel, which led to a huge cry from the assembled throng.

Ring Lardner in the March 6 *Tribune* opined that "those present at the festivities at Addison and Clark Wednesday morning think it was foolish to waste a bottle of champagne by breaking it over the spade." Referring to Weeghman's menu, Lardner continued, "A cup of coffee, [a] Boston, or a pint of oysters would have been less expensive and more appropriate."

The energetic Weeghman, ever the ham, took hold of the shovel at one point for the benefit of the photographers. As still cameras clicked and film cameras whirred, he furiously dug into the frigid ground "as if he would build his entire stand himself," the *Tribune* noted. When the pomp and circumstance were completed, police and workmen "assisted the crowd off the field," reported the *Herald*. William Sinek, the chief contractor on the project, immediately began to direct a hundred workmen in preliminary construction of the grandstand.

Oddly enough, former Cubs owner Charlie Murphy was in the news on that day as well. He and his wife were involved in a three-car crash at North

Avenue and Lake Shore Drive, Mrs. Murphy being thrown from the car and suffering a broken arm.

OILED

The next evening, March 5, the Chifeds organized a huge banquet at a downtown restaurant called States, where four hundred fans and club officials gathered. The room was festooned with baseballs and bats, manager and Mrs. Joe Tinker showed up, and Weeghman was at his usual crowd-pleasing best. Around midnight, the well-oiled guests began taking matches to souvenir balloons, which produced flashes of flame and, according to the *Daily News*, an auditory blast that "sounded like an attack at Fort Sumter."

Before everyone got drunk, Weeghman had told the press that he was planning to install potted plants atop the brick right field wall along Sheffield Avenue and that he intended the new park to be one of the prettiest in the nation. However, it does not appear that the potted plants ever showed up. Even so, Lucky Charley had already proven that he was serious about small details; in January, he hired away Mike Murphy, a former Tigers' groundskeeper with twenty years' experience, to tend his new park.

GIVE THE PEOPLE WHAT THEY WANT

The Chifeds' public spokesman was smart enough to know that baseball alone would not differentiate his club from the Cubs or Sox, or even the American Giants or the semipro clubs. A man whose entire business model was predicated on getting bodies through his doors amid fierce competition, Weeghman saw—as few others in baseball did at the time—that a pampered customer would, more likely than not, be a return customer.

As a relative outsider to the world of sports management, Charley looked at the way baseball was run and realized that he couldn't guarantee whether his club won. And with several other teams in town, he knew that he had to create a special product. He saw in the baseball of the time a gap between what was and what could be. He understood that if fans were treated with respect and goodwill, they would be more inclined to come back to the park. At that time, owners of baseball clubs often didn't feel that they had to spend money on their fans, because baseball was the top spectator sport in town; the bugs and cranks were already turning out in great numbers.

They came out despite filthy conditions. How bad was it at the park in those grand old days? Back then, there were no concession stands at sports facilities, and most parks had only spartan (and often disgustingly unusable) restrooms. Aisles and walkways at the park were rarely swept, and vendors crowded everyone's view in order to hawk their wares.

And it was noisy. Opined the March 5, 1914, edition of the *Post*, "Let's express a deep-seated hope that the new president of the Cubs (whoever he is, or even Charlie Taft himself) does something to stop the noise nuisance at the West Side park this season. The fans will greatly appreciate it if the popcorn, pop, program, and perfecto [cigar] purveyors are silenced."

Weeghman, no dummy when it came to marketing, was full of ideas to modernize, streamline, and decorate in order to satisfy his customers and add new ones. He would do *anything* to differentiate himself from the competition on the West Side. As he had done in his restaurants, Lucky Charley mandated that his park be kept clean and shiny and that every possible care be taken to show the customer that he, or, significantly, *she*, was boss. "It is my belief that in order to draw and keep the fans, a club management must show plainly that the first thought is for the fan's comfort," Weeghman told a reporter from the *Post*, which ran a lengthy story on the Fed owner's customer-friendly plans on February 23, 1914. "I have been a baseball fan for years . . . and many a time have I gone to a park all dolled up in my very best regalia, only to find that in order to occupy my seat, I must either buy a cushion or ruin my clothes." While most fans of the time were probably not as dapper or dandified in their choice of garb as the stick-pinned, bowler-hatted, bow-tied Weeghman, the point was well-taken: most ballparks were filthy.

"The dusty and generally dirty condition of several of the parks is not the only undesirable feature that the fan has been forced to tolerate," he noted. "The retiring rooms for men and women are generally a disgrace to a park . . . We will have the very best that is to be had in all branches, and will spare nothing in making the park one of solid comfort.

"There will be no abusive ushers to insult fans and there will be no dusty and dirty seats and filthy aisles for the fans to complain about. Every morning will find a corps of men at work dusting and cleaning the stands."

LOST TO HISTORY?

Charley told *Sporting Life* in April 1914, "We intend to have our plant in a condition that would be a credit to Spotless Town." Everyone who read that story at the time knew the reference. The phrase "Spotless Town" referred to an anti-germs marketing campaign by a popular soap manufacturer, Sapolio, which pitted its hygienically minded citizens against those dirty folks living in neighboring "Dingeytown." Infused with anti-infectious disease enthusiasm, actual cities voted to become "Spotless Towns" in the early 1900s.

Weeghman certainly believed cleanliness meant customers would come again and again. But he clearly also wanted to elevate the game of baseball to accommodate a more gentrified class: people like himself, the *nouveau riche* of go-go Chicago.

REFRESHER COURSE

Food, of course, was a major topic in any conversation with Weeghman. He outlined his plan briefly in *Sporting Life*: "We are considering the installation of a system for supplying our patrons with refreshments, which will lessen the annoyance caused by noisy peddlers."

In the *Post*, he discussed his plans with the same relish as one would while tucking into one of his huge dinner rolls:

> We are thinking seriously of adopting a system of passing refreshments around the crowd. This will do away with the old time-honored curse by which one is forced to do a Hercules stunt in holding up some obnoxious peanut vendor.
>
> The new system provides long rods, which are fitted with hooks for bags, and in which there is a lot running the entire length. The prospective purchaser makes known his desire, and whether it be popcorn, peanuts, or an ice cream cone, the stuff is attached to the end of the rod by the vendor and is extended out several feet. In return the purchaser drops his coin or coins in the slot and the money rolls into a cup at the receiving end of the rod.

This collection system didn't work out, but Weeghman soon came upon another idea to deal with the crush of leaning vendors. Weeghman's idea involved setting up small kiosks in the rear part of the grandstand. At these kiosks, customers could buy food unmolested and return to their seats. Thus was the permanent concession stand born.

THIS IS FOR THE GIRLS

During March 1914, Weeghman announced that he would institute Ladies Days at his new park. This was just another salvo in Weeghman's fight to draw fans away from the other two clubs—especially the Cubs, prohibited by National League rules from engaging in such a promotion.

On March 31, the Cubs announced that they would petition the league to renounce its five-year-old ban on Ladies Day. Although the American League had no such prohibition and the White Sox used the practice regularly, the Cubs were not successful in getting the NL to change its collective mind.

MYSTERY ACHIEVEMENT

Late on the morning of March 4, 1914, hundreds of construction workers began building what we now know as Wrigley Field. Holes were dug, foundations were poured, and steel, concrete, and wood were molded into a beautiful ballpark. In a period of just seven weeks, a park that lasts to this day was constructed. What is especially amazing is that anyone transported from 1914 to the present day would probably not have had much of a problem with the way Wrigley looked—at least until the lights were added.

Between March 4 and March 16, the construction men excavated the area, brought in materials, and dealt with the lousy weather. March 1914 was cold and blustery, as February had been, making it difficult for construction, but the work continued. The wood for the project, supplied by Herman Hettler's Lumber Company at 2601 N. Elston, provided the foundation for much of the bleachers as well as the scoreboard. On March 16, workers began erecting the structural steel for the grandstand, which was steel with a concrete foundation. By March 19, workers were laying the brick for the bleachers in right field. Just a few days later, by March 23, the more than four hundred workers had laid the complete foundation. Five days after that, all the rivets had been placed in the steel structure. Nobody from the league (or even the Chifeds organization) expected that the work would be done so fast, but Blome-Sinek whipped their workers into shape.

On March 29, the *Tribune* carried a large, revealing photograph of the park under construction. The shot was taken from center field. The first-base-side grandstand was nearly completed, while the bleachers appeared about half complete. The field, at this point nothing but a mass of dirt, was covered with wheelbarrows, large cranes, and woodpiles as workmen dotted the site.

WHILE YOU WERE OUT

With work under way, Weeghman, his wife, other Whales owners, and about thirty pals traveled to the club's training camp in Shreveport, Louisiana. Weeghman rented a huge train for the trip. Once in Louisiana, he donned a uniform and took batting practice with his charges.

Around this time, two Lake View residents, Herman and Margaretha Croon, filed suit, accusing the Chifeds of failing to obtain necessary consent from owners of property bordering the new ballpark. James Gilmore told the press, however, that the club had already obtained the necessary documentation and the scheduled work on the new park did not stop.

Another rumor, assumedly started by rogues from organized baseball, ran around Chicago saying Weeghman was broke. The amount of money he was spending for himself and his friends in Shreveport should have made that rumor a nonstarter.

STEE-RIKE!

On April 3 at 10:00 a.m., union construction workers at the park went on strike. Union bricklayers walked off the site, and the concrete reinforcement had to be halted as well. However, the work had already proceeded at such a furious pace that the soon-to-be-named Weeghman Park was actually ahead of schedule. When the striking workers returned on April 4, construction of the right-field bleachers and the grandstand roof was completed. Two days later, the chairs for the grandstand arrived. They were not immediately installed, however, because it took until April 9 before the concrete runways and seat slabs had set. It wasn't until April 20—three days before the park opened to the public—that the seats were actually installed.

A large space for cars was placed under the third-base grandstand, and much care was taken in constructing roomy walkways for visitors to get in and out of the park. Wrigley's walkways were open to the surrounding streets and thus not claustrophobic, in contrast to many ballparks of today.

RAVE REVIEWS

The day the strike was called, also around the time the press box was completed, Weeghman and Gilmore brought local reporters and officials to the site for a tour of the mostly done ballpark. According to Handy Andy in the April 4 *Tribune*, "All that remains to be done is to erect a stone wall, roll the diamond, and install some plumbing." He opined that once the just-arrived seats were installed, "the stands, as far as the spectator is concerned, will be as fit as any in these parts."

Bill Brennan, the Federal League's chief umpire, was part of the contingent that toured the ballpark on April 3. He gave the *Inter-Ocean*'s Walter Roderick a glowing review of the edifice. "It seems like a dream . . . and believe me, it is some park. Here's where the fellows sit that know the game," he continued, climbing up on the bleacher seats. "Here's where they call you 'robber.' It doesn't make any difference if you're up there at the plate and they're away out here, they know, and you can't tell 'em anything about the game they don't know."

As was noted at the time, the new park had a left-field distance of 310 feet to the fence and a right-field distance of 345 feet, making it larger than the West Side Grounds, which was 329 feet to straightaway right. The foul lines at West Side, a rectangular-shaped park typical of the day's baseball fields, were far shorter—around fifty feet shorter in left and sixty to seventy feet in right—than at Weeghman Park. The playing surface of the new park looked small to the reporters, but that may have been due in part to building materials lying on the field and several trees in left field that had yet to be removed.

The construction was already receiving rave reviews. Roderick noted in the *Inter-Ocean*, "The structure sweeps around in an elliptical curve so that none of the seats are very far from fair territory. The stand is very wide and slopes at such an incline that there are oceans of room and yet every one can get as good a view as the next fellow. There are no obstructions to cut off the line of vision from any angle."

THE PRICE OF BASEBALL

On April 8, Harvey Woodruff reported in the *Tribune* that Weeghman planned to charge "big league" prices for tickets at his park. Tickets for the Feds' Chicago games would cost seventy-five cents for grandstand seats and a buck for boxes—the same amount as the Cubs and White Sox. Woodruff also noted that the Feds planned to adopt the American League strategy of each visiting club taking an equal percentage from every game's box receipts. At the time, the National League distributed a *pro rata* of receipts from a game to each visiting team. Only a few seats were sold in advance at Chifeds games. Grandstand and bleacher seats were sold day-of-game, even for Opening Day.

The *Tribune* also noted on April 8 that Weeghman had ordered that the construction crew be increased in size from 450 to 850 men.

SCORES FOR ALL

The *Daily Journal* of April 14 noted that "preparations for the local Federal opening are being rushed along. The north side park is being completed in a hurry." A few days later, Blatz beer advertisements appeared in Chicago newspapers, topped by an artist's rendering of the new stadium. Shortly afterward, the Feds announced that all parks in the league would post the scores of the ongoing games of their town's major league clubs (including American Association games in Buffalo and Baltimore and International

League games in Indianapolis and Kansas City). The Cubs and White Sox did not reciprocate by listing Fed scores, even though Ring Lardner of the *Tribune* called for them to do so.

One last legal hurdle arose before Opening Day. As Handy Andy wrote in the April 23 *Tribune*, "The consent of nearly 1,000 more property owners of the neighborhood must be obtained before the Feds will be secure in their new park. Apparently everyone within 1,000 feet, or nearly three blocks, of the park must have his say in the matter, whereas the Feds have believed that only property owners immediately across from the four sides of the park need be consulted." The controversy was defused in time for Opening Day, with club officials racing around the neighborhood to collect signatures.

On April 9, the crew began building the brick fence that would surround the park. By April 18, the field-level scoreboard in left-center was completed. The next day, workers completed final work on the walls, restrooms, and clubhouse plumbing. Weeghman's directive that the facilities be top-notch was scrupulously followed.

A FIELD SITUATION

Only at this point, when the construction equipment had been moved from the field area, could head groundskeeper Murphy begin to roll the diamond, lay the sod, and map out the field.

Seeding of the grounds and smoothing of the field was being done up to the last minute. Pictures from the first game show that the infield dirt was "squared off," as was the norm, rather than rounded off as it is today. As was also customary at the time, a thin dirt track stretched between the mound and home plate.

The field was pulled together quickly considering that work on the playing surface began less than a week before the first pitch. Murphy could not lay the sod until a couple of days before the first game, and the cold and damp conditions made footing a bit soggy. By Opening Day, however, the surface was, in the words of F. A. McInerney in the *Tribune*, "level as a billiard table."

The field's location was a bit off from what we know today. During the off-season of 1922–23, the playing surface was rotated southwest to its present configuration, with home plate pointing directly northeast.

One hundred and fifty men from the George Wittbold Florist Company, located nearby at 727 Buckingham, served as landscapers at the new park. The gardeners from Wittbold brought in excess of four thousand pounds of soil and four acres of bluegrass.

HOW DID IT LOOK?

The Federal League Park appeared very much then as it does today as Wrigley Field—in fact, almost freakishly so. The shape of the grandstand, though single-decked then, would be familiar to current fans. The outfield fences and scoreboard looked nothing like the current park's, but the neighborhood landscape hasn't been altered significantly, and with grass and dirt on the field and mediocrities in the home dugout, how much really has changed?

The grandstands down the left- and right-field lines did not extend all the way to the foul lines. (Weeghman said in April 1914 that he planned on extending them the following year, but this did not happen.) In addition, spectators looked straight out; in other words, the seats farther down the line were not angled toward the field. Those adjustments came decades later.

However, the field was always intimate and the stands were always close to the action, although—believe it or not—the field is slightly nearer to the spectators now than it was in 1914. Some of the rooftops past the right-field wall already had advertising posted on them, one of them a billboard for the neighborhood Bismarck Garden tavern.

The grandstands had two sections: one of ten rows that sat closest to the field, and, behind a large aisle, another section of some twenty to twenty-five rows. There were bleachers from right field to center but no bleachers in left field where the scoreboard was located at field level. The flagpole, located in deep center field, was in play.

At that time, few ballparks had curved outfields, and Weeghman Park was no exception. Most of them were square or trapezoidal, largely because the parks were built on small parcels of land, surrounded by other buildings. But Weeghman's park was somewhat different. While some residences did abut the ballpark, the shape of the structure was singular and attractive. Only later did the playing field become round; at first, the park featured a very deep center field—440 feet—and the outfield took its current shape only in the late 1930s.

The outfield bleachers went up only about ten to twelve rows, with the bottom row just five feet above field level; therefore spectators in the third floors of nearby apartments had no problems seeing into the stadium. The bleachers were not exactly at ground level; they appear to have been built on top of a riser of two to three feet.

The local and visiting baseball writers would be comfortable as well. Only a few years before, they had formed the Baseball Writers Association of America (BBWAA) to protest lousy seating at many American League and National League parks. At Weeghman's, they sat in a small, covered deck atop the roof behind the plate. American flags were placed on twenty-two flagpoles atop the roof from the press box to the end of the grandstand where they remain today, with some adjustments.

A wire screen behind home plate protected fans from foul balls. The dugouts were much smaller and a bit farther toward the left-field and right-field lines than they are today. Just as they do today, Chicago bleacher fans sat on hard benches. Back then, they were made of wood. The dugouts were, as today, actually dug out into the structure down the first- and third-base lines. Oddly, however, they were covered only by canvas, rather than by a hard roof. Past the dugouts, on each baseline, a stairway led from the field to the box seats—presumably to help dignitaries get on and off the field. Even then, celebrities were a part of the game.

CHAPTER 2

Opening Day at Weeghman Park: April 23, 1914

PULL UP TO THE BUMPER

Suppose you're going to see the Chicago Federal League club play its first home game at the team's brand-new stadium on Clark and Addison Streets.

Perhaps you're a member of the Union League Club, the Rienzi Café Federal League Booster's Club, or the Bravo El Toro Club, North Side good-fellow societies of well-to-do businessmen and civic boosters who bought their tickets in blocks directly reserved for them by the Feds.

You might be a West Side businessman and friend of former Cubs business manager Charley Williams, who had recently been stolen away by Weeghman. As a member of the Charley Williams Booster Club (really!), you've already purchased your seats either at the West Town State Bank at Madison and Western or at the Garfield Park Bank, *way* out west at Madison and Crawford—as long as you showed your membership card.

Or maybe you're a North Side resident, a German, Swede, or Lithuanian living in or near Lake View, who has been waiting years for a chance to cheer your very own "hometown" club. You trekked downtown to Jack Shannon's sporting goods store at 54 E. Monroe in order to buy reserved tickets. Then you made plans to skip work to watch the game and maybe stopped by the nearby Bismarck Garden at Halsted and Grace for a beer.

You could be one of the utterly twentieth-century young women responding to Feds owner Charley Weeghman's push to bring respectability and comfort to baseball fans in his new palace. Women had recently been given the vote in Chicago and were feeling their power in new ways—one of which was to go out to the ball yard, make their presence known, and hoot and holler just like the men.

Whatever your background, it's almost certain that you had a first-class time at the new Federal League ballpark. Whether you took the "el" train (yes, it was called that even back then) from all points of the city to Weeghman

Park for just a nickel, or whether you walked, your admission was well spent. Even if you were a "swell" pulling up to the park in your black Ford Model T, Pierce-Arrow, or Studebaker, Charley Weeghman promised you plenty for your money.

Photos of the time show parking available for automobiles on the west side of Addison Street as well as right next to the ballpark—where, today, an outdoor café and a statue of Harry Caray are located.

With its clear sight lines, modern and clean facilities, and vibrant neighborhood feel, what would soon be known as Weeghman Park made great impressions on everyone who attended. The verdict was unanimous: this was a keen new plant.

DOG AND PONY SHOW

The pregame ceremonies honoring the opening of the new park were characteristically over-the-top, beginning with a huge parade starting downtown and heading north toward the ballpark.

Back in the 1910s and 1920s, with far fewer entertainment options (no TV, no radio, and only silent movies), sports—specifically baseball—were king. All sorts of hoopla marked important baseball games during the war years, led by the dizzying patriotic whirl of elaborate flag ceremonies, marching bands, and players trooping the field with bats held over their shoulders like rifles. Nonmilitary flash and filigree were in evidence as well. Flower horseshoes, large trophies, and gold-plated loving cups were presented to hometown players and managers. Sometimes, even well-loved opponents were fêted.

Given that Charley Weeghman, one of Chicago's *bon vivants*, was opening his new play palace, the celebrations greeting Weeghman Park's debut could have been expected to veer dangerously toward overkill. For instance, one hardly could have had a ballpark opening without music. At that time, there were no organs or public address systems at the park, so why not hire a brass band? A capital idea. But would Good-Time Charley Weeghman settle for just *one*? Of course not. On April 23, 1914, *ten* brass bands were present at the park. As the *Inter-Ocean* remarked, "Each band ought to be able to render one piece during the afternoon—that is, unless several plan to play at the same time."

PARADIN'

At Sixteenth Street and Michigan Avenue, south of downtown, dozens of cars met up to travel *en masse* to the new North Side ballpark. Headed by yet another brass band, the caravan of autos—remember, cars were still a possession of the moneyed class—was to drive north on Michigan to Jackson Boulevard, then west to LaSalle, north to Madison, east to Michigan, and north to the lakefront. The convoy would then jaunt north by the lake up toward Addison, then west to the ballpark.

This curious route was most likely taken to avoid the traffic jams found every weekday in downtown Chicago, then and now. However, it is fascinating to think of the sight of several dozen autos stuffed with the wealthy and powerful trying to fight their way through noontime traffic.

A LOT OF BULL

The Bravo El Toro Club's rooters didn't ride from downtown in the parade, begging off to ready themselves for their activities. Preparation consisted of a few beverages at the Bismarck Garden. The bar had already taken the intelligent step of advertising to its built-in audience, putting up a sign on one of the apartments overlooking Weeghman Park's right-field wall.

Once presumably well oiled, members of the Bravo El Toro Club departed the tavern and walked to the park, arriving during batting practice, three thousand strong, dressed in full toreador regalia with gold and red sashes. The rooters then staggered to their reserved section. Meanwhile, a hundred of the organization's finest, decked out in sombreros and long linen coats, made their way onto the field. Drummers and a full German band accompanied the comical parade.

As if that wasn't enough, the high-spirited group had a live bull in tow. Originally the bull was to be ridden into the park by actor Jefferson de Angelis, who was to mimic Victoriano Huerta, the embattled Mexican president. Eventually de Angelis chose to "not tempt fate by impersonating the much talked-of Mexican," wrote Handy Andy in the April 23 *Tribune*.

A proposed bullfight, which had been much publicized in the days before the game, did not come off; the well-fed and sleepy bull was less than enthusiastic. However, the resulting shenanigans were enough to cause an interruption to batting practice, according to George Rice in the *Daily Journal*, and amuse the fans to no end.

How in the world did these bozos even get on the field? Charley Weeghman was a member of the Bravo El Toro Club!

SO MANY NIFTS

Elsie Dabel, her mom, and her sister went to the opening as well but were shut out by the crowd. However, she did notice plenty of handsome men hanging around the ballpark that day:

Today was the opening of the Federal League Ball Park. . . . We didn't go in. I never saw such crowds in all my life. . . . There were *so* many nifts there. Before the game they shot some kind of thing into the air and a little parachute came out. . . . They had two bands there which kept playing "This is the Life," a very appropriate song for the occasion. The Chifeds won. There was an awful cute pennant guy there who kept fancying us. We bought a pennant for a quarter. We certainly had a fine time but I was wishing I could have gone in.

SINK (ONE AT) THE BISMARCK

The Bismarck Garden, known at the time as "Chicago's Pride," was a popular local restaurant and bar as well as a celebrated concert hall, holding concerts for many years every weeknight and on Sunday afternoons. The Garden was located at Evanston Avenue (changed to Broadway shortly thereafter), Halsted, and Grace. The musical programs included opera, light opera, lieder, military songs, and hymns and offered a full range of food from appetizers and relishes to steaks, rarebits, and seafood. They also had a huge wine list and featured such beers as Anheuser-Busch, Anheuser-Busch Budweiser, Falstaff, and Michelob.

When big league baseball came to the neighborhood, the crowds of hale-fellows-well-met were a natural fit for the establishment. For several years, baseball events in the neighborhood would always be preceded as well as followed by drinking and fun at the Bismarck Garden. While the Garden has long since disappeared, the location is still world famous. The intersection hosts an International House of Pancakes.

THE WAR SPIRIT RAN HIGH

After several other rooters' groups had marched onto the newly laid field, the real ceremonies began. Twenty members of the Daughters of the Grand Army of the Republic Relief Corps, dressed in white and led by GARRC President Ida Wright, toted a thirty-foot silk American flag around the ballpark. During the procession, one or more of the brass bands struck up "The Star-Spangled Banner," which was not yet the national anthem.

Weeghman and Walker accompanied the ladies on their jaunt as did players from both teams, assorted dignitaries, and probably fans simply swept up by the emotion of the moment. Hundreds of people crowded onto the field as fifteen of the ladies ran the flag up a pole in deepest center field.

Fans greeted the patriotic ceremony with great gusto. Soldiers fired a twenty-one-gun salute, and the club set off a barrage of fireworks when the flag reached the top of the pole. It was decided that the flag should be raised before every Chicago game during the 1914 Federal League season. The huge flag was made of an extremely thin, gauzy silk, and as a result did not last long in the Chicago winds. Local newspapers carry references to the club putting up "new" flags during both the 1914 and 1915 seasons.

Following the salute, the parade of players, ladies, and musicians headed to home plate, where Joe Tinker was presented with carts of flowers and, oddly enough, three dozen neckties. The usual awkward hilarity ensued as the manager "was compelled to smile amid the blooms for the benefit of the moving picture machine," according to Sam Weller in the April 24 *Tribune*. A grinning Weeghman received a gold loving cup.

A procession of a hundred cars, representing friends of Tinker from his west suburban hometown of Oak Park, also drove through the ball yard before the game began. Amazingly enough, wrote Weller, "the outfield was a bit soft, but the diamond looked fine" despite the pregame ruckus.

In what may have been a first, Weeghman paid to have thousands of baseball caps in different colors and decorated with the Chifeds logo passed out to incoming fans. Small felt flags were also given out. "Thousands of spectators donned the little caps distributed by the local management, while others waved Chifed pennants," noted J. G. Davis in the April 24 *Tribune*.

Contrast this early example of marketing savvy with the attitude of the New York Yankees, who for years refused to allow caps with their logo to be manufactured. Yankees management felt that its logo, and by extension its franchise, would be cheapened if just *anyone* could wear a Yankees hat.

WHO WAS THERE?

The park seated eighteen thousand at its opening, but nearly twenty-one thousand fans packed the single-decked stadium. Hundreds of others watched the game and ceremonies from windows and rooftops of buildings on Waveland and Sheffield Avenues, past the left- and right-field fences. Still more baseball bugs hung off the elevated platform at Addison.

Two large blocks of temporary "circus" seats were placed down the left- and right-field foul lines. (In fact, these seats actually jutted into fair territory!) They were jammed as well. Other fans lined up around the field and ringed the outfield. Some two thousand more were turned away because there was no room.

Celebrities attended in abundance, including chief contractor William Sinek, league president James and Mrs. Gilmore, Jefferson and Mrs. de Angelis (as themselves, not as Mr. and Mrs. Huerta), Louis and Mrs. Comiskey, and several local judges. Umpire-in-Chief Bill Brennan introduced the players from both sides to the fans, one hopes with the aid of a megaphone.

One significant outcome of the whole shebang was, as J. G. Davis wrote the next day in the *Tribune*, "the large number of women present." This was not lost on the Chifed owners, who had taken great pains to make the park acceptable to the fairer sex as well as to the seasoned male fan.

THE GAME

The weather was cold and damp in Chicago on Opening Day, and in true Windy City tradition, many spectators entered the park heavily fortified by various adult beverages. A harsh wind roared in from the lake. After John Sexton, corporation counsel of Chicago, threw out the first ball (Mayor Carter Harrison was out of town), the Feds took the field.

As a reminder that the Federal League was indeed a new, slightly disorganized aggregation, a bit of comic relief intruded. Following the conclusion of the second inning, Kansas City pitcher Chief Johnson left the game, not removed by his manager, but on orders from the authorities! Johnson, charged with double-dealing on a contract by the Cincinnati Reds, was served with papers by the NL club before the bottom of the second and was forbidden to pitch after the conclusion of the frame.

By then, the Chifeds had already tagged Johnson for three runs, and they went on to add another in the third, two in the fourth, two more in the sixth, and another in the eighth. Claude Hendrix threw a five-hitter at the visitors, and Chicago won 9–1.

THE PRESS BUYS IN

F. A. McInerney's words in the April 24 edition of the *Post* showed that the Feds had convinced at least some of the newspapermen:

> Charley Weeghman made a lot of friends yesterday.
>
> About 22,000 fans went to the Buns' North Side ball park, and they went away tickled to death with the treatment they had received . . . each was made to feel that he was welcome. Nothing in the park was too good for him. The fun was clean and amusing and the general effect was that of a huge family having a good time.
>
> This tone reflected Charley Weeghman's good fellowship, and it is significant because it indicates that those who went to the opening game will go again and again, and they will bring others with them.
>
> In other words, the North Side has good reason today to stand up and holler. It has something.

Even the *Tribune*, a paper not unconditionally in love with Charley and his Buns, weighed in with unreserved optimism: "Over 21,000 fans performed their part in making the opening one of the greatest in the history of the game . . . A glance at the wonderful setting for yesterday's combat brought the thought that someone must have rubbed Aladdin's lamp to effect such a magical transformation."

What the opening of Weeghman Park meant to Chicago's self-image is almost incalculable. The park's success on this day was the exclamation point to the new vitality of the North Side. The *Inter-Ocean* called it, with some hyperbole, "the greatest inaugural reception a baseball club ever had."

DON'T FENCE ME IN

After the first game, in which light-hitting Chifeds receiver Dutch Wilson belted two homers over Weeghman Park's 310-foot left-field fence, writers began to speculate that left field was a bit too inviting. On the off day following the first series at the new park, Weeghman hired a construction crew to move the wall back twenty-five feet. In order to make room for the additional outfield area, the crew removed the front porch of a mammoth brick house that stood across from the ballpark. The reconstruction also forced the club to relocate the left-field scoreboard.

Jack Ryder of *The Sporting News* sniffed in the May 7 issue that "the news that the Federal Park in Chicago, which was described by the press agents as a perfect marvel, is being enlarged, after the playing of three games on it, is amusing." Ryder went on to describe how eight homers were hit over the short left-field fence in the Sunday game and that orders were given to enlarge the area. He concluded, with the typical *TSN* slant, "It is sad to think of the money sunk in this venture that will never come out again."

It is not known whether Ryder or the other members of the establishment press felt that the Polo Grounds, which at the time sported rather cozy left- and right-field foul lines of 277 feet, or the West Side Grounds, which had a 316-foot right-field line, were equally inappropriate.

CHAPTER **3**

Heady Days: Weeghman Park, 1914–17

KISSING HANDS AND SHAKING BABIES

As the season progressed, it became clear that major league baseball would indeed be hurt by the new competition. As *TSN* reported on May 14, "The Cubs have fared pretty badly most of the time, because the Federals have weaned away so many of the dyed-in-the-wool Cubs supporters." On one occasion in early May, all three Chicago clubs were at home. The papers reported that the White Sox and Feds both drew around eighteen thousand, while the Cubs pulled in just ten thousand.

However, the new league was also finding it an uphill battle to bring in the bodies. Even after the exciting beginning to the Chifeds' season, Charley Weeghman still had to roust fans out to the park. This he did by many means: handbills, advertising, good customer service, and by apparently honoring every group with more than a few paying members with its own day. The July 7, 1914, *Sporting Life* reported that "Weeghman is working overtime with various stunts which are intended to edge into the good graces of the Chicago fandom . . . The boss of the local Federals has planned several days for the North Side park."

EVERYBODY IN THE POOL

Sporting Life wasn't kidding. On Friday, May 1, the Chifeds held their first Ladies Day. Elsie Dabel and a friend went to the park that day and experienced more than a little condescension among the male rooters: "We understood it perfectly. Our fans called the girls 'fanettes' and one fellow said that the girls think it's like playing tag. It got me sore because we knew just as much about it as he did. After this, every Friday is going to be Ladies Day and Em and I will be present at every one."

Manager Otto Knabe of the Baltimore Terrapins was honored before the first half of a doubleheader on June 14. Weeghman hauled in a German oompah band to entertain the fans before the 1:00 start, and plenty of locals came out to salute the popular Knabe, a longtime National League second baseman who would finish his career with the 1916 Cubs.

On July 11, Weeghman held a special "German Day" with a boatload of pregame entertainment: a fifteen-hundred-marcher on-field parade, led by Ballman's Band, and several vaudeville routines. Is it necessary to note that the parade began at the Bismarck Garden? Once the game started, a second band of ragtime-influenced musicians in comic clothing entertained fans in the bleachers while Ballman's Band played for the more upscale grandstand patrons.

Before the second game, a band played "Spanish fandangoes" (*sic*) in honor of the five hundred or so members of the Bravo El Toro Club who showed up, decked out once again in their fake bullfighters' togs, ready when the game let out to raid the local taverns.

June 18 was "Fisk Day" in honor of Chifeds hurler Max Fisk, a product of the South Side Roseland neighborhood. Several hundred of his pals from Roseland and nearby Pullman made their way north with, of course, their own band in tow. Fisk, a spitballer, pitched a complete-game, two-hit 3–2 win. One example shows just how the game was more intimate back then. When Fisk went up to hit in the third inning, several of his buddies jumped onto the field, strode to home plate, and presented him with a new gold watch.

Max's surname was universally spelled "Fisk" at the time, although he is now referred to in the record books as "Fiske." This was to be Fisk's sole big league season; he held out in spring 1915, refusing a five percent raise, and was quickly jettisoned.

On Saturday, June 20, the North Side Boosters came out in full force. Of course, they brought a band as well. Two days later, a quarter of the two thousand fans on hand were from the Graeme Stewart School. The following day, the pupils of Lake View High School were Weeghman's guests, with "more schools to be entertained later." July 15 saw a contingent of Elks honored at the park; both Weeghman and Tinker belonged to the fraternal organization. (Buried in small print next to this report in the *Tribune* was a short paragraph concerning the Boston Red Sox' purchase, from the Baltimore Orioles minor league organization, of a young pitcher named George Ruth.) On August 12, the YMCA brought a group of kids, who led organized cheers in an impressive fashion. A few days later, a Meiji University baseball club, from Japan, played the Mandel Brothers nine, representing the State Street Merchants League.

Another important group had made its presence known at the park on June 10. Labor unionists, angered that the Brooklyn Tip-Tops had used nonunion workers to build their grandstand in April, made sure that all trades-men in every Federal League city knew to boycott the Tip-Tops wherever they played. As a result, only twelve hundred fans showed up for the June 10 game.

On August 15, the Chifeds held National Union Day. Just a week later, the ballpark had a combined Flag Day/Masonic Day (Tinker was also a member of the Masons). Weeghman had obtained a brand-new, oversized American flag to raise, and two thousand members of the Masons marched on the field before the game accompanied by their own fifty-piece band.

On August 20, three Greek Americans, attempting a walk across the United States, were admitted free to the park by club secretary Charley Wil-liams. They were seated in a field box and "treated like curiosities" by the fans, according to the *Tribune*. September 1 was Cy Falkenborg Day. The In-dianapolis "Hoo Fed" pitcher, who had served for eight years with the Indi-ans and Senators, was a native of Chicago.

In addition to the myriad special days, Weeghman held successful La-dies Days on Fridays when the Chifeds were in town. When the club wasn't at home on a Friday, he pushed the date to Thursday. The sporting press of the day often referred to fans as "bugs," and the female contingent predict-ably became known as the "lady bugs."

During 1914, Weeghman brought his team to his hometown of Rich-mond, Indiana, for an exhibition game against a local club. (John Powers was bounced from the Federal League presidency in 1913 for doing much the same thing.) The favor was not forgotten; in a table-turning event, citizens of Weeghman's hometown held a "Weeghman Day" in Chicago.

Despite all of his hard work and marketing expenditures, Weeghman was having trouble drawing more than a couple thousand fans for weekday games. A good weekend turnout was six thousand, with the few crowds over ten thousand welcomed as godsends. Even on weekends, the bleachers were usually packed but grandstands sat only a third to a half full.

SUNSHINE AND SPEED

Charley Weeghman put the comfort of the customer first, even when it con-travened usual policy. June 15 was a chilly day, and Weeghman permitted the fans sitting in the grandstand to move into the box seats in order to catch some sunshine. He really did believe in making the fans comfortable.

Back on May 8, the Whales and Brooklyn Tip-Tops couldn't play their scheduled game at Weeghman Park, but fans were let in to watch the teams practice. According to Elsie Dabel, the Tip-Top players might have had something other than infield drills on their minds: "We got stung because they didn't play on account of wet grounds. But we saw the Brooklyns practicing. We sat in box seats and several times they looked over and smiled."

On July 13, with the St. Louis Terriers in town, the skies opened up. Weeghman allowed the bleacher fans into the covered grandstand. (The *Tribune* noted that some of the fans took advantage of Weeghman's good nature and "rushed right down into the choice box seats and sat there in spite of the rain, which was not so wet apparently as it was out in center field.")

Lucky Charley was also conscious of the time it took to play a game. With July 4 falling on a Sunday, Weeghman tried to pump attendance for the team's July 5 game (a holiday in Chicago) with ads in the local papers. With pregame entertainment featuring a fifty-piece band and singers, Weeghman wanted to make the day at the park a family affair. Conscious of selling the product as not only enjoyable but also convenient, his ad blared that "the Federal League is playing 'faster' and 'closer' ball than any other Major League this season . . . If you enjoy good ball and want to see a fast game, be a 'Fed' fan and join us at Weeghman Park to-day!"

Somewhere between five and six thousand fans showed up for the 2–1 Feds victory. Two days later, the Chifeds completed a game in a snappy eighty-four minutes.

LOOKING GOOD

Sam Weller of the *Tribune* laid bouquets at Weeghman's and groundskeeper Murphy's feet on May 31. "While the team was away," he noted, "the infield was skinned, leveled up, and re-sodded. The grass in the outfield is perfect." Weller went on, "It is doubtful if there is a ball field in the country which looks any better than Weeghman Park today."

Obviously the money Weeghman spent on upkeep was a big part of his strategy to get people to come out to the ballpark. His restaurants weren't sloppy; why should his baseball field be? Clearly the press appreciated the care he took, especially compared to the penny-wise and pound-foolish ways shown by the Cubs at West Side Grounds.

One benefit to having his own ballpark was that Weeghman could indulge himself in a little fun—a kind of fun certainly not found in ballparks today. Charley built a small stable under the third-base stands, where he kept a horse named Queen Bess. According to the *Tribune*, Bess was "an old, gentle, fat bay mare which had done service on a pie wagon in the loop for more than ten years." Weeghman, something of an animal lover, kept Bess fed and had her occasionally pull the lawn mower when the ballpark grass needed to be cut. At nights, with the team out of town, the mare was given the run of the diamond.

AND I'M TELLING YOU I'M NOT GOING

Even as his Feds fought for the new league's first pennant, Weeghman had to fight off more rumors that he was ready to split for the majors. The September 12 *Sporting Life* carried a story in which the Chicago owner admitted that four Federal League clubs would lose money on the season and that "it is a bad year in base-ball."

He denied once again, however, that he would desert the new league if he, Otto Stifel of St. Louis, and Robert Ward of Brooklyn were awarded franchises in the American Association. (Everyone in the press assumed that with the moneymen given such a guarantee, the Federal League would immediately be cashiered.)

Indeed it was a rough time for the baseball men. Weeghman noted in October that he had been informed by an American League owner that only two clubs in the junior circuit, Boston being one, had actually made money in 1914. Weeghman, perhaps edging himself closer to the majors—his true ambition—even claimed that the Feds and their signing of major league players were partially responsible for the public's lack of confidence in the game.

However, at least to the public, Weeghman was claiming financial victory. *Sporting Life* reported on August 8, "A dispatch from Chicago, under date of August 2, said: 'Over $5,000 in paid admissions to the Chicago-Pittsburgh Federal League game today . . . the receipts taken in put the club handled by Joe Tinker on velvet for the season. Chicago has played to good and paying crowds ever since the league started, and the receipts today were just enough to cover all the expenses for the remaining month. *From now on every cent taken in will be profit for the owners.'*" [Italics added.]

JUMP AROUND

With the Buffalo Feds in town on June 22 to play the Chifeds, first baseman Hal Chase of the White Sox jumped his contract and headed to Weeghman Park and put on the Buffalo club's blue suit.

"Jumping is old stuff for Chase," James Crusinberry noted the next day in the *Tribune*. But the fans, ten thousand strong, applauded the pockmarked defensive whiz, well known not only for contract jumping but also for gambling and even throwing games. Chase would go on to have his most impressive season for Buffalo in 1915, leading the Federal League with seventeen homers.

That Chicago baseball fans were a highly cultured crowd could be put to the lie by their love of Hal Chase. The *Tribune*'s account of the July 7 game offered more evidence that fans were as rowdy then as now: "Occupants of the right field pavilion had some sport with a bluecoat over a foul ball that one of their number attempted to retain as a souvenir. The policeman and a park attaché surrounded the bug and the ball was finally produced, but tossed out of reach. Others took up the game and passed the ball back and forth for several minutes before it was lassoed."

Eventually, in 1916, Weeghman started a trend by allowing fans to keep foul balls. It must have happened in midseason, because an article in the August 12, 1916, *Sporting Records* was headlined, "President Weeghman of Chicago Makes Big Hit With the Fans; Permits them to Retain Baseballs." The accompanying picture features a jaunty Weeghman decked out in a high-button suit and straw hat.

On August 20, a sign on the Weeghman Park scoreboard read "Hal Chase Tomorrow," touting the next day's contest with the Buffeds. Clearly, Chase was a huge gate attraction in his own right. The August 21 game was a Ladies Day, and the gentler sex made up most of the audience.

UNDISCIPLINED

Umpiring in the Federal League was a real issue; few of the arbiters were of high quality. On August 16, the Chifeds and Baltimore Terrapins' 1–0 game at Weeghman Park was delayed for nearly twenty minutes by a huge rhubarb. With a man on base in the eighth and Baltimore up 1–0, plate umpire Charles Van Sickle called time at Feds' coach Jimmy Block's request as Terrapin pitcher Bill Bailey began to deliver a pitch to Dutch Zwilling. The Chifed center fielder smacked the ball into the bleachers. Baltimore manager Otto Knabe ran onto the field and reminded Van Sickle that time had been called—the rule was clear. Van Sickle, however, wavered, discussing the situation with base umpire Monte Cross and trying to get all sides to agree rather than simply imposing the correct decision.

All hell broke loose. Tinker and his players were up in arms; the fans showered the field with garbage. The band entertaining that day tried to drown out the arguments and booing by playing popular songs. Imagine the cacophony. For eighteen minutes, Tinker refused to send Zwilling back up to bat and, during the fray, Weeghman made his way down on to the field and began yelling at Van Sickle as well.

Van Sickle was unable to restore order—he was reported as having said to Tinker, "Come on Joe, get the boys out there. Be a good fellow," rather than simply threatening to forfeit the game to the visitors. Weeghman and Tinker asked the local scribes, who had run down from the press box to cover the brouhaha, to explain the rules. Once the writers notified the Chifeds that they were in the wrong, the game resumed.

Van Sickle was fired the next day. He would appear in the news again in June 1915, when a player in the Western League slugged him.

INDECENT PROPOSAL

On August 14, Weeghman offered up a challenge to the Cubs and White Sox, who already engaged in an annual "City Series." The Feds wanted in on the action, and Weeghman said that he would pay twenty-five thousand dollars to either major league club if they defeated his Buns in a postseason tourney.

Neither the Cubs nor the White Sox wanted to give Weeghman the time of day, so the proposal fell by the wayside despite the fact that a good portion of the local baseball public certainly would have enjoyed such a spectacle. The Feds had nothing to lose by making such an offer; the majors had nothing to gain by accepting it.

DISAPPOINTED

The Chifeds appeared to be in the driver's seat for the 1914 Federal League crown, but a tough doubleheader loss to the sixth-place Kansas City Packers on October 6 turned the tide in the favor of the Indianapolis Hoosiers, who clinched the next day. Eventually, the Chifeds finished one and a half games out.

The result was disheartening to Weeghman, who had staked much of his pocketbook on winning a title. All winter, he pursued Walter Johnson, the greatest pitcher in baseball, and nearly got him. At one point, Johnson agreed in principle to playing in Chicago, but he was eventually convinced to return to the Washington Senators. White Sox owner Charlie Comiskey, fearing the gate attraction of the "Big Train" pitching in his hometown, agreed to the unusual step of kicking some money toward the Senators to keep Johnson in the nation's capital.

MODIFICATIONS

During the winter of 1914–15, Weeghman chose to change the seating of his ballpark. He scrapped initial plans that would have both brought the left-field seats all the way to the foul pole and double-decked the left-field bleachers. Instead, according to Ray Kush in the 1981 SABR *Baseball Research Journal*, Weeghman had Davis design a plan to tear down the existing right-

and left-field seats and construct a much larger bleacher in left field. The project, run by Blome-Sinek, cost the team seventeen thousand dollars.

The large left-field bleacher was fifteen to twenty rows deep and ended near center field. Distance to the left-center fence was around 340 feet. In right field, no seats remained, just a large brownish-red brick wall that ranged all the way to the scoreboard (which featured a *Tribune* advertisement) in deepest center. The March 6, 1915, *Tribune* noted that Weeghman was holding off traveling to Shreveport for spring training until he finished working out the details of tearing down the house that occupied part of the left-field territory.

In addition, the infield dirt behind second base was changed from a ninety-degree angle so that the infield no longer was a box. From where the second baseman played to where the shortstop played, the dirt behind second was changed to a straight line.

As a convenience for the fans, Weeghman had Illinois Bell place public phone booths inside the park.

As always, Charley Weeghman presented the change in the grandest possible terms. In the 1915 Whales game program, it was written that "the new and larger bleachers were erected and the playing field enlarged because there is nothing too good for the patrons of the Chicago Federal League Baseball Club."

HOW DID IT PLAY?

After early-season changes were made to Weeghman Park's short left-field fence, it became only a slightly above-average home run park. The Chifeds did lead the Federal League clubs in home runs in home games in 1914, with thirty, but other clubs had home totals of twenty-eight, twenty-seven, and twenty-five. Visiting teams hit only nineteen homers at Weeghman in 1914, which ranked third among FL teams.

Even with all batters combining for forty-nine homers in 1914, tied for the most in the FL, Weeghman still wasn't a good hitter's park; in fact, Weeghman was the *lowest*-scoring park in the league by a very wide margin. Meanwhile, the Chifeds led the league in runs scored in road games.

In 1915, Newark entered the league and had a huge park in which only six homers were hit *all season*. Batters slugged thirty-one homers at Weeghman, a total that tied for the fourth highest in the Federal League. While Weeghman wasn't the best pitcher's park in the league, it was still a pretty good place to be a pitcher; Chicago and its opponents scored 562 runs there, fifth in the loop.

THE NAME GAME . . . AGAIN

Early in 1915, Weeghman—always looking to keep his business in the public eye—ran a contest to name the Chifeds. Soon, the entries began rolling in to area newspapers. The club's new-name possibilities proved great fun for the newspapermen. The *Herald* reported that some of the possibilities included animal names such as Colts, Eagles, Swans, Condors, Pelicans, Zebras, Bunnies, and Rats; food jokes such as Spuds, Beefers, Chibuns, and Pepper Pods; and topical or local references such as Kaisers, I Wills, Navajos, Iroquois, Bismarcks, and Windy Lads. The writers had already used several of the nominated monikers—Tinx, Tots, Buns—in 1914. (In fact, when Joe Tinker returned to managing in the minor leagues in later years, his teams were called the "Tinx" as well.) This was a popular contest; the *Herald* claimed five hundred letters with 289 different names submitted, while the *Daily News* said they had received 368 letters with 287 names.

The February 5, 1915, *Daily News* reported that "Chix" was Weeghman's choice, but that a fan—having heard the rumor that this name would be chosen—wrote the club and said that he'd *never* return to see a team that could be mocked as "Chickens." So "Chix" was out and "Whales," Charley's second choice, was in.

D. J. Eichoff, who resided at 1451 Hood Street in the north side Edgewater neighborhood, was responsible for the name. Eichoff also sent in his suggestion for a logo: a whale with its large tail upturned, as if having just vanquished an opponent. "I certainly am delighted to learn that my title was adopted. I think it will become a popular name with the fans, too," he told James Crusinberry of the *Tribune* after being announced as the winner on February 4. The Eichoff family was awarded a set of season tickets as prizes. This made Mr. Eichoff very happy, as he and Mrs. Eichoff had been Fed fans ever since the club was playing at DePaul back in 1913.

Many historians have wondered what the "Whales" reference really meant. A note in the *Evening Post* in February 1915, shortly after the new name was adopted, made a joke of the name and referenced Weeghman's large sandwiches, which supposedly had to be cut "with a safety razor." But Eichoff's ideas were far more literal. His reasons given, as reported by the *Herald*:

◆ The best commercial whales (i.e., those used for meat and whale oil) are found in the frozen north, which means that the North Side should have the best team.
◆ Whales lash and drub their opponents.
◆ Anything marked a "whaler" is large and extraordinary.

With a new name came new duds. The club's new uniforms were a far cry from the austere pinstripes worn the year before. The 1915 Whales boasted cream-colored jerseys and pants when in Chicago, with blue stockings and caps and cherry-red sweaters. A large blue *C* on the left breast of the jersey held inside of it a blue whale. The logo looked as much like a submarine sandwich as a sea creature.

Weeghman, now being called "Whale Oil Charley" by the writers, certainly was happy with the hugeness and domination that the name intimated—big and brassy was his *modus operandi*.

FEDS FETED

On March 4, as spring workouts were beginning in Shreveport, Weeghman and the Whales were feted at a booster club banquet at Rienzi Café at Clark and Diversey. Diners, numbering at least 750 and possibly as many as a thousand, were served chicken. The crowd, in a jovial and most certainly drunken mood, heard singing, jokes, and speeches, including a very short one from Weeghman and a fiery one from James Gilmore.

The next day, Weeghman got off the best line of the year. Boston Braves hurler Bill James wanted to jump his contract and sign with the Federals, but when Weeghman saw that the pitcher's contract did not have the ten-day escape clause, he demurred. "I still have some respect for the law," Weeghman proclaimed, "even if I *am* a baseball club owner."

WORKOUT

The day before the Feds opened the 1915 season at home on April 10, they held a public workout at Weeghman Park. Admission was free, and John O. Seys in the *Daily News* noted, "President Weeghman, who was one of the early comers, gave orders to allow everybody to enter, and the front rows of the box seats were well filled with the admirers of the new north side team."

Seys also reported that "the remodeled outfield was a revelation to the players who were on the team last year. Dutch Zwilling and Al Wickland, who covered right and center fields last year, found they had been given a lot more room through the removal of the bleachers in right center."

There was another change for 1915 as well. During the year, a new firehouse for Engine 78's company was built at 1052 W. Waveland. It's still there and has been an integral part of neighborhood—and ballpark—history since. Sitting just across the street from the left-field gate, it's been a hangout for Cubs fans, locals, the press, and even the athletes and coaches themselves for years.

For their second season, the Whales had developed a system by which tickets for their games could be reserved by mail or phone. The tickets would be left downtown at Shannon's, at 54 E. Monroe, for pickup up until noon of game day, or at the park until 2:30 p.m. on game day.

OPENING DAY #2

April 10, 1915, saw another Opening Day parade of ballplayers, rooters, and officials. As in 1914, the trail began in the loop and headed all the way to the park. Some four hundred cars rode north. Manager Joe Tinker, decked out in a long coat and a Whales cap, rode in a car festooned with flowers. Several rooters clubs had cars in the parade also, riding vehicles swathed in Whales pennants, garlands, and other decorations. Some five thousand people were said to have greeted the parade, which arrived at the park sometime around 2:30.

By the way, those who think that things were less commercialized in the "good old days" might find discomfort in Chicago *American* reporter Jay Davidson's summing up of the parade: "Most of the cars were decorated with banners and signs, and the usual number of advertising dodgers were seen in line. It was interesting to the innocent bystanders to learn that John Pumpernickel's raisins constitute the chief diet of Whales, and that the Whales nightly wallow about at William Whosit's biggestcabaretinthecity [*sic*], but this natural history lesson soon was forgotten."

Unfortunately, the parade's late arrival at Weeghman Park wiped out batting practice, so both clubs hastily grabbed their gloves for a quick infield toss-around. The fences around the park were decked in American flags, and despite the chilly and wet conditions, an overflow crowd of twenty thousand was present.

Newly elected Chicago mayor "Big Bill" Thompson was on hand, getting to the premises just in time. Carter Harrison, the former mayor, was also at the park, as was Bob Sweltzer, the Democratic candidate vanquished by Thompson just days before. Thompson walked onto the field wearing a sombrero as a band played "Illinois" and other songs. The assembled crowd stood and applauded while the ubiquitous "motion-picture machines" recorded the event.

Weeghman, knowing what side his bread was buttered on, presented Thompson (who was, according to Mark Okkonen, a stockholder in the 1913 Federal club) with his own box seats—gratis—for the duration of the season. The "mayor's box" was located next to the Whales' dugout.

The mayor, accompanied by campaign manager Eugene Pike and some other aides, went to the mound and threw a perfect strike to catcher Dutch Wilson. Both Tinker and St. Louis manager Fielder Jones received flower garlands. Finally, at 3:15, the game started. The Whales won 3–1. (During the 1915 season, all Federal League games were scheduled for 3:00.)

ADVERTISING SECRETS

Want to go back to those innocent days when baseball was played for fun and not money? Let's take note of the Whales' 1915 scorebook, a forty-four-page, five-by-seven-inch, five-cent affair in which the club managed to cram in 114 advertisements. Some of these businesses appealed to the well-to-do. Car companies, steamship lines, and high-class hotels took out advertising in Weeghman's program, as did insurance companies, coal companies (including Collins and Weise, whose lot bordered Wrigley Field at 3637 N. Clark), tailors, haberdashers, banks, sporting goods stores, and the *Examiner*. Several types of liquor were represented, as were nearly a dozen different brands of cigars. Hollowed & O'Hara's, a restaurant and saloon downtown on Monroe near State, advertised "The Largest Bar in the World." The Rienzi Café, eight blocks south of Weeghman Park, was also a happy advertiser.

Everyone wanted into the inner circle. The People's Hand Laundry touted itself as the club's official laundry service; the Rittle Restaurant billed itself "Federal League Headquarters," inviting fans to its location just a few blocks from the park. The makers of Hydrox Ice Cream, which was served at Weeghman Park, stretched credulity to the breaking point by claiming that its nutritional value was such that humans could survive on it alone. Arthur Feilchenfeld's Hats offered a new model for 1915, "The Whale," a fairly ridiculous hat taller than a bowler but shorter than a topper. It looked for all the world like an expensive version of the silly green cardboard hats given away at St. Patrick's Day parties.

Whales manager Joe Tinker had his own brand of cigar, manufactured by Spector Brothers, while the G. V. Electric Truck Company claimed that its trucks were "Whales for Work." Of course, Weeghman also placed an ad for his ten downtown lunchrooms in the program. Several local concerns also bought ads, indicating that a hopping scene had already cropped up around the ballpark to serve the Whales' patrons. The Federal Ice Cream Parlor, located at 959 W. Addison, kitty-corner from the park, hoped that fans would come in for a frozen treat before or after a game. In addition, the Addison Buffet, directly across the street from the park at 1059 W. Addison, served hot and cold lunches and sandwiches to hungry fans. Just south of the park on Clark Street, the Bernstein Painting and Decorating Company touted its services, as did the Hemming Brewery at 3530 N. Clark (currently the location of the popular hangout Sluggers). Just a few doors up, at 3550, sat the American Plumbing and Heating Company, and close by at 3557—the southeast corner of Clark and Addison—was Reid's Buffet, offering both food and liquor. K & G Billiards, inside the still-standing Links Hall Building at Sheffield and Newport, bid fans to come by after the game and shoot a few rounds. There was even a new barbershop on Addison east of the park.

AT THE LINKS

Weeghman, as a man much given to leisure now that he'd made his name, didn't always spend his days at the ballpark. On May 27, he took a look at the skies and called off that day's scheduled game with the Newark Peppers, forcing a doubleheader two days later. Weeghman certainly didn't cry about it; instead, he just hauled his golf clubs out of the front closet. "Immediately after calling the game," remarked the *Herald*, "Weeghman hied himself to the Exmoor Links, but returned in time to bat .300 in the entertainment at Bismarck Garden at night."

The day turned out to be sunny.

ON THE ROAD AGAIN

Ninety to a hundred years ago, baseball players obviously lacked the union representation they enjoy today. Without long-term deals, for the most part, and with smaller team budgets, players were also far more tied in to the daily success or failures of the gate. Therefore, on days where a team wasn't playing a league game, it was just as likely to be on the road playing exhibitions. The Whales spent many of their home stand "off days" in towns like Ottumwa, Iowa, Richmond, Indiana, and Marion, Illinois, playing exhibitions against local nines and pocketing a chunk of the gate. Today, such games are rarely played. In fact, the 2002 collective bargaining agreement now bans such in-season exhibitions.

FUN AT THE NEW BALLPARK

On June 3, reported the *Daily Journal*, fans at the game were entranced by a hot-air balloon advertising a local tavern. Cubs fans familiar with the inflatable balloons installed on rooftops around Wrigley in the 1980s and 1990s know that in some respects times haven't changed that much. (One particularly hilarious incident on a windy day in the early 1990s had Budweiser's forty-foot inflatable Spuds McKenzie slowly deflating during a game.)

On June 6, a particularly zealous fan tried to keep a foul ball hit into the stands, attempting to fight off the police—then found that he was seated right next to club secretary Charley Williams. The embarrassed fan soon began to develop a greenish complexion, according to the *Daily Journal*, and appeared to wish he could disappear into the ground.

HIPPODROMIN'

Weeghman didn't keep his ballpark shuttered when his team was out of town. Early-season bad weather had resulted in a number of postponements (as well as washing out many games in the American League and National League), and the need to raise more money from the ballpark led to an interesting decision.

Early in 1915, Weeghman went east to see Barney Dreyfuss, the owner of the Pittsburgh Pirates, and was greatly impressed by a postgame exhibition of hippodroming at Forbes Field. What exactly *was* "hippodroming"? The term had two meanings. One was negative—it meant to make a farce of something serious, which in baseball terms meant "players throwing games for money." The other term involved entertainment—namely singing, dancing, comedy, animal acts, and other vaudeville-type shows. Originally, a "hippodrome" was an arena used for equestrian exhibitions (the term derived from the ancient Greek term for "horse racecourse") but ultimately came to represent entertainment in open-air stadia.

So when Weeghman saw Dreyfuss using his ballpark for popular entertainment, raking in profits, he figured that he could give the North Side another option for evening fun. Weeghman was attempting to compete with downtown shows, featuring ticket prices and number of acts comparable to those in the chi-chi theaters. Certainly it was a good option for those living in Lake View.

While the debut of Weeghman's hippodrome came on June 12, 1915, with the Whales on a lengthy road trip, there had been fireworks at the park on July 3, 1914, according to Elsie Dabel: "We couldn't get a seat because mother wouldn't go in the crowd."

For the June 1915 opening, Jake Stenard, a local vaudeville veteran, took charge of arranging the program. Star of the first night's show was Slivers, a local comedian renowned for his excellent baseball pantomime. "Everybody who ever went to a circus has had a real, genuine laugh with this baseball clown," opined the *American*. Slivers and the other acts performed on the third base side of foul territory facing the nearby stands. A large platform on wheels, used for animal acts, was installed near the pitcher's mound. Tickets for various seats were ten, twenty, and thirty cents, with the program scheduled to last from 7:30 to 11:00. Festivities opened with a parade. Appearing with Slivers on the first night were seven other acts with names that now seem like *parodies* of vaudevillians: The Six Royal Hussars, Holland &

Dockroll, The Holman Brothers, the Five Juggling Normans, the Armanto Trio, the Paul Rondas Trio, and the Three Fanchon Sisters.

Turning Weeghman's baseball field into an amusement park took some doing—particularly in making sure that people could see what was going on at 9:00 at night. Many people believe that lights didn't sully Wrigley Field until 1988, but in order to run the hippodrome, Weeghman found it necessary to have an entire electric lighting system constructed to illuminate the field. He even had a circus-type double spotlight system brought in.

The hippodroming continued at least through Independence Day, and probably longer. On the nights of July 4–5, Weeghman not only presented the usual hippodrome and cabaret acts but also blew off five thousand dollars worth of fireworks arranged into patterns portraying the Liberty Bell, the American flag, and even President Wilson!

ANOTHER PARK, ANOTHER SUNDAY

But singing, dancing, and comedy were not the only things going on at Weeghman Park with the Whales out of town. Charley Weeghman also let the park out to various organizations. The U.S. Army baseball team made frequent use of Weeghman Park during June 1915, playing the University of Chicago team at least three times as well as whipping the local semipro Modern Woodmen team and the squad of Billy Niesen's Gunthers. Niesen was the preeminent organizer of semipro baseball in Chicago at the time; in fact, during the 1910s, Niesen ran the Ogden Grove league, which included a team sponsored by Wrigley's Gum.

Lane Tech High, still just eight blocks west of Wrigley Field at Addison and Western, held its all-school field day on June 7 at Weeghman Park. In addition to various track and field contests, a color guard presented the flag, and a dance squad went through various routines on the infield.

RUMORS

On July 2, rumors were rife that Benny Kauff, already referred to as "The Ty Cobb of the Federal League," would soon join the Chifeds. Kauff had jumped his Brooklyn Tip-Tops contract and inked a tentative pact with John McGraw's Giants. Seeing Kauff disposed to moving around, Charley Weeghman immediately set about obtaining the low-market Cobb-lite for his own.

Kauff, however, never made it to Chicago. The more lasting news of import to Fed fans that day was the announcement that schoolchildren would henceforth be allowed into Weeghman Park for free one day a week, most likely a weekday.

DISASTER RELIEF

One of Chicago's most shocking disasters took place on July 24, 1915, when the cruise ship *Eastland* capsized while preparing to leave town. More than eight hundred drowned. Weeghman, always conscious of his place in the community, decided to hold an "Eastland Sufferer's Day" July 29. (A "Joe Tinker Day" planned for a few days earlier at the ballpark was canceled out of respect for the victims' families, and all city functions were shut down on July 27 for an official day of mourning.)

Other public entertainments—theaters, cabarets, and dance halls—were also lending hands to the survivors. For instance, a series of local actors put a show on to raise money for the victims' families at the Auditorium Theater the day after the Whales' benefit game. All gate proceeds from the July 29 Whales–Buffeds game, as well as the funds from concessions, were given to the families of the victims. Weeghman, who received some good notices in the press as well as a few barbs for exploiting the terrible event, said he hoped to raise ten thousand dollars.

Local actresses from two popular stage shows, "All Over Town" and "The Lady in Red," volunteered to walk through the stands and sell programs and flowers, as did society figures and wives of some Whales players. The proceeds, of course, were earmarked for the fund. In order to increase traffic, Weeghman lowered ticket prices to a quarter for the grandstand and fifty cents for box seats. "It will greatly please Weeghman," said the Chicago *American*, "if he has to stretch ropes around the playing field to keep the overflow crowds off the diamond."

The pass gate was closed. Everyone had to pay to get into the park that day: players, writers, telegraph operators, policemen, umpires, and Jim Gilmore. "I just want to look at the fellow who would begrudge spending 50 cents for such a cause," Weeghman sniffed to the *Evening Post*, offering to pay the admission cost out of his own pocket to anyone who couldn't afford it.

Another selling point to the game was the pitching matchup. Tinker used "Three Finger" Brown, the former Cubs hero, to start the game, while Buffeds skipper Harry Lord countered with his top pitcher, Fred Anderson. It was also noted that both player-managers would "participate in the game in some capacity." At one point, there was talk of asking Jake Sternad, who handled nighttime amusements for the Whales, to arrange a vaudeville show before the contest (including hippodrome acts, according to the *Eve-*

ning Post), but good taste seems to have won out. The 3:00 start was not delayed by "any frills or fussing," wrote Jay Davidson of the *American*.

Everything got back to business shortly thereafter. A few weeks later, on September 2, it was "Intercollegiate Day" at Weeghman, featuring an East versus West all-star college baseball game.

WHALES WIN!

The 1915 Federal League pennant race was one of the most fascinating in baseball history. Five of the eight teams remained in contention in mid-September; the final weekend saw the Whales, the St. Louis Terriers, and the Pittsburgh Rebels tightly bunched.

Eventually, the Terriers split the four games of their final series at Kansas City to end up in second place even though they won eighty-seven games, more than either the Whales or the Rebels. The Terriers played all 154 of their contests, with the Whales suffering two rainouts and the Rebels one, none of which was made up by the financially struggling league.

Therefore, the Whales' victory at home over Pittsburgh in a darkness-shortened second game of the October 3 doubleheader gave Chicago the crown by .0009 percentage points. The Whales' 86–66 record was just that much better than St. Louis' 87–67, while Pittsburgh finished 86–67.

The Whales' clinching triumph produced bedlam at the North Side park. Francis McInerney of the *Evening Post* doubted that "ever a World Series crowd had anything on that roaring, crowding, screeching turnout of 34,212 fans which [*sic*] watched Joe Tinker's Federal League Buns spike down the Federal League championship pennant at Weeghman Park." J. J. Alcock of the *Tribune* reported on "the deafening cheers of one of the greatest baseball crowds this city has ever seen."

Nobody expected this kind of crowd, least of all Charley Weeghman, and he and his staff were caught flat-footed. By the time Mayor and Mrs. Thompson showed up, secretary Charley Williams was sweating bullets as he escorted the dignitaries to their seats.

Two days later, Alcock noted in the *Tribune* that "Weeghman is lamenting the fact that he did not know how to distribute the fans, for he believes he would have broken the record for attendance at a ball game if he could have crowded in everybody who tried to get inside the grounds."

Four hours before game time, hundreds of fans were lined up to buy tickets. The trains and streetcars brought in thousands more hopefuls, and tickets were sold out an hour before the first pitch. Five thousand fans waited outside the stadium and added their cheers when alerted to the goings-on.

Fans stood ten deep in the grandstand. The aisles were jammed. The field was crammed with fans in a giant horseshoe, six people deep at its narrowest around the outfield. Young men sat on the brick outfield walls. Women in full fancy dress uncomplainingly sat on cushions. Fans even went under the stands to watch through small portholes. Some three hundred fans forced themselves into the press box, nearly crowding out the writers.

In game one, the Whales—up 4–1 with two outs in the ninth, just one out from the championship—showed the hysterical crowd a classic Chicago finish that Wrigley Field fans have come to know almost by heart: they blew the seemingly safe lead and fell 5–4 in eleven innings. This turn of events disheartened the crowd and made it a life-or-death concern that their pod of Whales capture game two before the sun went down. A Pittsburgh victory or a tie would give the Rebels the pennant.

Federal League Umpire-in-Chief Bill Brennan was running the plate that day. Brennan always seemed to be in Chicago, assumably because it was the signature city in the league, and possibly because Charley Weeghman would have demanded the best umpire be at his field. Brennan signaled at the beginning of the second game that the contest would be called off after whatever half-inning was completed after 5:24 p.m., the exact hour of sundown.

The Pittsburghers obviously tried their hardest to loaf their way through the game and produce a tie. But in the bottom of the sixth, Max Flack rapped out an RBI double to right that put the Whales up and sent the crowd into hysterics. By the end of the inning, the Whales led 3–0. Brennan looked at his watch and announced that the top of the seventh would be the last inning. With two out, Pittsburgh's Ed Konetchy stroked a lazy fly to center field. When Dutch Zwilling squeezed it at 5:25 p.m., the Whales had their pennant.

PILLOW FIGHT

In the words of McInerney, the fans then "went Borneo," tossing their seat cushions into the air.

"One of the biggest cushion fights ever staged in a Chicago ball park took place," wrote Alcock, suggesting that this type of event was not exactly a rarity at the time in the city's athletic fields. "The multitude on the field rushed for the Whale bench to congratulate the winners and were met with a steady fire of cushions from the stand. The men on the grass were prompt to accept the challenge, and within a minute there were a couple of thousand cushions sailing back and forth."

Mayor and Mrs. Thompson were caught in the crossfire. The muckety-mucks barely escaped being beaned by several cushions, which even came sailing from the hands of interlopers in the press box. McInerney wrote that "many were struck by the flying pads, and altho ground attendants and police got busy, it was several minutes before the frenzied fans became rational enough to seek the street and elevated cars."

Following the contest, Weeghman held court in his office, inviting in dozens of friends, all the writers, and plenty of fans just out for a good time. Weeghman's parents were there as well, "smiling as pleasant a pair of Hoosier smiles as one could picture," according to the *Tribune*.

IT'S ALL OVER NOW

So Weeghman finally had his flag, tattered as it was, but he had no luck leveraging it. "Now that you have it, Charley, whatinell are you going to do with it?" the *Tribune* asked.

In an October 5 telegram to the Red Sox and Phillies (the American and National League champs who were about to begin the World Series), Weeghman entreated the winning club to take on his Chifeds for the benefit not only of his players, but also for "the many thousand fans who have been patrons of the Federal League games throughout the season."

Everyone knew the majors wouldn't respond to Weeghman. "The best the Buns can do is claim the world's title by default. Empty honor," mourned columnist Howard Mann in the *Evening Post*.

Even the Chicago city council weighed in, passing a resolution urging Mayor "Big Bill" Thompson to call for a round-robin series between the Phils, Bosox, and Whales. But no go.

His calls for a true battle with the big boys unheeded, Weeghman again turned to the local city series. His team, he argued, was the only champion in town, but neither the Cubs nor the White Sox were interested in helping their rivals get more coverage and showed no interest in Weeghman's offer. Mann groused about the Cubs and Sox, "The winner will claim the city championship in the face of the fact that the Buns won a league pennant. It is to laugh."

Ring Lardner, as usual, had a verse for the occasion.

> The Whales have copped the Federal flag,
> As experts knew they'd do.
> And now that they have copped the rag,
> Whom can they sell it to?

As it turned out, they couldn't sell it to anyone. The Whales had played their last game. No sports franchise ever went out with such a bang. That week, the Whales held a huge ball at the Arcadia Hall in Lake View in honor of the team and Weeghman. Dancing, dining, and drinking were all part of the package, and after the party, the team disbanded for the year—and for good. The *Tribune* reported that the players on the club wrote up a hilarious skit for the occasion mocking themselves and their alleged financial tight-ness.

HOW DOES IT FEEL?

This is not to say, of course, that the Whales were above playing refusenik, too. Rube Foster, the man behind the American Giants Negro League club, challenged Weeghman and the Whales to a series, knowing full well that neither the Cubs nor Sox would take on the Federal League champions.

Weeghman's heart, however, was apparently as hard toward the Negro Leagues as the American and National Leagues' were toward the Feds. There was no Whales–American Giants series, quite possibly because Weeghman suspected that the American Giants would easily whip his squad.

THE DEATH OF THE FEDERAL LEAGUE

The 1915 Federal League race was one of the most exciting, down-to-the-wire affairs in baseball annals, but the young loop was still bleeding money at a furious rate. Even lowering ticket prices didn't bring the Fed fans out. Meanwhile, the major leagues continued to suffer decreased attendance, in-creased salaries, and less press coverage. Several minor leagues shut down, while others struggled just to keep the gates open. Everyone involved on the management side—the majors, the minors, and the Feds—wanted relief from the current situation.

The unexpected death of Brooklyn owner Robert Ward in October 1915 removed much of the impetus for the Feds to continue, and both sides began thinking about whether it would be best to negotiate a settlement. The Fed-eral League, however, had months earlier filed an antitrust suit against orga-nized baseball, which federal Judge Kenesaw Mountain Landis sat on all season. He didn't want to rule on the case. Both sides wanted peace, the ma-jors to be rid of competition and get salaries back under control, the Feds to recoup some of their losses and, in the cases of the most powerful FL fran-chises, to crowbar themselves into the big leagues.

In order to do this, Fed president Gilmore and some of the clubs—mainly Chicago and St. Louis—went on the offensive. In June 1915, the Fed leadership announced plans in the papers to plan an invasion of New York City for 1916, with an unspecified Fed team relocating to the Big Apple. This move, a bluff of the highest order, eventually had the desired effect of haul-ing the big leaguers to the bargaining table.

On December 22, 1915, in Cincinnati, the Feds and the majors inked a pact. In order to rid themselves of the Feds, organized baseball paid six hundred thousand dollars to be distributed among the upstart league's owners. Ward's heirs received four hundred thousand dollars of that, and the Pittsburgh club got fifty thousand. Some teams got nothing, including Baltimore, which became the only Federal League club *not* to drop the lawsuit against the majors.

Charley Weeghman and St. Louis' Phil Ball were allowed to buy major league franchises. Weeghman was awarded the right to buy the Cubs, with Ball given the opportunity to purchase the Browns. James Gilmore's role in the game essentially came to an end; without a league to command, he went back into private business.

Ultimately, the big winners were Weeghman, Ball, and organized baseball. The losers were most of the other Fed clubs (some of which received little or no money for their troubles) and the players, whose salaries returned to pre-1914 levels with the dissolution of the Federal League.

Another winner? Cubs fans. Stuck in a decaying ballpark on the West Side, with terrible ownership and a dwindling fan base, the Cubs would receive a jolt of fresh money, fresh attitude, and—perhaps most important— the ballpark that they still play in today.

WEEGHMAN BUYS IN

On December 14, 1915, eight days before the official end of the Federal League, the majors and Weeghman hammered out an agreement at the Waldorf-Astoria in New York. Weeghman was allowed to buy controlling interest in the Cubs from Charles Taft, a Cincinnati-based businessman (and half brother of President William Howard Taft) with a somewhat shady reputation. As an absentee owner in the fiercely proud and independent city of Chicago, Charlie Taft had been viewed as only a slight improvement on Charles Murphy. The fans weren't too unhappy to see him go.

On January 20, 1916, Weeghman handed over a check for five hundred thousand dollars, drawn from his account at the Fort Dearborn National Bank, to J. G. Wakefield of the Corn Exchange National Bank. This gave Weeghman control of the Chicago National League Ball Club.

Photos of the occasion show the dapper and confident Weeghman happily passing the check to Wakefield. At this point, Weeghman had achieved one of his great dreams: to own a club in the established major leagues. Truly it was remarkable that in twenty years, this self-made man had risen from filling the coffee cups at the tables of the rich and powerful to sitting down with them himself.

Half a million bucks was the highest price that had been paid for a major league team up till that time. For that sum, Weeghman obtained 90 percent of the club, with the remainder belonging to investor Harry Ackerland of Pittsburgh, a Cubs stockholder.

In mid-January, Weeghman announced that some of his shares would go to J. Ogden Armour, the meatpacking magnate who was one of the hundred richest men in the United States. According to Warren Brown's *Chicago Cubs*, Armour convinced William Wrigley, head of the dominant Wrigley Gum Company, to buy in as well. Both Armour and Wrigley paid fifty thousand dollars for their initial shares, with both taking a seat on the board of directors. In addition, advertising executive A. D. Lasker, sales magnate R. A. Cavanaugh, and C. A. McCulloch (manager of the Thompson's restaurant chain, a competitor of Weeghman's!) bought into the team. These three were also added to the board.

It is not clear whether Weeghman was struggling financially at this point; it may be that he simply wanted to have his friends involved. Other pals, such as Adolph Schutter and Al Plamondon, also bought in. The final deal wasn't sealed on the additional investments until April 7, 1916. At that point, the *Daily News* reported, "The club is now a million-dollar organization."

Weeghman's Whales were essentially folded into the Cubs. The St. Louis Terriers were also allowed to transfer their talent to the Browns, but the other six Fed clubs lost their players to the open market. Joe Tinker became the Cubs' new manager, replacing Roger Bresnahan; the best Whales players (Rollie Zeider, Max Flack, Les Mann, Dutch Zwilling, Claude Hendrix, Mike Prendergast, and George McConnell) wore Cub flannels in 1916 as well.

A new north side Rooters' Club was formed in early April. The group hoped to have five hundred members by Opening Day, and the club established a club and lounge at the Hotel Morrison. The lounge was festooned with baseball photographs, books, and newspapers for the members, as well as desks for any writers who wanted to come in, have a drink, and hang around.

CUBBIES ON THE MOVE

It made all the sense in the world for the Cubs to move from West Side Grounds to the North Side. West Side Grounds was older, had grown decrepit from years of poor care in the hands of Murphy and Taft, and was far from the tonier neighborhoods in which Weeghman and his friends lived. But it was also a sad day for those who remembered the Cubs' glories of the early 1900s and knew what might happen to the West Side once the club departed for greener pastures.

On April 20, 1916, the day the Cubs played their first game at Weeghman Park, Ring Lardner penned a bittersweet twelve-stanza tribute to West

Side Grounds, "Elegy Written in a West Side Ball Park," in the *Tribune*. It read, in part:

> Now fades the glimmering landscape on the sight.
> Save for the chatter of the laboring folk
> Returning to their hovels for the night,
> All's still at Taylor, Lincoln, Wood, and Polk.
> Beneath this aged roof, this grandstand's shade,
> Where peanut shucks lie in a mold'ring heap,
> Where show the stains of pop and lemonade,
> The Cub bugs used to cheer and groan and weep.

NEW KID IN TOWN

The Cubs hitters found, during their first practice at Weeghman Park on April 18, the outfield distances much to their liking. All the sluggers drove batting-practice pitches well past the fences.

Accompanying the Cubs from West Side Grounds to Weeghman Park was Pat Pieper, the legendary field announcer who served as the team's public-address man until he passed away in 1974. Originally a vendor at West Side Grounds back in 1904, Pieper had been hired as field announcer in early 1915, and he eventually took his place on the field at the North Side park and intoned the daily lineups with a megaphone. In the 1930s, he was finally given a microphone. By the 1960s, Pieper was seated inside the scoreboard.

Many of the old West Side fans stayed with the team as well. New location or not, true fandom isn't easy to give up, as the many sixty-year-olds who keep Brooklyn Dodgers caps in their front closets can attest. However, this was a new kind of game; Cubs fans were used to on-field success and off-field doings of a much less glamorous fashion. The loud, somewhat obnoxious, and often filthy quality of the West Side game and ballpark were giving way to a shiny, new, somewhat more polite form of baseball. Even the unofficial name of the park emphasized the difference between the old and the new. While everyone associated with the Cubs called the place Weeghman Park, the newspapers and fans were just as likely to refer to it as the "north side park."

The newfound cleanliness, or trendiness, or *je ne sais quoi*, didn't get rid of ticket scalpers, who were probably much happier that the Feds were gone; the extra club had created more seats than could be filled. Regarding the threat of reselling Opening Day ducats, Weeghman told the newspapers: "It is certain there will be attempts at ticket scalping. This cannot be helped, but the fans can see to it that the scalpers lose money if they refuse to be held up."

Of course, the scarcity of tickets and the buzz that the opening created didn't hurt Weeghman at all.

MORE CHANGES

Tickets for the Cubs–Reds opener were snapped up as soon as they were available, and a bursting-past-capacity crowd was expected. Therefore, more seats had to be installed. On April 19, "Weeghman was at the park for several hours," penned Oscar Reichow of the *Daily News*, "superintending the construction of extra seats that have been stationed in front of the grand stand, extending from the extreme left end to the extreme right, with a break behind home plate." These seats would hold three thousand additional fans.

The expansion didn't stop there. Just a day before the game, a group of carpenters was called in to construct another seating section on the field, this one in the only space not previously filled: directly behind the plate. Other extra patrons were to be ringed around the outfield, as usual, this time on two rows of benches. In addition, plans were made to place other fans down the right-field line. Some of the many rooters spilled into fair territory, and nine ground-rule doubles were hit into that crowd.

It had rained on and off for a few days before the opener, muddying up the park and giving groundskeeper Murphy quite a challenge to have the field in top shape for the opener. Stories in mid-April mention the Cubs covering the playing field during rainy times with "pieces of canvas that kept off a great deal of the water."

ONE MORE PARADE

Things began poorly for the Cubs in 1916; the club lost four of its first six games and had to return to Chicago "under cover of darkness" on April 18, according to James Crusinberry of the *Tribune*. Luckily, the bugs didn't sniff them out, so the players lived to see another day, and another ballpark.

Visiting Cincinnati dignitaries, including owner Garry Herrmann, paraded through the downtown streets upon their arrival in the morning after having spent the previous evening at the Bismarck Garden—or, rather, the Marigold Garden, as the tavern had been renamed in view of rampaging World War I anti-German sentiment.

For the Cubs' first game in their new park on April 20, Weeghman once more pulled out all the stops. He arranged a parade of city officials to ride to the new park from downtown. This time around, with a club in the National League rather than the ragamuffin FL, he was able to get a better parade going. A ten-motorcycle police escort guided the parade, which was scheduled to last one hour, from Grant Park at 1:00 p.m. The game was scheduled to begin at 3:00. Chief deputy sheriff Charles Peters served as grand marshal.

Two hours later (one hour tardy), the mile-long parade arrived at Clark and Addison. Six brass bands, cars stuffed with players from both the Cubs and the Reds, plenty of politicians (including Mayor "Big Bill" Thompson, and Illinois Governor Ed Dunne), and assorted flag-bearers and hangers-on comprised the procession.

FIRST DAY ON THE NORTH SIDE

Waiting for this illustrious group was a crowd of twenty thousand cold and impatient fans, some of whom had been there since the ballpark gates opened at noon. Once the players and officials finally arrived at Weeghman Park, the game was further delayed as everyone got out of their cars.

Pregame festivities took place in the usual Weeghman (or, perhaps, Wagnerian) manner. Bombs, fireworks, and six brass bands made the noise, drowning out a speech that a local judge was making on the field. Some three hundred visiting rooters from Cincinnati had hauled along their own German music makers as well. The Rooter's Club traveled "in tallyho" from the Hotel Morrison with their own band. And surely not the only ass on the premises was the live donkey that Chicago's Twenty-Fifth Ward Democratic Organization trooped out.

A twenty-one-gun salute again greeted the raising of the flag, and fans and the press were notified that a local tailor named George Kelly had offered a suit to any player who smacked a homer on Opening Day. Only one did: Cincinnati's John Beall.

J. Ogden Armour made a gift of a baby bear to the Cubs for the Opening Day celebration. The bear, named "Joa" in honor of its giver, cavorted in front of whirring motion-picture cameras as the players warmed up. The small bear lived in a cage at the corner of Clark and Addison, just outside Weeghman Park, during the 1916 season. At various times in Cubs history, baby bears were brought around to the park for photo opportunities, fed milk out of small bottles, and the like.

Armour, now one of the Cubs' chief shareholders, sat in a special field box with Continental Bank President George Reynolds. Armour had presented Weeghman with a floral bouquet grown at his Lake Forest home, just one of the many garlands and wreaths given out to players, officials, and managers. Charles Comiskey and James Gilmore also made appearances.

The game finally started at around 3:30. It ended after 6:00 p.m., with Chicago having won 7–6 in eleven innings. "It was another epochal day in the history of baseball," the *Tribune*'s Crusinberry wrote the next day, "and quite convincing that the Cubs have found a welcome to the north side.

There was a newness and a curiosity to things. It was the first time many of the players and doubtless many of the fans had ever seen the north side ball park. But they seemed to have no trouble in finding it."

The *Tribune* noted that several hundred fans watched the game "from the roofs and windows of flat buildings across the street from the ball park." The overflow crowd caused at least one near miss. During the seventh inning, Cubs outfielder Bill Fischer, attempting to catch a foul fly, accidentally ran over a small boy who was part of the overflow crowd. Neither party was seriously injured.

The day after the first National League contest at Weeghman Park, the Cubs–Reds game was canceled due to inclement weather. But on April 21, the city's men still had something to celebrate: city authorities ruled that it would now be permissible for women to wear bloomer suits without stockings on the beaches during the summer.

THE LAST TIME

Cubs manager Joe Tinker had earlier in the season called on thirty-nine-year-old Mordecai Brown, a star of the Cubs a decade earlier who had fashioned a 17–8 season with the 1915 Whales, to help fill out his pitching staff. Never a hard thrower, Brown had little left but guile and experience and would pitch just twelve games in 1916, the final campaign of his big league career.

But Brown didn't depart without filling the stands one last time. On September 4, the Cubs and the visiting Reds arranged a real Weeghman special—a matchup between Brown and Cincinnati manager Christy Mathewson, Hall of Fame hurlers famous for their duels in the first decade of the century. Mathewson had been dealt from the New York Giants earlier in the year.

With the Cubs and Reds out of contention, the decision to hold the game was a cinch. Neither pitcher was really on his game that day, but it hardly mattered. The memory-making special, the twenty-third matchup of the two immortals, drew a sellout crowd with the Reds defeating the home team 10–8. Mathewson went all the way for the win. It was the final performance in each of the great hurlers' careers.

Mathewson would die just nine years later of the aftereffects of tuberculosis he contracted after being gassed in World War I. Brown retired in 1921 to his farm in Indiana. Tinker would be relieved of his duties following the 1916 season, with Fred Mitchell brought in to run the Cubs.

CALIFORNIA DREAMIN'

In preparation for the 1917 season, the Cubs trained in California. This sun-kissed paradise became the Cubbies' spring home because of the persuasiveness of William Wrigley, part owner of the team. Wrigley's interest in this area was, writes Warren Brown, the first visible evidence that the gum magnate wanted to be more involved with the club.

Wrigley convinced the board of directors that the Cubs should train out west, where the team would enjoy clement weather, enough distance from the home fans to whet the appetite for the season opener, and ready-made opponents in clubs from the Pacific Coast League. Two years later, Wrigley bought Catalina Island off the coast of Los Angeles. He soon built the scenic isle into the Cubs' training base and, not coincidentally, a tourist destination. By November 1922, the *Tribune* opined that Catalina was "one of the best places for a ball club training in the country."

When the Cubs got home from the sunnier clime, they found advertising on the left-field bleacher fence, as well as the rendering of a huge American flag on the center-field scoreboard. In addition, outside of the park, atop the right-field wall, was a new sign reading "Chicago National League Ball Club."

NO NO SONG

One of the most remarkable games in baseball history took place at Weeghman Park on May 2, 1917. With dry understatement worthy of Dr. Johnson, Oscar Reichow of the *Daily News* scrivened, "Cub fans to-day saw one of the most remarkable pitching duels they probably ever have seen." Or *anyone* ever has seen. Jim "Hippo" Vaughn of Chicago and Fred Toney of Cincinnati each no-hit their opposition for nine innings. Never before and never since in the history of major league baseball has this feat been duplicated.

In the tenth, Vaughn's heart was broken. Reds shortstop Larry Kopf singled with one out. One out later, he went to third when Cy Williams dropped Hal Chase's long fly. Chase then swiped second. Jim Thorpe bounced back to the mound. Vaughn, hoping for a play on Kopf, fired the ball toward home, but catcher Art Wilson wasn't expecting the throw and let it get by. The play was ruled a hit. Kopf crossed the plate, but Wilson tagged out Chase attempting to score.

In the last of the tenth, with one out, Cubs first baseman Fred Merkle nearly got the run back. His deep fly backed Manuel Cueto to the left-field wall, but the ball stayed in the park. Cy Williams then whiffed to end the game, and Toney had a spectacular no-hit victory. Vaughn—who fanned ten men and walked just two—had nothing but a painful 1–0 loss on an unearned run. It was the first no-hitter thrown at what is now known as Wrigley Field.

Warren Brown wrote, years later, that there were "350,000 who wished they had been in the vicinity" when they read the papers the next day. Unfortunately, this great game, completed in just one hour and fifty minutes, was witnessed by between only twenty-five and thirty-five hundred souls. The next day, May 3, in horrible weather, the two teams drew just three hundred hardy fans.

On August 8, en route to a twenty-two-win season, Vaughn would two-hit Brooklyn and win 2–0, completing the game in a quick one hour, twenty-three minutes.

VIVE LA FRANCE!

During World War I, different cities in the United States sought to show their patriotism by forming strong relationships with European allies. When a group of French dignitaries announced a planned trip to the United States in early 1917, various civic organizations began scrambling to entertain them.

When the French visitors, including Field Marshal Joseph Joffre and former Premier René Viviani (both deposed from power and now in ceremonial positions), reached America in spring 1917, guess who wanted to take them out to the ball game when they reached Chicago? Yes, Lucky Charley.

The same day that Vaughn and Toney tossed their double no-hitter, Weeghman was in the newspapers requesting that the committee appointed to entertain the visiting Frenchmen consider bringing the party by his ballpark that Friday or Saturday to take in the national pastime.

Weeghman wanted to hold "France Day" over the weekend and fill his park, as well as add some money to the war relief fund. "I am sure the visitors would enjoy the game, knowing it to be a national institution, and the fans undoubtedly would give them one of the greatest receptions they could get in this country." Charley, never shy about pressing his case, claimed in the *Daily News* that the presence of such impressive foreign allies and the resultant pomp and ceremony would swell the ranks of the military! "I believe such a celebration would have an impressive effect on the younger men and stimulate enlistment in the national service."

Unfortunately, the visiting dignitaries never made it to the park; they already had too much on their plates. Even Weeghman's offer to donate an ambulance to the war effort couldn't draw the party to a Cubs game.

MASTERS OF WAR

As the war spirit reached new peaks, baseball tried to climb over all other public entertainments to show its patriotism. Friday, June 29, 1917, was "Red Cross Day" at Weeghman Park, and the Whales drew a big enough crowd to contribute $3,858 to the relief organization. The papers made note of the fact that Friday was a lousy day at the ballparks, with most people working to finish up the week and waiting to spend their money on the weekends. Today, Cubs fans can't wait for those Friday 3:05 games to *jump-start* their weekends.

On July 27, the Canadian Highlanders and their band came to Weeghman Park and were fêted by the fans. U.S. military personnel were also guests of the Cubs that day.

PIGGYBACK

Charley Weeghman loved to hitch his wagon to whatever parade was gaining the interest of passers-by. He may have outdone himself in late June. On June 22, the Pirates held "Honus Wagner Day" at Forbes Field. Two days later, with the Pirates and Cubs traveling back to Chicago for a series, Weeghman held his own celebration for Hans. The Cubs and Bucs drew ten thousand to Weeghman Park that day to celebrate perhaps the game's most beloved player. Wagner received a flower garland from Weeghman. Asked to make a speech, he simply replied, "Much obliged."

During July and August, Chicago was hit with a massive heat wave. As a result, a practice that still drives the working press crazy began to take root: some non-press patrons of the game were let into the press box, apparently at the behest of management. As a writer from the *Herald* noted with no little irritation, "It's getting so the workers have to do their work downstairs."

On August 5, a rainstorm broke out during the top of the ninth inning of the Cubs' loss to Philadelphia. Fans in the bleachers were allowed to run across the field in order to get to the grandstands and stay dry.

CHAPTER 4

1918: Weeghman Park and the War

BAD TIME

The year of 1918 was fateful for the Chicago Cubs and for Charles Weegh-man. The Cubs won the National League pennant for the first time since 1910, giving Weeghman his first taste of the World Series he had longed for. The crazy 1918 campaign had the potential to be Lucky Charley's biggest triumph; instead, it proved to be the final stage of the meteoric fall of the enthusiastic but undercapitalized owner. Several factors were responsible for Weeghman's financial fall:

◆ World War I's impact on the working population. With many working men serving in the military (instead of spending their days in downtown Chicago), far fewer people were eating in Weeghman's restaurants, going to his movie theaters, and frequenting his pool halls. Attendance at base-ball games was also way down.
◆ The influenza epidemic, a catastrophe that led the U.S. government to urge citizens to stay out of crowded places like restaurants and ballparks. Some self-appointed protectors of morality, both inside and outside the government, also used the panic and fear caused by the epidemic to drive home their agendas of "clean living" and "upright behavior."
◆ Weeghman's own plan to buy high-priced players for the Cubs. This strategy, which he had utilized since breaking into baseball, caused him financial woe when his other businesses began to struggle.

LIFE DURING WARTIME

The First World War changed human history. It was the first truly modern war, fought with much more lethal twentieth-century technology in an era when military tactics were still mired in the nineteenth century. Chemical weapons were major killers in the First World War, and since then their use has been banned. The horrendous casualties all over Europe, with the death and destruction brought instantly to the home front by newspapers, photographs, and newsreels, shocked European artists into creating the purposely absurd expressions of Dadaism and, later, Surrealism.

Americans, not cursed with fighting on their own soil, enthusiastically embraced the war spirit anyway. Newspapers of the day spread jingoism and urged aggression toward the rebels trying to overtake Mexico, for instance. For many Americans (especially businessmen who profited from the manufacture of armaments), the time couldn't come too soon for "our boys" to join the fight to "make the world safe for democracy" (in the quaintly pompous phraseology of the day). Newspapers of the time actually carried shameless headlines like "Doctors, Nurses Eager to Go to War."

The international instability brought about by the destruction of Europe's economy affected the United States. Even before America joined the war and men marched off to fight, people were further tightening their already cinched purse strings. This meant fewer people could afford discretionary spending on ball games, movies, or eating in restaurants—three businesses that Charles Weeghman depended on for his economic survival.

Most people at the time believed that baseball players, as hale and hearty men, should be among the first to fight. In these days before the advent of the broadcast media, the game may have been a national mania, but it was deeply rooted at the local level. While Major League Baseball was a national business, it was far less a focus of attention than big league sports are today, because the overwhelming presence of the mass media did not yet exist. Yes, baseball was important, but nobody would have felt that it was as important as aiding in what was believed to be a good fight. Ballplayers had long been encouraged to take part in pregame military-style parades on the field, shouldering baseball bats like rifles. There was no shortage of patriotism at the nation's ballparks, just as there is no such shortage at today's parks in the aftermath of the September 11, 2001, attacks.

One consequence of the war effort was a lessening of some of the game's fusty rules. The barrier against Sunday games in the nation's capital was struck down May 14, 1918, when baseball on the Sabbath was legalized in Washington, D.C.—largely to provide amusement for the many workers who could no longer attend weekday afternoon contests.

SHUTDOWN, PART I

In July 1918, Washington Senators catcher Eddie Ainsmith was drafted. He applied for a work-related deferment. Secretary of War Newton Burns soon ruled that baseball was a nonessential industry. This ruling caused baseball men to shake in their boots, as most of them believed that the game could actually be shut down indefinitely with players (and management) required to take "essential" wartime jobs. Most minor leagues did wind down by the end of August, as several opportunists lined up to fill the void expected to result from the shutdown of the major leagues.

At one point in late July, National League President John Tener— speaking without consulting the NL owners—was quoted as saying that he didn't favor a World Series. Charley Weeghman, probably reaching for the nearest oxygen machine, since his Cubs were in first place, gasped that he couldn't believe that Tener had been correctly quoted. The *Daily News* reported humorously on August 5, 1918, that "restoratives were being administered to [Charley] Weeghman" as Billy Niesen announced plans for a new semipro "city league" to meet fans' need for competitive baseball. Niesen, however, apparently never got his league off the ground.

The American and National Leagues told the press and the government that they would shorten the 1918 regular season so that everyday competition would end on September 1. After that date, all ballplayers would be required either to join the armed forces or get other "essential" war-related jobs. A wag in the August 29 *Sporting News* noted that Cubs players would have two choices of essential jobs: either managing a Weeghman doughnut shop or becoming cattle herders at the Chicago stockyards with weekend ball-playing privileges.

SHUTDOWN, PART II

Many major league owners, especially those with low-drawing clubs, were more than happy to close the gates of their parks, especially if they could blame the war. The war spirit didn't stop them from trying to keep their players tied up without paying them, however. As *TSN* noted on August 29, 1918, "Letters were sent to National League players last week notifying them that their services would not be needed after September 2 and that they would be paid off up to and including that date and dismissed until further notice. That 'further notice' stuff is what gets the players. If they are to be 'reserved' for an indefinite renewal they'd like to know why their contracts should not be carried out until the end of the season. 'If they want to reserve us, they got to pay us,' seems to be the player's slogan. It sounds reasonable."

Oscar Reichow in the August 14 *Daily News* wrote, "It would be a blow to President Weeghman and his associates if a world's series is prohibited. They have gone to a lot of expense to give Chicago a winner in the National league and would be hard hit if the team wins and cannot get into the games."

Shortly after the agreement was made to abbreviate the regular season, President Calvin Coolidge and Secretary of War Burns alerted the leagues that the World Series should indeed go on, but with some changes. To cut down on wasteful train travel, the first *three* Series games would be played in Chicago, with the next four slated for Boston. To make matters worse for Weeghman, the Series games would take place during the week in order to allow the players and press to travel on the weekend. Charley Weeghman, his face already gray from lost revenue, now had to adjust himself to the reality that these restrictions would cheat him yet again.

Photos taken during the 1918 season and World Series show Weeghman looking older and less chipper than a few short years before. Still nattily attired, the rapidly capsizing Weeghman put up a brave front for his friends in the press and in business, but everyone connected with the club knew that Lucky Charley was in trouble. Despite the club's success, everything was going wrong for him.

AIN'T THAT GOOD NEWS

One thing did go right for Charley Weeghman during 1918. Charlie Murphy, former president of the Cubs, filed a lawsuit in January to force the current management of the team to pay rent on old West Side Grounds. The case was dismissed on July 11, and Weeghman and his associates were found not liable for the rent.

David Rotroff of the *Daily News* noted on August 14 that "persons have seen a five-foot snake crawling around over at Des Plaines and West Madison streets. It is a relief to know that we don't have to go over on the West Side grounds any more to see the Cubs play ball."

THE 1918 IRREGULAR SEASON

It was a strange campaign, marked by low attendance, threats of shutdown, and assorted odd events. In a late May contest in front of approximately fifteen thousand at Weeghman Park, Earl "Greasy" Neale of the Reds (later a football great) socked Cubs catcher Bill Killefer in the jaw to culminate an argument about whether a ball was fair or foul.

A series against McGraw's Giants in early June attracted record crowds to the ballpark, and the Cubs were looking like winners. But even with the team playing well, fewer and fewer people could afford to catch a game, and Weeghman's spending began to grate on his partners. Since taking over the

Cubs in late 1915, Charley Weeghman had spared no expense to make his club a contender. In his Federal League days, he was never afraid to shell out a wad of money to obtain a player he considered crucial. Recall that Joe Tinker was the league's first significant signing.

Weeghman spent sixty thousand dollars to obtain superstar pitcher Grover Cleveland Alexander and his battery mate, Bill Killefer, from the Phillies following the 1917 season. This move didn't work out too well; Alexander ended up in the army and pitched just three games in 1918. The Cubs also made other deals to bring talented and expensive players such as Fred Merkle, Phil Douglas, and Pete Kilduff to the team.

"The deals that brought us Alexander, [Killefer], [Lefty] Tyler, and [Dode] Paskert are not the only ones we will pull this winter," Weeghman told *The Sporting News* in December 1917. "I want a heavy hitting, clever outfielder to add to my collection of trophies, and I'm willing to part with the price to get them. We would pay $25,000 or more for the right one. Nor have we given up the hope of landing [Rogers] Hornsby."

When his baseball and other business revenue began to drop off in 1917, the enthusiastic and somewhat imperial Weeghman (not many others would refer to their players as *"trophies"*) was instructed by his partners to tighten the belt. Even though overall player salaries had dropped in 1916 after the Federal League's demise, Weeghman was still paying a lot of money to his players as well as taking better care of his park than anyone else.

Weeghman still tried every trick in the book to get people to come out. From his fan-friendly concession stands to souvenir giveaways to what was viewed at the time as the outrageous practice of allowing fans to keep foul balls hit into the stands, Weeghman was a master at promotion. "Weeghman's success in the majors is fortunate for the game," said George Robbins in *TSN* on July 4, 1918. "It proves that a good business man who loves baseball, studies the game, and has the gift of seeking the proper advice is the fellow who should and will succeed in baseball." While Robbins, usually sharp as a tack, would turn out to be wrong about this one, it does show that Weeghman's profile had improved among the more conventional sporting publications.

REAL NIGHTTIME

At the same time Robbins was lauding Weeghman's hardiness, the Boston Braves were beginning a new venture—twilight baseball—to help bring fans to the park during wartime. What can legitimately be called the first night game in the history of the major leagues was held not on May 24, 1935, in Cincinnati, but rather on July 1, 1918, when the Braves began a game against the Brooklyn Superbas at 6:00 p.m. While the game was a success on the field—Boston won 5–3—the weather was threatening and only a thousand Hub fans showed up. The gray skies opened up on the small gathering in the eighth inning and kept pouring until the game ended and the fans had gone home.

The Sporting News enthusiastically supported the idea, opining that "twilight baseball is what we have in mind as the game's salvation" as a way to help working stiffs come to the games they'd miss if played at the usual start time of 3:15. However, the Braves were a bad team that year, and nobody wanted to come out to their games anyway. As a result, the idea was abandoned after the one attempt.

WITH A LITTLE LUCK

Baseball in the second decade of the twentieth century involved clubs playing long home stands and, in turn, taking long road trips. Clubs traveled by train, and the travel time on such voyages meant that road series were bunched together. Therefore, teams might not play their first home games until mid-April, or they might not have home games scheduled after early September.

This was the situation with the Cubs in 1918, who by the artificially enforced September 1 close of the season had played seventy-six of their seventy-seven scheduled home games but only fifty-three on the road. Therefore, the early end of the season helped stuff Weeghman's coffers and helped his team win the pennant. Nobody had played as many home games in 1918 as the Cubs; their chief rivals, the New York Giants, saw just fifty-six games at the Polo Grounds.

TICKETS, GET YOUR TICKETS

Demand for World Series tickets in both Chicago and Boston was running high, but Weeghman fretted over the possibility of more lost revenue. Rather than simply sell out the Cubs' fifteen-thousand-plus-seat ballpark and bemoan the blasted luck that thousands of other possible customers couldn't get in, smart young Cubs business manager Walter Craighead—who had replaced the popular Charley Williams that year—persuaded management to rent out White Sox owner Charles Comiskey's park, the "Baseball Palace of the World," for the postseason.

It would be nearly impossible in this day and age to imagine the Cubs playing home games at the grounds of their intercity rivals, the White Sox. Surely some North Side fans back in 1918 couldn't have been pleased at the specter of traveling south to sit in an American League park in order to watch their hometown heroes. Nevertheless, as one would expect, the Cubs' financial needs won out. By mid-August, Comiskey had agreed to rent his space. The Cubs were happy to print up the extra tickets.

However, the National Commission (the governing body of the two major leagues), wanting to appear patriotic and wanting to fill all the seats in both parks if possible, forced Weeghman to price tickets lower than usual. Box seats, five dollars during the 1917 World Series, instead went for three dollars this time around, with grandstand seats at one-fifty, pavilions at one dollar, and bleachers at fifty cents. Even with his team in the Series, playing in a bigger park, poor Charley couldn't get his pot of gold.

He did, however, win respect for a letter he sent to Comiskey (and released to the press) thanking the White Sox magnate for his warm welcome. "The many courtesies extended to us during the Series have added to your nationwide reputation for good sportsmanship and to our admiration for you." Comiskey had also won Weeghman's admiration by helping to convince other AL owners not to call off the World Series. Several junior-circuit clubs had wanted to shut down the season on August 20 to save money, but, luckily for the Cubs (and the Red Sox), common sense carried the day.

There is, of course, huge irony in that the Cubs' first World Series after the club moved into what is now Wrigley Field didn't even take place there. The park would have to wait until 1929 to be decked out in its first postseason bunting.

The *Daily News'* Oscar Reichow reported on August 20 that the Cubs had begun to implement a system of ensuring that their most loyal fans received a chance to buy World Series tickets. Walter Craighead again deserves much credit for inventing this system: "[Craighead] has put a crew of girls to work at listing the names of the Cub fans who have attended the contests regularly at the north side park and have dropped their rain checks in the boxes at the park to show they are entitled to consideration when the distribution of the tickets takes place." *TSN* reported that Craighead invented this system in order to better handle projected postseason crowds. "A bunch of rain checks held by a ticket applicant shows he has been a regular all season."

GREEDY PLAYERS?

Chicago played very poorly in the Series and lost in six games. Of the three games played in Chicago, the Cubs won just one. After Game One was rained out in Chicago on September 4, the contest was played the next day in front of 19,274 chilled spectators. The police were out in full force on this cold day busting up dice games near Comiskey, prompting David Rotroff to joke in the *Daily News*, "If a person wanted to shake the bones, he had to buy a ticket and go inside and shake his own."

All the expected patriotic hoopla took place before the game, but, to the consternation of Cubs fans, the home team lost 1–0 on a six-hit, complete-game shutout by Babe Ruth.

"The Star-Spangled Banner" (which wouldn't become the national anthem until 1931) was played during the seventh-inning stretch. This was yet another baseball first celebrated in Chicago. From that point, it would be played at *all* World Series contests, although it was not sung routinely before regular-season games for many more years. Even at Wrigley, the anthem was not regularly sung in peacetime until the late 1960s.

Game One's crowd was disappointing, but 20,040 fans watched the Cubs win the next contest 3–1 at Comiskey. The third game of the Series was played in front of 27,054, but the Cubs fell 2–1. While plenty of fans were on hand for the final Windy City contest, others were turned away. As remains the case today, fat cats bought up the reserved seats, and many of them refused to brave the cold and instead stayed home.

"It was unfortunate that many fans could not have had access to the reserved grand stand seats, which were sold out early in the morning," *The Sporting News* sniffed. "Hundreds of fans waited outside trying to get general admission seats and were finally turned away. Some seats went to waste."

Both clubs then boarded trains for Boston. Baseball writers criticized the men running the game for not playing one of the contests on a Sunday, which was a travel day. Once the clubs arrived in Beantown, the finish came soon for Chicago. Two of the final three games went to the Red Sox, and the Crimsons were the champions of the world.

Despite the Cubs' disappointing six-game loss in the makeshift 1918 Series to the Red Sox and phenom pitcher-outfielder Ruth, the season was viewed as an artistic success, if not a financial one. Manager Fred Mitchell received his bouquets from the press. Seen as a hardy soul who did his best to keep his club together in tough times, Mitchell's role would soon expand.

The scribes of the day believed the Cubs were overconfident and simply fell apart in the fall classic; they also wrote that players from both sides were overly concerned with their share of the slim profits engendered by the games. In fact, the players *were* unhappy to be receiving lower shares of the gate and were worried by rumors that they would get little—or even none—of the proceeds. As a result, the players from both clubs nearly went on strike prior to Game Five in Boston, holding up the start of the contest for nearly an hour and bringing down a shower of press criticism.

Such attention to mere money was seen as inappropriate during wartime, although nobody in the papers bothered to criticize Cubs management for its decision to move the games from the North Side to the South Side in order to jam more cheeks into the seats. Press outrage at player "greed" is not surprising, given the biased attitude toward labor–management relations held by the sportswriters of the time—a comfortable and urbane crowd regularly wined and dined by the owners.

GOOD TIME CHARLEY'S GOT THE BLUES

For his part, Charley Weeghman was not wining or dining many people in the 1918 season. Instead, he had been raising money to support his other businesses by selling shares of Cubs stock to the one man in the ownership group who appeared to have the *least* interest in taking over a baseball club: chewing-gum magnate William Wrigley. Wrigley's business did just fine during the war, and he had plenty of scratch. He also liked Weeghman and believed that he and the other Cubs' owners had something of a civic duty to ensure the success of the team.

Weeghman, with his fingers in plenty of inkwells, was a man whom we today would refer to as "overleveraged"—that is, his businesses were riding high but always on the edge of collapse. It's probable that he had to take out huge loans to pay for the expansion of his businesses, and even with his extra income gained from selling Cubs shares, Weeghman's financial situation remained bleak.

What could sink such a successful man so quickly? His empire was built on traffic, and the wartime economy reduced disposable income. In 1915, ten Weeghman's lunch counters served downtown Chicago; the Casino Theater at 58 West Madison and two downtown billiard rooms were his bailiwick as well. At the time, Weeghman's restaurant business had three main competitors: Messenger's, which at the time ran fifteen lunch rooms in a broad range of Chicago neighborhoods; Raklios', with ten counters; and Thompson's, which also boasted ten restaurants.

In 1914, Lucky Charley lived at 5627 N. Sheridan Road, a block from Lake Michigan in the then upscale Edgewater neighborhood. His residence stood just a block north of the Edgewater, a huge pink structure that was for many years one of the ritzier addresses in Chicago. (The building, which still stands, was at one time home to George Halas, owner and coach of the Chicago Bears.)

What Weeghman—who, it was said, worked fourteen hours a day—needed to survive was a constant flow of people coming in and out of his restaurants, bakeries, ballpark, theater, and pool halls. With thousands of Chicago's working men in the military, the number of people lunching at one of Weeghman's clean and shiny lunch counters decreased sharply. Many breadwinners also could no longer take their families to the movies, couldn't shoot pool, and couldn't go to the ballpark. And the glut of quick-lunch restaurants, now less populated with diners, began to thin—this was, as the analysts call it, a "market correction."

When every break started to go bad for Weeghman, it became apparent that his businesses were built on a weak foundation. He owed a lot of people a lot of money, and when his incomes dropped, he couldn't keep up. The real estate magnates who controlled the high-rent property on which Weeghman's restaurants sat were in no mood to feel sorry for the suddenly troubled entrepreneur. The rents had to be paid.

A BAD INFLUENZE

To make matters worse, the influenza epidemic that blazed across America in late summer 1918 had terrible consequences for businesses where the public gathered. The flu killed approximately 195,000 Americans in October 1918 alone, including many prominent members of society. The resulting panic led government authorities, as well as self-appointed masters of public morals and safety, to urge citizens not to frequent places in which people gathered in large numbers and germs could be spread.

Clearly the government needed to educate its citizens and urge them to fight the spread of infectious diseases. Unfortunately, the money spent on hosing down streets and buying protective masks for citizens, as well as the business lost by restaurants, theaters, and other public places, hurt an already struggling economy. Edicts to stay at home were issued just as loudly by religious groups who supported the government in an attempt to rid America of what they considered sinful behavior, i.e., dancing, drinking, billiards, and gambling. This didn't help owners of quick-service restaurants one bit.

The spread of disease was enhanced on military bases where tired and overworked young men, their immune systems weakened by hard physical labor, were housed in tight quarters. Soldiers sailing across the Atlantic helped spread the flu to Europe as well. Chicago, as a major rail center, also served as a locus of the pandemic. By mid-October, the disease had officially been declared an epidemic in Chicago, where more than two thousand citizens had died. All theaters, night schools, and pool halls were shuttered, and bars were often cited for violating capacity rules. Schoolchildren were sent home from parks, and church services were shortened.

In the winter 1990–91 edition of *Chicago History*, David E. Ruth wrote: "In closing dance halls, theaters, and cabarets, [health officials] aimed a traditional weapon of social control—enforced adherence to a middle-class moral code—at the new realm of commercial leisure. Activities that had recently shed their lower-class stigma and had gained middle-class acceptance, or at least toleration, became unacceptably pernicious during the emergency. The healthy society was austere; frivolity invited disaster."

Chicago Health Commissioner John Dill Robertson was at the forefront of this movement. According to Ruth, "The primary motivation for closing the theaters, Robertson admitted, was not to control the spread of germs, but 'to discourage the late hours kept by most adults.'" Obviously, such pressure from the city hurt Weeghman's businesses, even though citizens rebelled against some of what they perceived as heavy-handed, dictatorial measures. A ban on smoking on train cars caused considerable consternation, according to Ruth: "The *Daily News* reported that 'while church, school, and other anti-smoking elements' supported the ban on smoking, most commuters 'strongly opposed' it. During cold weather, train operators had to nail open car doors to comply with the order for adequate ventilation after passengers ignored signs to leave the doors open."

Despite these efforts, thousands perished. Approximately eighty-five hundred Chicagoans passed away from the "Spanish flu" before the disease ebbed during the summer of 1919. Later that year, Illinois ratified the Eighteenth Amendment, banning the sale, manufacture, and transport of liquor. This misguided effort further assisted the mob in expanding its base of illegal activity and closed more than seven thousand bars in Chicago alone.

CHARLEY AND THE MOB?

Charley Weeghman was known to have big-time gamblers among his friends and probably had been friendly with their kind for quite a time. Chicago in the first decades of the twentieth century was full of corrupt politicians, mobsters, and grifters—plenty of them at the highest levels of society. This was a time of greased palms and inside deals, the times and events that cemented the city's reputation of dirty politics and graft that dogs the "City That Works" to this day.

How closely was Weeghman associated with the mob? He ran businesses in food service, entertainment, construction, and sports. It would have been difficult for him *not* to be in contact with the criminal element. In fact— and we are getting just a bit ahead of the story for a bit—Weeghman was called on to testify at the Black Sox trial in 1920. The authorities wanted to know about his friendships with New Yorker Arnold Rothstein (believed by most scholars to be the biggest financial beneficiary of the 1919 World Series fix) and gambler Monte Tennes, the top dog in racetrack bookmaking in Chicago for many years. Tennes and Weeghman were old friends, as both testified during the trial.

According to Steven Longstreet's *Chicago*, Tennes was "the Daniel Boone of big crime, a forgotten pioneer of the methods the Capone mob, and their rivals, and today's Mafia groups were to use with such success, from Vegas to narc peddling." Charley Weeghman had spent much of the summer of

1919 vacationing at Rothstein's home in Saratoga, New York, and he seemed to know an awful lot about Rothstein's and Tennes' wagering habits. At the trial, Weeghman said, "[Tennes] told me that the series had been fixed. This was in August [1919], mind you. Seven White Sox players had agreed to lay down . . . but [Tennes] didn't want it because he liked baseball and didn't want to go in on such a crooked deal. I understand that in spite of the tip, he bet thirty grand on the Sox!"

Tennes denied ever having spoken to Weeghman about rumors of a fix, and the matter was—incredibly—dropped, though it is difficult to imagine *anything* that would disgust a drug runner, cheater, and swindler like Tennes enough that he wouldn't want in on some of its easy action. Did he hate the racetracks that he corrupted?

Weeghman also said, presumably with a straight face, that he didn't even remember whether he had discussed the matter with National League President John Heydler. With a club owner and a big-time gambler hanging out at the latter's resort, also frequented by Arnold Rothstein, one would think that the three principals would have merited more than a cursory cross-examination. It's likely that what Weeghman said about Tennes was crafted in the best possible light to make his friend appear innocent while avoiding telling an easily disprovable lie (that Tennes never bet on baseball games). At the time, sportsmen openly wagered money on horse races, golf tournaments, and the like, and everyone in baseball knew that gambling on the game was a problem.

So, was Charley a rube or a sap? Was he hung out to dry by Tennes, or did the two previously corroborate their testimony in advance? It is difficult to believe that Weeghman could have made as much money and been so successful if he was a rube, but the press clearly felt that Weeghman was a fair dealer who was not accustomed to lying. Is it coincidence that Weeghman had only good things to say in his friend's defense? It is difficult to tell. Certainly with his empire destroyed, Weeghman had plenty of reasons in 1920 to curry favor with any friend with money.

The relevant question is whether Charley Weeghman's financial troubles of 1917–18 were caused at all by his mob connections. Weeghman made a Herculean rise in the business world and took a Herculean fall. Those events warrant investigation. He could well have borrowed mob money to expand his businesses and then struggled when the loans were called in.

Whatever the case, Weeghman kept selling more shares of the Cubs to William Wrigley in a desperate attempt to stay afloat. But shortly after the World Series ended, it became clear that Lucky Charley's fortunes had irrevocably turned and that he would have to give up the Cubs. By November, he had sold Bill Wrigley all of his stock. That month, fares on the Chicago elevated train system increased from five to six cents.

GOODBYE, CHARLEY

On November 18, 1918, the Cubs put an end to nearly a year's worth of rumors with the formal announcement that Weeghman would step down as president of the Chicago Cubs. Bill Wrigley, who held all the cards, engineered Weeghman's departure. In buying unlucky Charley's shares, he told him, according to Harry Neily in *The Sporting News*, "If I help you out, you must retire from baseball and devote all your time to business." So Wrigley had engineered the events that would ultimately put him in charge of the Cubs, then helped bail out the sinking Weeghman as well.

Fred Mitchell would take over the duties previously held by Weeghman—who retired for what were termed "business reasons"—as well as remaining field manager. The men behind the scenes would be William Wrigley, who himself presented Weeghman's resignation at the club's December 1918 board meeting, and former sportswriter Bill Veeck. Mitchell, apparently a real pip, "had to do nearly all of Weeghman's work last summer," wrote Oscar Reichow of the *Daily News*, "while the latter was looking after his restaurant interests that were in a precarious condition owing to war conditions."

TSN's George Robbins opined in the November 1918 that Weeghman's real downfall came from leaving the West Side for the North: "Weeghman went to the North Side, was the active force in constructing a modern baseball plant, and ran the capital stock into big money to meet expenses . . . The coming on of the war may have had a lot to do with the failure of the Cubs, though champions, to make money . . . but the general opinion is that the desertion of the great West Side, hotbed of baseball, was the chief item in the financial failure."

Talk about the "great West Side," deserted by the moneyed classes decades ago, now seems odd. But it was once a classic Chicago neighborhood. Of course, one can easily point out that the Cubs' determination to depart the crumbling, rocky, bug-and-snake-infested old West Side Grounds in favor of the newer, fresher, and greener pastures of Weeghman Park was a sensible business decision—as well as one of the early nails in the West Side's coffin. The construction of Weeghman Park was great news for the Chicago Cubs and for their new neighborhood, though. Situated near the lake, in a tonier and up-and-coming locale, the ballpark ensured success both for the team and for the Lake View neighborhood in the coming decades.

Upon the not-unexpected announcement of Weeghman's departure from the Cubs—and, it would turn out, from Chicago and the sporting world—the papers carried tributes to the man who had brought so much vitality to the city and to its sporting scene. Charley and Bessie would divorce in 1920, and Weeghman ended up on the East Coast, where he tried to revive his career in restaurants and movies without much luck. He remarried in 1922.

Most everyone in the press was sorry to see Weeghman go and lauded his good spirit, sense of fun, and general bonhomie. *The Sporting News*, never a booster, even tossed him a small bouquet: "He was never accused of not being a splendid fellow personally and a game sportsman, and good wishes of the fan public generally go out to him . . . If he may be lacking in baseball acumen he is a master in his business, out of which he arose from a $12 a week waiter to one of the best known and most popular restaurant magnates in the country."

CHAPTER 5

Two Bills, Two Series: Cubs Park/ Wrigley Field, 1919–32

GUMMY BEAR

William Wrigley dropped out of school at age thirteen in 1874 to help run his father's soap manufacturing company in Philadelphia. Later, the Wrigley Company began to sell baking powder as well. Young Bill proved an able study and popularized the idea of offering premiums with purchases, helping revolutionize the retail industry. One of the premiums he used to sell baking powder? Chewing gum. The chewable compound proved such a good sales tool that Wrigley decided that chicle was his future. He chose to devote his time and energy to producing, advertising, and selling gum.

Using solid sales techniques, low cost, and efficient distribution, Wrigley soon made the company (incorporated in 1910) the largest vendor of chewing gum in the world. By 1925, when Wrigley handed over day-to-day management to his son Philip, the Wrigley Company had assets of $60 million. In February 1914, Wrigley bought a $175,000 mansion in Pasadena, California, joining the "Chicago Colony" of businessmen wintering in the sunnier clime of the West. The *Chicago Daily Journal* called Wrigley's new home "one of the most pretentious in the city." (At the time, the word "pretentious" had a less negative connotation.) Not forgetting his home base, Wrigley also constructed a huge office tower on Michigan Avenue overlooking the Chicago River. The beautiful Wrigley Building remains one of the most identifiable landmarks in America.

WON'T YOU COME HOME?

When Charley Weeghman gave up the Cubs, William Wrigley—despite owning the biggest share of the club—seemed an unlikely caretaker for the franchise. "I'll never attend a meeting," he was reported to have said when named to the team's board of directors in 1916. But this may be so much folderol. In an article entitled "Owning a Big League Ball Team," published in the September 13, 1930, *Saturday Evening Post,* Wrigley claimed that since childhood, his dream had been to own a major league baseball team. During the 1917 and 1918 seasons, Bill Wrigley began to take a greater interest in the doings of the club—especially as he continued to buy more and more shares from the increasingly insolvent Weeghman.

Early in 1919, Wrigley was dining with a group of Chicago sportswriters at his home in California. One of them, Bill Veeck Sr. (the *American's* "Bill Bailey"), made some cutting remarks relating to the fashion in which the Cubs were being run. Warren Brown, in his 1946 book *The Chicago Cubs*, reconstructed the conversation this way:

> "Could you do any better?" inquired Wrigley.
> "I certainly couldn't do any worse," said Veeck.

Wrigley was more than intrigued—he was *sold.* He knew the Cubs needed strong management and put together his new team. With Fred Mitchell as president and manager, Veeck as vice president, and John O. Seys, another former ink-stained wretch, as secretary, the Cubs had, for the first time in many years, a management group with enough baseball sense to win the respect of the writers.

VEECK—AS IN WHAT THE HECK

Bill Veeck Sr., according to Warren Brown, knew baseball. His "acquaintance with ballplayers in major leagues and in minors was perhaps as large as anyone's." Born in Indiana, he married his childhood sweetheart, Grace. Having started his newspaper career in Louisville, Veeck went to Chicago in 1902, first to write for the *Inter-Ocean* and then for the *American,* establishing a reputation as a smart man with flair.

Veeck *père* was not a great writer, according to his son, but "a good, solid reporter" as well as being "dignified without being stuffy" and extremely well respected in the game. Fair-minded, honest, and scrupulous, he was well suited for his new job. However, like all in power, he had his favorites, and he had his quirks. For one thing, despite his outward appearance, he—like another somewhat stuffy and successful baseball man, Branch Rickey—fielded teams full of gamblers, hard drinkers, and reprobates. Veeck knew that gambling was deeply embedded in baseball, but he seemed more interested in making the game *look* clean in the early 1920s than actually having it *be* clean.

Veeck's influence quickly grew. Fred Mitchell was forced to give up the presidency of the Cubs in June 1919, apparently because the National League was not inclined to have a manager-president. Wrigley was happy simply to hand the position over to Veeck, who held it until his death in 1933 at age fifty-six. Mitchell had made one critical move, however. On March 1, 1919, Bobby Dorr—a friend of Mitchell's from Rochester, when the skipper had been there—was hired as Cubs groundskeeper.

ROLL WITH THE CHANGES

With Charley Weeghman out of the picture, things began to change at what, following the 1918 season, was called Cubs Park. For one thing, photos from 1919 show what appears to be an uphill climb toward the center-field scoreboard. It's not clear why this was necessary, as the ground had always been level at Weeghman Park. It simply may have been a design feature.

Another big change in the park in 1919 was an advertising sign against the right-field wall hawking sporting goods. It was probably an ad for either The Fair, a huge downtown department store with a big sporting goods department, or Wilson's Sporting Goods, which had a long-standing ticketing connection with the Cubs. Past the right-field wall, on the same Sheffield Avenue roof as before, was an ad for the recently renamed Marigold Garden. More advertising dotted the center-field scoreboard, including a large mention of the *Tribune*. The left side of the scoreboard in these years featured the data on the Cubs' game: ball/strike count, outs, and the score. The center of the board featured advertising, while the right side listed out-of-town contests.

Two figures, one throwing a ball and one getting ready to hit it, sat atop the scoreboard in 1919. They resemble the Wrigley's Gum "Doublemint Twins" figures on the board in the early 1920s. This would be the earliest sign of Wrigley's advertising at the park.

At some point in 1920, American League scores were posted on a board attached to the brick wall in right-center field. This may have been intended to allow more advertising on the main scoreboard. Finally, at some time before 1921, the Cubs cut a space out of the wall down the left-field line, past the home dugout, in order to store a tarpaulin. The outside of the ballpark had been decorated as well; attractive awnings with art-deco designs covered the ticket windows on the park's Clark Street entrance.

DOUBLEHEADER

Morning/afternoon doubleheaders were not uncommon in the teens, and the Cubs hosted the Reds in a Labor Day twin bill on September 1, 1919. Ten thousand came to watch the morning contest, while an unexpected throng of twenty-four thousand overstuffed the park for the 3:00 game. James Crusinberry in the *Tribune* opined that "probably it was the biggest holiday attendance the Cubs ever had."

Speculation had many of the spectators as fans of the just-about-to-clinch-the-AL-title White Sox, who came up north expressly to scout out the Reds (who in turn were close to nailing down the NL championship). Whatever the neighborhood of the fans, "All the seats in the grand stand, pavilions, and bleacher were filled. Space clear around the outfield was roped off and the mob herded upon the field until an enormous horseshoe of humanity, a dozen deep, was formed. Besides that, a host stood in the grand stand and the right wall was fringed with fans."

LISTEN, MR. HAT

"[Yesterday] one Cub fan was lucky. It was the last day of August, the last day of straw hats, according to tradition. This fan had his hat busted by a foul ball during the batting practice and went into the office, filed a complaint, and got an order for a new hat." As evidenced by this story in the September 1, 1919, *Tribune*, ball clubs hadn't yet defined the legal risks of entering a ballpark. Imagine a fan entering the Cubs' offices now and complaining that a batting-practice ball destroyed his hat.

Back in the early 1900s, men would buy new straw hats each spring, and at the end of August, each would dispose of his in whatever way he wished. (The hats were meant to last only one season.) Around the Labor Day weekend, stage comedians all over the land regularly made hay of destroying large amounts of straw hats in their routines. Today's practice of whipping twenty-dollar caps onto the field is much more devoted—and much more ridiculous.

KNOW WHEN TO FOLD 'EM

While William Wrigley was a brilliant, sympathetic owner (at least as wealthy magnates go), he wasn't completely savvy to take over the Cubs in 1919. In fact, Wrigley walked face-first into a beehive. The demise of the Federal League following the 1915 season, and its resulting cutback on salaries and elimination of ballplaying jobs, caused resentment among players, and eventually some of them began to throw games. (Of course, some players had been gambling away at-bats and even games for years, but the frequency of such mischief increased after 1915.) While the White Sox were obviously the most heavily tainted by corruption, throwing the 1919 World Series, the Cubs were hardly untouched.

"In the Cubs camp, as well as in New York, a number of ballplayers had been in touch with not only players but booking and betting agents," wrote Warren Wilbert in *A Cunning Kind of Play*. One of them was Lee Magee, a thirty-year-old infielder-outfielder traded to the Cubs from Brooklyn in mid-season 1919. He was soon implicated for helping Hal Chase and Heinie Zimmerman fix games the previous season, when Magee was in Cincinnati. In particular, the final contest of the 1919 season, a Cubs–Giants tilt, was said to be well off the level. Magee was tossed from baseball for life.

The *Daily News* reported on September 4, 1920, that earlier in the summer, a gang of gamblers "suspected of betting in the stands and bleachers at the north side park" had been arrested and hauled east a few blocks to the Town Hall police station. Apparently, gambling had been going on at Cubs Park for quite some time, but only now did Veeck and Wrigley feel some pressure to clean things up.

SCANDAL

The problem was far from over. On August 31, 1920, just a couple of weeks before the Black Sox story broke, the Cubs and Phillies were scheduled to play at Cubs Park. At the time, both clubs were well out of contention, but the Cubs were a better team. Oddly, however, the gambling odds favored the pathetic Phillies. Several telegrams addressed to Bill Veeck, most from Detroit and signed by those who called themselves "concerned fans," arrived at Cubs Park informing him of rumors that the day's game was to be thrown. (Unfortunately, as the police later ascertained, the addresses given by these "concerned fans" were bogus—nobody by the names given on the telegrams lived where they claimed.)

What seems to have happened is that gamblers got to some of the Cubs, including starting pitcher Claude Hendrix, and promised money if he and his teammates threw the game. Once the cooperation of certain Cubs was assured, the gamblers spread the word that a fix was in. After myriad bets were then made on the Phillies to win, the intrigue *really* began. An hour before the game was scheduled to start, the telegrams began to arrive. A group of gamblers from Detroit—probably the original gamblers, but possibly a group of double-crossers—sent the telegrams and made phone calls informing the Cubs that the game was to be fixed.

This news prompted Veeck and Fred Mitchell to immediately remove Hendrix from the slab in favor of Grover Cleveland Alexander. Mitchell even gave Alexander a five-hundred-dollar bonus to bear down. By forcing the situation, the gamblers responsible hoped to make the Cubs a sure winner, then bet on the Cubs at high odds and clean up. Unfortunately for them, the Cubs lost anyway, 2–0, due in part to a crucial error by Buck Herzog on a sure double-play grounder. Eventually, four Cubs were implicated in the scheme: Hendrix, Herzog, first baseman Fred Merkle, and scrub pitcher Paul Carter. Veeck threw open the investigation, asking his former press colleagues to dig the dirt.

The Cubs left Hendrix behind in Chicago when the club went east for a road trip in early September. Although everyone associated with the club said that the pitcher stayed behind because he was ineffective against Pittsburgh, Hendrix clearly was no longer trusted by management or by his teammates. He probably would have been the victim of endless taunting by crowds as well.

On September 7, Judge Charles McDonald of the Criminal Court of Chicago ordered a grand jury investigation of the incident. The court subpoenaed the entire Cub team, as well as Veeck, Mitchell, and William Wrigley. Three days later, certain gamblers began to spread a rumor that Babe Ruth had died in Cleveland in an auto accident. From the very start, most fans rejected the rumor, as public interest in the August 31 Cubs–Phillies affair was at a high pitch and fans were already more than suspicious of the effect of big-time gamblers on the game.

On September 21, the Cubs and Braves played a fifty-eight-minute nine-inning game at Cubs Park. The Braves' 3–0 win is the shortest complete game in Cubs history. The next day, Veeck told the grand jury what he knew about the gambling scandal. Then, on September 23, pitcher Rube Benton of the Giants—no choirboy himself—implicated Herzog, as well as the already bounced Chase and Zimmerman, in throwing the 1919 game. Other players, including Art Wilson and Tony Boeckel, also made affidavits.

On September 25, Monte Tennes was in the papers. This paragon of society told a *New York Daily News* scribe that he had given up betting on baseball. "I won't say I won't bet on it any more, but I made a good big bet last year and lost. I haven't made any this year." Asked if he knew anything about rumors of a fix of the 1919 World Series, he simply remarked, "I do not care to talk until I get back to Chicago and see just what the situation is there." When he got to Chicago, the situation was hot. On September 28, eight White Sox players were indicted for throwing the 1919 World Series. Tennes, and his connections to Charley Weeghman, Arnold Rothstein, and the Black Sox, became much clearer to the general public in the ensuing days.

The Cubs–Phillies affair was wiped off the front page as the Black Sox scandal unfolded. But the wheels of justice didn't stop grinding. Following the season, Merkle retired. Herzog and Hendrix both became, as Bill James has written, "persona non grata," unwelcome in the majors though not officially banned. Kenesaw Mountain Landis, in his autobiography, insisted that he *had* banned Hendrix from baseball. Since Landis's is the only opinion that counted, it was indeed an unofficial banning. Herzog played in the minors after 1920, but the hapless Carter was simply bounced from the game.

Perhaps a key piece of the puzzle of game-throwing is that most of the players involved in the betting scandals were veterans, hard-bitten from the baseball wars, cynical from broken promises, and—in the case of Chase, Zimmerman, and Magee—just plain corrupt. For instance, in the Cubs' case, Merkle had played since 1908; the thirty-one-year-old Hendrix was an old Chifeds pitcher. Herzog, thirty-five, was a popular figure who had even served as player-manager of the Reds for two years.

GAMBLING SHOCK—A BRIEF RANT

What is amazing about all of this is that anyone was surprised at players throwing games. The gambling culture was omnipresent in sports; wagering on all types of competitive sport was a common activity among players, managers, fans, and even writers. John McGraw had part ownership in a gambling house—with Arnold Rothstein! Players of the time routinely claimed to gamble on other sports. The biggest spectator sports of the time, aside from baseball, were boxing, horse racing, and golf, all of which featured significant gambling subcultures.

Major league teams outwardly tried in the 1910s to discourage gambling, calling for an end to the practice, occasionally asking the police to bust the most obvious gambling rings, and even posting signs in the ballparks that no wagering was allowed. But owners also knew that a significant portion of their audience came to the games *expressly to bet.*

As Bill James has pointed out, every big baseball story of the 1910s concerned money, from the "$100,000 Infield" to the founding of the Federal League to the crashing and burning of the nascent Players' Fraternity. Once the Federal League was bled out of existence and overall salaries decreased, many players felt betrayed by baseball. In such an atmosphere, it's not hard to understand why some of the greedier players of the era instigated game-throwing.

And that's one part of baseball infinitely better in 2002 than in the 1910s and 1920s. Purists may cry foul, for instance, that the bleachers at Wrigley Field are currently stocked with rich, sun-worshipping, baseball-challenged yuppies, and indeed the cost of a bleacher seat is outrageous. Furthermore, not everyone at the park really cares whether the Cubs win. But that's not a new phenomenon. Plenty of people have gone to Wrigley, and other parks over the years, not really caring what team wins. Families go for sunny fun. Teenagers go looking for someplace to ogle each other and have a smoke or a beer. But yuppie bleacher bums and overpriced tickets and disinterested fans, though annoying, don't compare with money changing hands based on player performance. That environment almost ruined baseball once. Gambling on baseball has no place at the ballpark.

Unfortunately, gambling has been romanticized over the years. A story written by Jack Griffin in the April 19, 1963, *Sun-Times*, covering the previous day's Cubs home opener, contained these heartwarming bits:

> "Whadaya mean ya wanna lay sevenny-five?" a man in a plaid cap said scornfully. "I got eighty goin' the other way now. So you gimme two runs. Big deal."
>
> "So you wanna action on the Dodgers," said one. "So all right, I give ya the Dodgers. It's a cold day."

Fan gambling began to be "all right" again in the 1930s, once everyone figured that the games were clean. Following Judge Landis's death in 1944, the Iron Grip of Morality loosened and gambling became more and more accepted at the ballparks. And that's too bad. What intelligent observer would want to go back to the days that lasted even to the late 1970s and early 1980s, when the Wrigley Field bleachers—often half-filled—served not as a place where families enjoyed the game, but as a center of gambling between a bunch of dysfunctional "fans"? The popular early 1980s Chicago-produced play "Bleacher Bums" seemed to get it right, treating the game as a sort of Greek tragedy, with nobody but the gambler happy at the end of the game when the Cubs lost. But does anyone who really cares about baseball want Wrigley Field to be like that?

For whatever reason, some people romanticize the 1950s and early 1960s, as well as the mid 1970s, when "crowds" of seven thousand dotted the park and the Cubs were awful. What in the world is romantic about a game being attended mainly by gambling addicts betting on the next pitch, the next home run, or the day's attendance? Give us bleachers filled with people enjoying themselves, not worrying about their next twenty-dollar bet. If people are going to bet on baseball—and obviously some people can do it without letting it control their lives—let them engage in online betting or fantasy baseball, or go to off-track betting salons and do it there. Keep gambling out of the parks, and you've gone a long way toward making the ballpark experience more honest, more wholesome, and better for baseball. At least in this regard, the good old days are clearly now.

Of course, if Pete Rose is let back into the game, we can assume that the good old days are over.

AND TO MAKE THINGS WORSE . . .

Beginning the morning of January 16, 1920, America went dry, a result of the Eighteenth Amendment to the Constitution and the soon-to-follow Volstead

Act. The forces of moral good inveigled the government into declaring the sale, manufacture, and drinking of alcohol illegal. Therefore, without actually *meaning* to destroy the country, the efforts of the well-meaning reformers put thousands of Americans out of jobs, increased violent crime, lowered the quality of life for millions of taxpaying citizens, and helped organized crime gain its foothold in liquor production and distribution. So when the Black Sox scandal drove fans to drink, most of them couldn't even do *that*, or at least not legally.

An anonymous *Chicago Daily News* reporter conveyed, on September 25, 1920, the sad news of a busted shipment of beer.

> "Gurg-urg-urg-urg-urg."
> In a long, melancholy monotone, it poured to-day [*sic*] from the necks of 21,600 bottles into the Chicago River.
> "Gurg-urg-urg-urg-urg-urg."
> One bottle after another, all 6 or 7 per cent in alcoholic content, all the best product of a Kenosha brewery.
> "Gurg-urg-urg-urg-urg-urg."
> In amber colored beauty, it descended upon the dreary expanse of water, spattering into creamy foam, wasting its wild bitterness upon its unappreciative antithesis.
> Deputy Marshals Murray and Sheehan officiated. It was all from a cargo which was brought to Chicago in August 1919 by the good ship Mineral City and caught at the dock. Thomas Young was fined $500 for bringing it. The order for its destruction came to-day [*sic*] from Judge George B. Carpenter. And, on the word of Mr. Young, it was all first-class beer.
> "Gurg-urg-urg-urg-urg-urg."

WRIGLEY'S POWER

The Black Sox scandal, and its associated baseball gambling affairs, threw baseball men into a panic. Major league owners searched for someone—something, *anything*—to help restore public confidence in the game. When Cubs shareholder A. D. Lasker came up with an idea for a tricornered group to run baseball, Bill Veeck and William Wrigley listened. But they tinkered with the idea, suggesting instead that *one* man have absolute power over the game.

Wrigley, on Veeck's recommendation, pushed for Judge Kenesaw Mountain Landis, a well-known, respected, authoritarian arbiter known for his business verdicts. Landis, who lived in Chicago, ended up a happy visitor to Wrigley Field on many occasions, his chin resting on a bar in front of his box seat.

By 1920, the fifty-seven-year-old Wrigley was becoming more powerful in the game. Soon after, Lasker—never, according to Warren Brown, a fan of

Veeck as a general manager—sold most of his shares in the club to Wrigley. Around the same time, J. Ogden Armour sold five hundred of his shares to Wrigley as well, making the latter nearly the sole owner of the club. Veeck, meanwhile, would continue as a strong supporter of Landis, even at one point, according to David Pietrusza in *Judge and Jury*, finagling to get the commish's salary raised. Later, the two would fall out when Landis suspended Cubs second sacker Rogers Hornsby for gambling.

In 1922, Veeck came up with an idea that *didn't* fly. He proposed that baseball undertake a series of midyear interleague exhibitions. The first All-Star Game didn't come until eleven years later, and interleague play in the majors would wait for more than seventy years, though Veeck continued to propose the idea until his death in 1933.

PLAY THE GAME

Back in the days where a good turnout was fifteen thousand fans, you didn't just go home when the weather turned a little wet. On May 14, 1922, rain delayed the 3:00 start, and the makeshift tarpaulins apparently provided little protection for the field, which was muddy and nearly unplayable. But with a crowd of some eighteen thousand in the stands, the Cubs and Giants soldiered on.

In the top of the fourth, the rain began to fall heavily, causing delays between pitches and plays as well as sloppy fielding and running. Fans in the left-field bleachers, perhaps driven mad by the conditions, began tossing pop bottles, popcorn boxes, and seat cushions onto the sodden outfield grass in protest. Still the game continued. In the bottom of the fourth, Charlie Hollocher doubled past Giants third sacker Heinie Groh, who fell in the mud trying to field the ball. Left fielder Irish Meusel also slipped into the muck retrieving the hit. Hollocher then tried for third on a short grounder; when he slid, he kept sliding through the mud and was tagged out when he went right on by. Two plays later, Ray Grimes, who had doubled, was also out when *he* overslid third.

In the sixth, Jess Barnes of the Giants hit an easy grounder, but first baseman Grimes couldn't hold the wet ball when it was thrown to him. Umpire Paul Sentelle ruled Barnes safe, which caused a huge argument as the rain became a deluge. "Fans in the bleachers started a roughhouse act," said the *Tribune*, "tossing boxes and cardboards on to the field until Umpire Klem was forced to call the contest until the obstructions had been removed."

In the eighth, the rain became interminable, and many in the bleacher crowd began climbing over the fence. Swells in box seats had already rushed under the roof to stay dry, and the bleacher fans ran on to the field, attempting to climb into the grandstand themselves and get dry. Unfortunately for the four-bit fans, the policy of the 1910s, allowing them access to dry areas during deluges, had apparently been changed. The *Tribune* noted, "It took the efforts of ten coppers to shoo them back."

After ten innings, this hellish game finally ended, the Giants escaping with a rain-drenched 5–4 win.

DAFFINESS IN REVERSE

On August 19, fans rushed the field after the Cubs' 2–1, eleven-inning win. But that was normal for the weird 1922 season. It was the Brooklyn Dodgers who often got credit for inventing the "three men on third base" play, but on August 24, 1922, at Cubs Park, the Dodgers were the beneficiaries of some weird Chicago baserunning. According to Retrosheet's "Strange and Unusual Plays" file, in the last of the third, Ray Grimes stole second. He then attempted to swipe third, but apparently forgot the situation; when he arrived at the bag, Charlie Hollocher was already there. Furiously improvising, Hollocher tried to score but was tagged out.

Three days later, transportation authorities announced a plan to let Chicago residents ride the elevated trains on an unlimited basis for the princely sum of $1.25 a week. Currently, the el costs $1.75 a ride.

26–23???

The very next day, things got even weirder. The Cubs have hosted some big slugfests over the years, but none top the game of August 25, 1922, when the Phillies were in town. Seven thousand fans witnessed a ridiculous game that shattered all sorts of records. The 26–23 Cubs win still holds the major league record for most runs scored by two teams in a game.

Trailing 3–1 in the last of the second, the Cubs piled on against pitcher Jimmy Ring, scoring ten times. Two innings later, already up 11–6, Chicago scored fourteen more times. Cubs right fielder Marty Callaghan batted three times in the inning, singling and scoring twice and whiffing for the last out. Ring left the game in the fourth in favor of Lefty Weinert, who absorbed the rest of the pounding. Yes, the Phillies allowed just two pitchers to give up twenty-three runs, twenty-six hits, and ten walks.

Hack Miller homered twice for Chicago, while Cliff Heathcote went 5-for-5, walked twice, and crossed the dish five times. But in true Cubs style, the win didn't come easy. The Phillies trailed 26–9 after seven innings but began to beat up on Chicago relievers Euel Eubanks and Ed Morris, tallying eight times in the eighth inning. In the ninth, the first four Phils reached base against Morris, which led manager Bill Killefer to bring in Tiny Osborne, who was hardly better. The Phillies, who left sixteen men on base on the day, scored six times and fought back to 26–23 but finally ran out of gas.

Before the game, the *Tribune* dutifully noted, Cubs outfielder Jigger Statz was presented with unique gift: a rubber-tired baby carriage. One assumes—one *hopes*—that the popular Statz was about to become a father. The gift came courtesy of eight showgirls currently appearing in a local production of "The Dancing Honeymoon."

STALEY DOWN, DECATUR STALEYS

Following the close of their disappointing 1922 season, the Cubs defeated the Sox in a rain-soaked City Series (tickets available, as always, from veteran Cub ticket seller Rube Cook at Wilson's Sporting Goods store downtown), then vacated their field, leaving it to the Chicago Bears. The football club, formerly known as the Decatur Staleys, had moved to Chicago and into Cubs Park the previous season. This would be the first year that the football aggregation would officially be known as "Bears," a name chosen expressly to gain favor with Cubs fans. In fact, some newspapers at the time actually referred to the *Cubs* as "Bears."

The football Bears made their 1922 Cubs Park debut on October 15 against Rochester, winning 7–0. By October 21, a new scoreboard for football—featuring a clock—had been installed, and grass had been laid over the baseball baselines and the mound. The next day, the Bears defeated Buffalo, again rolling up the score to a 7–0 count.

THE FIRST BIG RENOVATION

When the Bears' home schedule was completed on December 3, the Cubs began a three-hundred-thousand-dollar renovation program designed to boost capacity in the park from around nineteen thousand to more than thirty-one thousand. Crowds during the late teens and early twenties had convinced management that the time was right to expand.

Zachary Davis, the original architect in the Weeghman days, was contracted to help design and engineer the renovation, a project to be carried out in a way that retained the feel of the park while expanding it. News of a possible expansion of Cubs Park had leaked out back on May 2, 1923, when the *Daily News'* Oscar Reichow hailed, "Cheer up, Cub fans! There may soon be room to seat 30,000 at the north side park." Reichow noted that "the plans are to cut the main grand stand in half, move it back to Clark street and the railroad tracks, and extend it north to the bleachers." When the plans were finalized months later, the existing concrete grandstand, which at the time seated approximately fifty-five hundred in the boxes and eleven thousand in general admission, was actually sliced into *three* parts.

The right- and left-field "wings" were separated from the home plate section. The third-base and left-field grandstand was placed on rollers and pushed northwest toward Waveland Avenue and Clark Street. The home plate section was moved south about sixty feet toward Addison Street. The first-base/right-field stands stayed where they were. The act of moving the stands around, and having to reattach them in a new place, created the odd "curve" in the grandstand near where the first-base dugout is now located. As for the dugouts themselves, they were not much larger but at least were now covered with cement rather than canvas. In addition to the grandstand being rolled around, it was also lowered several feet. A new fence was installed around it from foul line to foul line. (When built, the grandstand was several feet above the ground; there would now be no need for a stairway to get in and out of the stands.) The retaining wall was about two feet high, with a two-foot heavy wire fence atop it.

With all that extra room, the club installed ninety-three hundred new box seats and seventeen thousand general admission seats. Cubs Park was now, in terms of seating capacity, the largest single-decked ballpark in the country. However, according to Bill Veeck, there would be no upper deck: "Fans do not like the top seats, and we find we can get enough by splitting the main structure."

Veeck also stressed to Reichow a secondary goal in making the changes: to enlarge the playing field. "It will increase our playing space to excellent proportions. Right field, which is now the shortest, will be the longest, for by moving the stands back to Clark and the railroad tracks we will get more than 100 feet additional."

The expansion came not a year too soon. On August 17, the Cubs and Giants played "before the largest weekday crowd that had been to the north side park in years," reported the *Daily News* the next day. "It was estimated that 22,000 were present. The jam was so big that ropes were put in the outfield to handle the overflow. . . . This is the first time in many years that the Cubs have had spectators on the field on a weekday." It was Ladies Day, which certainly helped explain the high numbers.

But the next day, another twenty-five thousand fans paid to see the two clubs, and on Sunday, August 19, twenty-six thousand crammed the ball yard for the final game of the series. The crowd on Sunday, according to the *Tribune*, was "probably the greatest crowd that ever witnessed a game at the Cubs' north side park." Fans stuffed the outfield, sat on the high right-field wall, and even perched themselves atop the scoreboard some forty feet above the ground. More than three thousand fans were left outside. During the contest, fans protested an umpire's decision by hurling their seat cushions onto the field.

THINGS WILL BE BETTER

"The grandstand with its sweep from wall to wall looks like the finest in the big leagues in its newness, its green paint, and [its] graceful curves," extolled the *Daily News'* William H. Becker, when given a tour of the nearly finished product. "From the promenade at the foot of the grandstand seats to the concrete wall about the field, the boxes are ranged twelve deep. These boxes sweep right and left to the full extent of the grandstand."

Becker also wrote that enlarging the grandstand (note the change to one word, "grandstand," in stories of the time) indicated a big change in the financial standing of ballpark patrons. The Cubs were increasing the number of boxes and general admission chairs because their buying public could, and would, happily pay higher prices for the more rarified seats. On the North Side, as in many parks across the nation, baseball had become more lucrative. Noted Becker, "The old bleachers [are] looking painfully small and inadequate when one looks back a score of years and remembers when the bleachers in ball parks predominated and the grandstands were small and apologetic."

OUTSTANDING IN THEIR FIELD

The playing field was moved toward Addison, lowered, and replanted. This had the effect of making the field larger (especially in right field). It is believed that the current location of the pitcher's mound is where home plate was before 1923. By April 7, according to Becker, the infield and outfield had been sodded; steamrollers ran incessantly over the turf in order to mash it down sufficiently. As Opening Day neared, the crew shaped and rolled new base paths filled with fine clay.

The new seats were being installed and were to be painted green, but not all of the freshly decorated chairs dried by Opening Day. In fact, newspaper stories of the time refer to the common annual inconvenience of getting green paint stains on one's clothing at the season's first game. The twenty-five hundred bleachers in left field were rebuilt from purely wood to steel-framed wood. They ranged from near the left-field line to left center, leaving straightaway center and the scoreboard open. In addition, twenty-five hundred brand new bleachers were built from right center to close to the right-field foul line; this would be the first time since 1914 that the park featured any sort of seating in right field. As with the original 1914 construction, bleachers were separated from the field by a see-through wire fence. This allowed the bleacher seats to reach field level. The bleachers in right field were twenty rows deep.

On both foul lines, a section behind the fence did not include bleachers;

photos of the time show tarpaulins being stored there, and one assumes the spaces housed other groundskeeping equipment as well. Both foul poles, inside these areas, were actually out of play.

Dimensions in the "new" Cubs Park were measured at 325 feet from home plate to the bleachers in left, a whopping 447 feet to deepest center, and 318 to right. Interestingly enough, fans were allowed in Cubs Park during April, while the Cubs were still at training camp, to watch the workers fix up the field and the stands.

FINISHED?

On April 5, the *Tribune* reported that construction work on the stands was complete. All that was left to do before the April 17 home opener was to install seats and gussy up the playing field. Tickets for the home opener went on sale April 5, with new seats installed and painted by April 11.

All the newspapers at the time referred to the park as "new." It wasn't just a matter of a few cosmetic changes; more than ten thousand seats had been added and right field was much larger. A hundred flags were hoisted on poles around the park and would be raised every day henceforth.

But not everything about the reconstruction went as smoothly as the Cubs management would have led you to believe. On March 1, 1948, the *Tribune* published an interview with groundskeeper Bobby Dorr, then entering his thirtieth year on the job. He said that finishing the playing field for Opening Day 1923 went right down to the nub:

> Dorr's biggest operation at Wrigley Field started in mid-October 1922 and was finished a few minutes before Opening Day in April 1923. This was a 6-foot-6-inch bite into the entire field, or 52,000 yards of dirt. . . . The job was complicated by strikes in the building unions and much of the material was left in nearby alleys under cover of darkness. . . . One hundred men each worked on day and night shifts in the race against time.
>
> "On the morning of Opening Day," says Dorr, "there was a hole 30 feet square around shortstop. . . . We even had to scrape up dirt out of the alley for this last fill-in, but we made it."

By April 7, large figures representing "The Doublemint Twins," Wrigley Gum mascots, had been installed atop each end of the center-field scoreboard. In photos, they appear to be different than the figures on the scoreboard back in 1919. One of the pixies, on the left-field side of the scoreboard, held a bat, while another, on the right, wound up to deliver a pitch.

It was also around this time that white-coated ballpark vendors began wearing Wrigley Gum hats while peddling their wares.

OBLIGATORY BATHROOM REFERENCES

Even the day before the "new" park was set to open, things were still a mess—literally. Nonunion contractors had built much of the spanking-new plumbing system at Cubs Park, and local unions—which at the time had no problem resorting to violence to fight for their rights—were not happy. On the night of Sunday, April 15, a wrecking crew affiliated with the aggrieved union workers broke into the park and did ten thousand dollars worth of damage to the plumbing, scattering the scabs' tools around the lot. Nobody associated with the union bothered to deny responsibility.

The next day, six more angry union members attempted to break into the park and stop the nonunion workers from repairing the busted plumbing, but the ruffians were thrown out. By 5:00 p.m., most of the pipes and fixtures had been repaired. Given the vandalism, a large squadron of police was on hand for Opening Day to make sure nothing fishy went on. No exploding commodes were reported.

FINISHED!

Bill Veeck had been quoted in the *Daily Journal* on April 12 as planning to give fans "fewer frills and more baseball" on Opening Day, April 17, 1923. But it would have been impossible to escape from all ceremony. Jack Bramhall's band, on hand for their twenty-eighth straight Cubs opener, began playing at 1:00 p.m., and at 2:45, a battalion of blue-and-red-clad U.S. Marines from Fort Sheridan headed toward center field, picking up first the Cubs from their dugout and then the Pirates from theirs. The parade marched out to the flagpole where Old Glory was raised in front of the scoreboard's large advertisement.

The "inevitable" (said the *Daily News*) pink roses were laid around home plate, and the Cubs presented floral offerings to manager Bill Killefer and outfielder Hack Miller. Mayor Bill Dever, who arrived at the park at 2:45, threw out the first pitch from his box behind home plate. Somewhere around thirty-five thousand fans stuffed the "new" ballpark, but the Cubs lost 3–2. Thousands of fans were stuck outside because they couldn't fit in the park. With new bleachers built in left and right field, there was no room for extra standees in the outfield.

It was a cold day marked by sloppy baseball. Hugh Fullerton of the *Tribune* cracked that "the frappéd crowd witnessed a fricasseed contest." Fullerton also noted that the crowd on this Opening Day was one of high class. "The leaders of social, business, and political life of Chicago were there, and the proportion of women was large." Contrast this with the already foundering post–Black Sox White Sox, who were in the nether regions of the

American League and would not contend again until the 1950s. The trendy North Side was now the place to be for Chicago's baseball fans.

SCORES IN GILEAD

The Chicago *Tribune*, usually a step ahead of the competition, opened up the first sports telephone update line in the city—just in time for the 1923 baseball season. In this, one of the last years before radio broadcasts of games began, fans who wanted to know lineups, current scores, and the like but who couldn't be at the park could call ST6110 (phone numbers had just six digits back then) and get the information from a *Tribune* staffer.

"Telephone baseball fans began limbering up the score wires before 10 AM yesterday with requests for the lineup, opening hour, and other details," wrote Anna Garrow, the newspaper's chief phone operator on April 18. "For the fans who cannot attend the games in person, there is still 'balm in Gilead,' the *Tribune* score department, State 6110."

By the 1930s, twenty trunk lines were devoted solely to the *Tribune*'s score service, with a new number: Superior 0220. Even into the 1980s, every major newspaper had a score line, usually using tape-recorded messages to give out the previous day's totals.

DRAINING

During the 1922 season, Dorr helped improve the Cubs Park drainage system by installing an eight-inch pipe, made of tile, under the playing field from home plate to deepest center field, with two pipes shooting off toward the foul lines. The field was configured to rise from foul line to foul line by sixteen inches, allowing for improved two-way drainage.

WHITE RIOT

The increased capacity in Cubs Park had negative fallout on September 16, 1922. A Sunday crowd of around twenty-six thousand, which included Commissioner Landis and National League President John Heydler, provided one of the most dangerous demonstrations of misguided loyalty ever seen at the field. When Cliff Heathcote of the Cubs was ejected for arguing an "out" call in the fourth inning, the shouts began for umpire Charlie Moran's head and a few bottles were pitched onto the field. In the eighth, Moran's close call on a force play, which went against the Cubs, set the crowd alight.

"Bottles came from the bleachers," wrote Irving Vaughan of the *Tribune*, "and in a moment the outfield was floored with them. From the grandstand came others, some sailing as far as second base, whence Moran had retreated to be out of range."

The broken glass on the field caused a fifteen-minute delay, as the Cubs refused to take their positions for the ninth until the pieces were picked up. Finally, the crowd decided to let the game continue. Fans also tossed bottles at Giants outfielders in the bottom of the ninth, but New York walked away with a 10–6 win. Not much could be said for the bugs' accuracy; the only player hit by a bottle was Cubs third baseman Barney Frieberg.

After the final out the fans roared and hooted anew and some one hundred police were called to escort Moran from the premises. John McGraw also had to be hustled out of the stadium by the bluecoats. Vaughn continues, "Even Commissioner Landis, who attended the game accompanied by President Heydler of the National League, didn't escape the choice remarks of the 'sports.' Landis merely shook his cane at the mob and moved on."

It certainly was a day for the ages, but not a positive one. "The scene surpassed anything ever seen on a local field," noted Vaughn. "Even after the show was over, the pop-eyed fans failed to cool off, hundreds whooping and howling like wolves outside the umpires' dressing room and thousands camping outside the main entrance waiting for something to happen."

1924

In 1924, William Wrigley purchased the land that the ballpark sat on. Prior to the season, he and Bill Veeck elected to remove advertising from the center-field scoreboard, using the extra space to post American League as well as National League line scores. In addition, the Cubs installed a new drainage system in the outfield, which measurably improved the ability of the field to dry, and a new field tarpaulin.

As reported by the *Tribune* on Opening Day, April 23, "The customers will find the park as tidy as a doll house. The stand and bleachers have been given a new coat of paint, [and] the field is in perfect trim." A hundred boys from Senn High School's ROTC were along to raise the flag at 3:00, following the customary concert from Jack Bramhall's marching band. The Cubs clouted St. Louis 11–1 before twenty-seven thousand fans.

For the first time, the Cubs wore red sweatshirts under their uniform tops. (This was a big topic of conversation among the press at the time.) We also get, in 1924, early evidence of gamesmanship among the fans at Cubs Park. On April 26, during the top of the seventh inning, a Cubs fan in the right-field seats, using a small mirror, attempted to direct sunlight into the eyes of the Pittsburgh hitters. "Big Ed" Konetchy, probably a Pittsburgh coach at the time (although not listed as such in *Total Baseball*), complained about this illegal tactic, and Umpire-in-Chief Bill Klem took care of it.

The next afternoon, the Cubs and Pirates played a wet, error-filled 4–2 game after a morning of pouring rain. Most of the fans left the park before the start, thinking the contest wouldn't go on, but the clubs waited out the storm. Apparently the new drainage system wasn't up to a true deluge; groundskeeper Bob Dorr and his crew actually spent time before the game *shoveling* water off the field and into wheelbarrows.

"President Veeck, after the game, declared that any fan who held a seat check could get his money refunded," noted the *Tribune*'s Frank Schreiber. "There were less than 4,000 customers in the stands when the game started, and there had been a big advance sale. This action establishes a big league precedent."

The Cubs finished fifth, at 81–72, despite allowing one more run on the season than they scored. This odd course of events evened out in 1925, when the Cubs finished last.

IF THEY ONLY KNEW . . .

On July 18, 1924, the city of Chicago dedicated a statue of Civil War General Philip Sheridan at the corner of Sheridan Road and Belmont Avenue, just off Lake Michigan, four blocks south and six blocks east of Wrigley Field. The statue depicts the general riding high on his steed. Hundreds of artillerymen and infantrymen were present at the dedication of the grand statue, to say nothing of the spectators on hand, and a seventeen-gun salute rang out to honor the occasion.

This statue is intertwined with Cubs history—though not for anything to do with the good general's accomplishments in the 1860s, or even anything having to do with baseball. Rather, the statue's relevance to our story lies in the "boys will be boys" realm. Nobody knows quite when the tradition started, but players on teams from both leagues are quite familiar with General Sheridan and his equine escort. Most clubs, on their road trips through Chicago, have a peculiar ritual where several members of the team—oftentimes rookies—are commanded to paint, in luminous blue, the testicles of General Sheridan's horse.

THE LONG TERM

Doing things right, for William Wrigley, meant doing them sensibly. Polish your product, get your name out, and treat your customers well. While he lacked Charley Weeghman's unmatched ability to get his name in the papers, Wrigley was methodical and smart, and he had plenty of pals in the press himself. And he was an ideal caretaker for Cubs Park.

During the first few years of any new structure, it is critical to maintain it, clean it, and make necessary repairs early and correctly. The amount of money the Cubs poured into the park in its first few decades is one reason it remains functional while other, newer parks have fallen apart. In a 1930 *Saturday Evening Post* article, Wrigley laid out his qualifications as a custodian of the park—and showed that he, like Weeghman, understood that to bring in a higher and wealthier class to the ballpark, you had to make nice: "Persons used to refined surroundings will not voluntarily go to places for entertainment which offend their sense of cleanliness, comfort, and decency. Therefore I spent $2,300,000 to make Wrigley Field clean, convenient, comfortable, and attractive to the eye—a place in which any woman accustomed to refined surroundings would feel safe, comfortable, and in a frame of mind to enjoy the game."

WRIGLEY AND BASEBALL

William Wrigley belonged to a class of businessman who felt a civic obligation to keep people employed, happy, and—not coincidentally—actively spending in America's capitalist system. As a civic leader and successful businessman, he already had his money and now wanted the esteem that public acceptance would bring. Wrigley was said to be proud of the jobs he had created, both in the gum industry and in other businesses he pioneered, and in how much he gave back to his community. As the *National Cyclopedia* stated in 1933, "He was a liberal contributor to many hospitals, charities, and organizations working for the education and welfare of boys and girls of all races and sects."

His belief about the national pastime was that "no man is qualified to make a genuine success of owning a big league team unless he is in the game for the love of it." But despite his charitable streak, Wrigley was no cream puff; he pushed his business and had a hardheaded and realistic approach to baseball. Wrigley had no reservations about making healthy profits; the First World War helped spread his product throughout the world, and he saw people of all nationalities as potential customers of his chewing gum. Wrigley felt that his primary business fit quite nicely with the uniquely American phenomenon of baseball.

As William Wrigley's son Philip K. Wrigley told his own biographer, Paul Angle, former president of the Chicago Historical Society, in the 1970s, "The customers of the Cubs were exactly the same people that we sold most of our chewing gum to." In *Veeck: As in Wreck*, Bill Veeck Jr. noted that William Wrigley "practically invented chewing gum, [and] was the last of the super salesmen, a man who made his name synonymous with his product. He was a well-upholstered, jovial man who liked people and knew what made them tick."

William Wrigley appears to have indeed been jovial, but more importantly he was a visionary, capable of seeing long-term results and choosing to invest in his businesses. A believer in the power of advertising, he was one of the first to enthusiastically embrace radio broadcasting of games in order to publicize his product, first allowing Cubs games on the air in 1925.

RADIO KILLED THE VAUDEVILLE STAR

Radio scared the hell out of a lot of people—the movie moguls, the theater industry, the concert hall promoters, and the baseball men. (As it turned out, vaudeville did not survive the assault; it was on its way out anyhow.)

Many in baseball believed that "giving away" the game via the new medium of radio would kill attendance. But Wrigley, having done great business in new markets because of advertising, i.e., *getting the product before the public*, understood that putting Cubs home games on the box would keep baseball in people's minds and draw a whole new class of customers to the park.

There were times in the 1920s and 1930s, before the Cubs granted one station exclusive rights to the broadcasts, when multiple channels—WGN, WCFL, WBBM, WIND, and WCFL at one point—aired the contests from Wrigley Field with different announcers. Instead of selling the rights to one station, the Cubs threw the gates open. Wrigley believed that the more people heard the games, the more people would be interested. It was only in the mid-1940s that the Cubs chose to auction off rights to the highest bidder for radio, and the team didn't award exclusive TV rights until 1949.

Such broadcasting greats as Quin Ryan, Hal Totten, Pat Flanagan, Russ Hodges, and Bob Elson lent their voices to the Cubs in those years. And attendance at Cubs games in the 1920s and 1930s—with radio helping to spread the word—exploded, forcing the club to continuously increase capacity at Wrigley Field.

The first broadcast came on Opening Day, April 15, 1925, with WGN's Ryan bringing the game to listeners from Cubs Park's roof. There wasn't anywhere else to put him; according to the next day's *Tribune*, this was the biggest attendance to that time for an opener in Chicago. "They were in the seats and on the seats, on the field and in the aisles, and even on the fences and the iron girders—in fact, no vantage point was in need of an occupant."

Before the game, the *Tribune* had predicted that the North Side park, "newly painted and looking as neat as a Dutch bakery," would be packed. "Useless, timeworn opening ceremonies will be dispensed with," the paper continued. "The exceptions will be a couple of bands that probably will try to drown out each other."

JUBILEE

The Cubs celebrated the fiftieth anniversary of the National League on June 9, 1925. The date had no logical connection to the actual anniversary of the loop's organization, but the party went on anyway.

Approximately seventy-five former players were invited to Cubs Park for the event, including seventy-five-year-old Deacon White, the catcher in the first game the NL Cubs ever played, on April 25, 1876. White would live until 1939, passing on in nearby Aurora. The only other survivor of that team at the time, crusty first baseman Cal McVey, was not in shape to travel from California. He died about fourteen months later in San Francisco.

In front of fifteen thousand fans, Jack Bramhall's music-makers serenaded a parade of players aged and current, and a special pennant marking the occasion—which actually had first been raised on Opening Day—was flown in center field. Commissioner Landis was on hand to present floral pieces to several of the players, and the Cubs promptly went out and lost to the Giants 9–7, allowing three home runs.

GOODBYE, BLEACHERS

Long balls at Cubs Park were a common theme. All season, the Chicago nine had been victimized by what were called "cheap" home runs into Cubs Park's left-field bleachers. (Surely the Cubs hit plenty of them as well, but sabermetric research hadn't blossomed at the time. Even *weekly* averages in the papers were a luxury.) The left-field line was a cozy 319 feet from home plate, with straightaway left just 325.

Things finally reached a head on July 28, when the New York Giants slugged five home runs in a 10–3 shellacking of the Cubs. Irish Meusel's second homer of the game bounced off the back wall in left field and landed on Waveland Avenue. In the seventh inning, while the Giants were busting the game open, William Wrigley looked at his watch, rose from his seat, and hurriedly departed the park. James Crusinberry of the *Tribune* wrote. "One rumor was that Mr. Wrigley had rushed to city hall with the hope of ιosing a couple of streets and enlarging the field before the game today."

On August 2, Brooklyn's Elmer "Dick" Cox smashed a three-run homer to left to beat the Cubs 3–2. Crusinberry pined in the following day's *Tribune*, "If that left field bleacher could just be lifted up and put over the right field one as a double deck, there would be the same space for the four-bits guys and there would be some room out in left for the Cub outfielders to go and catch about two-thirds of the homers that are hit there."

Talk about power of the press! That very day, the Cubs' board of directors heeded the growing cries from the fans and the writers and voted to rip out the inviting left-field seats. Fifteen hundred seats would be lost, leaving just a small, sixteen-row-deep section of fifty-cent bleachers—to be known as the "jury box"—in left-center field.

The left-field line, after the removal of the bleachers, was 370 feet away rather than 319. Distance to the jury box in left center was 353 feet. As a result of the changes, far fewer cheap homers would travel out of left field. Workmen did the construction while the Cubs took an eastern road trip in early August.

This construction work decreased capacity in the outfield for sitters but increased the space for standees. On big-crowd days, the Cubs regularly allowed fans to stand in the deeper parts of the outfield, which brought "ground rules" into effect for balls hit into the humanity; the effect of moving the seats out to help the pitchers was somewhat lost on well-attended days. E. M. Swift of *Sports Illustrated* wrote about this in 1980 and detailed a particular home-field advantage: "'When the Cubs were up,' remembered an old fan named Papa Carl Leone, who spent much of his time from the 20s through the 80s in the right field bleachers, 'We'd all step forward and pull the rope up. When the other team was up and hit one deep, we'd pull it back and let the guy catch it.'"

IS IT MY NAME?

Following the 1926 season, Cubs Park was renamed for its owner. The name change was announced on December 3. The park would now be known as Wrigley Field—a reasonably appropriate act, since William Wrigley was about to pour another vat of money into fixing up the premises.

DECK THE HALL

On October 14, 1926, the Cubs announced a plan to double-deck the park. "Several times during the season just closed," the October 15 *Evening Post* noted, "Cubs Park was filled to capacity and thousands were turned away." Huge crowds during the fall's City Series between the Sox and Cubs also convinced William Wrigley and Bill Veeck that more seats were necessary. The White Sox were also expanding Comiskey Park.

The Lanquist Construction Company was booked to handle the building work, and the design came courtesy of Graham, Anderson, Probst, & White. The Cubs hoped to have the entire project, which had a projected budget of six hundred thousand dollars, finished by the start of play in 1927. The fifteen thousand new upper-deck seats would raise capacity to forty-five thousand. The plan involved no changes to the field, the bleachers, or the seating in the lower deck. The new upper tier would feature box seats in the lower half, with general admission in the back.

The first step in the process was to remove the current roof support, then replace it with stronger steel that would support an upper deck. This work was begun during the football season, and the heavy building commenced after the Bears' home season ended with a 3–3 tie before ten thousand against the Green Bay Packers on December 12. By Opening Day 1927, though, only the third-base stands had been doubled. The team announced that a "delay in materials" caused the slowdown and that the Cubs would complete the project by 1928.

The reason for the shift of the project from a one-year cycle to one of two years, however, may have involved more than a delay in materials. On November 9, 1926, the *Daily News* reported, "There is not the progress [at Wrigley Field] as evident at the domicile of the White Sox." The paper went on to note that Bill Veeck had returned to the city from a vacation, and that "there will be action, and more of it, on the north side." Did the mice play while the cats were away?

When the snow melted and springtime rolled around, the writers were invited in. The Chicago *American*'s Jimmy Corcoran, reporting on April 7, 1927, wasn't especially impressed by the half-done job, although he did cut the Cubs a little slack: "An expert in design, symmetry, or equilibrium likely would walk into Wrigley Field next Tuesday when the Cubs pop open the season against the Cardinals and comment on the fact that the Cub officials had lost their sense of what constitutes beauty in a ballpark. Such a comment, however, would be extremely moist."

The new almost half-deck, which ranged from the left-field corner of the grandstand to close to home plate, raised the capacity of the park to forty thousand. The chairs in the park were not especially wide at that time, which allowed for a much larger crowd (albeit one with smaller tushes). One assumes that the Cubs hoped, by adding this new seating, to fit more people in the ballpark and, just as important, charge more for seats than they could by simply sticking extra spectators on the outfield grass.

What is especially fascinating is that the upper deck, which compared to those in today's ballparks is very low, was seen at the time as being almost unbearably high. Corcoran again: "It will be well for those who use the upper deck at the Bruin orchard to maintain their balance at all times. When you start to climb you can't get away from the feeling that you are going up in the air—and no fooling."

The ramps built to take spectators to the upper deck were attractive in their simplicity, and they still stand today. The upper deck at Wrigley has been added to, reconstructed, repainted, and reconfigured, but it is essentially the same deck built more than seventy-five years ago.

As the deck was being finished, John Seys supervised the laborers painting, building, and adjusting various factions of the park. Corcoran noted that this was being done "with the avowed purpose of fulfilling owner Bill Wrigley's intention, and that is to make the park the prettiest in the major leagues."

The beautification effort, which eventually became an annual ritual, included repainting the bleachers and reserved seats in their typical Irish green and the trim around the park in cream and red. Pictures taken in early April 1927 show that the field was not in the best of shape; the Cubs blamed this on the presence of the Bears the previous winter.

Opening Day, April 12, 1927, was c-o-l-d. Mayor Thompson was on hand, arriving at the park five minutes before the game was to start. He joined the forty-two thousand or so fans crammed into every available space. The double-decked, third-base grandstand was jammed, and the outfield was full of standing patrons. Uniformed policemen stood in front of the outfield standees to try and maintain order. Photographers and movie cameras set up on the first-base roof.

"Other thousands were clamoring at the gates for admittance," Wayne Otto wrote in the *Daily News*. A band from Senn High School, located in Edgewater about twenty-five blocks north of Wrigley Field, played during the flag raising. In addition, Jack Bramhall's combo played.

The 1927 season was good on the field for the Cubs, who finished 85–68 in fourth place. It was an even greater fiscal success. The new half–upper deck allowed 1,159,168 paying fans to enter the gates, the first time in National League history that a club had busted the million mark.

SHATTERED

On September 27, 1927, Pittsburgh pitcher Carmen Hill delivered a pitch to Charlie Grimm. As the umpire called "strike two," one of the lenses from Hill's eyeglasses fell to the Wrigley Field mound and shattered. Hill was forced to depart the game.

THESE WAVES ARE ALL AROUND US NOW

In 1927, baseball games were still starting at 3:00. Most radio broadcasts of games began with pregame announcements and hot gossip at 2:45. Hal Totten was the city's top baseball broadcaster at the time. Totten broadcast all home games of both the Cubs and White Sox on WMAQ. The *Tribune*'s sponsored radio station, WGN, put Quin Ryan behind the mike on a full-time basis to challenge WMAQ's dominance. Other stations followed suit.

Until the 1950s, most clubs had their announcers work only home contests, with road games recreated in the station's studio for economic reasons. In this scenario, the announcer read a ticker-tape feed of the play-by-play, aided by an engineer using canned sound effects to supply crowd noise and the crack of the bat.

BALLS TO YOU

Pat Pieper, the Cubs' field announcer, was also responsible for counting the number of baseballs used in the team's games. During the 1926 season, Pieper reported, 3,004 balls had been used—a rate of nearly forty per contest. Just a few years earlier, such a number would have been unheard of. Dirty, scuffed baseballs were kept in the game as long as possible to save money. When Ray Chapman was fatally beaned in 1920, the press began to push for clean balls and the banning of illegal pitches.

"It costs the front office no little money to keep the two teams supplied with throwing material for 77 contests," wrote William Becker in the *Daily News* of November 1, 1926. (Uh, Bill, these are known in business as *operating expenses*.) But there were differences in how balls were distributed. Becker noted, "On July 2, when [Ernie] Quigley was behind the bat, only 17 balls were taken out of the boxes and handled by the players. But on May 9, when [Bill] Klem was calling strikes, 60 balls were given the once-over with the batters. The arbiters didn't have anything to do with the differences in totals; it was due to the fouls or scuffing or homers."

That the umpires had *nothing* to do with the total of balls used seems unlikely. Klem, often said to be the best umpire in history, probably adhered to a more rigorous standard of what constituted a clean baseball.

DECKED

The first-base upper deck at Wrigley Field was finished in time for 1928's first game, on April 18, and interest ran high in the new, double-decked ball yard. All 15,300 box seats for Opening Day sold out well in advance. The thirty thousand grandstand and bleacher tickets, put on sale at 11:00 a.m. the morning of the game, went quickly. The crowd of more than forty-five thousand was the largest ever, to that point, to watch a baseball game in Chicago. "Paid admission was approximately 44,000," noted the *Tribune* the next day. "Another couple of thousand seeped through the pass gate, which from 2 to 3 o'clock p.m. was the busiest spot in the park."

Opening ceremonies, which used to take two hours or more with Charley Weeghman at the helm, had been pared down with Wrigley in charge. The lid lifter began at 3:00 after a reasonable fifteen minutes of ceremony. A squadron of ROTC cadets from Senn High provided the pomp and circumstance; Jack Bramhall's fifty-piece band provided the light entertainment. "Prof. Bramhall promises to have a corps of sterling tooters out," opined the *Tribune*'s Frank Schreiber, "and threatens to play his two cornet solos—he's played the same pieces for the past thirty-five years—as an added feature."

Cubs manager Joe McCarthy and fan favorites Grover Cleveland Alexander of St. Louis and Gabby Hartnett of Chicago received flowers. According to the *Tribune*, "Alex also drew a traveling bag and a large gourd that was the exact shape of a bat." What Alexander was supposed to do with that, a gift from a barbershop quartet from Grand Island, Nebraska, was anyone's guess.

The *Tribune*'s "Wake of the News" column waxed romantic about the Cubs and their fans on April 19: "There are some owners who attach more importance to the making of money then they do to winning. The Cub management is not in that category. We venture to say that Bill Wrigley, whose fortune is not dependent on baseball earnings, would rather see his team in a world's series than see a ledger profit of $250,000."

It's hard to believe that anyone could write that with a straight face, but then again Veeck was friends with the newsboys, and Wrigley certainly went to a lot of trouble to make the park beautiful and satisfy the fans with good baseball. A good-faith pact had developed between the Cubs and their fans.

HACKED OFF

Hard-hitting and hard-partying Cubs slugger Hack Wilson had taken about all he wished to take. It was June 20, 1928, and the Cubs were hosting the Cardinals in a doubleheader. The Cubs won the first 2–1 but were losing the second game 4–1 in the ninth. Despite two walks and a single, Wilson was receiving the business from some of the fans.

One particular rooter, seated in a box behind the Cubs' dugout, really got Wilson's goat. In fact, Wilson was so angry that after grounding out for the second out in the bottom of the ninth, he rushed into the stands to attack the fan. After landing a few punches, Wilson was pulled away, but a riot had already begun in the section. Fans, policemen, and players all joined the fray, and it was several minutes before order was restored and the Cardinals got the third out.

Even with fans occasionally being belted, 1,143,740 of them paid their way into Wrigley Field in 1928 to see a club that went 91–63 and finished just four games behind pennant-winning St. Louis.

MAKING THE WORLD SAFE . . .

In the Prohibition days, Chicago was where one could get a fill of any poison, human or other. A cursory glance at the arrest logs of Lake View in 1928 and 1929 prove that there was no shortage of poison-providers in the area. On August 22, 1928, the sewers at Grace and Damen Avenues, just a bit northwest of Wrigley Field, were fortified by several barrels of contraband beer, seized as part of a vice crackdown. "Scores of men watched the proceedings wistfully," wrote a reporter from the *Lake View Booster*.

The vice squad hardly calmed down over the winter, either. Over a two-week period from February 12–26, 1929, the *Booster* reported that authorities confiscated 170 gallons of wine and 175 bottles of home-brewed beer at an ice cream parlor at 3657 N. Southport. Next, they arrested and fined a man one hundred dollars at 2853 N. Burlington for running a beer flat in his home. Following that, they closed down Lindy's Café, at 3733 N. Halsted, for possessing intoxicating liquor and running a boudoir, resulting in fines of three hundred dollars. Finally, authorities went four blocks south to 3337 N. Halsted and arrested a woman there for running a boudoir as well.

It was a rough time. Speakeasies all over the city, including in Lake View, were doing great business, often with the cooperation of certain paid-off police officers and federal cops. One such club was the Green Mill, a jazz hangout still open at Lawrence and Broadway, about twelve blocks north of Wrigley Field. Joe E. Lewis, a singer (and, later, a famous comedian), had a residence at the club, which was run by one of Al Capone's henchmen, "Machine Gun" Jack McGurn. Lewis was offered a higher-paying gig at another club, the Rendezvous, at Clark and Diversey (eight blocks south of Wrigley Field). Despite threats from McGurn, Lewis took the gig and shortly afterward was beaten and razored to within an inch of his life at the nearby Commonwealth Hotel. Some sources have McGurn himself, as well as noted mob boss Sam Giancana, administering the punishment.

A BIG SEASON

Hal Totten, trained a sportswriter and on holiday from his radio gig, wrote in the April 6, 1929, *Daily News*, "Wrigley Field already presents a most pleasing sight to visitors. The entire plant is dressed in new coats of green and cream-colored paint." The Cubs had also obtained a new peanut roaster for the park, which handled two hundred pounds of nuts at a time. Estimates had fans eating two hundred fifty thousand bags of peanuts at the park a season, as well as sucking down three hundred thousand bottles of soda and filling out six hundred thousand scorecards.

Two new flagpoles, each close to 90 feet tall, graced the end of the foul lines, and a brand new 110-foot pole was placed in a newly laid eight-by-eight, twelve-foot-deep concrete slab in deep center field. While Totten remarked that little about the park had been altered for 1929, he pointed out that a fifteen-foot-high corrugated steel wall had been built from the end of the left-field bleachers to the right-field open seats. This new wall replaced a previously standing wood fence. Certainly the change was critical for outfielders who actually had the misfortune to run into the new wall.

Photos from April 1929 show that box seats at the park were far from providing contemporary standards of comfort. The wooden chairs, featuring four slats of wood on the seat and just one supporting slat up the back, are far narrower than today's chairs—seven chairs sit where five or six would now be used—and the chairs were removable. The Cubs did not actually bolt down some of their box seats until the late 1960s.

Reports of Opening Day 1929 had more than fifty thousand fans watching the Cubs fall 4–3 to the Pirates. Some twenty-two thousand general admission seats were put up for sale on the morning of the game, while the box seats and the first twelve rows of the grandstand sold out well in advance. The crowd surged on the field, noted the *Tribune*, "making ground rules necessary an hour and a half before game time."

According to contemporary reports, the ubiquitous Jack Bramhall Band played the popular song "Avalon" incessantly before the contest. It must have been hard to play the brass instruments, as the temperatures reached only forty-seven degrees with winds whipping down from the north.

During the game, Town Hall police arrested two men—one from Lake View, one from the northwest side—for betting in the ballpark. One of the fans was a well-known gambler recognized by the cops when he left his seat and went underneath the grandstand to place a wager.

PENNANT FEVER

The Cubs' 1929 pennant push started when they got the one player they'd been chasing for years: second baseman Rogers Hornsby, who had batted .387 for the Boston Braves in 1928. Eventually the Cubs pried him loose from Boston for four players and $250,000 of William Wrigley's money.

Hornsby, a great hitter but (to put it mildly) a tough guy to be around, combined with a productive outfield—hard-drinking Hack Wilson, line-drive producer Kiki Cuyler, and American League castoff Riggs Stephenson—to give the Cubs a fearsome attack that battered opponents at home and on the road. The 1929 team is one of the most storied in Cubs history. Several of its players, including Charlie Grimm, Gabby Hartnett, Zack Taylor, and Hornsby, later managed in the majors. Others, such as Charley Root, Woody English, Pat Malone, and Guy Bush, remained local heroes for years.

The club got hot in the summer; they went 24–9 in July, and after July 24, they had first place to themselves. And the fans came out. Wrigley Field welcomed 1,485,166 paying customers in 1929, a major league record that stood until 1946. After an ugly road trip in late August, the Cubs came home (still well in front) and were greeted by a huge crowd at Union Station. On September 1, forty-three thousand fans came out to the first game of a Cubs home stand. "Every player was given a tremendous ovation on his first appearance," wrote Ed Burns of the *Tribune*. "In the course of all of this, a ton or so of straw hats was cast upon the playing acreage."

Two days hence, eighty-one thousand showed up for a morning/afternoon Labor Day doubleheader sweep over the Cardinals. The thirty-eight thousand fans at the morning game were said to have broken all records for a.m. contests in the history of the game. More straw hats came down from the stands in the afternoon contest following Hornsby's three-run homer, his thirty-second of the campaign.

While the high quality of the club's play that season led to a huge throng of fans, the high numbers could not have been accomplished without an adjustment. The Cubs chose during the season to change to eight—rather than the customary six—chairs in each box-seat section. This increased capacity but reduced comfort.

THE BIG BOSS LEADS THE WAY?

Bill Veeck Sr. even joined in the on-field fun on August 31. The Giants, winners of eleven in a row, were in Wrigley. A half-hour rain delay helped chill the big crowd. As his son Bill wrote in *Veeck: As in Wreck* years later, in discussing the 1929 season:

> We were playing the Giants to break a tie for first place, a game of such importance that we found Judge Landis sitting with my father. The Giants seemed to have the game sewed up right into the ninth inning when the Cubs scored four runs to tie it up. The Giants bounced right back with four runs in their half of the tenth.
>
> In our half, the first two batters went out. Mark Koenig kept us alive with a home run. The next three batters got on to load the bases. Up came Kiki Cuyler, representing the winning run. And Cuyler belted one. The ball was still climbing over the fence when William Veeck Sr. let out a rebel yell and vaulted over the railing . . . By the time we got onto the field, my father was in the very center of a mob scene, grabbing for Cuyler's hand.

Unfortunately, this great story is not true. Veeck is conflating two, or maybe more, separate events. First off, Mark Koenig wasn't even *with* the Cubs in 1929. In addition, Kiki Cuyler's only Cubs grand slam came on September 17, 1929, off fireballer Dazzy Vance of the sixth-place Dodgers—in the fifth inning. Not much tension there.

The game to which Veeck may be referring actually occurred on August 31, 1932, in which Cuyler hit a *three*-run homer in the last of the ninth to beat the Giants 10–9. And it wasn't a game swimming in tension; the Giants were a seventh-place team in 1932, and the Cubs were already well ahead of the second-place Pirates at the end of August. Unfortunately, nobody bothered to check Veeck's book for accuracy, and the error has been repeated in subsequent Cubs histories.

TEMPORARY LIKE ACHILLES

With the Cubs far enough in front to make early World Series plans, the club applied for a special dispensation from the city of Chicago to make more seating available. The club asked for, and on September 11 received, permission to build temporary bleachers on Sheffield Avenue, past the right-field wall, and on Waveland Avenue, past the left-field wall. The construction started on September 15, once the materials arrived.

The project completely shut down the two streets at the points where they bordered the ballpark. The temporary bleachers stretched from the back of the ballpark wall approximately forty feet, reaching halfway into each street. On both the left-field and right-field sides, the bleachers ranged from the scoreboard out well past the foul poles. These interim bleachers, which could accommodate eight thousand extra fans, rose high above and behind the existing bleacher seats in right field and left-center field. The builder, the Patent Scaffolding Company, promised that the bleachers would be constructed with the utmost safety precautions. Bill Wrigley said in 1930 that the bleachers cost forty thousand dollars to build. The temporary seats rose nearly to the level of the "Atlas Special Brew" sign on the roof beyond right field that before 1928 had sported a billboard promoting the Marigold Garden.

These "circus seats" went for one dollar each. The Cubs sold them all, making sixteen thousand dollars for two games' worth of tickets, a rate well below their cost. However, the bleachers clearly were more profitable than that; Bill Veeck Sr. claimed at the time that the bleachers would cost "90 percent of the greatest amount the club possibly could derive from it," indicating that the Cubs were counting on selling a lot of concessions to bleacher fans. There is no record of any fans in the buildings past the outfield walls filing lawsuits against the Cubs for blocking their view.

FOR THE LOVE OF MONEY

The first two games of the Series, to be held in Chicago, were scheduled on October 8 and 9, with early starting times of 1:30. Ten thousand bleacher tickets were sold on the day of the game. In addition, twenty-five hundred standing room ducats were made available at two and three dollars apiece, depending on where one wished to stand. If you were driving to the game, you'd have to fork over one dollar for protected parking.

Box seats were $6.60 each, with the sixty cents going to Uncle Sam. Reserved grandstands went for $5.50, including fifty cents tax. Box and grandstand seats were sold only by mail, in advance, for three games (One, Two, and Six if necessary), making the outlay for a box seat $19.80. In 1929, this was a *lot* of money.

Arch Ward, in the *Tribune*'s "Wake of the News" column on September 12, noted that while this probably felt like a skinning to most fans, it wasn't as bad as it seemed. "Of course, Wrigley Field would be a sellout if admissions were $10 or even $15 per game." Ward's article, however, argued that postseason ball wasn't such a financial windfall, claiming that "[owners'] profit in victory is increased drawing power the following season." Ward posited, therefore, that prices for World Series tickets should be reduced. "To the regular fan of all season, who must take seats for three games to get any, they are too high . . . Perhaps they already have passed the limit fair to regular customers."

Clearly the teams weren't doing this for love. The cost of the tickets for Game Six would be refunded if the game wasn't played, but the money would have sat in the bank for a week gathering interest for the Cubs. And you thought that underhanded ticket policies began recently?

While a group of Boy Scouts trooped the field before the game of September 12, the tens of thousands of applications for box and grandstand seats arrived at Cubs Park. In order to be fair, the team's ticket office employees simply picked envelopes out of a huge grab bag and filled orders.

HANGING OUT, DOWN THE STREET

The rush to get bleacher tickets, which sold for a buck apiece (a good chunk back then), began early. One enterprising fellow got in line just after the Cubs and Pirates played the year's final contest on October 6. According to the *Chicago Daily News*, "James Macek, of 2459 Washtenaw Avenue, parked himself on a cracker box beneath the ticket window just after yesterday's final ball game of the regular season." Macek, who spent thirty-six sleepless hours in line, ultimately did get in the bleachers before anyone else.

By the afternoon of October 7, approximately thirty people were camped out in the ticket line, "passing the time by playing rummy over a box, passing remarks with the wisecracking bystanders, and trying to place small wagers on the outcome of the big event." Hot-dog merchants descended upon the area to feed the crowd, which had swelled to the thousands by evening.

There was little modesty as both women and men waited out the day and night of October 7. Ladies with smudged makeup and wrinkled clothes and hats did their best to stay dignified. Men talked, smoked, and played cards. One assumes that the bathrooms of any surrounding bars and stores were perpetually filled, and that plenty of red hots were consumed. (One hopes that the fans didn't do to the neighborhood what some intoxicated fans with full bladders do these days.)

In order to clear the streets, the bleacher gates were thrown open at 7:00 a.m. on October 8, sending twelve thousand "sleepy-eyed individuals," as John Keys of the *Daily News* called them, into the park. "The action brought a sudden splurge of wild activity among the waiting thousands. Boxes, chairs, cushions, and other paraphernalia were joyfully kicked aside as the waiters jumped into place to begin the happy scamper through the gates."

WRIGLEY'S FIRST SERIES

Once inside Wrigley Field, Keys noted, the fans "sat jammed in a towering wall of drab-colored humanity," awaiting the contest. The bleachers were completely stuffed by 11:00 a.m. Before the game, Bramhall's band tootled away, and baseball clowns Nick Altrock and Al Schacht did their crowd-pleasing routines. Fans waved pennants, stomped up and down, and did cheers to stay warm. Blankets and heavy fall coats were plentiful, especially in the grandstand where the sun was barely evident.

Nobody thought that the cool winds whipping in from the west were an omen of bad things to come. But the harsh breeze, according to Keys, "bestirred a ragtag carpet of torn newspapers that littered the streets and sent a shivering chill through the huddled forms of at least 10,000 red-eyed, sleep-hungry but hard souls" hoping to enter the park. There was little relief in Wrigley Field, where "firemen patrolled the wooden seats to see that none of the fans there built fires to keep warm." Policemen lingered on the field to ensure that nobody jumped onto the green, while vendors distributed peanuts, soda, and popcorn.

Temperatures rose to the fifties by game time. Approximately fifty-one thousand fans saw the contest, and not everyone was present by the time Charley Root threw the first pitch; plenty of grandstand ticket-holders were still in line. Eight men trying to scalp tickets were arrested outside the park, while another group of men hustled tickets downtown to be made available at the last minute to well-to-do, under-the-table buyers.

At least one man saw the game for free. A fellow named "One-Eyed" Connolly, "the country's best-known gate-crasher" according to the *Daily News*, "Houdinied himself in with the crowd" at the Addison Street entrance.

"How did I get in?" he was asked. "Oh, just walked in. Me, a ticket? I should say not."

DISASTER

The 1929 World Series was a crusher for Chicago. Favored to win over Connie Mack's Athletics, the Cubs were instead vanquished in five painful games. In the lid lifter, thirty-five-year-old Howard Ehmke's slow-slower-slowest deliveries baffled Chicago hitters. Ehmke, whose 3–1 win was his last in the majors, whiffed thirteen Cubs to set a record. Chicago also dumped the second game, 9–3, when starter Pat Malone couldn't get out of the fourth. A baker's dozen of Cubs hitters fanned in this contest as well.

Once in Philadelphia, the Cubs improved, winning Game Three 3–1, and appeared to have turned the momentum around. In Game Four, Chicago was up 8–0 in the last of the seventh, looking certain to knot the series at two apiece. But the Athletics staged a rally for the ages, posting a spectacular ten-run comeback in the seventh, and won the game. They took the series the next day, coming back from a 2–0 bottom-of-the-ninth deficit and winning 3–2.

Hack Wilson hit .471 in the Series but fielded poorly, especially in Game Four's ten-run inning. In 1930, Wrigley Field fans began to roll lemons at him when he came to bat. A tremendous hitter who had already paced the league in home runs in 1926, 1927, and 1928, Wilson went on to smash fifty-six homers in 1930 and drive in 191 runs—a record that still stands. By 1931, however, he fell prey to the sauce and wore out his welcome with manager Joe McCarthy.

WORKING FOR SOMEBODY ELSE

The Cubs employed 499 people in 1930, most of them on a part-time basis. Thirty-one were uniformed personnel; twenty-three were members of the grounds crew; seventeen were on the executive level. The remaining 438 were game-day workers: ushers, ticket sellers, concessionaires, and the like.

In 1929, Wrigley admitted to having sold 694,954 score cards, 539,938 bottles of soda, 482,364 rolls, 425,820 hot dogs, 388,410 ice creams, 266,900 bags of peanuts, and 132,650 sacks of popcorn. The team ran its own in-house concession operation at the time, both to guarantee quality of the goods and to manage expenses more efficiently. The Cubs' sales income from concessions in 1929 was $233,450.

THE GIRLS WANT TO BE WITH THE GIRLS

As Warren Brown wrote in 1946, "This gesture of setting aside an afternoon each week in which the gentler sex might watch a ball game as guests of the club had been tried by the Chicago National league club as far back as the days of Pop Anson. . . . [but] Wrigley not only invited 'em out, he practically insisted on it. . . . Not even a sale of nylons in early 1946 was as productive of mass turnouts of women as were these Ladies Days at Wrigley Field."

During the late 1920s, the ladies would simply show up on Friday after-noons, causing an unpredictable (and often huge) crowd. At one time, the Cubs tried having the "fanettes" show up at Wrigley Field on Wednesdays to claim the Friday tickets. In 1930, three downtown stores took over the duties, serving free passes to the female fans.

On June 20, 1930, half of the thirty-five thousand at the game were women. Before the game, a new silver flagpole, which would hold the forth-coming 1929 NL pennant, was installed. On Saturday, June 21st, somewhere around forty-two thousand fans came to the park to see Cubs players, led by a military processional, troop around the unfurled championship pen-nant. Once everyone had marched out to center field, the pennant was run up the new flagpole. The Cubs then went out and whipped the Boston Braves twice.

THERE IS NOTHING LIKE A DAME

William Wrigley wanted to make the game of baseball safe for women at his park, just as Charley Weeghman had done. But at the same time, Wrigley noticed that not all the ladies who came to the park were proper. "It is easier to control a crowd of 100,000 men than of 10,000 women," he told Forrest Crissey in the *Saturday Evening Post*. Wrigley found that no matter what he did, the ladies who crashed the gates for free on selected Fridays were sur-prisingly rough: "The ladies listen to a speech urging them to take their time and assuring them that each applicant will be accommodated; then they storm wickets, sweeping aside policemen and guards in a way to make men gasp and wonder how the phrase 'the gentler sex' ever originated. What they do to one another in the process of crashing the gate is astounding to male spectators."

The Cub management had to live with several contradictions during those years. One was that ladies, who were supposed to make things more genteel, were among the rowdiest and uncontrollable fans Wrigley Field saw. Other contradictions of the time included the need to stamp out gambling, although many fans engaged in it, and the desire to bring in higher-income fans, although they weren't as passionate about the game as the less affluent. Ultimately, the sides of the arguments that won out were the ones facilitating the clicking of turnstiles.

THE BIGGEST EVER

One record that will probably never be broken at Clark and Addison was set on Friday, June 27, 1930. The largest crowd in the history of Wrigley Field—51,556—attended a game between the Cubs and the Brooklyn Dodgers. Of that more-than-capacity crowd, 30,476 women entered free. Several thousand more ladies were unable to get into the park, and at least ten thousand male customers with tickets were left holding the bag as well. Today, fire regulations wouldn't permit such a crowd.

"Mothers standing in the deep extremities of center field with babies in their arms. Little tots purring, scrambling on the green in right, center, and left fields, where the jam pack ran twenty deep. All aisles packed to a point where navigation from one end of the stand to the other was impossible," commented Jimmy Corcoran in the *American*.

Proper ladies, some bouncing children on their knees, sat in wool skirts on the concrete slabs at the fronts of seating sections. Families picnicked on the grass in deep left field. Gentlemen sat down in the pasture, or hunched down in their seats and removed their hats in order to provide ladies with a better view. Despite cloudy skies, the huge crowd began descending on the park by noon, three full hours before game time. Management began herding the excess fans onto the outfield grass at 2:00, and the ladies and kids kept coming. During the game, which ended 7–5 (in the Cubs' favor), several hard-hit balls ricocheted into the outfield standees for ground-rule doubles. For the first time in the history of the park, according to Corcoran, the aisles were so jammed that paying patrons in the first six rows of the grandstand were forced to stand up in order to watch the game.

On capacity-plus days before 1937, fans were all over the field. Some of them even perched themselves atop the left-field wall, although it is tough to tell how they got up there. To ease the crush and panic and make sure that paying fans weren't to be disappointed, the Cubs *again* altered the Ladies Day policy for 1931. Fans wishing their free Ladies Day ducat had to send the club a request, along with a self-addressed stamped envelope, for the game in question. Only one pass was available per customer, and the previously unlimited free supply was brought down to a more reasonable twenty thousand.

GIRLS BEHAVING BADLY

The Ladies Day custom continued into the 1970s. However, the day on which women were admitted free fluctuated. In 1940, the Cubs held Ladies Days on Fridays. During the 1941 season, they were held on Tuesdays. By 1957, it was back to Friday. During 1961, ladies were allowed in free on Saturdays. By 1963, they were again on Fridays. In 1969, the day was changed to Thursday.

The generous Ladies Day policy created a ground swell of female support for the Cubs that remains to this day. Much of the team's fan base is built around teenage girls who grow up, continue to go to Cubs games and, later, bring their children, grandchildren, or nieces and nephews. Which is not to say that the ladies *ever* became a high tea, peaches-and-cream set. As P. K. Wrigley told Paul Angle years later: "We couldn't get a policeman to work up there. We couldn't get an usher. We had to *drive* them up, because if a man talks back to a policeman or an usher, they are liable to get punched in the nose, but women can say anything with impunity, and they abuse these fellows something terrible."

DON'T BLAME ME

The burnishing of William Wrigley's legacy was in full effect with his 1930 *Saturday Evening Post* article. Already loved and respected, Wrigley was now crediting himself with Charley Weeghman's innovations. "When I entered upon my experience as a ball-club owner back in 1916," the article read, "the typical ball crowd was generally considered rather rough stuff. . . . The socially elect of our city did not then crowd the ticket lines. A Ladies Day at that time would have been a joke—a target for the gibes of sports writers and columnists."

This is demonstrably incorrect, and Wrigley (and the editors at the *Post*) should have known better. Weeghman had worked as hard as anyone during the teens to make baseball cleaner and safer, especially for women, and Ladies Days at the time were far from a joke. In addition, Wrigley's comments about the social order are incorrect—Weeghman had brought all sorts of goodfellows and social gadflies to the park, and Wrigley knew this.

This article served, to an extent, to paint Wrigley as a champion of the game and as a custodian of an extraordinarily successful franchise, and he qualified on both counts. But he doesn't deserve credit for being the first to make baseball a classier sport, and he doesn't get points for making over baseball for women. Such a movement well predates even Weeghman. For instance, Jack Norworth's "Take Me Out to the Ball Game," featuring its female protagonist, was written in 1908, six years before the advent of the Federal League, and had been a smash hit. Team owners had courted women customers since at least 1886, when Cincinnati's Tony Mullane, "The Apollo of the Box," set hearts fluttering when he would take the mound. Of course, not all owners wanted women at the park, and Weeghman's innovations were groundbreaking for the time. But Weeghman wasn't the first, and Wrigley *certainly* wasn't.

Wrigley did make some interesting points in the article. He noted that every employee at the ballpark wore "an attractive uniform," and that on every weekday game save Friday, four thousand children under sixteen were admitted to the park free—even on school days, "through the cooperation of the school board and the athletic committee of the city council."

Not only did Wrigley help kids cut school, but he also cultivated future Cubs fans. No wonder people thought he was a genius!

HACK'S EXIT

Hack Wilson, formerly a fan favorite, was increasingly helpless in the field, difficult to live with, dependent on alcohol, and less effective as a hitter. The Cubs tired of Wilson's act by summer 1931. Already skidding at the plate, Wilson did not help himself by repeatedly breaking curfew. The final straw came on a train ride from Cincinnati to Chicago in early September where he encouraged pitcher Pat Malone to punch out two sportswriters, then informed teammates that club management could go to hell. Once informed of Wilson's transgressions, the Cubs suspended him for the balance of the season. Bill Wrigley, incensed at Wilson, made the decision himself.

Wilson showed up at Wrigley Field on September 7 and sat in the stands to watch the Cubs and Cardinals. The *Tribune* reported, however, that management didn't welcome him. "The club is definitely through with the home run hero of 1930. He has been told to remove his belongings from the clubhouse."

GOODBYE BILL

William Wrigley suffered a stroke on January 18, 1932. A heart seizure soon followed, and he passed away at age seventy-one in Phoenix on January 26. Asked about his feelings concerning Wrigley, Bill Veeck Sr. simply stated,

"It's a terrible shock. It's like losing a parent. Mr. Wrigley was the finest man that ever lived."

The death of the magnate surprised and saddened the baseball community, and it threw those associated with the club into no little panic about whether his son, Philip K. Wrigley, was ready to take over. But P. K. was the logical heir. As Irving Vaughan wrote in the January 27 *Tribune*, "It was [William Wrigley's] wish, often expressed, that after his death, his son, Philip K. Wrigley, should conduct the club on the same high plane. That the son will do so, for several years at least, seems certain."

At his death, William Wrigley owned about 70 percent of the club, having bought out A. D. Lasker some years before. William Walker, stockholder Adolph Spielman's heirs, and P. K. himself owned most of the remaining Cubs stock.

William Wrigley, it is said, begged his son on his deathbed never to sell the team, to keep it forever in the family. While it is not crystal clear that this is true, it makes as much sense as any other explanation when one asks why P. K. held on to the club in the first place.

CHAPTER **6**

Dead at the Top: Wrigley Field, 1933–65

P. K. FAQ

Philip Knight "P. K." Wrigley was born on December 5, 1894, in Chicago, one of two children of William and Ada Wrigley (P. K. also had a sister, Dorothy). Wrigley was born at the southeast corner of Clark Street and North Avenue, about twenty-four blocks south of the ballpark, in the Plaza Hotel. Mitchell's Restaurant and the Village Theatre are now the key tenants at the corner.

While William Wrigley loved his son enough to name a brand of gum ("P. K.") after him, he also let it be known early on that the son was expected to work for his position, not just inherit everything. Although there was clearly a deep love between father and son, the two Wrigleys were not alike. Bill Veeck Jr., who knew and worked for both men, wrote, "It is hard to understand how a father and son can be as completely different as William and Phil Wrigley." Of course, Bill Veeck Jr. was hardly a carbon copy of *his* father . . .

Quiet young Philip lacked the smiling bonhomie and the love of the social ramble that characterized his father. He was interested in the mechanical—engines, machines, cars, and airplanes. It has been written that P. K.'s favorite activity in life was to strip down a car, upgrade it, and put it back together. He also would whip out a screwdriver and repair the malfunctioning watches of visitors.

P. K. graduated from Phillips Academy in Andover, Massachusetts, in 1914 and soon joined the navy. During World War I, he served at Great Lakes Naval Station in the northern suburbs of Chicago. In 1918, he married Helen Atwater, who gave birth to three children. In 1925, Philip succeeded his father as head of the Wrigley Gum Company. Another piece of William

Wrigley's empire, the baseball club, was heretofore of little interest to P. K. But this would change on the elder Wrigley's passing; Bill left all of his Cubs stock to his son, and thirty-eight-year-old P. K. assumed control of the Cubs in 1932.

Again, Bill Veeck: "His father left the club to him personally . . . and so Phil Wrigley assumed the burden out of his sense of loyalty and duty. If he has any particular feeling for baseball, any real liking for it, he has disguised it magnificently." Clearly, P. K. Wrigley was no pip at baseball. In 1943, Stanley Frank wrote in the *Saturday Evening Post* that "the chewing-gum magnate is astonishingly naïve in baseball matters and is given to impulsive decisions which seem to be splendid ideas at the moment, but never quite work out."

Veeck's judgment may be more than a little unfair. Veeck *fils* and Wrigley *fils* were two fish from different oceans, or maybe a fish and a bird. But Philip Wrigley did care whether his team won or lost, although it seemed like more of a personal quest to burnish his father's image than a need to win based on competitive zeal. "The club and the park stand as memorials to my father," P. K. Wrigley told the *Daily News* in 1933. "They represent all the sincere and unselfish ideals that actuated him in all his public contacts . . . I will never dispose of my holdings in the club as long as the chewing gum business remains profitable enough for me to retain them."

He also told Warren Brown, "We aim to have the Cubs pay their own way, just as if they were my only interest. In this the Cubs are no different from any other major league club whose owners have no outside interests. Actually, the Cubs do make their way on their own, too; but it is hard to get anyone to believe that this is so."

WHY IS THIS SO COMPLICATED?

Part of the reason Philip Wrigley could afford to think this way was that the Cubs and Wrigley Field were actually two separate business entities. The Chicago Cubs were a Delaware-based corporation under the Wrigley family ownership. P. K. Wrigley was controlling stockholder, but not the *only* stockholder. In contrast, P. K. privately owned Wrigley Field; William had willed the ballpark and property directly to his son. This meant that the club actually paid the Wrigleys rent.

This explains why the Tribune Company had to make two separate transactions for the team and ballpark during the 1981 sale and also gives us a clue as to why P. K. Wrigley paid so much loving attention to the ballpark at the expense of the team for forty-five years. The ballpark, not the club, was his personal inheritance, and Wrigley was its thorough—maybe even fussy—caretaker.

BACK TO BUSINESS

April 20, 1932, was Opening Day at Wrigley Field. A Senn High School ROTC unit trooped onto the field, and players from both sides, as usual, marched to center field for the flag-raising. The banner was then lowered to half-mast in honor of the late William Wrigley.

This would be another fun year at Wrigley despite the departure of Hack Wilson for Brooklyn. The Cubs were playing great ball, remaining near the top of the league as the Pirates, Dodgers, and Phillies did their best.

GRIMM DAY

First baseman–manager Charley Grimm of the Cubs was given a "day" at Wrigley Field on August 16. "Jolly Cholly," a popular, banjo-playing jokester, received flowers, a platinum watch, and a set of silverware (a common ballpark gift of the time). Grimm had already been the beneficiary of two such "days" in St. Louis and Philadelphia that year.

The Cubs were down to Boston 3–0 in the bottom of the ninth but jumped off the mat with one out. Three straight doubles made the score 3–2, and then Riggs Stephenson singled in Kiki Cuyler to knot the game. A hit and an error later, Billy Jurges rapped out a hit to deep center that brought in Stephenson and gave the thirty-two thousand or so fans on hand a thrill. The Cub win kept them a game ahead of hard-charging Pittsburgh.

Hundreds of straw hats sailed from the stands, according to the *Tribune*, but "the owners of more expensive Panamas are going to wait a while to see how times proceed before they let enthusiasm carry them away."

MARATHON—BEST IN THE LONG RUN

The following day, the Cubs and Braves played nineteen innings at Wrigley Field, with Chicago finally winning 3–2 on Frank Demaree's sacrifice fly. On August 18, the two teams played fifteen *more* innings, this time with the Cubs taking a 4–3 decision.

The pennant tangle continued August 20, when newly acquired Mark Koenig slammed a three-run homer with two out in the ninth, capping a four-run rally that gave the Cubs a 6–5 win over the Phillies. Koenig's homer went deep into the right-field bleachers, sending sixteen thousand fans into hysterics. As Koenig reached home, "The ushers had to drive back several hundred fans," each of whom wanted a piece of Koenig to take home, according to the *Tribune*'s Ed Burns.

BABY GOT BACK

According to Paul Angle, one of the first big changes that the Cubs made in 1932 was cutting the number of seats in a box from eight to six. P. K. Wrigley figured, correctly, that it wasn't good business to annoy the highest-paying customers just to achieve short-term financial benefits by jamming them in too tightly.

As the Cubs moved closer to the flag, Wrigley approved the construction of temporary bleachers on Waveland and Sheffield Avenues, as had been done in 1929. The cost of such work was estimated again at forty thousand dollars and began long before the team actually nailed down the pennant.

THE WINNER

The Cubs clinched the 1932 flag by taking the first game of a September 20 doubleheader at Wrigley. The 5–2 win, over the second-place Pirates, came courtesy of a three-run triple by fan favorite Kiki Cuyler in the seventh that broke open a 2–2 nail biter. Before the game, fans gave popular outfielder Riggs Stephenson assorted gifts.

Despite both Sheffield and Waveland Avenues being blocked from traffic by bleacher construction, the fans came out. The papers reported that thirty-eight thousand rooters jammed the ballpark on a misty, warm day. As game time drew near, it became clear that the Cubs could cram thousands of extra fans onto the field if they wished, but Bill Veeck, according to the *Tribune*, said, "No customers on the field today."

Unfortunately, the overflow crowd caused a ruckus. Once all the seats were filled, around fifteen thousand fans, denied the chance to gain standing room privileges in the outfield, began to agitate. Several hundred fans stormed the pass gate. Scores of policemen were called to the scene in order to quell the near-riot.

The decision to keep the fans off the field was a break of sorts for the Cubs; an overflow crowd would have meant that Cuyler's big triple would have been a ground-rule double instead. As second baseman Billy Herman threw out Pirates pinch hitter Gus Dugas to end the game, fans threw hats onto the field and the Chicago dugout emptied. Photos taken at the time show groundskeepers immediately heading toward the infield to get the park ready for game two of the twin bill; so much for celebration.

More than half of the fans remained at the park for the second game despite a heavy rainfall. "They must have thought that maybe Charlie Grimm would rush across the field with the pennant and climb the flagpole with it," the *Tribune* opined. Most Cubs regulars, spared playing the night-cap, chose to fill up on ice cream in the clubhouse.

THE LOVE PARADE

Mayor Anton Cermak and the city council arranged a parade for September 22. Fans with motorcars who wanted to join in the fun were encouraged to do so; the parade was estimated to be several miles long. The party began at 9:00 a.m. at Wrigley Field, where Jack Bramhall's band clambered to the top of a bus and played. Taking Addison to Sheridan Road, then Sheridan south to downtown, the team was showered with ticker tape on LaSalle Street, home of the brokerage houses. Several popular old ballplayers, including Jimmy Archer, Jimmy Callahan, and Jimmy Slagle, were on hand as well.

A FISTFUL OF DOLLARS

The love reached all the way to the financial district, as the 10 percent of Chicago Cubs shares that were actually on the market gained in value. (In 1932, the Wrigley family owned 60 percent of the Cubs.) From an in-season low of 125, Cubs stock opened September 20 at 265 and closed at 350. Five shares were being sold at 400. During the clinching game, prices fluctuated, rising 50 points to 350 immediately following Cuyler's three-run triple. The age of updated stock information clearly didn't begin with the Internet.

Following the Cubs victory, a Cincinnati gambler named Frankie Moore walked into a Chicago establishment and offered seven thousand dollars against five thousand dollars that the American League champion Yankees would beat the Cubs in the World Series. Moore, reported the papers, had sued former Chicago manager Rogers Hornsby several years earlier to collect unpaid wagering debts.

The *Tribune* estimated that the ballplayers, fans, and media traveling to Chicago for the Series would bring in ten thousand dollars a day to the hotels and restaurants in the city. In addition, local telegraph companies would earn fifteen thousand dollars a game laying down lines to transfer the 1.5 million or so words sent back to newspaper offices from the ballpark each game. The Cubs assigned three hundred press credentials at Wrigley for the Series.

YOU WON'T SEE ME

The temporary outfield bleachers killed the view for the men at Company 78, the firehouse just past Wrigley Field's left-field wall. In the past, the men had been able to watch games from the station's rooftop, but the bleachers meant that now the firemen couldn't see much more than the mound and home plate. Meanwhile, the Chicago Department of Revenue announced plans to tax any fans watching the games from the roofs or windows of local buildings. This was not a high-income operation for the revenue department, apparently pulling in just enough money to pay the collectors. The revenue department's chief collector, Gregory Van Meter, also told his deputies to collect a 10 percent tax on all ticket brokers charging more than list price.

TIX, TIX, TIX

The Cubs began selling World Series tickets before the pennant was actually clinched. This time around, fans could reserve tickets at the windows and then have them mailed to their homes. Owing most likely to the depressed economy, seats didn't sell much until the flag was won. As usual, mail-order tickets for the Wrigley Field games were sold in three-game packages only.

Two fans were at the bleacher window more than three days before Game Three at Wrigley Field. The bugs took turns sleeping on a cot, with the other guarding their place in line. Later on, two young ladies, fourth and fifth in line, were treated as the fairer sex, given—courtesy of the Cubs—a spot sheltered from the cold while being allowed to keep their "places" in line. The $1.10 bleacher tickets actually went on sale at 6:30 a.m. the day of Game Three, as did twenty-five hundred standing room tickets at $2.50. The bleacher seats for Game Three did not sell out until around 12:30.

ANOTHER SERIES, ANOTHER DISAPPOINTMENT

The overpowering Yankees, AL champs by thirteen games, won the first two contests in New York, 12–6 and 5–2, before coming west to Wrigley Field. The fans, to say nothing of the Cubs, were already deflated by the Yankee bats of Lou Gehrig and Babe Ruth, and few thought that Chicago had a chance.

For Game Three, at 1:30 on October 1, the skies were cloudy but the temperatures warm. The wind blew out to right field all game, and 49,986 fans were on hand. The Board of Trade American Legion band entertained the faithful before the first pitch. The Yankees jumped ahead 3–0 in the first inning off Charlie Root, and the rally included a home run by Babe Ruth. Many fans missed it. Arch Ward of the *Tribune* noted that "hundreds of fans who arrived after 1:15 o'clock yesterday were unable to get to their seats until after Babe Ruth had knocked his first home run." Ward blamed the congestion on poor entrance facilities, which "forced many to stand in line for 20 minutes." Bill Veeck denied that the Cubs did anything wrong. He said that all turnstiles were in use, but that "it is impossible to eliminate congestion when thousands attempt to enter at game time. There is no way we can provide more entrances."

The Cubs tied it 4–4 off George Pipgras in the fourth, which set the stage for one of baseball's most famous home runs. In the Yankees fifth, Babe Ruth clubbed a monstrous laser beam to center field off Root. This was his "called" shot, which almost nobody who was at the game actually believed that he "called." Ruth's prodigious drive, which came in the teeth of some vicious bench jockeying by the Cubs, sailed past the flagpole on the right-field side of the center-field scoreboard and smashed into the box office at the corner of Waveland and Sheffield. Ruth yelled, cursed, and pointed at the Cubs bench as he rounded the bases. Sportswriter Warren Brown later wrote that following the game, seven different folks on the streets claimed to have the ball Ruth drove from the park.

Following the Yankees' 7–5 win, the AL champs hosted Bill "Bojangles" Robinson in their locker room. Robinson danced atop a trunk while the New York players yelled and clapped their hands.

SWEPT AWAY

Prior to Game Four, on October 2, fans arrived earlier, leading to little of the crowding that marred the start of the third contest. This time, 49,844 stuffed themselves into Wrigley Field hoping for a miracle. Prior to the game, Babe Ruth—who had won over the crowd with his two homers in Game Three—went out to the left-field "jury box" bleacher and had some fun with the fans. Cranky-sportswriter-turned-right-wing-screedist Westbrook Pegler, who took great pains to criticize the Babe's fielding as well as his tonnage, was mortally offended, and said so the next day in the *Tribune*: "[Ruth] had the naïve effrontery to take a stand before the left field bleachers, whose occupants pelted him with lemons on Saturday afternoon, leading them in rousing cheers for Babe Ruth. It was the first incident of the kind seen in the sport business since Joie Ray, the runner of the American Olympic team, hopped up on a chair in a café in Amsterdam and called for three cheers for Joie Ray."

After the Cubs took a 4–1 first inning lead, knocking out Johnny Allen, their pitching slowly fell apart. Battering Chicago hurlers Jakie May and Burleigh Grimes, the Yankees scored four in the seventh and four more in the ninth to break open what had been a close game. The final was 13–6, and by the last inning, the Cubs were being booed loudly by their own fans.

Before the third inning, a huge cloud of gnats descended on the fans in the box seats, causing several minutes of consternation.

JEFFERSON, I THINK WE'RE LOST

Popular actor Jefferson de Angelis, an honored guest at Weeghman Park's opening back in 1914, died aged seventy-three on March 20, 1933, in Orange, New York. De Angelis's connection to baseball didn't end with Weeghman; one of his pallbearers was DeWolf Hopper, the famous actor who performed countless recitations of the poem "Casey at the Bat." Other well-known sporting and entertainment figures attended the funeral, including Milton Berle Sr., Al Spink, George Barnum, and Charles Stoneham.

Bigger news came just two days later.

BACK TO THE BARS

One of the first initiatives of the Franklin D. Roosevelt administration, which came to power in the November 1932 elections, was to repeal Prohibition. All concerned realized that the morally based movement had failed in practical terms. The first step in ending Prohibition was the Beer Revenue Act of March 22, 1933, which legalized beer and wine with alcohol content up to 3.2%. The government planned to tax liquor sales in order to refill depressed federal coffers.

Beer and wine became legal again across the nation at 12:01 a.m. on April 6, 1933, and Chicago vendors that night sold alcohol for as little as a nickel a glass. Restaurants and hotels planned all-night parties to sell the beer being furiously bottled in Chicago by seven breweries: Prima, Atlas, Schoenhofen, Bosworth, McDermott, Monarch, and United States Brewing.

BEER . . .

Oddly enough, prior to Prohibition, nobody had ever bought a glass of alcohol at Wrigley Field, even back in the hazy, good-time Charley Weeghman era. John Carmichael noted, in the March 24, 1933, *Daily News*, "In the old days at the west side park, and even in the present spot, beer was never sold."

Why would this be? It's not as if the Lake View neighborhood was dry, or was even faintly squeamish about drinking—witness the nightly debauchery at the Bismarck Garden. There are several possibilities for the lack of alcohol sales at Wrigley before Prohibition. These include neighborhood protests; club magnanimity in protecting local bars; a decision that selling beer was unprofitable; a lack of suppliers; and anti-selling laws.

Most of these possibilities hold no water (or liquor). Few in Lake View opposed drinking. There is also no evidence that the Whales or Cubs held back sales to protect local businesses. Concerning the profit motive, selling beer has always been good business, and there was certainly no lack of breweries before Prohibition. It's possible that a city ordinance prohibited ballpark beer sales. The White Sox had never sold alcohol at Comiskey Park, which opened in 1911. The Pale Hose had last vended beer at the 39th Street grounds, where they played from 1900 through 1910.

The city might have been working on a form of protectionism for local businesses by prohibiting beer sales at the ballparks and racetracks. But by 1933, everyone had had enough of over-regulation, and the gates to beer selling were thrown open with force. During the latter part of the Prohibition years, the Cubs had sold beer substitutes, such as Prager, from taps at the concession stands under the grandstand seats. Wrigley opted to have those taps outfitted for the 1933 season to serve 3.2 beer.

"We are going ahead with beer for the ball park," Wrigley told Carmichael. "But as far as I know it will be draft beer only, served down at the bars along there under the grandstand. I think most fans like a sandwich or two with their beer. So, for the present, at least, there will be no bottle beer sold at the ballpark." Wrigley was probably worried that fans would drain their beer bottles and drunkenly pitch them onto the field.

The sale of beer at Wrigley made an immediate impact on Opening Day 1933. "The volume of business in beer alone far surpassed the soft drink sales under the stands on Opening Day last year, according to attendants," reported Arch Ward of the *Tribune*. "The bar on the third base side was crowded even while the game was in progress."

Prohibition was fully repealed on December 5, 1933. During this time, new businesses, including bars and restaurants, opened (and re-opened) around Wrigley Field. The southeast corner of Waveland and Sheffield became home to Ernie's Bleachers, a hot dog stand that also sold beer in pails. During World War II, Ernie's was converted into an actual tavern. Ernie sold in 1945, and the bar was known as JB's for a couple of years before Ernie bought it back. In 1965, Ray Meyers purchased the bar and renamed it Ray's Bleachers, which it remained until 1980. That year, Jim Murphy bought it and renamed it Murphy's, the name it carries today.

. . . . AND SEX

Yet another innovation at Wrigley Field for 1933 was even more attractive to many men than the heretofore-illegal pleasure of standing at a bar. The *Tribune* noted that "a comely young woman attired in white dress and bonnet dispensed cigarettes to the box seat patrons. This is the first time the Cubs have had a girl vender [*sic*]. Her high French heels gave her the appearance of walking on stilts."

Jack Bramhall was on board again with his band, reportedly for his fortieth straight opening (the number of years he and his band served tended to get confused over the years). Arch Ward reported that "they're still playing some of the pieces that were popular in 1895."

DRINK IT UP

On July 4, 1933, the Cubs dedicated a new marble and bronze drinking fountain behind home plate to William Wrigley. The fountain remained in operation at this location until the 1980s, when the Tribune Company decided to put a souvenir shop at the spot. The fountain was then moved down the first-base line and currently stands near the Friendly Confines Café.

Just two days after the fountain was dedicated, the first baseball All-Star Game was held on the South Side of Chicago at Comiskey Park. *Tribune* sportswriter Arch Ward thought that such a spectacle would be a great addition to the World's Fair, held in Chicago that summer. Ward also saw the contest as a benevolent event for indigent former players.

Eventually, Ward convinced Judge Landis that a gala midseason exhibition, with its attendant fan balloting and extra publicity, was good for the game. The All-Star classic was so well received that the previously reticent owners were forced to make it an annual event. What is not generally known is that a simple coin toss decided the location of the contest—Comiskey Park or Wrigley Field.

GOODBYE, MISTER VEECK

Bill Veeck fell ill in September 1933, catching a chill in poor weather at Wrigley Field, and was home in bed for a week. When he didn't improve, Veeck entered the hospital, where an exam led to a diagnosis of leukemia, a relatively new disease for which there was no known treatment. The fifty-five-year-old Veeck went quickly downhill and passed away on October 5, 1933, at St. Luke's Hospital, with both the Giants–Senators World Series and the Cubs–Sox City Series in progress. Bill Veeck Jr. says that in order to help ease the misery of his father's last days, he went to an unimpeachable source to get the best bootleg liquor in town. "The last nourishment that passed between my daddy's lips on this earth," he wrote, "was Al Capone's champagne."

When Bill Veeck Sr. passed away, the flags at Wrigley Field and at Griffith Stadium in Washington, D.C., were lowered to half-mast. The following day's City Series game was canceled, and the tributes flowed in as everyone wondered who in the world would run the Cubs now.

The press admired Veeck. He had been one of them and therefore understood that the flow of information was important. Veeck rarely stonewalled when a story broke. An Associated Press report written on his passing noted that "Veeck was a firm believer in taking the public into his confidence in all baseball affairs of general interest, despite the protests of many of his associates." The *Tribune* noted, in its eulogy, that "the doors were never closed against any baseball writers seeking news. . . .[Veeck] never was known to complain to a writer about any unfavorable comment published about the Cubs."

There are cases in baseball history of famous and talented fathers being outrun by their sons—Ken Griffey Sr., Bobby Bonds, Cal Ripken Sr., and Gus Bell come to mind. Bill Veeck is another such figure. Few people today know how much Bill Veeck Sr. helped the Cubs become a great team in the late 1920s and 1930s. Will Harridge, the AL's president, best summed up Veeck's impact: "He was forceful. He made friends. Baseball is a tremendous loser in his passing."

THE LONG DOWNWARD SLOPE

P. K. Wrigley was completely unprepared to deal with life after Veeck. In desperation, he hired former Cubs owner William Walker as president. However, Walker didn't work out; he was intractable on marketing ideas that Wrigley wanted to implement, and an ill-advised trade of Dolf Camilli to Philadelphia brought down a hailstorm of criticism. In 1934, Walker was eased out of the position, and according to Paul Angle, P. K. Wrigley bought his 1,274 shares of the club for $150 each.

Phil Wrigley ultimately chose to man the post himself. Warren Brown recalled in the March 17, 1938, *Sporting News* that when Wrigley called the press together in 1934 to announce the news, he told the writers, "I don't know much about baseball, and I don't care much about it, either." Wrigley was convinced—by the *writers*—not to allow that comment out for publication.

At first, Philip Wrigley took the job of team president reluctantly but eventually grew so attached to it that he refused to hire anyone else. Once in control, Wrigley was able to work on his own marketing projects, one of which was to let all children in for half price. Other clubs in the league thought this was a terrible precedent, but eventually they all followed. By 1938, Brown conceded that Wrigley "seldom misses a game any more, if his many other duties permit" and that he, indeed, truly had gained knowledge and passion for the game.

On the field, the Cubs after Veeck's passing were solid through 1938, as they had a good base of talent and in the past had been unafraid to spend money. But as Wrigley became more and more entrenched in his position, and as he realized how over his head he was as a baseball man, he relied more and more on yes-men, hangers-on, and loyalists, few of whom had any ability to run a baseball club.

THE REMAKING OF WRIGLEY FIELD

While P. K. Wrigley was no baseball man, he was a smart and innovative marketer who understood the value of advertising. His goal was to make Wrigley Field not just a place to watch winning baseball, or a destination for a guy's day out, but a place for *families* to spend a healthy, happy afternoon in the sunshine. Key to understanding Wrigley's achievement is to realize that this goal was, at the time, unusual. While getting families to come out to the park may not sound like a big deal to us now, this was an extremely radical position to take at the time.

Even in the 1930s, baseball was still seen by many as the property of hard men, ruffian kids, bettors, and the working class. People gambled, smoked, cussed, and (legally, at least, after 1932) drank at games. Baseball parks were one of many places where women and children weren't especially welcome in the 1930s—even at Wrigley Field, which had a history of Ladies Days—and many male fans wanted ballparks to be sacred territory. *Winning* was what mattered, not spending a sunny afternoon at a clean, well-kept park. For years, the NL refused to allow its clubs to have Ladies Days, even though their decision was probably less about sexism than about wanting to attract *paying* visitors rather than *free* ones.

P. K. Wrigley believed that pushing baseball as a healthy, American activity would be his best advertising tactic. "Our idea in advertising the game, and the fun, and the healthfulness of it, the sunshine and the relaxation, is to get the public to go to see ball games, win or lose." During the winter following the 1934 season, the Cubs took out advertising in the Chicago papers urging fans to look forward to spending time at Wrigley Field the next summer. It had been several years since the club had taken out ad space in the papers; Charley Weeghman had done so often.

Charles Drake, at one time assistant to the president of the Cubs, told Paul Angle, Phil Wrigley's biographer, that "Wrigley had looked out of his office window onto Michigan Avenue and asserted: 'See those people going by. They are all consumers of chewing gum. They are all baseball customers if we can convince them they ought to see the Cubs play. We are going to sell them baseball.'"

In simple terms, Wrigley was controlling what he could. He understood that baseball was hard, but upkeep was easy. Even if you couldn't guarantee the fans a winner, you could make their ballpark experience positive if the place was clean, the food good, the facilities first-rate, and the attendants friendly.

(I WANT TO GO TO) BEAUTIFUL

The caveats to selling a "beautiful" park were making and keeping it beautiful, and Phil Wrigley didn't disappoint. He inherited—and even expanded upon—his dad's mandate to make Wrigley Field the nicest-looking plant in baseball. As George Castle wrote in *The Million-to-One Team*, "Wrigley did one important thing right as owner. He kept a regular schedule of ballpark upkeep that preserved Wrigley Field for decades to come."

Nearly every season, the park was repainted in its trademark green, red, and cream. Seats were regularly replaced. The plant was swept, rinsed, and mopped. Overall fan comfort—including clean restrooms, polite ushers, well-stocked and clean concession stands, and the like—became the first priority.

"In the general area of promotion, Wrigley and I agreed on only one thing: keeping the park clean," wrote Bill Veeck. "Phil Wrigley carried it even further; he made the park itself his best promotion. Wrigley kept the park freshly painted. He threw out the sidewalk vendors, newspaper boys, and panhandlers. He stationed ushers out front to guide people to their sections. He insisted that ticket sellers be polite and courteous. We sold 'Beautiful Wrigley Field.' We advertised 'Beautiful Wrigley Field.' The announcers were instructed to use the phrase 'Beautiful Wrigley Field' as often as possible."

In his devotion to comfort and cleanliness, P. K. Wrigley was a later incarnation of Charley Weeghman, although advances in technology and increased space made Wrigley's vision possible in a way that Lucky Charley's never could have been realized. Even when the Cubs were lousy, in the early 1940s and into the 1950s, they still drew well—far better than their performance would have indicated they should. "Those were the years," Warren Brown noted about the early 1940s, "which proved beyond any reasonable doubt that P. K. Wrigley's plan of selling baseball amid pleasant surroundings was a happy thought and a profitable one."

HIGH FIDELITY—CAN YOU HEAR ME?

The Cubs installed a new public address system in time for two preseason 1934 Wrigley Field exhibitions against the defending AL champion

Washington Senators. Unfortunately, during the April 7 game, which the Cubs dropped 8–3, the new system exploded.

MY VACANT CHAIR

Arch Ward of the *Tribune* noted that all the regulars came to Opening Day 1934, on April 24, except one. "The seat between the screen and the Cubs dugout, which for 16 years had been occupied by the late president of the Wrigley baseball forces, was vacant." The other Opening Day customs were observed. Jack Bramhall's band showed up for its forty-first straight Cubs opening; the Senn High School ROTC presented the flag; and Cubs manager Charley Grimm received a huge floral horseshoe.

Two particularly silly things happened that day before the Cubs beat the Reds 3–2. Prior to the game, Cubs hurler Lon Warneke tried to catch a fungo and inadvertently swallowed his chaw of tobacco. Around the same time, a bass drummer in Bramhall's band was almost brained by a foul ball. In response, the band struck up a song entitled "Was That the Human Thing to Do?"

Ward wrote, "The answer was in the affirmative."

TRAINING

Since the 1980s, baseball fans have heard rumors that major league clubs will desert their spring training homes in Florida for the southwest. Back in March 1935, the Cubs—who had still been training on Catalina Island all these years—considered leaving the west for the south. The reason given at the time by the Cubs for considering a move was that Pacific Coast League clubs—whose seasons started earlier than the majors—no longer wanted to take the bloom off their own rose by scheduling so many exhibitions with high-drawing major league clubs. In addition, PCL owners were said to be unhappy with the mediocre level of intensity showed by the big leaguers in the games.

But the Cubs remained on Catalina. It would take World War II, and restrictions on travel, to keep the Cubs off the island. In the years from 1942–45, they trained in French Lick, Indiana, and returned to Catalina for 1946–47 and 1950–51. During 1948–49, the Cubs trained in Los Angeles. Beginning in 1952, the Cubs have trained in Arizona every year except 1966.

SO UNUSUAL

April 16, 1935, Opening Day at Wrigley Field, was, according to the *Tribune's* Arch Ward, "the most unusual in Chicago's history. . . . Not a single floral tribute was presented at home plate before the game." Perhaps all the flowers had died. It was cold, and snow sat in the upper reaches of the stands. While advance sales for the game were brisk, the turnstiles did not turn quickly, largely because of the chill.

Mayor Ed Kelly was there to toss out the first ball, which he did from the stands rather than on the field. Bramhall's band was there, for (it was said) the forty-third consecutive year. The band was involved in a rather silly episode when, after Dizzy Dean of the Cardinals was injured by a line drive, the musicians insensitively struck up "Happy Days Are Here Again."

Al Campion, who ran the Cubs' press gate from 1905 to 1934, was off the job and instead given less strenuous duties. He didn't have much to do on June 5; apparently, nobody did. Just 1,229 fans paid to see the Cubs at Wrigley Field. The team announced that this was the lowest paid attendance in at least a decade.

ON 1935

The Cubs hung around the top of the NL standings all summer in what eventually became a four-team race. Chicago found itself scrambling with the world champion Cardinals, the Giants, and the hard-charging Pirates. Local fans weren't fascinated with this Chicago squad, but an August 6 game beginning a home stand brought out six thousand paid fans, along with forty-five hundred school-age kids let in free and ninety-five hundred women given special passes because they hadn't been accommodated the Friday before.

As late as September 4, the Cubs were in third place, behind St. Louis and New York, but a long home stand would prove to be the tonic. On September 5, the Cubs defeated the Phillies 3–2 at Wrigley in front of just 4,780 fans for their second straight win.

Two days later, before another victory over the Phils, first baseman Phil Cavaretta was honored by local friends, who gave him a new car, a basket of flowers, and a guitar, which came from a fellow Lane Tech High School alumnus. Before the game, the Cubs announced that they had placed a piece of canvas on the left-field side of the center-field fence. According to manager Charlie Grimm, the canvas was installed to give left-handed hitters a better look at deliveries from right-handed pitchers. It's not clear when this piece of canvas was taken down.

21 STRAIGHT

Upon coming home in early September, the Cubs caught fire. The hitting of Augie Galan, a series of strong pitching performances, home cooking, and a schedule packed with below-par opponents carried the team. On September 7, in front of 8,642 paid and three thousand school kids, the Phillies fell 4–0, protesting plate umpire George Barr's ball–strike calls by tossing bats out of the visiting dugout and eventually suffering three ejections. Three days later, just forty-five hundred came out to see the Cubs win their seventh in a row, shutting out the visiting Braves 4–0. The streak went to nine with two more wins over the last-place Bostons.

The Cubs finally started to capture the city's imagination. On September 14, 13,328 paid to see the Cubs take first place from the struggling Cardinals with a loony 18–14 win over the Dodgers, and the next day, 28,890 fans saw the Bums fall again, 6–3. Chicago's winning streak stood at twelve.

The quickly sinking Giants were next, and they suffered four straight pastings from the streaking Cubs by a combined score of 34–10. The fourth game, the Cubs' sixteenth consecutive win, was a 6–1 decision over Carl Hubbell. On September 18, when the Cubs stomped the Giants 15–3, P. K. Wrigley himself was photographed at the park, sipping lemonade.

Crowds between 29,740 and 32,885 saw the games, and more tried to enter through the pass gate. The Cubs were the hottest ticket in town. On Saturday, September 21, the Pirates invaded and were vanquished 4–3 before 38,624 (including 12,500 women admitted free because Friday, usually Ladies Day, had been an off day), and on Sunday, 40,558 crammed in to see the Cubs close out their home season with their eighteenth consecutive win, 2–0. For the last game, the Cubs probably could have sold fifty thousand tickets, but according to the *Tribune*, "P. K. Wrigley . . . ordered that general admission ticket sales be stopped as soon as the grandstand was loaded to capacity. The ticket windows shut down more than an hour before starting time, leaving thousands on the outside with money in their hands, but no place to spend it." Scalpers were out in force that day—keep this in mind, by the way—and did a raging business before a group of *federales* swept in and nailed every speculator they could find. In addition, keepers of local parking lots made big money; they charged a dollar per car during the series.

Chicago then went to St. Louis and won three more to clinch the NL before finally dropping the last two games of the season. WGN radio, which had been broadcasting only Cubs home games during the year, arranged to have announcer Bob Elson travel to St. Louis to bring those contests live to listeners in Chicago.

REGULARLY TEMPORARY

For the third time, the Cubs decided to have temporary bleachers built past the outfield walls in case of a World Series. Some fans, by September 18, had already begun to send in World Series ticket requests, but the Cubs simply had them redelivered to the early senders.

The twenty-nine-thousand-dollar project, undertaken by the R.C. Weiboldt company, began immediately following the Cubs' last home game on September 22. The next day's *Tribune* reported that "cranes, lumber, and tools were moved onto the scene last night, and actual construction will begin this morning. The seats will begin at the top of the walls in left field and right field and extend more than halfway across Waveland and Sheffield avenues. They will be nearly 800 feet long and will accommodate 12,000."

P. K.'S FIRST BLUNDER

These days, plans for the World Series—dates, broadcasting arrangements, and, until 2003, home cities—are mapped out months or even years in advance. But back in the 1930s, arrangements for the World Series weren't made until late in the season. On September 17, representatives of the four National League and two American League clubs still in contention met with Commissioner Kenesaw Mountain Landis in Chicago to iron out plans. The NL was putatively scheduled to host the first two and last two games of the fall classic, but Landis saw a problem. St. Louis was already hosting a large convention on October 2, the date of Game One, so the city couldn't promise enough hotel rooms for visiting press and baseball people. Landis decreed that, as a result, the AL would host the first two contests. This seems a bit ridiculous now—by September 16, the Cubs were two games up and rising—but it was Landis's way. Whether something actually made sense was not always relevant to him; the appearance of fairness and logic was paramount.

Meanwhile, Cubs manager Charlie Grimm was furious, according to the *Tribune*, "because Cubs representatives at the meeting for the purpose of making World Series arrangements did not hold out for opening the series in a National League park." Who represented the Cubs at the meeting? P. K. Wrigley and John Seys.

P. K.'S SECOND BLUNDER

When it came time to sell World Series tickets, Philip Wrigley believed that there had to be a better way than by mail, which was an extremely labor-intensive rush job. So Wrigley decided on a public sale of tickets for the battle between the Cubs and the American League champion Detroit Tigers. This clearly was a recipe for trouble, but, as Irving Vaughan noted in *The*

Sporting News of October 10, "As he is the club owner, none of the other officials questioned it."

Prices remained at 1932 levels: $16.50 for a one-ticket, three-game block of grandstand seats and $19.80 for box seats. The twelve thousand $1.10 bleacher tickets and the standing-room certificates did not go on the market until the day of the game. The sale was scheduled to start October 1 at 8:00 a.m. Ten thousand or so fans arrived at Wrigley Field the day before to line up for reserved and box seats. The *Tribune* reported that industrious local carpenters "did a thriving business in makeshift shelters—wooden screens that could be attached to the walls of the ballpark in case of rain."

"Many of the men in the crowd brought along shaving equipment. One had a portable gasoline stove and kept himself and friends supplied with hot coffee." Some of the crowd simply sacked out on the sidewalk near Clark and Addison, wrapping themselves in blankets, while others stayed awake. "Card games were numerous and plenty of bottles were sighted, although few contained milk."

The *Tribune*'s story also carried a note of foreboding. "Many boys and young men who were well up toward the windows last night frankly admitted that they had no intention of seeing the series themselves, but were holding places in the line at anything from 10 cents to $1 an hour. Not so talkative were representatives of ticket speculators, who hoped to carry away enough tickets to make their employers a substantial profit."

THE CORRUPT ONES

At the scheduled time, the sale commenced—and it was a shambles. The Cubs and Wrigley apparently failed to factor in the shameless avarice of their fellow man. As a result, the team didn't set up even the most rudimentary precautions against cheaters and bullies. "No effort was made to ferret out suspicious-looking characters," reported Irving Vaughan. "Twenty-four hours before the ticket booths opened, there were about 200 in line. About 75 per cent was made up of seedy-looking youths, who obviously couldn't have been shaken loose from a dime if turned upside down. They were merely fronting, in most cases, for scalpers. These were the fellows who could have been spotted if the club had properly safeguarded itself."

Approximately twenty thousand were on hand when the ticket windows opened. Thousands of fans, hoping to get tickets, had shivered all night in line but were cut out of the process by scalpers and their representatives. The police presence was light, and the finest of Chicago's Finest apparently stayed at home. Noted the *Tribune* on October 2, "Two or three dollars in the hands of a policeman or an usher enabled all of the young men to return to the front portion of the line and repeat the business of buying another set [of tickets], and from there it was just a matter of going to head of the class again and again."

Abuses in the process were rampant. Two ticket sellers were fired for giving one hundred tickets to a known scalper. Rich fans with ready money bribed cops and ushers to get to the front of the line. Perhaps happiest were the downtown ticket brokerages, which almost immediately began fetching prices of fifty dollars or more for each three-game block—this despite a new anti-scalping law on the books for just a few months. The *Tribune* reported, "Through the morning hours, the patient legions who were a block away from the front office in many cases continued to stand and amuse themselves, unaware that they were being rooked in the matter of preferred position by the speculators' stooges, who must have numbered nearly 300."

To make matters worse, the club never announced how many tickets would be sold to the public, leading to suspicion that other, more moneyed interests were being given first crack at the ducats. Public outcry was swift and intense as the press and fans excoriated P. K. Wrigley. In Vaughan's words, "Wrigley, who was sincere in his belief he was doing the right thing by ordering a public sale, was greatly agitated over the repercussions."

REPERCUSSION

The controversy affected the box office. Only 45,532 of a hoped-for Game Three crowd of fifty thousand showed up despite good weather and predictions of a sellout. Several thousand bleacher tickets went unsold. In addition, according to Arch Ward in the October 7 *Tribune*, at game time, "There were plenty of empty box seats. Most of them were occupied before the first inning was over, but it appeared the scalpers had been hooked slightly, at least."

Even as early as October 5, the day before the Series reached Wrigley, some brokerages were unloading their seats at box-office prices. Ward noted that before Game Three, one fan was able to buy two box seats at game time for the grand total of twenty-five cents.

POLICE ON MY BACK

Even with the smaller crowd, traffic was heavy around Wrigley Field. The police had decided previously to deactivate all traffic lights in Lincoln Park and on Sheridan Road before and after each Series game. Uniformed policemen served as traffic controllers at the streets without lights. The city dreamed up a series of complex northbound and southbound traffic routes to help alleviate the congestion.

Chastened by the poor performance of some of their officers at the ticket-buying debacle, the police were out in full force shutting down the more heinous scalpers. The cops arrested Harry Cohen, who had a ticket agency at 63 West Randolph, for trying to sell two sets of box seat tickets at seventy dollars. Cohen had forty-three other sets of tickets in his possession. Just a few doors down from Cohen, a hapless northwest sider named Philip Schwartz was nailed for trying to scalp two sets of tickets to visitors from Kansas and Missouri. Schwartz had eight sets of tickets on his person.

Police were also on the lookout for anyone climbing to the top of the roofs of local buildings in order to see the Series. It was still illegal to be on a rooftop, due to concerns about the safety of buildings under the pressure of extra weight, and Police Commissioner James Allman ordered any violators arrested.

THE EDGEWATER BEACH HOTEL

The opposing Detroit Tigers were staying at the Edgewater Beach Hotel, about twenty blocks north of Wrigley Field. The choice of hotel was no accident. Previous Cub-beating World Series clubs had stayed there; the 1929 Athletics and the 1932 Yankees had found the lodgings comfortable. Tigers manager Mickey Cochrane, an alumnus of the '29 A's, was said to be quite superstitious.

Ed Burns of the *Tribune* commented, however, that the New York Giants bunked at the Edgewater Beach during their trips to Chicago in 1935, and they had lost their last eight games at Wrigley.

GAME THREE

Prior to Game Three, with the series tied 1–1, the American Legion Band of the Chicago Board of Trade, led by Armin Hand, entertained the fans. The musicians wore dark jackets, white pants, and white helmets and brought their own like-outfitted flag guard. The band walked on sod, freshly laid by groundskeeper Bob Dorr and his crew when the Cubs were on the road at the end of the regular season, and played "The Star-Spangled Banner."

Meanwhile, P. K. Wrigley, in clear flouting of tradition, had the Cubs' NL pennant raised before the game. (Usually this was not done until early the following season.) After the ceremony and controversy, the game was outstanding. The clubs traded leads, with the Cubs up 3–1 after seven. In the eighth, the Tigers used a walk, four hits, and a steal to score four runs, but the Cubs knotted it in the bottom of the ninth. In the eleventh, an unearned run off Larry French gave the Tigers a 6–5 win.

Despite the efforts of the police, the park and surrounding areas were completely jammed with cars. The closing of Waveland and Sheffield due to the temporary bleachers didn't help.

AND THE REST

It was not to be the Cubs' year, as they dropped their third Series in nine seasons. In Game Four, a much larger crowd—49,350—witnessed an outstanding pitching duel between General Crowder of Detroit and the Cubs' Tex Carleton. Both hurlers went the distance, and only a sixth-inning unearned run gave Detroit a 2–1 win. The traffic jams, patrols of rooftops, and arrests of scalpers continued (four more were arrested before Game Five), and the Cubs at least won one at home, taking Game Five 3–1 behind the pitching of Lon Warneke and Big Bill Lee before 49,237. Chuck Klein's two-run homer provided the difference.

Both teams then trained it back to Detroit, where the Tigers won the sixth and final game 4–3. Goose Goslin's single in the last of the ninth plated Mickey Cochrane with the Series-clinching run. Chicago had not played badly; the club led at one point in five of the six games and was only blown out of one, but it was just another disappointing Series for Cubs fans.

RAZZBERRY SHOWER

The Cubs, expected to repeat as National League champions, sagged in 1936. The club fell back into the pack in August and finished five games out. The low point of the season? It may have been Memorial Day, May 31, when the Pirates whipped the Cubs 7–5 and 11–7 at Wrigley. The 43,332 fans overflowing the park were a cantankerous bunch, and the crowding caused tempers to rise.

"The crowd became pretty peevish," reported *The Sporting News*, "and manager Charley Grimm was treated to the noisiest booing ever heard at the Cubs' park. He couldn't make a move without precipitating a choice round of razzberries. Maybe some of the fans were sore because, after spending their money to get in, there was no place to sit and in many cases not even room for a glimpse of what was going on, so they took it out on the boss."

"WESTERN UNION, DIT-DIT-DIT-DIT-DIT"

For the 1936 season, P. K. Wrigley worked with Western Union to design an innovative ticketing process. At each of the 102 Western Union offices in

Chicago, operators were supplied with blocks of blank Cubs tickets and Wrigley Field seating diagrams. Customers could travel to their local Western Union office and inform the operator where they wished to sit. The operator would then phone the Cubs' box office at Wrigley Field to ascertain whether the seat was available. If the seat wasn't taken, the Western Union operator would fill out the seating details on the ticket and validate it with a signature, collect the customer's money, and send the customer on his or her merry way. Western Union would, at regular intervals, turn over the ticket revenues to the Cubs. The Cubs installed fifteen operators and a twenty-line switchboard at Wrigley Field to handle the demand.

NOSTALGIA FOR 1876

In accordance with the National League's sixtieth anniversary, the Cubs held an 1876-style baseball exhibition at Wrigley Field on Saturday, August 22, 1936. Boston's Braves had already held their 1876 celebration, as the *Tribune* reported on August 19: "The feature of that event for the Cubs was a gentleman on an old high-wheel bike, who as he pedaled past the dugout yelled, 'How do you get off this thing?' The Cubs couldn't answer. The gentleman afterward fell off and his problem was solved."

The three-inning exhibition, held before the scheduled Cubs–Reds contest, featured young men in the uniforms of the times: "thickly-padded pants, high-collared blouses, and flapping neckties," noted the *Tribune*, which also reported that the players "entered the ball-field in barouches, buggies, and victorias, the horse drawn equipage of the nation's centennial year." At 1:15, the parade began, led by Jack Bramhall's band. A huge cardboard cake was rolled out to center field. Mordecai Brown cut it, and, said the *Tribune*, "Out sprang the 1876 athletes in the full glory of mustachios and padded uniforms." The 1876-styled game commenced at 1:30, with the Cubs vanquishing Cincinnati 3–1. Relevant rules differences and customs in vogue in 1876 were explained to the fans via the public address system.

Prior to the whole affair, P. K. Wrigley fêted a band of old-time players with a luncheon at the Congress Hotel, then invited them to Wrigley to watch the exhibition from box seats. Some of the players from the past on hand included Jack Pfister, Jimmy Slagle, Jimmy Archer, and Mordecai Brown of the Cubs, Ginger Beaumont of the Pirates, and Fred Luderus, one-time first baseman for the Phillies. Even Art Nehf's father, Charles, was also on hand. The one surviving member of the 1876 Chicagos, ninety-year-old catcher "Deacon" White, was ill and could not attend.

While the regularly scheduled game was delayed by the ceremonies, and it was very hot at the park, the *Tribune* reported, "The time was well put in by the customers and there was no impatience manifest in the stands." The Cubs then fell to the Reds 6–4.

INCIDENT AT WRIGLEY

On August 30, 1936, the surging Cubs met a buzz saw at Wrigley Field in the form of the Giants. New York's 6–1 and 8–6 doubleheader win knocked Chicago from the National League race for good. The wins raised the Giants' August record to 24–2. The crowd was a sellout; 45,401 paid to get in, and another two thousand pass holders entered free. And more wanted in. According to the *Tribune*: "At 11:50 o'clock yesterday the thousands around the portals of Wrigley Field were advised that all boxes, general admission, and bleacher tickets had been sold. The locked out crowd was orderly until almost 1 o'clock. Then a group tried to batter down the gate at Waveland and Sheffield Avenues."

As was customary, fans were strung around the outfield, roped off from play. On this day, the ropes were forty-three feet from the wall in left field, thirty-five feet from the scoreboard in center, and twenty-five feet from the right-field screen. This made the dimensions for the day cozy: just 325 to left, 405 to center, and 331 to right.

THE DORR WAY

The November 19, 1936, *Sporting News* published Ed Burns's profile of head groundskeeper and park superintendent Bob Dorr, on the job since 1919. In the article, Burns reported that Dorr and his family lived in a six-room house, designed by William Wrigley in the early twenties, built into the left-field corner of Wrigley Field. The home, which longtime Cubs employee Bob Lewis lived in following Dorr's death, is now used by the Cubs' concession department. When Dorr lived there, the front door of the house let out onto Waveland Avenue. The article notes the effort that it took to keep the field in baseball shape, considering it was also used for football in the winter: "After the close of the baseball season, Dorr levels off and sods his infield so that there is no trace of the skinned area, the base lines, the pitcher's box, or the batter's box. The transition this year will cost $4,000 before the place is returned to its baseball status. Dorr and his crew take one and one-half inches of soil off the skinned portion of the diamond, ten inches of clay from the area around home plate, and 18 inches of clay from the pitcher's box. Some 1,500 yards of sod were laid [in October 1936]."

At the time, Dorr had a staff of sixteen workers, all of whom were part of the Theatrical Janitors' local union. They were each paid six dollars per day. Of the sixteen-man crew, five were, at the time, retained for seven months at full-time status. Eight of them were ten-month employees, and three of them worked year-round.

In order to prepare the field for baseball following the end of the football season, Dorr would lay between five thousand and sixty-five hundred feet of bluegrass and red sod every December. In later years, the new sod would not be laid until March or April. A distinguishing characteristic of the time was the mixing of the infield dirt to an attractive reddish-brown hue, rather than the gravel-like brown-gray seen in most parks. The infield dirt matched the park's cream, buff, and green color scheme extremely well.

During the baseball season, the crew began work at 8:00 a.m. on game days. They also worked when the club was on the road, though for only a few hours a day. Dorr wasn't crazy about using a tarp to cover the field, preferring instead to keep the grass as wet as possible. He "will lay the canvas, 3,150 feet of it, only when ordered to do so by Cub officials." Dorr felt little need to keep the field overly dry, because he believed the drainage was better at Wrigley Field than at any other park. Burns quotes Dorr as saying the field drained well because "there are 85,000 feet of land tile under the field."

As park superintendent, Dorr was also responsible for repairing the non-playing areas of the park and for keeping the stands clean. He had 135 tools stored at Wrigley for his and his crew's use. Burns noted that Dorr was a fanatic about keeping the park painted and "probably would run about the place with a paint brush in his hand but for the rigid union policy of the Cubs." Burns would write later that year in *TSN*, "there's always some painting being done at Wrigley Field. The paint is so extensive, in fact, that the groundskeepers after each game have to eject Ira Hartnett, a paint salesman, who lives in constant terror that someone will chisel the account."

GALLERY 37

Opening Day 1937 saw a crowd of just 18,940, even though the club had forecast up to forty-two thousand. The weather wasn't great—nobody tried to climb to the rooftops, due to a chilling wind from the east—but it wasn't miserable, either. Mayor Kelly showed up to toss out the first ball, Jack Bramhall's band entertained for approximately their forty-fifth Cubs opening, and Senn High School sent over its ROTC corps to lend the required dignity to the flag raising.

In addition, there were two other less than dignified ceremonies. First, the Cubs presented a large bouquet of flowers to Paul Dominick, the team's official mascot. In that era, "mascot" meant a full-grown, uniformed, non-playing adult around four feet tall. Second, manager Charlie Grimm was herded over to the Cubs dugout to pose with two small bear cubs and feed them from baby bottles. According to Harvey Woodruff, longtime *Tribune* sports editor who wrote the "In the Wake of the News" column that day, the little bears, a gift from American Airlines pilot A. D. Ator, were hauled in from Sonora, Mexico.

This was to be the last Opening Day before Wrigley Field underwent the changes that made it recognizable to today's fans. On Opening Day 1937, the dimensions were 354 feet to the left-field line, 364 to the "jury box" bleachers in left center, 440 feet to center, 356 to right center, and 321 to the line in right. The scoreboard was still in deep center with the Cubs' game data on the left, NL line scores in the middle, and AL line scores on the right. Just off the right-field foul line, the Sheffield Building, which in previous years had boasted advertisements for the Marigold Garden, now carried a sign hawking Prager Beer, a brand lost to history.

For 1937, the Cubs unveiled new uniforms, the first in many years to use the logo with a large "C" and little "u-b-s" that adorns Chicago players' chests to this day. Otis Shepard, the art director of the Wrigley Company, designed the new suits in collaboration with Wrigley. Shepard, an outstanding graphic artist, was responsible for the spectacular game program designs the Cubs used from the 1940s through 1971.

CONTROL

The Andy Frain Company began serving Wrigley Field with game-day ushers in 1925. By 1937, Frain had bought uniforms for the young employees ("Andy Frain's Stylists") who flipped the turnstiles at the ballpark. Andy Frain ushers and security served at the ballpark until the early 1980s, when the Cubs chose to hire and train their own security force.

Around this time, the Cubs instituted a new crowd-control innovation: ringing the playing field at game's end with ushers. *The Sporting News* noted in June 1938 that the Cincinnati Reds had adopted "two Chicago Cub innovations—building many field boxes and stationing ushers around the diamond to protect the infield from the crowds when the game is over." This practice kept fans under control and protected the playing surface.

PRESENTING . . . THE OUTFIELD!

The Cubs announced in June 1937 plans to again fiddle with the outfield, choosing to ring the entire spectrum, from foul pole to foul pole, with seats. This time, the changes would stick. Management estimated the cost of the project at between $150,000 and $200,000.

Philip Wrigley made the decision, which would increase the bleacher capacity from thirty-five hundred to approximately eighty-five hundred, partially because the Cubs were involved in a pennant fight. Irving Vaughan reported in the July 1, 1937, *Sporting News* that "the bleachers are being enlarged sufficiently to add seating space for 5,000, which space will come in handy if a World's Series is played here."

Ed Burns of the *Tribune*, however, wrote in December 1937 that money wasn't Wrigley's chief motivation for expansion. "The desire for scenic distinction probably was more of an incentive than the desire to spring the capacity of the field." While it's difficult to believe that an objective sportswriter could write such a thing, Burns's article does point out Wrigley's belief in aesthetics. One assumes that Wrigley thought it was a better idea to spend the money on permanent bleachers than to go to the trouble of building temporary ones every few seasons. The city of Chicago, forced to close down streets to accommodate the temporary bleachers, might have thought so as well.

ENTER JUNIOR

P. K. Wrigley signed off on the idea to expand the bleachers, then turned the project over to Bill Veeck Jr., who had been working at the park since 1934. When Veeck *fils* began to make his name in Chicago, many in the press refused to take him seriously. But despite his goofy demeanor, overblown presence, and sometimes scene-stealing antics, he did good things for Wrigley Field and his presence is still felt.

Veeck loved baseball, and he loved nightlife. Following his frequent nights on the town, he would often sleep at the firehouse near the left-field gate. Marketing and promotion were his areas of interest—he constantly argued with Wrigley on behalf of new ways to bring people to the park. This customer chasing was undignified, Wrigley felt, and Veeck fumed.

In spring 1937, Wrigley asked Veeck to start negotiating with different architectural designers, and eventually Holabird & Root were retained to do the work on expanding Wrigley Field.

CUBS HALL OF FAME?

On June 16, the Cubs introduced a bat rack in their home dugout. No more would the team's bats lie in front of the dugout, in foul territory, where fielders chasing pop flies might trip over them. A week later, on June 23, the Cubs unveiled a plaque of former first baseman and manager Frank Chance. This was to be the first exhibit in a planned Cubs Hall of Fame. Both Johnny

Evers and Joe Tinker, the late Chance's double-play partners, were on hand for the ceremony, along with "Three Finger" Brown and Jimmy Archer.

This date also marked the end of an era for Wrigley Field; the next day, workers began constructing a temporary left-field wall.

ANOTHER BRICK IN THE WALL

On Thursday, June 24, workers began the first phase of the bleacher project. The first step was to install a nine-and-a-half-foot-tall wall about nineteen feet in front of the current left-field brick wall. This fence was put in on a trial basis so that the Cubs could evaluate how the shorter dimensions would affect the game. "I remember a green partition in 1937 as part of the new wall," recalled Chicago radio veteran "Red" Mottlow. "I believe the partition was where the actual new bleachers wall would be. I saw [Cubs outfielder] Frank Demaree hit the ball over the partition in batting practice."

Left field would be shrunk considerably any way you sliced it. The original plan called for left field, at its closest point to the hitter, to sit just 335 feet away. The new wall would slant backward before reaching the foul poles so that each foul pole would be 341 feet from the plate. This plan was altered just two weeks later, apparently based on some feedback from players and/ or the press. The July 4 *Tribune* reported, "The new plan calls for stands built on the bias so as not to shorten the left foul line as much as had been intended when the scenic fence was erected."

Irving Vaughan, in the July 15 *TSN*, put in his two cents: "The revamping plans . . . have been altered, either because the officials didn't like the criticism of the short fences which would be created or because somebody erred in figuring the distances from home plate."

The new plans meant that straightaway left (and right) would be farther from the hitters and the new bleachers would curve toward the foul poles, making the distance to the poles deeper as well. The final foul line measurements of 355 and 353 feet, which remain to this day, give the Cubs the deepest foul lines in the major leagues. The wall would now be twelve feet high, rather than the original nine and a half feet. One assumes that pitchers everywhere breathed a sigh of relief.

Holabird & Root designed the new bleachers, with both Otis Shepard and Wrigley involved. Wrigley's new bleachers, according to the July 10, 1937, *Tribune*, would be made of "reinforced concrete construction supported by an open steel framework. Smooth pipe railing and woven wire fences will afford protection where required." The new seats, again constructed from slats of wood, were this time made of a longer-lasting cypress.

The shortening of left field was to be balanced by an increase in the size of right field. The removal of the old right-field bleachers, and the installation of new ones, would give the pasture some extra playing room. Center field, long a Death Valley in Wrigley, would be chopped to a more hitter-friendly four hundred feet. As a result of the new bleachers, fans seated in the outfield would no longer be on ground level; all the new bleachers would be located above the twelve-foot wall. This was a significant change; since the park's construction in 1914, there had *always* been some field-level bleacher seats.

The left-field bleachers were built first, and following that, the Cubs tore out the right-field seats and installed new ones.

GET ON UP

The decision to build the new outfield seats high above the ground was made for several reasons. First, the grounds crew needed covered space in which to store their mowing, rolling, chalking, and planting equipment, as well as the tarpaulin and batting cage. At the time, Bob Dorr had been forced to store most of his gear in the uncovered space down near both foul lines, and the equipment suffered whenever rain fell. Dorr wished, for example, to keep his state-of-the-art lawn mower, which was capable of the unprecedented speed of thirty miles per hour, from getting rusty. The mower got enough moisture anyway; at times, after morning rain, the grounds crew would immediately cut the lawn so that the field would dry more quickly.

The new brick outfield wall featured six embedded metal doors for purposes of allowing the grounds crew to move equipment on and off the field. The storage section also housed pitching machines, batting cages, and the like. The doors, reddish-brown for years, were painted green in the 1980s. Second, the space under the bleachers near the corner of Waveland and Sheffield Avenues would provide room for restrooms, kitchens, and ticket windows. Third, in accordance with Wrigley's standards of upkeep and conformity, the Cubs simply wanted to present a new look, an outfield design more modern, slick, and consistent than the charming but frankly slapdash look that Wrigley Field had sported for twenty-four years.

So out went the field-level bleachers, the slightly ramshackle 440-foot center-field fence constructed of corrugated metal, the old-styled scoreboard, and the small left-field jury box jutting from a harsh brick wall. In came a smooth, tailored, more symmetrical outfield design.

Distances to the outfield walls were displayed on white-painted plywood numbers screwed into the wall. In the late 1940s, the numbers were at ballplayers' waist level but were moved higher in the 1960s. By the 1980s, the Cubs simply decided to paint the dimensions directly on the brick, this time in yellow.

Last and probably not least, the Cubs almost certainly wanted to control the crowds. The reserved P. K. Wrigley couldn't have thought much of the fans-rushing-the-field custom, common when Weeghman and even William Wrigley owned the team. Things were different in America by the late 1930s; emerging from the financial crisis of 1929, the land was becoming increasingly conservative. P. K. Wrigley, though he was something of a maverick concerning the way organizations and machines should operate, believed in uniformity as it related to his products.

The new bleachers changed the game considerably for fans; they would no longer be as close. But the new view from the Wrigley Field bleachers was equally beautiful. Change in the field also affected the players, who would now have to deal with a hard brick wall all around the park, rather than just in left field. The eventual addition of ivy didn't make the outfield wall any less painful to run into.

BOARD WITH IT ALL

The final Wrigley Field contests before new bleachers were actually built came July 6, 1937, when thirty-nine thousand fans watched the Cubs sweep St. Louis in a doubleheader, 13–12 and 9–7. The first game went fourteen innings, which meant that the second game didn't even *begin* until after 6:00 p.m.

On July 9, the John Griffiths & Son Company began deconstructing and reconstructing the bleacher seats. The center-field scoreboard, still sporting the Doublemint Twins figures, was the first order of business. The builders ripped the scoreboard in half, disposed of the portion including the American League line scores, and reinstalled what was left about fifty feet off the left-field line, where it would remain in operation until the end of the 1937 campaign.

As a result of this surgery, instead of "Wrigley Field, Home of Chicago Cubs," fans beyond the ballpark fences now saw on the back of the scoreboard, "ey Field, ome of go Cubs."

I CAN'T REACH YOU

On August 13, the Cubs whipped the Reds 22–6. During the game, the public address system went down, forcing field announcer Pat Pieper to use a hastily procured megaphone to communicate lineup changes.

WHITE SHIRT

The new bleachers opened for the first time on September 5, 1937, for a doubleheader against the Pirates. The Cubs lost both games, 7–0 and 4–1. Only a three-thousand-seat center-field section of the new bleachers was available, but the new layout immediately proved a problem. With the Cubs still fighting for first place and a huge crowd in the new outfield seats, hitters immediately noticed that they couldn't see the ball coming from the pitcher's hand. Before the new bleachers, the dark-hued center-field fence had served as a helpful hitting background.

Ed Burns wrote, in the September 8, 1937, *Tribune*, "The Cubs are worried about the new bleachers, opened for the first time last week. When the plans were first announced, the Cubs figured it would have a depressing effect on their hitting when any except a sidearm or underhand pitcher was facing them. After Monday's experience trying to hit into the shirtsleeve background against Paul Derringer and Lee Grissom, both of whom are more overhand than otherwise, the Cubs are convinced their early fears are justified."

Players were upset at having to adjust to an entirely new hitting background during the season. In May 1937, Mickey Cochrane had sustained a career-ending skull fracture when Bump Hadley drilled him. Most of the sportswriters of the time treated the players' complaints on this issue with contempt, insinuating that they were just whiners more concerned with their batting averages than with winning. Few in the press bothered to really analyze the issue; otherwise they would have understood that making such a severe change virtually overnight was bound to affect the way hitters performed.

In addition, it wasn't just .180-hitting scrubeenies who were complaining. In September, Ed Burns noted that both Cubs and Cardinals players were already complaining that the bleacher fans' white shirts were too close to the color of the baseball. But little of consequence was done to address the hitters' concerns for nearly four years. The new bleachers were too lucrative to shut down, even on a trial basis.

BREAKDOWN

The Cubs led the National League by six and a half games on August 12, but poor performance that month against second-division teams and a disastrous road trip allowed the Giants to catch and pass them in September. But the Cubs still clung to hopes of winning, and on September 18 they began accepting applications by mail for World Series tickets.

Chastened by the nightmare of 1935's abortive "public sale," Wrigley went back to the old by-mail plan. With Games Three, Four, and Five scheduled for play in the NL winner's park, the Cubs sold tickets, two to a customer, through the post. Available in strips of all three games, they cost $19.80 for boxes and $16.50 for reserved seats.

The ducats wouldn't be used. The Giants came to town on September 21 up two and a half games. After the Cubs won to slice the lead to one and a half, 41,875 fans crammed into the "new" Wrigley on September 22, filling the entire outfield bleacher section, which had been thrown open on September 19. Fans lined the catwalks down the left- and right-field lines and even sat on the fences overlooking the catwalks. The *Daily News* reported that the warm weather meant that the bleacherites were "in their shirtsleeves, making it look like a mid-July afternoon. And, incidentally, making the hitters moan a bit more about 'them white shirts.'"

All seats in the bleachers were fifty cents. P. K. Wrigley had special ticket windows designed for the bleacher section—"cupolas so elegant," wrote Ed Burns in *The Sporting News*, "that the boys in the $1.65 end of the park, the main entrance guys, are jealous."

Unfortunately for the fans, the Giants won 6–0 on September 22, then won again the next day.

IVY, IVY

P. K. Wrigley decided late in 1937 that he wanted to plant ivy on the entire outfield wall. He asked Bill Veeck to implement the change. "I had planned on planting it at the end of the season, after the bleachers had been completely rebuilt," Veeck wrote in his autobiography. "By the time the new season came around, the ivy would have caught and Mr. Wrigley would have his outdoor atmosphere. The Cubs were ending the season with a long road trip, returning home only in the final week for one last series. The day before the team was to return, Mr. Wrigley called me in to tell me he had invited some people to the park to watch the game and gaze upon his ivy." So, according to Veeck, overnight he and several assistants planted the ivy just for the last Cubs series of the year, against the Cardinals, which began on October 1.

Another terrific story, but not true. Either Veeck's memory was off when he wrote his autobiography, or he was exaggerating for dramatic effect. The planting was done prior to the last series of the year. Cubs historian Ed Hartig notes that the September 14, 1937 *Chicago Cubs News* publication contains a photo of some scraggly-looking planting on the outfield walls. In addition, newspaper photos from the Cubs–Giants series of September 21–23 clearly show the vegetation, and it's in the same pattern as existed on the outfield walls on Opening Day 1938.

Most of the growth was actually at the bottom of the outfield walls, because the planting was done, of course, from the ground up. s not clear exactly when the landscaping was done, but Ed Hartig estim s that it might have been planted on September 3, 1937. Since the official team publication of the time ran a story about it, this was no big secret, as Veeck might have us believe.

Second, as Veeck himself noted, it wasn't even ivy. Whatever the reason for P. K.'s insistence on having the planting done, a call to the Elmer Clavey Nursery in northwest suburban Woodstock confirmed that ivy could *not* simply be planted overnight. Informed that the answer to their problems was a fairly hardy and quick-growing vine called bittersweet, Veeck and groundskeeper Bob Dorr got to work. Under a string of lightbulbs attached to the top of the brick outfield wall, Veeck, Dorr, and a few others, including twenty-year-old Gordon Clavey, covered the wall with the newly purchased bittersweet.

Per Wrigley's orders for a beautiful green wall, 350 Japanese bittersweet were planted to give the bleachers some color for the short term—although the result was, in September 1937, far from the lush growth we have grown accustomed to today. Two hundred strands of ivy were also planted in between the bittersweet, and eventually ivy, which grows slower but more thickly, became the dominant plant. On April 18, 1938, Wayne Otto of the *Herald and Examiner* noted that the ivy wasn't yet fully grown. "Don't overlook the shrubbery and vines that will decorate the bleacher walls this summer."

Gordon Clavey, who lived until 1998, eventually became president of the family nursery in Woodstock.

CONCESSION SPEECH

By the late 1930s, Wrigley Field's concession stands were believed to be the best in the business. This wasn't accidental. P. K. Wrigley gave Bill Veeck Jr. the freedom and necessary funds to design the right kind of concession stands, and according to Veeck (who, at times, exaggerated), it took more than one try.

> Concessions are a whole little world in themselves, a world that has continued to fascinate me. You would be amazed how much sheer psychology is involved in selling a hot dog and beer. In designing the new concession stands at Wrigley Field, I wanted to install fluorescent lighting. I was told that fluorescent lighting could not be used outdoors because, as everyone knew, the lights wouldn't work in the cold.
>
> Well, baseball isn't exactly a winter sport. I told them to put in the fluorescents anyway and we'd see what happened. What happened was that the lights worked fine . . . what also happened was that our business immediately fell off drastically.
>
> I had made the mistake—in the luck of the draw—of choosing a hard blue-white fluorescent, a lighting particularly cruel to women. Women seem

to be born with some tribal instinct about these things; they would not come to the stands no matter *how* hungry they were. We changed to a soft rose-white, which is flattering to women, and quickly picked up the old business and more besides.

KNOW THE SCORE

The new hundred-thousand-dollar scoreboard, completed late in 1937 and installed atop the new upper-center-field bleachers, was, and still is, a marvel. Combining a slick late 1930s design with a smart rendering of all the information a fan needs to know, the seventy-five-foot-wide, twenty-seven-foot-high structure remains one of the best boards in sports. The game information is located in the center of the board, with eyelets conveying the ball and strike count, the outs, and the batter's uniform number. Line scores from both leagues fill either side of the board. Oddly enough, the man who designed the scoreboard for the Cubs didn't follow through with the project. He skipped out on Veeck and the team, forcing Veeck to do a lot of the work himself.

A helpful innovation, especially for the sportswriters of the time, was the use of yellow numbers on the line scores to indicate innings in progress. This tradition began in 1938. When an inning was finished, the number would be posted in white.

In 1938, a game clock for football was strapped to the bottom of the scoreboard. It was only in 1941 that the clock, which still stands today, was moved atop the board. This clock initially sported a white face with dark numbers and hands, but eventually was changed to the familiar green-faced, white-numbered, white-handed model.

A ton of steel was necessary to install the clock atop the scoreboard. Around the same time, the club painted the entire board the green with which we associate it today. Previously, the board had been a reddish-brown, but the new look gave the park even more consistency.

The new scoreboard was put into operation for the first time on Friday, October 1, 1937, with a Ladies Day crowd of 15,667 on hand. The Cubs lost 4–1. While the press was effusive in its praise of the scoreboard's design, they were equally disappointed with the board's lack of utility; the inning-by-inning numbers were too small for anyone to see clearly. By Opening Day 1938, this problem had been addressed. By that day, an auxiliary scoreboard—this one electronic—had also been installed in the middle of the upper-deck grandstand. This was done so the folks in the upper deck wouldn't have to strain their necks and eyes toward center field if they had lost track of what was going on.

THERE IS A LIGHT THAT NEVER GOES OUT

Even if you haven't gotten to the Cubs game, you can still tell who won or lost hours after the finish. White and blue flags fly above the field from the center-field scoreboard after the game's completion to tell who came out on top. Back in the 1940s, when the practice began, the winning flag was blue; now the winning flag is white with a large blue "W" on it.

In addition, you can tell who won the game by checking the light bulbs outside the scoreboard. This innovation came courtesy of Bill Veeck. As he wrote in *Veeck—as in Wreck*:

> There was only one promotional gimmick I ever got away with. Mr. Wrigley permitted me to install lights on top of the flagpole to let homeward-bound Elevated passengers know whether we had won or lost that day. The flagpole was on top of the new scoreboard, and at its summit I put a crossbar with a green light on one side and a red light on the other. The green light told the El passengers we had won, the red that we had lost . . . it wasn't much, but it was all I had and I was proud of it.

In the 1980s, the two lights' colors were changed to match the flags. A blue light doesn't mean a K Mart special—it means the Cubs have lost. A white light means a Chicago victory.

MARGARET DONAHUE

Margaret Donahue began working for the Chicago Cubs in 1919 as a stenographer. She eventually became club bookkeeper, responsible for collecting, counting, and maintaining the cash on the premises. She was one of the first women to assume this level of responsibility for a major league team.

The November 4, 1937, *TSN* ran a profile of her, written (per usual) by Ed Burns. Ms. Donahue noted that P. K. Wrigley had instituted several recent changes to make going to the ballpark easier for most fans: "After a three-year fight, he has been successful in introducing special tickets for children under 12 years of age, something which never before had been permitted. He has continued the idea of a beautiful park and always has before him the fans' comfort. In striving to provide comfort for them, he has replaced all the box seat chairs with larger and more comfortable ones, and has installed the more modern legless chairs in the grandstand."

It is interesting to note the Cubs' philosophy concerning ballpark seating. At the time, fans paying more money for box seats were put in portable chairs and could be crammed more closely to one another during a World Series. Meanwhile, the fans in the grandstand were in bolted seats that *didn't* move around. One would assume the "legless" chairs to be more comfortable.

The Cubs apparently believed that their box-seat fans valued proximity to the action rather than seating comfort. While in most new parks, the highest-priced tickets are for plush seats, Wrigley Field still adheres to a more democratic process—seats in the different sections are identical.

SAVED YOUR NECK

In January 1938, the Cubs began a project to help their fans avoid painful neck strain. As Irving Vaughan wrote in *The Sporting News*,

> Work will start shortly on another improvement at Wrigley Field. . . . approximately $125,000 will be spent rearranging some of the [left field] seats so that the occupants thereof will be able to see the game without having to look over their right shoulders. Next year, the right-field end will be curved in similar fashion.
>
> The plan provides that the last couple of sections of the left field extremity, involving about 5,000 seats, be curved toward the bleacher, thus turning the chairs in the direction of home plate by about 30 degrees. As it is now, the fans in the ends of the stand see only the left and center fielders if they look straight out from where they are sitting. Visibility also will be improved by slanting the boxes in the regular section up to a point level with the left field wall.

While the Cubs fully intended to turn the right-field bleachers in 1939, the money apparently wasn't there to do it. Then the war came. The project wasn't completed until after the 1951 season.

Warren Brown also commented that "the size of the chairs was increased, with a resultant drop in the park's seating capacity, but a tremendous increase in the comfort of patrons who had been jammed together on big days." Box seat capacity was reduced to 14,097, and there were now only 19,343 grandstand seats.

The dressing rooms for the players and umpires were also upgraded, with new facilities and improved plumbing. The tiles in the shower rooms were rendered in a striking shade of orchid. Brown noted that in addition, "More attention was given to sound equipment and other details connected with the proper presentation of a ball game."

Vaughan also commented that players would have a new and better place to, er, expectorate: "It is possible that even brass cuspidors will be provided in place of the Bowery-like gobboons which now serve as targets." Times certainly have changed. These days, players just spit their tobacco juice on the dugout floor.

ANOTHER BRICK IN THE WALL PART II

Prior to the 1938 season, the Cubs made additional renovations. One of them involved constructing an attractive brick wall from foul line to foul line, which replaced the earlier stone and wire fence. Wrigley Field's brick wall remains today and is such an identifier of the "good old days" that the Houston Astros, for one, have installed a similar wall in their new park.

Gone also in the new setup was the foot-high barrier rising above the dugouts; fans now had a better view of the field from the box seats.

When the seats were turned down the left-field line, they had to be raised somewhat from ground level. As a result, the brick wall, four feet high at most parts, rose sharply as it moved down the left-field line toward the foul pole.

In addition to the cosmetic changes, the park also received a structural boost. The Cubs replaced the original building materials from 1914 with brand-new steel and concrete and also took the opportunity to improve their concession stands under the grandstand. Fans lining up to buy food and beverages now stood beneath attractive red and orange awnings.

Public address announcer Pat Pieper was given additional responsibilities for 1938. From this point on, every player's name and position was to be broadcast into the microphone the first time in the game that the player came to bat.

PERFECT NIRVANA

Another renovation made to Wrigley was the outdoor paint job. The entire park had been repainted in gray and reddish-brown, the last color matching the scoreboard. All of the park's chairs had been repainted in an attractive Kelly green.

Wrigley's 1938 lid lifter, an April 15 City Series tilt, saw the "bleachers filled almost to capacity," noted John Carmichael of the *Daily News*. But despite the new bleacher design, the crowd was no better behaved than usual. "Customers had fights over two home run balls by Rip Collins and 'Bozey' Berger before the game was halfway along."

All in all, Wrigley had spent $350,000 in repairs from fall 1937 to spring 1938, and he reaped plenty of benefits from the enthusiastic local press, who agreed that the Cubs indeed were in Nirvana. Carmichael waxed, "The Cub park glistened like a newly turned out streamlined train. A new seat arrangement, fresh paint everywhere, and refurnished dressing rooms caught the eye. There isn't a layout in either league to touch it for class at the moment."

The *Herald-Examiner*'s Wayne Otto called Wrigley "the ultra in outdoor sports palaces." Warren Brown, in 1946, made these notes: "Here was now the most beautiful of all the country's ballparks. It possessed a distinct type of bleacher, skirting the outfield. In dead center, high above the top row of the stands, was a mammoth scoreboard, perhaps the outstanding feature of the face-lifting job . . . In this streamlined setting, every wish of the patrons for comfort was satisfied. Concession stands and restrooms for the bleacher-ites were above what was considered standard in other ballparks for grand-stand and box-seat patrons. There was a blending of colors within the field which enhance the beauty of the place."

The idea that Wrigley's spartan, at best, bleacher facilities were better than those in box seat sections at other parks sets the mind reeling.

THE ARRIVAL OF DEAN

On Opening Day 1938, the Cubs debuted Dizzy Dean, the sore-armed, wily, and phenomenally popular right-hander, newly acquired from the Cardinals for $185,000 and three players. Red Mottlow remembers: "I saw Dean in the home opener in 1938. They played it up pretty big. Fortunately my father, Harry, got box seats behind first base. It was a wonderful day, the place was packed. It was an exciting home-opener crowd."

Mottlow's memory fails a bit. Dean pitched the season's *third* game, against the Cardinals on Sunday April 24, and shut out his former team-mates 5–0 in front of 34,520 fans. Dean couldn't pitch often, having devel-oped arm problems by adjusting his motion to deal with the pain inflicted by a broken toe. P. K. Wrigley knew, however, that the extra customers Dean brought in would more than compensate for the money spent acquiring him.

Wrigley Field's official 1938 NL opening came on Friday, April 22. Wrig-ley was noticeably absent, having traveled to Los Angeles to look over the Angels' ballpark. "He is going to miss Jack Bramhall's band today," joked Warren Brown in the *Herald and Examiner*, "when it blares forth those dulcet notes that make conversation within a range of a quarter of a mile impossi-ble." Bramhall's band was, as usual, seated behind home plate deep in the lower grandstand, which bothered the press corps, situated just above, to no end.

ELM DALE

Sometimes P. K. Wrigley didn't know when enough was enough. One of his less brilliant schemes to beautify the "new" Wrigley was to install fully grown Chinese elm trees on the concrete "steps" leading to the scoreboard on the upper center-field bleacher level. Wrigley wanted *full-grown* Chinese elms, and he wanted them yesterday.

Bill Veeck was put in charge of this project. He noticed that the high winds around the park would continually blow the leaves off the newly planted trees. "It took about ten sets of trees before Mr. Wrigley began to spot a trend," Veeck wrote later. "The trees were quite inexpensive; the footings cost about $200,000." As a result, this part of the beautification process was abandoned in the early 1940s.

DULL AND UNINTERESTING IN COMPARISON

Margaret Donahue's *TSN* profile gives an idea of what a big crowd at Wrigley Field was like in those days.

> There is plenty of excitement in handling capacity crowds as well as heartaches when you have to close the gates and turn down thousands who are waiting to get in, some of whom had stood in line for hours. The pleading for tickets, standing room or anything, is pathetic, as there is nothing you can do once the capacity is reached. With thousands of people milling around, shoving, and crowding, there is always danger of accidents, as frequently gates are crashed and people pushed and shoved and almost walked upon. It is queer how throngs of people little realize the danger at a time like this.
>
> I remember a woman and small child narrowly escaping injury when the gate fell as the crowds crashed one of our main entrances. The big days are the ones I enjoy most, however, the others being dull and uninteresting in comparison.

It must not have been much fun to work for the team at that point; everyone wanted a favor, a ticket, or something. "In the 1929 series we turned down enough ticket requests to sell out the park a second time," said Donahue. "After it is all over you will find you haven't a friend left in the world, no matter how many you may have taken care of."

Sometime before 1938, the Collins & Weise coal yard directly west of Wrigley Field was abandoned. This allowed for increased fan parking; more people had started driving to the ballpark. In addition, this further opened up Seminary Avenue, parallel to the park, for autos. A train line and a trolley line, still cutting through the Clark and Addison intersection, caused plenty of traffic jams, but a large parking lot on the northwest corner of Clark and Addison stored hundreds of cars.

PENNANT RACE?

Every Cubs fan believed that the 1938 National League pennant was a cinch even before Dean was brought on board. But the Pittsburgh Pirates started the season hot and held the league lead. The Cubs were three and a half games in back of the Bucs on September 18. But the Cubs began to win, and the Pirates began to lose. At one point, the Cubs took seventeen games in a twenty-game stretch.

On September 26, eight photographers on the field got in the way of a possible run-scoring wild pitch. According to the *Tribune*'s Ed Burns, "The hypo squad was banked solid a few feet from the right of the plate . . . when Davis caromed a wild pitch off Owen's glove. Owen plunged into the huddle and got the ball. Hack could have scored easily had he been able to see just where the ball was." Burns went on to note, "The umpires, however, scattered the photogs, but with sympathetic appreciation that the lads simply were earning an honest dollar."

While photographers no longer are found in the playing field—most of them are in specially constructed "photo wells" past the dugouts—they are *not officially banned* from the field. Rule 3.15 states: "No person shall be allowed on the playing field during a game except players and coaches in uniform, managers, news photographers authorized by the home team, umpires, officers of the law in uniform, and watchmen or other employees of the home club."

WALK THE PLANK

Pittsburgh came to town on September 27 just a game and a half ahead. As the *Tribune*'s Ed Burns wrote, "42,238 giddy guests" were at Wrigley Field for the Cubs' 2–1 win. Among the giddy were league presidents Will Harridge and Ford Frick.

Dizzy Dean, who missed most of the year with various miseries, went $8^2/_3$ innings for the win. Bill Lee came in to strike out Woody Jensen to end the game and send the fans into a tizzy as Al Todd, the tying run, stood on third base. The Pirates' lead was now the slimmest of margins—just a half-game.

GABBY ST.

The game of September 28 would go down as one of the greatest in Cubs history—and if not for a prescient decision made the previous day, things might have turned out very differently. It was announced in the morning papers of September 28 that the game's starting time was moved from 3:00 p.m. to 2:30 in order to ensure that extra innings wouldn't result in the game being called on account of darkness. Critical late-season games at Wrigley had previously been started early—for instance, the Cubs–Giants show-downs of the previous September.

September 28 was already dark and threatening as 34,465 fans entered the park. The Cubs went up 1–0 in the second, but the Pirates scored three in the sixth to take the lead. The Cubs knotted things 3–3 in the bottom of the sixth, but the Bucs went ahead 5–3 in the eighth before three Chicago pitchers stemmed the tide.

Darkness was beginning to fall at Wrigley Field, but the Cubs came back in the eighth. With two men on, old pro Tony Lazzeri doubled home Rip Collins, and Stan Hack knocked in Billy Jurges for the tie. At this point, the ballpark resembled an insane asylum. As Ed Burns wrote in the *Tribune*, "Mob ecstasy was choked by bitter disappointment, only to be supplanted by more ecstasy with more disappointment."

Before the bottom of the ninth, the score still 5–5, the umpires, looking at the sky, realized that this would have to be the last inning. With the Cubs having used six pitchers already, a doubleheader the next day did not appear to be a winning proposition. Pittsburgh's Mace Brown retired Phil Cavaretta on a fly to center field and Carl Reynolds on a ground out to start the home ninth. He got two strikes on Gabby Hartnett, and some fans began to gather up their belongings.

Next, Brown threw his signature curve, and Hartnett swung. Years later, Hartnett would tell Jim Enright of the *American*, "I've read and heard it said that I closed my eyes and swung the bat with everything I possessed. That is only half true. I was swinging for the downs, but my eyes were never more wide open because I had a good look at the curve ball Mace served up." Hartnett belted the ball deep to left field, where it disappeared in the growing darkness. Plate umpire George Barr watched the ball soar and eventually raised his right arm—home run.

"You have seen them rush out to greet a hero after he touched the plate to terminate a great contest," Burns wrote. "Well, you never saw nothin'. The mob started to gather around Gabby before he had reached first base. By the time he had rounded second, he couldn't have been recognized in the mass of Cub players, frenzied fans, and excited ushers but for that red face, which shone out even in the gray shadows."

Thousands of delirious fans helped escort Hartnett around the bases, with dozens of blue-suited Andy Frain ushers doing their best to protect the Cub hero, pushing rooters out of the way and giving Hartnett some sort of path to each bag. Years later, public address announcer Pat Pieper recalled, "That was the only time I ever lost my head. I ran to third base, carrying my ball bag, and escorted Gabby across the plate."

"There was new hysteria," according to Burns, "after Gabby reached the catwalk [behind the third-base dugout] that leads to the clubhouse. But this time the gendarmes were organized. Gabby got to the bath house without being stripped by souvenir maniacs." Meanwhile, Mace Brown, the league's best relief pitcher, sat in the Pirate clubhouse and sobbed.

Hartnett, a six-time All-Star and Hall of Famer, is one of the greatest Cubs ever. In 1969, retired nearly thirty years, he was number two in an all-time Cubs popularity poll, finishing behind Ernie Banks. And on September 28, 1938, he probably could have been elected prime minister of Ireland, mayor of Chicago, and pope at the same time.

And how in the world would this game have turned out if it had been started at the regular time of 3:00?

THIS IS JUST TO SAY

The Cubs whipped the demoralized Pirates 10–1 the next day, then went to St. Louis and clinched the flag. On October 3, the Cubs were beneficiaries of a huge parade that began at 11:30 a.m. at Wrigley Field and picked up steam as it headed downtown. The party moved down Addison to Lake Shore Drive, then south down Michigan Avenue toward City Hall. Around a million people watched the parade.

Once downtown, the accumulated throng listened to music from the Chicago Police Band and cheered the players, who were individually introduced to the crowd from a platform as Mayor Ed Kelly looked on. Meanwhile, the grounds crew quickly readied the park for the first two games of the World Series against the powerful New York Yankees. The field had to be fixed after the post-Hartnett riot.

To prepare for the onslaught of writers arriving for the Series, the Cubs strung up a special intercom system from the main press box to the overflow press box in the upper deck (as well as to the radio booths) to ensure that everyone knew the official scorer's decisions. According to Arch Ward in the October 5 *Tribune*, more than one hundred wire connections were installed in the press areas to allow newsmen covering the games to file their stories.

Ward also reported that Ray Kniepp, concessions manager at Wrigley Field, ordered "72,000 redhots, 1,600 pounds of baked ham, 1,600 pounds of roast beef, 6,000 dozen rolls, 800 two-pound loaves of bread, 42,000 bags of popcorn, 3,000 cases of pop, and 400 pounds of coffee" for the first two contests.

DOLLARS

In the ticket department, the typical "pay for three games, maybe get two" setup of tickets-by-mail was in effect, with costs remaining $6.50 for box seats and $5.50 for reserved grandstand. Regular season prices in 1938 had been $1.65 for boxes, $1.10 for reserved grandstands, and 55 cents for bleachers.

Reversing his regular policy of box-seat comfort, largely because he knew he'd make a lot more money doing it, Wrigley chose to cram more and smaller chairs into the swell sections, expanding seating capacity for the Series to more than forty thousand rather than the usual 37,500.

Fans snapped up all 32,660 pre-sale tickets almost immediately. According to the *Tribune* of October 4, the Cubs raked in $659,000 in advance ticket sales. The eight thousand bleacher seats went on sale for $1.10 at 9:00 a.m. before each Series game. (There were also three thousand standing-room-only ducats at $3.30 apiece, which were sold at 10:00 a.m. the day of each contest.) Some fans stood in line for several days in order to get a good seat in the bleachers for Game One on October 5. By the evening of October 4, some two thousand were in line, and ten thousand others strolled or drove their cars around the neighborhood, just wanting to be in on the fun and excitement.

HALF STAFF

The press made a big deal out of the fact that for the first time, both league pennants would be unfurled and displayed at the Series. "Until 1935, no team ever raised its pennant until the following season," gasped the *Tribune*. "That year, the Cubs raised theirs before the first series game in Wrigley Field."

By this time, the Wrigley Field practice of displaying the flags of NL clubs by their standing, on yardarms on each side of the 190-foot-tall center-field flagpole, was already established. This remains one of the park's most charming customs. Close to the scoreboard was a large sign advertising "Baby Ruth" chocolate bars. The sign, erected in the middle 1930s, was located on a building on Sheffield Avenue past the right-center-field wall. Some believe that the sign was put up there because it's close to where Babe Ruth's 1932 "called shot" homer sailed.

GAME ONE

A complete sellout—43,660 fans—stuffed Wrigley Field for the first game, which began at 1:30 p.m. Bleacher seats sold out in ninety minutes, and the standing-room tickets were gone by noon. The American Legion's Board of Trade Band supplied the music (where was Jack Bramhall?), and pleasant weather greeted everyone—including dozens of fans who sat on curbs around the ballpark and looked up at the scoreboard in order to follow what was going on. Some fans tried to perch in the trees around the park to get a good view, but the cops kept busy flushing the climbers back to the ground.

Arch Ward of the *Tribune* reported that Andy Frain hired 737 ushers, including six captains each from his Los Angeles and Brooklyn operations, to handle the World Series crowds. Additionally, 656 Chicago policemen were also assigned to traffic duty around the park. Andy Frain's men appear to have done their jobs quite well, at least in one documented instance. One-Eyed Connolly, the non-paying Houdini from 1929, did not get inside this time. Ward noted that the gate-crashing legend "was still on the outside when [Frankie] Crosetti stepped to the plate to start the series."

Maybe Frain should have brought in a few new ballplayers. Perhaps worn out from their tight pennant race, the flat Cubs lost 3–1 to Red Ruffing.

THE LEDGE

Far more than 43,660 fans saw the game—and far more than 43,660 paid. The buildings on Waveland and Sheffield Avenues once again became private businesses. Marcia Winn penned a piece for the October 6 *Tribune* in which she sorted out this 1938 version of the underground economy: "Peanut galleries, known also as window boxes or observatories, are what has become of windows space in homes fronting on the park. In these the right of gazing is rented out at scalpers' prices, usually to latecomers or fans from out of town. For an ordinary ballgame, a window sells for 50 cents. Yesterday standing room ten feet behind a crowded window—where you could manage to see if you could find a ladder to stand on—sold for a minimum of $2. A box seat, one directly in front of the window, sold for $4.40 and up."

According to Winn, Mrs. Fred Nelson of 3625 Sheffield had forty-three viewers crammed into two front rooms. Another housewife on Waveland stuffed fifty-seven paying customers into her front rooms. The same humanitarian spirit that led Wrigley to place more chairs in the box sections also led this woman to open her doors if the visitors came with money in hand. "I'd hate," the woman said, "for anyone not to see the game. It makes me so excited, baseball, that I almost jump out the window."

Winn went on to note that fans also were seated on table leaves propped in tiers in front of windows, on ledges, and on fire escapes. Police, however, remained vigilant in their efforts to keep fans from watching the games from rooftops—even their own. Lieutenant Michael Ahern of the Town Hall Police Station told Winn that the practice of standing on the roof to watch is "illegal and it is dangerous."

SCALPED

The ticket brokers did just fine. Before Game One, a set of one ticket for each of the three games was going for as much as eighty dollars. But, as always, if you hung around for a while, you might do better. An hour before game time, the agencies at the downtown hotels were selling ducats for only a little more than list price. At least one well-known local politician was a beneficiary of this tactic. "At 1 o'clock Assistant State's Attorney Richard Devine paid $7.70 for a choice box seat at the Sherman hotel office," noted the *Tribune*. "The elevated railroad then transported him to the baseball park just in time for the beginning of the game."

Interest was also high for Game Two. According to the *Tribune*, "The highest price asked last night for a $6.60 box seat for the Cubs-Yankees baseball game at Wrigley Field today was $20 and the lowest was $11."

I'M SO DIZZY, MY HEAD IS SPINNING

The Cubs' backs were against the wall in Game Two as sore-armed Dizzy Dean took the mound before 42,108 fans. In the second inning, with the Cubs up 1–0 and two men on, Yankees second sacker Joe Gordon grounded a ball through the left side. Shortstop Billy Jurges and Stan Hack collided going after the ball. As Joe DiMaggio and Lou Gehrig crossed the dish, Dean himself had to track the ball down in short left field. The Cubs came back, however, to score twice in the third and still led 3–2 in the eighth. With Dean wearing down, New York shortstop Frank Crosetti homered for two runs. The exhausted Diz also allowed DiMaggio's towering two-run bomb onto Waveland in the ninth before exiting the mound to be relieved by Larry French.

The 6–3 loss broke the Cubs' spirit; they went to New York and lost 5–2 and 8–3, suffering their fourth Series loss, and second sweep, since 1929.

THE LAST OF CHARLEY

Charley Weeghman died on October 2, 1938. He was sixty-four. Weeghman had been vacationing in Hot Springs, Arkansas, with his second wife, Carol, and had stopped over in Chicago on the way back east. There, at the Drake Hotel, he suffered a stroke on September 27 and passed away.

In his last years, "Lucky Charley," who had severed his connections with the Weeghman's restaurant chain in 1923, managed the Riviera restaurant and dance hall in Fort Lee, New Jersey. While he had done all right, Weeghman did not die wealthy. He was buried in his hometown of Richmond, Indiana. Nobody associated with the team memorialized him or proposed naming any part of Wrigley Field in his honor, and since his death came at World Series time, the local press didn't waste much space honoring him.

Harry Neily, however, wrote a lengthy eulogy in *The Sporting News* that summed up Weeghman quite well: "Baseball has settled down since the Weeghman era, but if there were more Charley Weeghmans in the sport today, the duties of the scribes would be lightened, there would be more frivolity and mirth . . . Charley Weeghman was a showman and lived by the standards of that picturesque profession. He ran a shoestring into a million and when luck turned, nobody ever heard him complain. He really had a greater depth of character than his associates suspected, for he could take it when the going was tough."

NEIGHBORHOOD NEWS

The Germanic population of Lake View, which made up a majority of the neighborhood for many years, was pro-American during World War I. But now, two decades later, prior to World War II, some of the nationals were less interested in freedom and democracy. The Depression hit Chicago hard, and in tough times, people come up with some strange ideas.

In October 1938, some local Nazis held a meeting at Lincoln Turner Hall at Diversey and Halsted celebrating the annexation of the Sudetenland. The meeting, from which reporters were barred, was protested and picketed, mainly by German Americans and Bohemian Americans. The Nazis had rented the hall under the guise of putting on an "ordinary" meeting. Steven Bedell Clark, in *Lake View Saga*, notes that "members of neo-fascist groups like the German-American Bund openly paraded down *Lincolnstrasse* [Lincoln Avenue], and even staged a [Nuremberg]-style extravaganza one evening at [local fairground] Riverview Park. Lake View's traditionally easygoing German community seemed for a time bitterly divided over whether Hitler deserved their active support, cool neutrality or vigorous opposition."

The next year, another form of annexation was celebrated as locals held a Golden Jubilee festival in October 1939 to commemorate the annexation of Lake View by the city of Chicago. A mile-long parade served as the centerpiece to the eleven-day festival. Fifty thousand folks turned out to see the parade.

ANOTHER YEAR

The Cubs' 1938 success meant that 1939's Opening Day, set for April 18, had the biggest advance sale for an opener in many years. Unfortunately, rain kept the Cubs from beginning the season at Wrigley until April 24. When Chicago finally did play its first home game, there were no Opening Day ceremonies, no band, no nothing. The Cubs did install a microphone for the official scorer for the first time during a regular-season game, and a brand-new bar behind home plate won the admiration of fans. Large action photographs of infielder Billy Jurges were installed over the bar.

During the year, Addison Street between Clark and Sheffield was widened. A Standard Oil service station stood on the southwest corner of Clark and Sheffield, a site currently rented to a convenience store. As would befit a major intersection, several service stations dotted the area; Texaco had a station at 3553 N. Clark, and a new parking lot opened just west of Clark on the south side of Addison (where the Cubby Bear tavern is currently situated).

The Cubs, never serious contenders in 1939, finished fourth, thirteen games out. Nobody knew it, but the golden age of the Cubs had ended.

A CHANGE WILL DO YOU GOOD

The year 1941 was one of change at Wrigley Field. On Opening Day, April 15, Al Balder took over as scoreboard operator, replacing Charles Taubman—the Cubs' board operator since the nineteenth century—who had passed away over the winter.

In addition, reported Arch Ward in the *Tribune*, "For the first time since memory of man runneth not to the contrary, Jack Bramhall's band was missing from the Opening Day exercises." The previous year, 1940, the music-makers had entertained for the (allegedly) forty-eighth time at a curtain-raising Cubs contest. Bramhall's group apparently was a victim of the changing times. Instead of the old-time favorites his assembly provided, a swing band parked in the upper portion of the center-field bleachers provided the pregame entertainment. Ward noted sarcastically that Bramhall's band would still have been employed by the Cubs "if someone in other years had been so thoughtful as to remove them as far as possible from the customers."

Just 17,008 fans turned out on a cool and windy day to see the Cubs beat the Pirates 7–4. Of course, the ivy was not yet in bloom on the outfield wall, "which is a tough break for the hitters," according to Arch Ward, "who will have to wait until the leaves come out to enjoy a good background for the pitchers' slants."

The first batter of the game, Pirates second baseman Frankie Gustine, whistled a line drive off Cubs pitcher Claude Passeau's left shin. The hurler went down like he'd been shot, although he remained in the game, and players from *both* teams rushed to the mound. Rarely do you see that these days.

Many fans expected the Cubs to win the pennant in 1941, if only because of mathematics: they had won it every three years from 1929 to 1938. But by now, the rot had set in. After capturing the 1938 National League title, the Cubs suffered through nearly five decades of frustration, winning again only in 1945 when the war-depleted NL was especially weak. Over the next twenty-nine years, the Cubs enjoyed only *three* winning seasons.

KNIGHTS OF THE KEYBOARD

At least Wrigley continued to improve the scenery. On April 26, 1941, the Cubs instituted yet another innovation by installing the first organ at a ballpark. Roy Nelson was the man behind the keyboard at Wrigley Field when the pipe organ was installed. According to the May 1 *Sporting News*, Nelson "played a varied program of classic and soulful compositions at the premiere." The innovation was so popular that other clubs rushed to copy it. During the first home stand at which he tickled the ivories, Nelson had to stop playing at 2:30 when the radio pregame shows began. Rules at the time forbade songs from the ASCAP song publishing service from being played over the radio—even in the background—without compensation.

The *Tribune* reported on June 28 that in addition to the Nelson's usual popular and sacred songs, "In prospect is a Cub theme song entitled, 'When the Midnight Choo Choo Leaves for T-U-L-S-A.'" Fans were invited to submit other titles for possible Cubs themes as well. Following Nelson, the Cubs have employed several talented organists. In the late 1960s, it was Jack Kearney. During the 1970s, Frank Pellico, Vance Fothergill, and John Henzel entertained the fans. Ed Vodicka came aboard in 1982, and then Bruce Miles in 1984. Gary Pressey has been in service at Wrigley since 1987.

PROBLEM SOLVED

Former Cub Dolf Camilli came up with a novel solution for the white-shirt problem in the bleachers. In the May 19, 1941, edition of the *Daily News*, he told Howard Roberts (later a White Sox public relations man), "Why not reserve the three middle sections of the bleachers for fellows wearing blue shirts? Make a blue shirt a requirement for admission to that portion of the bleachers." Roberts continued, tongue firmly in cheek, that "the Cubs could carry the idea farther, of course, by inaugurating a sort of Cub cheering section that would wear blue shirts while the Cubs were batting and then do a rhythmic change into white shirts to confound the enemy batsmen."

LIGHT UP OR LEAVE ME ALONE

The night baseball story at Wrigley Field has not been served well by the mythmakers. Until a few years ago, it was widely accepted that Phil Wrigley, standing alone against the rising tide of that demon, night baseball, never considered soiling the hallowed roofs of Wrigley Field with light towers. In *Veeck—as in Wreck*, Bill Veeck puts it this way. "Old men, playing dominoes around the hearth, like to say that Phil Wrigley is the last of the true baseball men because he is the only owner who still holds, in the simple faith of his ancestors, that baseball was meant to be played under God's own sunlight."

Since the first game under the lights, which took place in Cincinnati in 1935, more and more teams had embraced the idea of night baseball. Both the minor leagues and Negro leagues had cavorted under artificial light for years, but the slow-as-molasses owners of major league clubs were reluctant to take to the idea. The Depression certainly kick-started the movement toward night baseball—almost *anything* that would get people to the park was considered—and high attendance at the contests meant the idea was here to stay.

And the Cubs were ready to join the party. By early December 1941, management had secretly ordered the steel, electric cable, and lighting equipment to install towers for the next season. Night games would, hoped the Cubs, pump up sagging attendance. Cubs general manager Jim Gallagher, like Bill Veeck Sr., a former sportswriter, was a fervent supporter of the project and ready to give workers the nod to start the building. Gallagher, interviewed by Jerome Holtzman in 1984, affirmed that "Mr. Wrigley didn't like the idea. He had his quirks. But he had authorized me to go ahead. This was in 1941, right after the season. It was a bad year. We were going over the books, suffering, wondering what the hell we were going to do and so he said, 'All right, we'll put in lights.'"

Unfortunately, on December 7, 1941, a Japanese squadron bombed Pearl Harbor, and the United States was suddenly at war. Gallagher noted, "I called Mr. Wrigley. He said, 'Call the War Department the first thing tomorrow morning and ask them if they want the material' . . . He was delighted to have an excuse to call the whole thing off. Mr. Wrigley always thought baseball was a daytime game."

Wrigley himself said many times over the years that he didn't want night baseball. He believed, for one thing, in the health benefits of daylight and sunshine. Second, he said that he didn't want to disturb the neighborhood. But concern for the neighbors didn't keep Wrigley from renting the ballpark out for other night events, using portable lighting.

The Cubs gave their steel to the War Department intending it to go to a defense plant. While Gallagher isn't certain where the steel went—it was rumored to be headed to a munitions plant—he told Holtzman that he suspected that it wound up as part of a local racetrack. Ironically, the horse racing industry was instituting night racing at the time.

While Gallagher's explanation is borne out by history, Veeck also thinks that Wrigley didn't go for night baseball for more ego-inflated reasons. He claims that Wrigley continued to brush off night baseball as a passing fancy, and Veeck finally decided that "having blown the chance to be first with lights, Mr. Wrigley just wasn't going to do it at all."

THE PINK POODLE

Wrigley Field was the place to be for baseball people in the late 1930s and early 1940s; Chicago was a great town for players and writers to visit, and a central location meant that plenty of business was conducted in the Windy City.

Prior to the 1941 season, the Cubs built an anteroom off the press box overhang, a fun place for the press and management that soon came to be known as The Pink Poodle. A 1941 article in *The Sporting News*, credited to "La Petite Gourmet" but probably written by the portly Ed Burns, laid out the benefits of such a "recreation parlor": "General manager James Gallagher and Manager Jimmie Wilson are available there after every game, thus removing the necessity of clubhouse ferreting. Visiting managers have also been dropping in, especially if they win . . . Matt Mack, a talented chef, is in charge of the snack department and in addition to fixing routine victuals can bake a charming pie or cup cake."

Interesting to note how the writers didn't think it important to talk to players themselves after games. This attitude wouldn't change until Dick Young made the postgame interview a staple in the 1960s.

ROPED OFF

Despite years of protest from hitters on both the Cubs and opposing teams, it took until July 1941, with the moribund Cubs in the middle of a terrible slump, for GM Jim Gallagher to close off a section of the center-field seats. On July 3, the Cubs and Cardinals began a three-game series at Wrigley Field. Three sections of seats in center field were roped off, and the gray stonework on the aisles and step lifts was painted a shade of brown.

And did the papers ever have a ball. The July 17, 1941, *TSN* ran a smarmy editorial titled "Laundering the Cubs' White Shirt Excuse," which tells you exactly how the "Bible of Baseball" felt. Much was made in the press of the Cubs drawing a crowd of forty thousand on July 4 and having to turn away fans who otherwise would have sat in the roped-off bleacher sections.

By the next Opening Day, the policy was already beginning to slip from the club's control. According to the April 18, 1942, *Tribune*, bleacher fans "swarmed into the space in the first inning and no attempt was made to dislodge them." Ed Burns wrote in the September 22, 1943, *Tribune*, "Somebody ought to do something about that background, most of the Cubs believe. The bleachers can't be remodeled this season, however, because of priorities, and it can't be torn down, because of the labor shortage."

G.I. BLUES

The Cubs were just terrible in the early 1940s, and attendance suffered as a result. The war also put a big bite into American wallets. As a result, professional baseball teams engaged in all sorts of promotional activities to bring the fans out—war bond drive days, recycling days, G.I. days, military all-star games, and the like. May 18, 1941, was "I Am an American" Day. Even before the war, the Cubs held days for the benefit of the military. July 22, 1941, was Aluminum Day at Wrigley Field. The *Tribune*'s Irving Vaughn noted that "women fans bringing aluminumware would be admitted to today's game on the payment only of the tax. The material collected will be turned over to the government for defense purposes."

And once America joined the war following the attack on Pearl Harbor, baseball once again embraced the patriotic spirit. April 17, 1942, was Opening Day at Wrigley Field. At 12:30, nearly two hours of pregame ceremonies began. Bob Strong's orchestra played patriotic airs, and 480 marines and sailors marched around the field to the accompaniment of a forty-piece band from Navy Pier. The marines held a bayonet drill. The *Tribune*'s Cubs notes column of the next day reported that the Cubs were presented a Minute Man flag by the defense department "for the club's 100 per cent cooperation in the purchase of defense bonds."

As an ominous sign, however, the Opening Day crowd numbered just 10,149.

NEGRO LEAGUERS IN WRIGLEY

A special all-star benefit was arranged for May 24 with the Cubs out of town. Retired hurler Dizzy Dean fronted a team of all-star players currently serving in the army; this squad took on Satchel Paige and the Kansas City Monarchs, reigning three-time champions of the Negro American League. For some reason, the game was billed as a tribute to Zeke Bonura, a popular former White Sox player then a soldier based in Louisiana, but the money from the 29,775 paid admissions went to the war effort. The Monarchs, with Paige on the mound for six innings and Buck O'Neil at first base, beat the all-white army all-stars 3–1.

Three days later, on Wednesday, May 27, the Cubs hosted the Reds in a doubleheader. It was a benefit for the army and navy; prior to the regularly scheduled contests, the Great Lakes Naval Air Station baseball team played the Camp Grant team. These two clubs had enjoyed a fierce rivalry during World War I. Ninety-three sailors stationed at Navy Pier actually went door to door delivering tickets that had been ordered in advance for the event. The tickets were available at regular-season prices at Wrigley Field, the *Tribune*'s offices, and at the usual Western Union outlets.

MORNING HAS BROKEN

During the war years, baseball clubs experimented with different starting times for games to entice different populations of fans to the park. Contrary to P. K. Wrigley's reputation as a traditionalist, the Cubs tried just as hard as anyone else to raise attendance. To pull in fans working night shifts, the Cubs decided to hold morning games. On June 11, 1943, the first pitch came at 10:00 a.m., but the novel start time pulled in only fifty-three hundred spectators. On June 22, another morning contest drew but thirty-seven hundred. The experiment was discontinued.

Part of the Cubs' attendance problem was the war. Another was that the club stunk. "Wrigley gave his product a resplendent wrapper, only to make a rather discouraging discovery," wrote the *Saturday Evening Post's* Stanley Frank. "The customers weren't buying the inferior product, the slipping ball club, he was selling."

DAY FOR NIGHT

Another innovation, the "twilight" game, came to Wrigley Field just a few days later, on Friday, June 25, 1943. The 6:00 p.m. scheduled start, another novelty designed to spark interest in a last-place Cubs team, was a first for Wrigley, although plenty of games had concluded later than that in the past. By today's standards, this would be considered a night game; this was the first major league night game ever played at Wrigley Field.

Hi Bithorn pitched the Cubs to a 6–0 win over the St. Louis Cardinals, allowing but two hits. Just 10,070 fans came to the park, with nearly thirty-five hundred of them Ladies Day freebies. The game took just two hours and seventeen minutes, ending before 8:30 p.m.

The twilight concept failed to capture the imagination of the fans or the press and, as a result, was not repeated. Stories in the papers the next day barely mentioned the odd start time.

INDIGNATION

Two days later, on Sunday, June 27, the fans at Wrigley revolted after the club lost both ends of a twin bill against the Cardinals. The Cubs had led both contests in the late innings. The outcry was significant enough that the *Saturday Evening Post* led off its September 11, 1943, issue with a story titled "The Decline and Fall of the Cubs": "A crowd of 37,792 reared back on its hind legs and howled its indignation at the floundering Cubs on the field and the blundering in the front office . . . Old inhabitants of Wrigley Field say it was the most violent demonstration against the Cub management since the wolves attacked Rogers Hornsby in 1932."

NOBODY HOME

Attendance at Wrigley Field continued to lag, as it did all over baseball in 1943, the nadir of the wartime economy. July 28 saw yet another benefit, with the Dodgers in town for a doubleheader. "The entire receipts will go to the Red Cross and the War Relief Fund," wrote Edgar Munzel of the *Sun*. "Everyone who enters the ball park, including players, newspaper, and radio men, will have to buy a ticket." In attendance were 25,735; this poured $29,733.55 into the fund. Before the game, a guard from the Glenview Naval Air Station (P. K. Wrigley's old naval haunt) presented the colors, and the Glenview Station band played. Cubs field announcer Pat Pieper himself sold seven hundred tickets to the contest.

On September 24, just 314 fans kept the faith at Wrigley for a rain-shortened Cubs victory. The Cubs' final 1943 attendance was just 508,224, their lowest total since 1921. They have not had a season total that low since. Even with this poor showing, the Cubs still ranked third in the NL in attendance; this should give an idea about baseball attendance during the war. Some teams played in front of fewer than four thousand fans a game in 1943; the Boston Braves drew just 271,289, while only 214,392 saw the St. Louis Browns.

The Cubs did pull in 18,739 fans on August 11 for "Charlie Root Day," a salute to their forty-two-year-old moundsman. Root, who lost 3–1 to the

Reds, was given several gifts before the game. He received a live pig from longtime Cubs trainer Andy Lotshaw, a station wagon purchased from fan contributions, a custom-woven blanket and a desk clock from his teammates, fishing equipment from the team's broadcasters, fifty dollars in gasoline coupons from White Sox players, and a twenty-two-hundred-dollar check from Phil Wrigley.

A WOMAN'S PLACE IS . . . LEFT FIELD

By 1942, Phil Wrigley believed that the war would last a good while, and knowing that Cubs receipts would be down, he sought ways to keep his ballpark busy. No one wanted to consider shutting down the major leagues, but just in case the apocalypse came, Wrigley wanted to be ready. Therefore, he decided to co-opt a popular local activity—girls' softball—and professionalize it.

"In 1942," Paul Angle wrote, "it was estimated that more than a hundred million spectators watched softball games each year." Lois Browne, in *The Girls of Summer*, writes that during that year, one Chicago women's softball league drew 250,000 fans.

Wrigley formed a corporation to implement the plan. Members of the group included Cubs general manager Jim Gallagher, public relations man Art Meyerhoff, longtime baseball executive Branch Rickey (who agreed to be a trustee), and Cubs employee Ken Sells. While the concept proved sound, Wrigley realized that softball would be too slow to retain large-scale interest. Therefore, the new league would play with a hard ball, just a bit larger than a regulation baseball. The All-American Girls Professional Baseball League (AAGPBL) debuted in 1943.

"By insisting that the women play baseball, not softball, Wrigley hoped to sustain interest in baseball as a spectator sport," wrote Susan Cahn in the spring 1989 *Chicago History*. Wrigley set about raiding the amateur leagues for the best players—at least those who fit his criteria. The game was to be played by feminine girls, not the so-called "mannish Amazons" so derided by the sexist press of the time. Yet the game was expected to be fast and competitive.

Laughably, the league's players wore short skirts. While these outfits certainly afforded spectators marvelous views of the players' legs, the skirts did nothing to protect the ladies, who dove and hustled all over the field, from injury. "Sliding strawberries" were a common problem.

On May 17, 1943, the league held tryouts at Wrigley. Photographers clicked away as the young ladies pitched, hit, and fielded in hopes of landing jobs. Six weeks later, on the evening of July 1, the WAAC (Women's Army Air Corps) held a rally at Wrigley Field. The rally, held with the intent of boosting recruitment, included two exhibits of ladies' baseball. One featured the women of local bases Fort Sheridan and Camp Grant, while the other pitted AAGPBL All-Stars from Wisconsin against those from Illinois and Indiana. The 6:00 p.m. game ended up with Fort Sheridan whomping Camp Grant by a ridiculous 33–5, while in the second game, the Wisconsin AAGPBL All-Stars mangled their opponents 11–0. Approximately seven thousand fans attended. In addition to the games, fans were treated to calisthenics, precision drills, and the twenty-eight-piece Fort Sheridan band.

The contest was, Lois Browne wrote, "notable for several reasons. For one thing, it was the first [baseball game] ever played at Wrigley Field under lights," as a temporary bank of floodlights was strapped to the top of the grandstands. Visibility was poor; player Dorothy Hunter recalled to Browne, "You were lucky if you could see who was sitting next to you. The outfielders were dead ducks."

P. K. PULLS THE PLUG

Unfortunately, putting on the girls' league in major league or high minor league parks tended to remove the neighborhood-styled intimacy necessary for the game to succeed. It wasn't major league baseball and suffered in comparison when played in Wrigley Field or in the large parks of Milwaukee and Minneapolis. Tickets were a dollar each for the games, a price that possibly kept some fans away.

Following the 1944 season, Wrigley, who felt that the war would end soon, sold the AAGPBL to Meyerhoff for a reported ten thousand dollars. Wrigley had spent some $135,000 on the league. Paul Angle wrote that "the venture had been costly for [Wrigley] personally, and from his point of view, nothing was to be gained by further expenditures."

In 1948, Chicago, for the first time, hosted an AAGPBL team: the Colleens. But the club soon became a touring squad and dropped out of the league following the season.

COLONEL MUSTARD

The Cubs opened the 1944 Wrigley Field season on April 13 with an exhibition against the White Sox. "The only military touch wasn't contained in the servicemen scattered throughout the park," wrote Lyall Smith in the *Daily News*. The outfield bleachers had been painted a new shade of mustard-green to better match the color of the scoreboard. Smith compared the new color to that from "a left-over can of paint from a General Grant tank." General manager Jim Gallagher noted that the new paint job was meant, among other things, to help improve the hitting background—at least on days when the bleachers weren't full.

On April 17, the Cubs held a high-school student war bonds day. Twenty-five thousand teenagers who had sold war bonds were admitted free of charge to the game—no adult spectators were present. Selling twenty-five dollars worth of bonds admitted the kids to bleacher seats. Fifty dollars worth got them into the grandstand. The big sellers—anyone with more than one hundred dollars of war bonds sold—were awarded box seats. Army and Navy bands were on hand to entertain.

THE LAST PENNANT

While nobody expected the Cubs, fourth-place finishers in 1944, to contend in 1945, the defending world champion St. Louis Cardinals got out of the gate poorly. After a hot start by the New York Giants, the Cubs came alive; Chicago's stretch of twenty-six wins in thirty games during June and early July catapulted them into first place. On July 15, the Cubs swept a double-header from the visiting Giants, 5–3 and 7–2, to move four games up in the NL race. An overflow crowd of 48,803, the biggest of the season, was at Wrigley. With many baseball fans still at war, money at a premium, and some turned off by the poor quality of play, the Cubs had pulled in only around twenty thousand fans for most of their big contests down the stretch.

PAFKO DAY

Chicago slumped in late August and was on-and-off through most of September. On September 23, with the Pirates in town, the Cubs held "Andy Pafko Day" for their young center fielder, and 43,755 packed the ballpark. All of the box seats had been sold out since the middle of the month. Before the game, Pafko was gifted with two large suitcases and a watch from the Chicago Slovak Good Will Club. The fan favorite responded in kind; his third inning grand slam homer gave the Cubs a 4–3 lead in a game they went on to take 7–3. The win kept the Cubs one and a half games ahead of the Cardinals.

ORDER UP

With just seven games to play, the Cubs entertained the Cardinals on September 25. With the weather gloomy after days of rain, just 20,438 fans came out to see a game on which the NL pennant race would surely turn. The

Cubs, down 3–2 in the seventh, broke through for four runs. After the Cubs tied it on a single by Don Johnson, Phil Cavaretta's bases-loaded single scored Stan Hack to put the Cubs up 4–3. Pafko then doubled in two more. Chicago held on for a 6–5 win, then went up the ramp to their clubhouse cheered on by hundreds of raucous fans. As Lon Warneke and Roy Johnson broke into the team's traditional victory song, "John the Baptist," the Cubs made for the beer tub.

That morning, the Cubs had announced plans to accept World Series ticket orders by mail—first come, first serve. Only two sets of tickets for three games each were to be sold to each applicant. One grandstand ticket for three games cost $18.35, with a small discount for two sets ($36.35). For box seats, one ticket for the three-game set was $21.95 and two tickets cost $43.55. Early the day of each Series game, all bleacher ($1.20) and standing room tickets ($3.60) would go on sale.

CLINCH

The next day, with better weather, 42,289 Cub crazies came out, but the Cardinals won a zany 11–6 game to trim the lead to one and a half with just five contests left. On the morning of September 26, the Cubs announced that all Series tickets had been sold and that one hundred workers had been hired to return all the extra ticket applications.

Chicago went to Cincinnati and swept a twin bill from the Reds, 3–1 and 7–4, on September 27. (On the year, the Cubs won twenty-one of twenty-two from the hapless Reds.) The next day, the Cubs traveled to Pittsburgh to make up a rain-canceled doubleheader originally meant to be played in Chicago. On the September 29, the Cubs swept their twentieth doubleheader of the season, 4–3 and 5–0, to wrap up the NL crown.

While the Cubs were not a particularly good team—no wartime aggregation was—they were relatively deep, especially in starting pitchers. Five Cubs hurlers finished in double figures in wins, including Hank Wyse, who paced the NL with twenty-two wins, and Ray "Pop" Prim, who led the league in ERA at 2.40. Midseason acquisition Hank Borowy, bought from the Yankees in an odd waiver deal, was 11–2 for Chicago. And his good looks won the hearts of thousands of Illinois women.

The twenty doubleheader sweeps set an all-time National League mark, pointing to the Cubs' depth and their ability to eat up second-division clubs. While they were just 6–16 against the second-place Redbirds and 11–11 versus third-place New York, the Cubs finished an incredible 81–29 against the remainder of the National League.

COME GO WITH ME

Unfortunately, wartime travel restrictions again worked against the Cubs. The first three games of the Series would be played in Detroit, with the remainder held in Chicago. This meant that the Chicagos might have as few as *one* home date. Fans were sold tickets (in strips) for the fourth, fifth, and sixth games. Game Seven tickets would be sold only if the game became necessary.

Prior to Game Four, the first to be held at Wrigley Field, Andy Frain himself gave the press a series of suggestions for fans to avoid problems at the park. Frain, who would be in charge of 525 ushers (100 of them women) for the Series games, advised that fans follow three simple directions: 1) go to the gate specified on the ticket; 2) bring only the ticket for Game Four; and 3) leave home early.

At the time, Wrigley had five main gates, not counting the bleacher entrance. Gate One was at Sheffield near Addison, in the right-field corner; Gate Two on Addison, near Sheffield, also close to the right-field corner; Gate Three, the home plate gate, was at Clark and Addison; and Gates Four and Five were located by the left-field corner on Waveland near Clark.

Frain noted that in 1938, several people bringing their tickets for all three games had either lost them or had ushers tear off the wrong ticket. In addition, there was always a risk of theft. He noted also that fans should think of arriving at the park at noon to avoid crowding or traffic. The city had once again closed down some streets on the North Side and planned to open express lanes for Wrigley-bound cars at 11:00 a.m. each game day.

WALKIE-TALKIE

As Ed Prell of the *Tribune* noted, Wrigley Field was the site of yet another innovation during the 1945 World Series. "For the first time in sports, a crowd will be directed by walkie-talkies. Girls with the radio gadgets will be posted at strategic points in the park in contact at all times with Frain, who will station himself at a vantage point. This will lessen the strain on Frain, whose practice in the past has been to dash all over a park or stadium in his capacity as supervisor."

These girls were certainly in no danger of being missed. Frain's ladies were kitted out in navy blue skirts with gold stripes down each side, powder blue blouses, and capes of blue and gold (the Frain service's signature colors).

TAKE ME HOME

After winning Game One 9–0 and Game Three 3–0 in Detroit to move up two-to-one in the Series, the Cubs arrived home on a special train on Friday, October 5 at 10:15 p.m. to a huge, cheering crowd at Union Station. They had left Detroit on a high: Cubs right-hander Claude Passeau threw one of the great games in World Series history at the Tigers in the third contest—a one-hit, one-walk shutout.

The Cubs decided, for the 1:30 starts to Games Four, Five, Six, and (if needed) Seven, to open box and grandstand gates at 10:30 a.m., while five thousand bleacher seats priced at $1.20 apiece went on sale at 7:00 the morning of each game. If the bleacher tickets sold out, twenty-five hundred standing-room tickets were to be vended at $3.60 apiece. Fans started gathering in line for bleacher seats the morning of Thursday, October 4. Art Felsch of Milwaukee, a factory worker, came by at 8:00 a.m., surviving on cans of cold chili and sleeping on an army-styled cot, in order to be first in line. Two army vets from the Italian and North Africa campaigns, on three-day passes from Kentucky, told a *Tribune* reporter that waiting for bleacher seats was "no worse than being in a chow line."

By Friday night, five thousand fans had gathered around the park, five hundred of them in line for bleacher seats and the others just enjoying the fun. Some of the kids in line were just holding places to sell to the highest bidder; one wanted fifteen dollars from a would-be buyer. Men walked around selling wooden boxes to tired standees for a quarter or two. Two hundred bleacher seats had been reserved for wounded servicemen from local Vaughan Hospital. The soldiers, who arrived in five buses, ate box lunches supplied by the Cubs.

It took only until 8:00 a.m. Saturday for the remaining bleacher seats to sell out. But only sixteen hundred standing-room ducats went, bringing attendance to 42,923—less than the expected 44,200 capacity. (All the standing-room seats were gone for Game Five, but Game Six again was less than a sellout.) To deal with the crowd, three hundred of Chicago's finest walked the area, along with forty-three navy patrolmen and twenty-five army MPs.

HITCHIN' A RIDE

Despite express roads being opened, newspapermen and broadcasters covering the game still had trouble getting to the park. The press bus, leaving from downtown at the Palmer House Hotel, broke down on Lake Shore Drive near Belmont Harbor, meaning the reporters had to grab their typewriters and notebooks, get out, and catch taxicabs to reach the park.

When the reporters got to Wrigley Field, they found P. K. Wrigley—who often wouldn't even *show up* for critical games—in an unexpectedly jolly mood, entertaining NL owners at the Pink Poodle.

THE PERFECT KISS

Most of Game Four was played under rainy gray skies. The tarp wasn't even taken off the field until 1:25, eliminating batting practice, and drizzle fell through the early portion of the game.

Before the first pitch, actress June Haver, appearing in the current film "Dolly Sisters," ran onto the field and kissed manager Charlie Grimm and pitcher Hank Borowy. According to Arch Ward, "It was good clean fun and all that, but we wonder what would happen if Grimm and Borowy dashed onto a set at the 20th Century-Fox studio and reversed the procedure."

CURSED

Fans have often heard about the "Billy Goat" curse, but its origins are less well known. David Condon told the story in 1972 of an event that occurred before Game Four of the 1945 series.

> One of the merriest fans was William (Billy Goat) Sianis, keeper of the [Billy Goat] saloon and a prominent herd of goats. Billy had unique intentions.
>
> Governor Dwight Green was in Wrigley Field the next afternoon. Mayor Ed Kelly was present, too. Mr. Billy Goat Sianis and his blue-ribbon goat, Sonovia, also appeared.
>
> Mr. Sianis presented a pair of box-seat tickets and escorted Sonovia to choice pews. The Frain ushers started squawking on those newfangled handy-talkies and very quickly both goats, Billy and Sonovia, were being rushed exitwise. Sonovia's ticket was retrieved. Presently it is mounted in the Billy Goat Inn.

The goat had come into Wrigley Field with the best of intentions; Sianis, a huge Cubs fan, had put a blanket over Sonovia reading, "We Got Detroit's Goat." But apparently, the Cubs weren't humored. Condon continues, "When the Tigers surged ahead by winning both the fourth and fifth games, Billy Goat placed an eternal hex on the Cubs. As an afterthought, he telegraphed Owner Philip K. Wrigley: 'Who smells now?'"

Sianis visited Wrigley in 1973, again with goat in tow, but was once more turned away. But in 1981, William Sianis's son, Sam, came by the ballpark with a goat and was allowed in. He again came in 1984 and 1986, and in a pregame ceremony early in 1994, Sianis and a goat were invited on to the field in order to "officially" end the hex.

ONE-EYED CONNOLLY

Remember One-Eyed Connolly, from the 1929 and 1938 fall classics? Andy Frain actually hired the well-known gate crasher to work as an usher for the 1945 Series. Apparently believing that someone who knows all the tricks of getting in free makes the most efficient gatekeeper, Frain placed Connolly at the front gate before Game Three and told him to keep the riff-raff out.

Unfortunately, Connolly's new career was short-lived. Before Game Six, according to Arch Ward in the *Tribune*, he did his job a little too well, refusing to allow P. K. Wrigley, whom he did not recognize, into his own park. Connolly submitted his (forced) resignation after the game.

BURNED

Wrigley had his own issues to deal with besides being recognized. Realizing that the phenomenon of scalpers made many fans angry, Wrigley took out an ad in the Chicago papers headlined "We're Burned Up Too, Cub Fans, about Scalping of World Series Tickets." The ad went on to state, "The Cubs went to a lot of trouble and extra expense to engage outside office space and a large force of bank tellers and clerks to try and do an extra good job of distributing evenly and fairly the comparatively limited supply of World Series tickets . . . Once the tickets are in the hands of the public, there is nothing to prevent individuals from selling their seats at a neat profit through scalpers . . . We all know this to be true, but as we said to start with—we do not like it."

SCALPER'S BLUES

Perhaps egged on, or pressured, by Wrigley's public stance, bluecoats kept busy nailing scalpers. The day before the Series started in Chicago, twenty city detectives and twenty-five revenue department deputies began to canvass the streets. Six speculators were arrested near Wrigley Field before Games Four, Five, and Six for selling above the printed price. Some of them were trying to move the $1.20 bleacher seats for as much as $10.00, although most of the hapless capitalists were probably the low feeders on the scalping food chain; no arrests of downtown ticket agency employees were reported.

One scalper, Louis Pike, owned Pike's Texaco at 3553 N. Clark, just kitty-corner from Wrigley Field. Another man arrested for scalping said that Pike rented him a space in his gas station from which to operate his ticket-reselling operation.

GAME SEVEN

Wrigley truly believed that he had done his best to distribute tickets fairly and evenly, which is why scalping bothered him so much. He realized that the whole process reflected badly on him, the Cubs, and the entire sport of baseball. (Would that current ownership realized this; in 2002, the Cubs themselves started their own scalping agency.)

When the Cubs, who had lost Games Four and Five to fall behind three games to two, forced a Game Seven with a wild twelve-inning 8–7 win in Game Six, Wrigley sprang into action. Since he had sold tickets for only the first three games, he was somewhat worried about a riot during a public sale of Game Seven seats. Therefore, to reduce the number of tickets to be sold, Wrigley used the off day before the deciding contest to contact as many as possible of the fans who had been left out of the previous ticket sales and offered *them* tickets for Game Seven. He explained it to Ed Prell of the *Tribune* as "attending to the wants of his own 'personal customers and rooters.'"

Thirty-six thousand tickets, minus the ones marked for previous lottery losers, went on sale October 9, the day before Game Seven, at the normal Series prices: $7.20 for boxes and $6.00 for grandstands. It is well known that when asked which team would take the Series, Chicago *Sun* editor Warren Brown noted, "I don't think either of them can win it." Cubs rooters, however, believed that their team was better. Fans began lining up by the ticket windows on Addison Street almost immediately after Game Six ended, and by midnight two hundred fans were in line, burning paper and wood in garbage cans to keep warm in the sub-forty-degree temperatures.

Wrigley and several members of his staff were up all night after Game Six preparing for the mass sale. Andy Frain was on hand as well, having called as many staffers as he could to the ballpark. Frain himself was the recipient of several bribe offers for a good place in line, including, according to Prell, a freshly caught six-pound fish.

The well-behaved crowd couldn't have known that they were in line for tickets to the last World Series game the Cubs would ever play (through 2003, at least), but they apparently were somewhat solemn. Few, if any, rooters were drinking, and the standees agreed to have their places in line marked by chalk numbers on the backs of their coats. At 8:00 a.m. October 9, the sale began, and the tickets were gone by 11:30.

JUVENILE DELINQUENCY

The five thousand bleachers for Game Seven sold out in an hour or so on October 10. While many kids staked out their places in line, some saw their only chance to view a Cubs World Series game dashed on the rocks. According to Ed Prell:

> At 11 p.m. there was an appreciable dwindling of the bleacher population when the police ordered all school boys and girls to leave for home. There were some murmurings of disapproval. One disappointed lad said, "That's a pretty dirty trick—the World Series happens once here every seven years and we can't see it."
>
> A philosophic policeman [said] . . . "Look at 'em," pointing to dozens of youngsters lying on blankets or quilts. "Those kids are running a risk of getting sick. I was a boy once—but I wouldn't want one of my kids out in this chilly weather."
>
> The cops let those youngsters remain who were occupied by their parents. It may be reasonably assumed that there were more than a few on-the-spot adoptions last night.

"IS THIS A BUST, OR WHAT?"

The authorities made more busts the morning of Game Seven and creatively disposed of the tickets. Several young men were caught in the lobbies of the Sherman and Morrison hotels attempting to scalp tickets. Judge J. M. Braude ordered the tickets sold in an impromptu fashion to locals. The original ticket value was then given back to the scalpers, who were also forced to donate money to the Red Cross or the Victory Loan drive. (Proceeds from the tickets sold to locals also went to war relief efforts.)

Meanwhile, outside the park, the glut of scalped tickets meant that prices dropped lower and lower at game time. Finally, after the game began, the prices fell below list. Unfortunately for Chicago fans, Detroit scored five runs off Hank Borowy and Paul Derringer in the first inning. The game was never close, and the Tigers cruised to a 9–3 win and a world championship.

WHAT WAS IT LIKE, DADDY?

In July 1972, *Tribune* columnist David Condon wrote that getting to Wrigley Field in the summer of 1945 was an adventure. "I rode the Clark Street surface cars, an experience likened to Russian Roulette with a carbine." The neighborhood was becoming modernized: more cars, more people, more businesses. And, apparently, more fun. By 1945, laws against sitting atop one's roof to watch a game had apparently either been changed or simply forgotten. One fan perched on a slanted roof on a Kenmore Avenue house to take in the World Series in his winter overcoat and hat.

As they always have, a few local residents decided to cash in on the success of the Cubs. After Game Six, city inspectors—following up on complaints—sued thirteen parking lot operators for asking more than they were licensed to charge. Some lots were demanding two dollars per car, when they were legally permitted to charge only fifty or seventy-five cents per space.

Commerce was in the news during this Series, which broke all sorts of records for box-office receipts despite what most in the press felt was low-quality baseball. Before Game Four alone, 180 vendors sold fifty-four thousand sandwiches. During the four games at Wrigley, the Cubs sold ninety-one thousand programs.

THE POSTWAR ERA

Despite winning the 1945 National League title, the Cubs were expected to slump in 1946, when the Cardinals and other clubs got back plenty of good players from the military. On a very cold April 20, 1946, 40,887 fans came to Wrigley Field to watch the defending NL champions inaugurate their season. Cubs manager Charlie Grimm received the NL pennant from league president Ford Frick as well as a small jar of Japanese soil from a twenty-one-year-old Chicagoan, Warren Jungwirth, who had spent thirty-eight months overseas. The crowd was the largest for an Opening Day at the park since 1929. Armin Hand's band, dressed in spanking new blue uniforms, were "further decorated by the presence of six slightly frostbitten drum majorettes," according to the *Tribune*'s Ed Prell.

Yet another innovation at the park was revealed. At close to 1:00, half an hour before game time, Grimm pressed a buzzer mounted in the dugout that called Cubs players out of the clubhouse and onto the field for their pregame drill. With the players on the field, Frick presented the Cubs the league flag. A small tractor drove the pennant to the right-field corner, where it was raised on the foul pole. The band, Prell wrote, "perhaps in the spirit of peace time, substituted 'God Bless America' for 'The Star-Spangled Banner.'"

WHO'S MINDING THE MINT?

It wasn't just school kids who played hooky for Opening Day. A group of Merchandise Mart businessmen, fifty-eight strong, rented out a trolley that drove them up to Wrigley Field for the contest. One assumes they took the Clark Street route north from downtown. These good fellows stuffed themselves on the way up with hot dogs and peanuts. Once at the ballpark, festooned in special gold-hued baseball caps, they yelled and made noise with cowbells and horns.

THE CHICAGO CUBS ARE OFF THE AIR!

Celebrating the first Opening Day since the end of the war, WBKB television was on hand, hoping to air the game to the few thousand Chicago-area owners of television sets. It would be the first telecast ever of a baseball game in the Windy City. Interference interfered, however. An item in the next day's *Tribune* noted that things didn't come off as planned: "Station WBKB's effort to televise the Chicago Cubs game with the Cardinals at Wrigley Field yesterday failed. The station's mobile unit televised the game successfully at the field, but electrical interference in the State-Lake building, where the transmitter is located, resulted in such poor images after the relay that William C. Eddy, director, declined to put them on the air. . . . Eddy blamed the interference on elevator operations in the building where the studios and the transmitter are located."

THE CHICAGO CUBS ARE ON THE AIR!

WBKB tried again on July 13 at Wrigley Field. This time, everything went swimmingly. Larry Wolters of the *Tribune* reported the next day that "tele-viewers saw the game from an upper tier position looking across home plate down the first base line, with the pitcher in view on the mound. Excepting when the camera was swung to follow action, they missed the activity at second, third, and in most of the outfield."

The game, won by the Dodgers 4–3, featured a ninth-inning Cubs rally that fell just short, as well as an argument involving Dodgers manager Leo Durocher. The commentator was Jack Gibney, who would *not* go on to become one of the great names in Chicago baseball broadcasting. On this day, however, Wolters found him adequate for the job; he "judiciously let the pictures speak for themselves."

Despite the use of just one camera, all parties judged the WBKB telecast a success. Viewers as far away as Michigan City, Indiana, picked up the transmission. WBKB broadcast several more contests that year, including the Giants game of July 15.

CHANGING COLORS

When Jackie Robinson made his first visit ever to Wrigley Field, on May 18, 1947, 46,572 paid to get in. At the time, it was called the largest paid regular-season crowd in the history of the park and certainly the largest gathering overall since 1936, when fans were banned from standing on the field. The fans "jammed all available spaces to see Jackie Robinson," according to the *Tribune*. "There was no doubt that the new paid record was set because Robinson, the much discussed Negro athlete, was making his first baseball appearance in Chicago as a big leaguer."

Oddly, though, no accounts in the white papers of the time note whether a large segment of the fans were black. Even the *New York Times* did not mention that Robinson was a center of attention. Perhaps back then, you didn't need to; everyone knew how momentous each game with Jackie was. But it still seems rather strange. Perhaps the Chicago papers did not want to alarm any of the local fans by painting a picture of hordes of blacks streaming off trains and streetcars and invading what had been an all-white playground.

In its May 17 issue, the weekly Chicago *Defender* implored African American fans going to Wrigley Field to be respectful and leave the liquor at home—a plea made by black newspapers in most National League cities—in order to leave a good impression on the press and on white fans. While the white papers didn't make mention of black fans, Mike Royko did years later, noting in the *Daily News* that he was among African Americans "by the thousands, pouring off the northbound els and out of their cars."

Most Chicago blacks at that time lived on the South Side. Those blacks that did go to big league games usually patronized the White Sox, whose home park, Comiskey, hosted many a Negro League All-Star game. It's likely that this trip to Wrigley was the first that most African American fans had ever made.

Mike Royko himself was at the first Jackie Robinson game. He sat next to a middle-aged black man who, when Robinson batted, was "beating his palms together so hard they must have hurt."

CUBBIE BLACK

For many years, the Cubs were one of the least integrated clubs in baseball. From 1947 through 1952, the Cubs had no blacks and only one Latino: Sal Madrid, who played eight games in 1948. It was a white club in a white neighborhood, and Phil Wrigley seemed in no mood to change things. "We aren't going out and hire a Negro ball player just because it is popular to have a Negro ball player," he said at the time. "When we have a Negro ball player, he will be an outstanding ball player. He has to be outstanding . . . He has to be better than any white boy because he will be under the microscope."

This assertion, of course, begs the question of just how much better any

Negro would have had to be than the white boys composing the execrable Cubs teams of the era. Was Wrigley tacitly admitting that he felt that his customers were racists? (Some in the media felt that he was, and that they were.) Or was Wrigley just stonewalling to avoid the issue because of his own feelings?

Several historians have claimed that Wrigley, like many in the establishment, simply believed in slow progress: nothing too radical, nothing too shocking, everything in its proper place and time. Perhaps Wrigley overestimated his club's ability to succeed when others had expanded their market for talent by going to blacks and Latinos in the late 1940s and early 1950s. The White Sox, for example, integrated much more quickly than the Cubs did—and their willingness to do so helped them vault from the AL's doldrums to the top for the first time in decades.

Eventually, Ernie Banks and Gene Baker came along in 1953–54. From that point, the Cubs gingerly embraced integration. Wrigley, as a marketing genius but a baseball outsider, probably felt it was more important not to risk offending the fan base by bringing in too many players of different colors. Cubs fans of the time probably wished he hadn't been so worried.

In the early 1960s, the Cubs had as many blacks as anyone but began trading some of them for white players. For most of the 1960s and 1970s, the Cubs were considered a desert for blacks, unless they were quiet like Billy Williams or jolly like Ernie Banks or Willie Smith. And, indeed, the organization's historical record on race is poor. Bill Madlock was disposed of when he had the temerity to ask for more money. The Cubs dumped Oscar Gamble and Bill North and Lou Brock and Andre Thornton, often for very little in return, presumably to be rid of "trouble" players whom other clubs were very happy to have. Most of them weren't stars when they were traded; they only became stars for other teams. And it wasn't until the mid-1970s that the Cubs had a serious Latino presence of any kind.

Were the Cubs afraid that they'd lose their audience by playing more blacks? Well, by the late 1950s and early 1960s, they didn't have blacks or Latinos, and they stunk, and they had lost their audience anyway.

WHY WERE THEY SO AWFUL?

For one thing, the Cubs were bad because they lagged far behind the curve on black and Latin players. Another reason that they fell behind in the 1940s was Wrigley's belief that the minor leagues should remain free from ownership by big league teams.

Bill Veeck, who owned a Milwaukee club in the 1940s directly subsidized by Wrigley, noted admiringly that Wrigley "did not believe in farm systems. It was his belief—and he was right—that baseball could only remain healthy if the minor league clubs were free to develop their own players and sell them to the highest bidder. He put his money where his mouth was. He subsidized Milwaukee, through a direct cash grant, and renounced all rights to their players."

As a result of this magnanimity, the Cubs had far less talent in their system than many other clubs who had less money to play with—the Cardinals and Dodgers, for example. By the early 1940s, the press was already pointing out that the Cubs had a substandard minor league system. Irving Vaughan in the July 27, 1941, *Tribune* wrote an article entitled, "Backward Cubs Begin to Learn About Farming—Crop is Poor": "The Cubs' officials were sustained, first off, by the fact that a few pennants had been won. Maybe they thought this would go on indefinitely, completely oblivious to the patent fact that men grow old whether they are playing baseball or sitting in a rocking chair . . . Nothing had been done about making minor league connections, either through purchase or agreement."

Vaughan concluded by noting that Wrigley's argument was silly, that teams needed to do whatever they legally could to compete; only players trapped in deep systems could possibly have a beef. Of course, the free minor league owners had a beef, too—their businesses were being destroyed. But the major leagues' greed and the rise of television eventually squashed them. The Cubs, late to the party, suffered for years.

STARS ON 47

The Cubs were awarded the 1947 All-Star Game, scheduled for July 8, the first midsummer classic in Chicago since the initial contest in 1933. Wrigley Field was well positioned at the time to house fans, baseball people, and the media. With six ladies' rooms, which had been doubled in size the previous year, and five men's rooms, as well as adequate concession facilities in several locations and even a first-aid station, it was as well-appointed as any major league facility.

Which isn't to say that Wrigley Field in 1947 was of the quality of Wrigley Field in 2003. Back then, both teams' clubhouses were on the mezzanine level. The current visitors' clubhouse, the smallest (and smelliest) in the league by far, is still in the same spot. Clubhouses were not built adjacent to, or accessible from, dugouts until much later. When games were finished in those days, clubs left their tiny dugouts—which were, indeed, small shelters simply "dug out" of the dirt—and walked down the foul lines to access their clubhouses, the Cubs down the left-field line and their opponents down the right. The very small umpires' room was located next to the visitors' clubhouse. (The arbiters would get a new space in 1955.)

On July 8, a heartening crowd of 41,123 came out to see the All-Stars.

Fans were now able to buy tickets at new windows on Clark Street, down the third-base line, as well as on Addison down the first-base line. Attendance at the midsummer classic had flagged somewhat since the event's initial novelty wore off; the 1942, 1943, and 1944 contests had meager crowds of 33,694, 31,938, and 29,589, respectively, and 1945's contest was canceled outright. The Wrigley Field All-Star crowd was the largest since 1941.

LITTLE PLASTIC CASTLE

Two weeks after the All-Star Game, the Cubs announced a pair of improvements. First, the photos overlooking the main concession stand, which dated back to the 1930s, were removed in favor of baseball action pictures from the current season. Second, the Cubs again tried to address the problem of the distracting hitting background in the bleachers without actually closing the seats off. This time, head groundskeeper Bobby Dorr installed a large piece of blue plastic either on top of or hanging from the outfield wall in dead center field. The screen was installed in time for the July 22 doubleheader. The plastic screen was intended to cut down on glare from the white shirts worn by spectators in the bleachers, but the "innovation" was removed without much ceremony on July 29. During the nine games the screen was used, the Cubs plated thirty-one runs and the visitors forty-eight.

HACKING MASS

On the suggestion of a loyal fan, Mrs. Margaret Barnard of Chicago, the Cubs honored veteran third baseman Stan Hack, who had announced plans to retire, on August 30, 1947. Hack, one of the most popular Chicago players ever, received a carload of gifts—including the car. In addition to a shiny new gray sedan, Hack was presented a thousand-dollar TV set, which had a screen the size of an Etch A Sketch®. He also got a freezer, two radios, fishing tackle, two pen and pencil sets, a traveling bag, a cigarette box, a crate of fruit, a humidor full of cigars, a wristwatch (from the Cubs), and presentations from five Chicago florists.

A crowd of 27,523 turned out for the game between the fifth-place Cubs and sixth-place Pirates, which Pittsburgh won 8–5. Hack went hitless in three at-bats and walked. One fan who came by, Mike Devore from McHenry, Illinois, checked in at ninety-eight years of age—just sixty-one years senior to Stan Hack.

When asked to speak, Hack said, "As far as I am concerned, there is no greater city in the world than Chicago, no finer team to play for than the Cubs, and no greater fans in the country. Cub friends, I love you all."

SHOWERING OF TOKENS

Irving Vaughan wrote, in his story concerning Hack's day, "The showering of tokens will be resumed this afternoon when Nick Strinchevich, who is scheduled to start for the Pirates against Doyle Lade, will be presented with an automobile by his Gary, Ind., neighbors. Tomorrow, Bert Haas of the Reds will receive a car from fans of his home town, Naperville."

PROPPING OPEN THE DORR

On March 1, 1948, the *Tribune* published an interview with groundskeeper Bobby Dorr, who said that the Cubs were about to plant fifty-five hundred square yards of sod on the portion of the field that had been used by the Bears the previous fall. Several spots in the outfield were also chewed up from drills and the use of blocking-and-tackling equipment. At the time, Dorr's chief assistant was Harry "New York" Hazelwood.

THE BIGGEST PAID CROWD

In the middle of dreary postwar Cubs history came the biggest paid crowds ever to attend a game at Wrigley Field. On May 18, 1947, 46,552 fans paid their way in. A bit more than a year later, on Memorial Day, May 31, 1948, a throng of 46,965 stuffed Wrigley Field to see the Cubs and Pirates split a doubleheader. On that day, major league baseball shattered its all-time single-day attendance record. There was nothing particularly momentous about the games, and the papers barely commented on the attendance record—or the crowd—the next day. It was as if the bloom was coming off the rose as far as the press was concerned; even though people still loved the Cubs and loved coming to the ballpark, it was no longer *a story*.

What was a story was the near-riot on August 26, 1948, with the Boston Braves, who would go on to win the National League flag. This time, 27,315 were on hand for the doubleheader. After the Cubs took the first contest 5–1, Phil Cavaretta came up in the third inning of the second game with Chicago down 1–0. With two men on, Cavaretta lined a shot to left field. Jeff Heath, Boston's left fielder, couldn't find the ball; he thought it had gotten stuck in the ivy. Cubs catcher Bob Scheffing, sitting in the bullpen, claimed that the ball was on the ground the whole time. Cavaretta circled the bases for an apparent three-run inside-the-park homer. The Braves protested, and the umpires ruled the play a ground-rule double, which allowed just one man to score.

"Straw hats, bottles, and paper sailed out of the grandstand and bleachers," reported Harry Warren in the *Tribune*. "Umpire Jocko Conlan tried to take command and raced across the diamond to berate a policeman in the Cubs' dugout for not stopping the noise." After Charlie Grimm came out of the dugout to protest Conlan's actions, the fans booed again, throwing more hats, bottles, paper cups, and scorecards. "Because of the debris in center field," Warren continued, "the umpires announced that any ball that fell in the paper would be a double. [Boston] Manager Billy Southworth protested this and refused to permit the game to continue until the field was cleared. This was done."

After Andy Pafko was intentionally passed, Peanuts Lowrey hit a bases-clearing triple off Vern Bickford. Chicago went on to win 5–2.

GIRLS, GIRLS, GIRLS

A September 13, 1952, photo essay on Ladies Day at Wrigley in *Collier's* showed that many of the ladies were teenagers. Some just wanted autographs; some spelled out players' names in masking tape on their blue jeans. Some fought hard with each other to reach foul balls hit their way. This was not a particularly genteel crowd. "There's a lot of shrieking, and screaming," said then-manager Phil Cavaretta, "but you know the women are behind you on every play."

Not all of them. One young lady impacted the team in a much more negative fashion. Miss Ruth Steinhagen, born in suburban Cicero in 1929, was an obsessive young Cubs fan. First, she had a crush on outfielder Peanuts Lowrey, many years later a Cubs coach; later, she turned her attentions to Eddie Waitkus, a slick-fielding first baseman who joined Chicago in 1946.

The Cubs dealt the popular and handsome Waitkus to the Phillies in December 1948. By the next June, when Philadelphia visited Chicago, the disturbed Miss Steinhagen was obsessed with Waitkus—whom she had never met. She hatched a plot to kill her favorite, believing that if she couldn't have him, nobody could.

On June 19, Steinhagen booked a room at the Edgewater Hotel, just twenty blocks north of Wrigley Field, and lured Waitkus upstairs by leaving him a note signed by a "Ruth Ann Burns," whom the player thought might be a relative of an old ballplaying friend of his from Boston. When Waitkus got to Miss Steinhagen's room, she pulled out a shotgun and fired, hitting his chest.

Waitkus survived the incident, but barely. It scarred him for life, both physically and emotionally. According to John Theodore, who wrote 2002's *Baseball's Natural: The Story of Eddie Waitkus*, Ruth Ann Steinhagen was institutionalized in Kankakee, south of Chicago, until 1952. Today she lives with her sister Rita, reclusively, on the near northwest side of Chicago, unwilling to talk about the incident.

This wasn't the first time that a Chicago player had been gunned down by a female fan. During the 1932 season, a showgirl named Violet Valli shot Cubs infielder Billy Herman at the Hotel Carlos, just a little bit north of Wrigley Field. Valli had wanted a relationship with Herman, but he had demurred. Herman was not seriously injured and in fact did not even wish to prosecute the case.

SOME OLD BUSINESS

Prior to the beginning of the 1951 season, the Cubs finally got around to turning the box and grandstand seats down the right-field line toward the playing field. (The left-field seats had been shifted back in 1938.) The project involved ripping out huge sections of the grandstand and boxes, rebuilding the cement foundation, and installing new seats at different angles. The change was made to only the lower deck, although the Cubs did install new bolted-in folding chairs for the upstairs patrons.

On April 14, the day of a City Series game against the White Sox at Wrigley, and three days prior to Opening Day, the Cubs announced that the repairs were complete. The very poor late winter and early spring weather held up the process. In addition, the outfield grass did not grow well and had to be re-sodded close to Opening Day.

In addition to the right-field seat-turning project, the Cubs also spent the 1949–50 and 1950–51 off-seasons building new box seats in various sections. The new lower deck, of monolithic reinforced concrete, was completed just before the 1951 season opened. A crew of 150 worked tirelessly through March and early April to get things ready for the season. The workmen, and their wives and/or girlfriends, were invited by the team to attend the Cubs–Sox exhibition held at Wrigley on Sunday, April 15. Unfortunately, the temperature was just thirty-seven degrees, and many of the workers elected to stay home. The April 16 *Sun-Times* reported that the Cubs sold six hundred gallons of coffee to the sixty-three hundred fans on hand.

SNEAD, JOLLY

The Cubs' 1951 Opening Day ceremonies on April 17 included a 450-foot hit that sailed over the huge center-field scoreboard. Unfortunately the drive came not from one of the Cubs, but from golfer Sam Snead, who—in his street clothes, with a recently broken left hand, and not using a tee—used a four-iron to hit a golf ball off the scoreboard, then a two-iron to clear it.

It was a cold day, but the 18,211 fans left happy because the Cubs beat the Reds 8–3. Old-timers Gabby Hartnett, Freddie Lindstrom, and Charlie Root were all on hand—Root as the Cubs' new first-base coach. Also present was semipro entrepreneur Billy Niesen, spry and full of vinegar at seventy-eight. As president of the local Old Timers' Baseball Association, Niesen watched over many an annual off-season banquet and beer bust for Chicago fans, writers, and players.

OLD-TIME BASEBALL

The 1952 season started soggily. After a week's worth of rain, which canceled some of the preseason Cubs–Sox series and made a mess of Bobby Dorr's newly seeded field, the Cubs opened at home on April 18, bare patches in the outfield and all. "The Cubs are introducing one refreshing novelty to the usual opening-day ceremonies," noted the *Sun-Times*' Edgar Munzel on Opening Day. "There will be no first-ball pitching by any of the politicians who are posturing and mugging with or without benefit of television in this election year."

Cubs general manager Jim Gallagher decided that rather than handing the ball to some dignitary, a loyal fan should be given the privilege of tossing out the ceremonial first pitches. The initial rooter chosen for this honor was fifty-three-year-old Eric Johnson of upstate Rockford, attending his thirtieth straight opener at Wrigley Field. After the first pitch and the customary band music and flag-raising, the Cubs—down 4–1 in the last of the ninth—rallied for four runs and won 5–4 on a two-run double by Bill "Willie the Whip" Serena in front of 20,396.

CLOSED FOR GOOD

On April 20, 1952, the Cubs announced that they were closing off four center-field bleacher sections at the request of Cardinals manager Eddie Stanky. "Eddie Stanky . . . has 2,200 individual enemies in Chicago," stated the *American* the next day. "That's the number of persons a Stanky request deprived from sitting in the sun yesterday at Wrigley Field."

The Cardinals skipper claimed that he wanted the sections blocked off because his hitters couldn't see the ball. It cost the Cubs eighty-dollars extra in ushers to patrol the bleacher section and keep it unoccupied during the game. According to the *Sun-Times*, when Stanky requested that the Cubs keep the bleachers unoccupied for a hitting background, Chicago manager Phil Cavaretta was all for it, and GM Jim Gallagher said OK. Cardinals superstar Stan Musial was pushing for the change, too. "When people are sitting in the middle sections of the center-field bleachers, it's just impossible to follow the ball," he said. "That's why Roy Campanella was beaned here last fall."

This time, the decision to reduce the bleacher count from fifty-two hundred to just three thousand would stick. It stuck because the Cubs themselves forced the decision. Cavaretta, as well as Pirates slugger Ralph Kiner, had previously appealed to Phil Wrigley to close down the bleachers once and for all. It's likely that the team decided to put the onus on Stanky in order to deflect criticism for what was actually an internal decision.

On April 25, with the Cubs entertaining Cincinnati, Jim Gallagher announced to the press that a total of twelve hundred seats—three sections—of the bleachers would be shuttered for the remainder of the season. "Closing the sections will mean a sacrifice of $750 on days when the bleachers ordinarily would be jammed," the *Tribune* reported on April 27th.

With the improved visibility for hitters, home runs and runs scored at Wrigley Field almost immediately increased. Wrigley didn't, however, become one of the *best* hitter's parks in baseball until smaller parks, such as the Polo Grounds, Ebbets Field, Braves Field, and Shibe Park, were abandoned and larger ones, such as Chavez Ravine, County Stadium, and Candlestick Park, were built.

SINKING

The Cubs in the early fifties were a joke, nearly irrelevant in their home town as the White Sox got off the mat in the junior circuit. That doesn't mean that nobody came out to see the Cubs; it's just that often, the Cubs had to *give* tickets away. Ladies Days (Wednesdays in 1953) remained staggeringly popular, with 1953 the first year that the ladies did not have to pay tax or service charges on their freebies. For several years after World War II, the Cubs also distributed up to five hundred tickets per game, through the USO, to military veterans. They did this at least through 1956.

Cubs general manager Jim Gallagher continued to let longtime fans throw out the first ball on Opening Day. For 1953, just a few days after a potential vendors' strike was settled, Mrs. Adele Karstrom, a widow living in suburban Evanston, tossed the first wild one of the season. Ms. Karstrom had seen every Cubs home game since 1933 with the exception of the year 1942, when she lived in Los Angeles—and saw every contest at *that* city's Wrigley Field.

The following year, sixty-one-year-old South Sider Dan Kelly tossed out the first ball, just a few days after three thousand fans welcomed the Cubs and White Sox home from spring training with a downtown ceremony. During these years, Opening Day festivities at Wrigley Field were trimmed to the minimum. Ceremonial first pitches and the raising of the American flag by marine color guards were all that was left of the elaborate ceremonies (flower arrangements, gifts, parades, and the like) of previous decades.

BRAVE COMBO

The Braves' move from Boston to Milwaukee in 1953 proved a boon to the Cubs. In the middle and late 1950s, when Milwaukee was manic over its club, busloads of fans would travel down to Wrigley Field for Braves–Cubs contests. Chicagoans would journey to Milwaukee as well, although not in such great numbers.

On August 16, 1953, 39,903 fans crammed into Wrigley to watch the surprising Braves, second in the NL, sweep the Cubs in a doubleheader. Fan loyalties were divided. It was Pat Pieper Day, in honor of the Cubs' longtime announcer. He got in a good one after a surprise rain delay, which caught fans unprotected. Many fans were hanging their wet shirts from the outfield walls to dry, and Pieper advised them over his microphone to "take in your laundry."

PAY FOR PLAY

Prior to the Cubs' 1954 home opener, Chicago player rep Ralph Kiner announced to the media that he and his teammates would forthwith demand a fee of one hundred dollars for any appearances on radio or television interview shows. Kiner stated that this was not intended as a shakedown. Rather, he explained, "Most of the players would just rather not go on those programs which come when we have to interrupt fielding or batting practice before games."

Amazingly enough, Cubs personnel director Wid Mathews stated that he agreed with the players in this regard. (Imagine the front office today telling the press that they'd have to pay for interviews.) Broadcasters, unhappy with the idea of having to pay players for their time, probably used this opportunity to begin soliciting gifts (clock radios, etc.) for prospective guests on pregame shows. And the issue didn't go away quickly, either. In a juicy irony, Kiner, while a broadcaster for the Mets, attempted in 1964 to interview Phillies pitcher Jim Bunning, who had just tossed a perfect game. Bunning greeted Kiner with a request for payment before he went on screen.

BLOW-UP

Opening Day 1954, April 15, was a bit odd. The Reds blasted the Cubs 11–5 in front of 17,271 fans. Rains delayed the start of the game, chopped batting practice in half, and made the field a mess. In addition, the spectators were surprisingly rowdy. Ed Prell in the *Tribune* called it "one of Wrigley Field's most exuberant Opening Day crowds" and noted that it was quite raucous. Pat Pieper had to warn the fans repeatedly not to throw papers onto the field. Several fans exploded firecrackers in the stands.

SAUER TIMES

Outfielder Hank Sauer was one of the most popular players ever to patrol Wrigley Field's pasture. He was given a day on August 22, 1954, with the Braves in town. The president of his local fan club, a young lady named Mary Joseph, presented her hero with a huge tub of sauerkraut, and he also was given a sports car, a hunting dog, and other tokens.

During the game, a 12–6 loss to Milwaukee in which Sauer went an inconsequential 1-for-5, fans threw packets of chewing tobacco onto the grass in right field. This gifting delayed the game for about two minutes while Sauer and center fielder Dale "Bob" Talbot collected the packages and, according to the *Tribune*'s Irving Vaughn, "stored them in the ivy vines on the right-field fence for safe keeping until the end of the game." One wonders whether Braves right fielder Andy Pafko, himself a popular former Cub, grabbed a pack or two.

These sorts of celebrations, in which fans, fellow players, club officials, and sometimes even members of the press contributed to buy gifts for popular star-quality performers, disappeared from the American sports scene by the early 1970s. With baseball players now making ridiculously higher salaries than most fans, writers, and even team officials, there is no need to give them anything but applause and respect.

ROBBERS' QUARTERS

Prior to the 1955 campaign, the Cubs repainted most of the ballpark, as they often did between seasons, this time doing the lower exterior of the park and the ninety-foot-tall foul poles, among other things. The winter of 1954–55 was surprisingly mild, which allowed grounds chief Bobby Dorr to re-sod the entire field with uncommon success; the field was in remarkably good shape by Opening Day.

But the biggest change at Wrigley Field for 1955 was a new room for umpires. Previously pent up in a small anteroom off the visitors' clubhouse behind first base, the arbiters were given new quarters under the stands down the left-field line. This thirty-thousand-dollar room was, according to the *Tribune*, "plush with a capital P." Unlike any other umpires' quarters in baseball, the Wrigley Field sanctuary included a TV, a new shower room done in marble, natural birch cabinets, a separate shoe bath, and a sitting room with Naugahyde cushions, end tables, and a writing desk. Otis Shepherd designed the room.

KILL YOUR TELEVISION

During the 1955 season, the Cubs had another technology-assisted brainstorm. It was decided that the audio portion of the Cubs' TV broadcasts would be piped in via speakers to a section of the left-field bleachers. This "TV audio section," which featured the tones of Jack Brickhouse, was proudly reported on in the Cubs' official newsletter. The audio broadcasts appear to have continued until the early 1960s.

SAD SAM

Sam Jones, nicknamed "Sad Sam" both for his expression and his demeanor, and "Toothpick" for the ever-present wedge of wood between his teeth, was one of the Cubs' more memorable pitchers of the 1950s. As a rookie with Chicago in 1955, he paced the NL in both strikeouts and walks; he would win two more K crowns before his career ended in the early 1960s.

Before Jones's May 12 start, WGN-TV's Harry Creighton bantered with him, promising to buy him a solid gold toothpick if he could no-hit the visiting Pirates. Jones apparently took Creighton seriously. Only 2,918 fans were at the ballpark on the overcast afternoon, but all were on their feet in the ninth. Jones hadn't yet allowed a hit and had gone 2-for-4 with an RBI as the Cubs led 4–0.

Jones walked the first three hitters he faced—Gene Freese, Preston Ward, and leadoff man Tom Saffell. Rearing back for a bit extra, he then struck out Dick Groat and right fielder Roberto Clemente, then in his first season. Frank Thomas, the club's key slugger, stepped to the plate. Jones whiffed him on a 1–2 count and became the first African American to toss a major league no-hitter. The gem was the first at Wrigley Field since 1917.

And Jones got his gold toothpick.

STEPPIN' OUT

America in the 1950s was a time of great innovation, whether or not the innovation was actually *helpful*. Philip Wrigley presented another ballpark "first" on July 21, 1956, when the Cubs debuted a "speedwalk" in the aisle leading to the upper deck on the right-field side. As do the moving walkways used today at airports, this device allowed fans to be carried upstairs without having to use an ounce of muscle (they could also walk up the ramp in conventional fashion). The speedwalk, however, did not carry fans down from the upper deck.

The first day the speedwalk was in operation, a torrential rainstorm visited Wrigley Field. In high winds, a huge bolt of metal snapped off one of the eight-foot flagpoles on the grandstand roof and tumbled into a box seat. Two spectators, a twelve-year-old boy and a thirty-seven-year-old man, were slightly injured. The game between the Giants and Cubs was eventually called off.

The speedwalk was fraught with mechanical problems, and it never really caught the fans' imagination. Longtime park doyen E. R. "Salty" Saltwell recalls that it was shut down around 1960.

LEGAL PRECEDENT

At least one youngster got permission to cut school for Opening Day 1956 from a higher authority. Judge Wendell Green allowed Jack Kron of Chicago to take his son Larry to the first game of the season, but Kron's estranged wife said no. Green, himself a baseball fan, ruled in favor of father and son.

In forty-one-degree temperatures, the Cubs whipped the Reds 12–1. No-hit Sam Jones threw a complete-game four-hitter. The first ball was tossed by Everett Gregerson, a local cabbie who had gone to all but twelve games at Wrigley since getting out of the army in 1946. Gregerson's pitch was made with a replica of the balls manufactured by Spalding for the National League back in 1876.

The following season, 1957, saw eighty-one-year-old William Klose, who had seen his first Cubs game back in 1886, granted ceremonial first-pitch honors. Klose whipped the ball from the mound on the fly to Cubs catcher Cal Neeman. A Marine Corps reserve corps raised the flag, and Mayor Richard J. Daley, Illinois Governor William B. Stratton, NL President Bill Giles, and 23,674 fans watched the Cubs lose 4–1 to Milwaukee.

The newspapers were especially abuzz because for the first time in many years, the Cubs took to the field in pinstriped uniforms, a style they have kept to this day. The Cubs' 1957 caps, though, were another matter; the odd-looking hats featured six white pipes running from top to bottom.

LAKE VIEW PRIDE . . . AND PREJUDICE

Residents of Lake View have always been proud of their community and have provided the city with some of its most tireless activists. Lake View has also done a good job charting its history and attempting to make sure that it remains a high-quality-of-life area. Helen Zatterberg was the secretary and historian of the Ravenswood–Lake View Historical Association. In *A History of Lake View*, published in 1937, she wrote, "Because Lake View's business life is outstanding, it must not be supposed that home life does not play an important part in the community. The eastern section of Lake View has many large apartment buildings of almost skyscraper appearance, while the western section is a purely residential district made up of blocks and blocks of small homes owned and well cared for by the people who live in them."

In the 1940s, however, some businesses began to close down. The legendary Bendel Bakery at Lincoln and Belmont, in operation for fifty-seven years, closed in 1949. The Best Brewing Company, at 1301 Fletcher, which had been delivering beer to homes and businesses since 1891, also did not survive long past the war. After World War II, young whites flocked to the suburbs to build their families as more African Americans and Latinos moved to the city. Lake View was affected, though not on the surface; in 1953, the Illinois Bell building on Sheffield served seventy-six thousand local customers and 109,000 telephones. Its 1954 retail sales were over $145 million. And by 1957, the area had 132,800 people.

Home ownership in Lake View had declined steadily, according to a 1957 University of Chicago study, however, and industrial and commercial use of the area increased. As the area began to slide, and more stores closed down—especially at Lincoln and Belmont—long-term residents began to age and younger ones moved away. It's not necessary to go into the reasons for the white flight from Lake View, but it *is* important to acknowledge that white flight *did* alter the area. In reality, the neighborhood didn't change for the worse, in terms of the people who came in when the long-term residents left, but the area definitely declined in the opinion of the press and much of the public. Not many blacks have ever lived in Lake View, but lower-income whites and Latinos began moving in during the 1950s. In an article about the history of Lake View, the September 1, 1957, *Tribune* obliquely referred to "problems [that] also plague this neighborhood of Wrigley field, famed ball park and home of the Chicago Cubs." One can assume that these problems had to do with the shifting population and its effect on home values, businesses, and perceived safety.

And Phil Wrigley had been letting the ballpark slip. Bill Veeck Jr. knew this when he bought the White Sox in the late 1950s, and wrote in *Veeck—as in Wreck*: "By 1959, Wrigley was no longer keeping the park freshly painted. The neighborhood had deteriorated badly. None of that mattered. People came into Wrigley Field *knowing* they were comfortable. Just as people who had not been to Comiskey Park in years *knew* it was a crumbling ruin."

There is some truth to his statement, but Veeck is overstating matters so that we will better admire his achievements after he bought the White Sox. People *weren't* actually coming to Wrigley to be comfortable; not many were coming at all. Attendance at Wrigley Field by the late 1950s was quite poor. From 1956 through 1958, the Cubs' attendance was seventh among eight NL clubs. They then ranked sixth in 1959, last in 1960, seventh in 1961, and last among the league's twelve clubs in 1962. In fact, between 1953 and 1967, the White Sox' attendance ranked better among AL teams than the Cubs in the NL *every single season*. And this had little to do with Veeck, who took over the Sox in 1959 and was out just a couple of years later.

These are the days that few people recall as "glorious" in the history of Wrigley Field: the days when the Cubs were a horrible team watched by progressively fewer people. The Cubs *had* started another park improvement program in 1958, replacing much of the original brick walls from the 1914 construction with a buff-colored concrete structure. Wrigley budgeted $1 million for the effort, which also included improving the ticket windows.

There was a perception at the time, however, that the Cubs had become irrelevant to the greater goings on of baseball, and this perception lingered until the Cubs became competitive. The lesson of the 1950s and early 1960s for the Cubs is one that they should have learned in the 1940s—that building a good team was difficult, but necessary. At that time, with entertainment options coming out of every wormhole, you couldn't just give fans sunshine.

PASS THE SALT, PLEASE

E. R. "Salty" Saltwell worked as an executive in Des Moines and other outposts in the Cubs farm system during the 1950s. In 1958, he was summoned to work in Wrigley Field as the team's assistant secretary-treasurer. His first order of business was to straighten out some shady business practices in the Wrigley Field ticket and concession offices. Apparently, some individuals in the offices had been siphoning revenue, although Saltwell never publicly disclosed the names of the guilty.

After longtime traveling secretary Bob Lewis fell ill, Saltwell was assigned to take over his responsibilities for the 1959 and 1960 seasons. When replaced as traveling secretary by Don Biebel in 1961, Saltwell returned to his true bailiwick, park operations. At that point, he pushed for and helped oversee several critical improvements to the park, including permanent seating, new painting, and new restrooms, in the space of a few years. When the Cubs became competitive again in 1967, the park was ready.

But it would be a long while until then.

TAKE ME OUT TO THE BALL GAME

Miss Lavon Carroll threw out the first song of the 1958 season at 'rigley Field at 1:00 p.m. on April 18. But rather than singing "The Star-Spangled

Banner," she belted out "Take Me Out to the Ball Game." Five marines marched out to the right-field corner and hoisted the flag. Seventy-three-year-old Frank P. Carter tossed out the first pitch. "Pitcher Carter, a brown-suited, white-haired fellow, removed his topcoat and hat, seized the baseball, and lofted it from his third base box into the north wind and onto the field," reported David Condon in the *Tribune* the following day. In his column, Condon also found it necessary to mention—twice—that Miss Lavon Carroll had a twenty-three-inch waist. And oh, yes, the Cubs won 11–6. After a hot start, they cruised to an eventual sixth-place finish.

Even the sportswriters were complaining. Robert Cromie wrote in the *Tribune* on July 2, "Heaven knows how many ulcers or cases of extreme dyspepsia got their start in press boxes during those interminable double headers from the cold cheese sandwiches on stale bread, tepid hot dogs, and acid coffee." Of course, Cromie and the others had little reason to complain; in those days, food was provided free to the press.

SUBWAY DOUBLEHEADER

The words "subway doubleheader" are two of the sweetest words in the English language to many a Chicago baseball fan. Those rare days when both Chicago teams are at home, one playing in the afternoon and the other at night, provide a great contrast between ballparks, neighborhoods, and styles of play.

The first such day came on July 1, 1958. The White Sox pulled in 16,639 fans for a night game at Comiskey Park, while the Cubs and Giants drew 16,549 at Wrigley Field. The day game went to the Cubs, 9–5, with the biggest kick coming in the home half of the first inning. Tony Taylor grounded a ball past third base and toward the left-field corner. As Giants left fielder Leon Wagner chased the ball, he lost sight of it. Cubs pitchers sitting in the bullpen down the line jumped from their perches and made it seem as if the ball were rattling around the bench. Wagner took the bait, looking behind the bench, thinking that the ball would be a ground-rule double—not realizing that the ball was sitting some ten feet past the bench near the foul line.

One fan tried to point Wagner in the right direction while Taylor sped around the bases. It was only when Taylor had rounded third that Wagner found the ball. The Giants protested, but the home run stood.

ECCCH

Since 1945, the Cubs had finished third once (in 1946) and fifth once (in 1952). Otherwise, it was sixth, seventh, or eighth. *Every season.* That means that except for 1952, the Cubs didn't rise above sixth place between 1947 and 1966.

In 1959, the Cubs altered their game starting times to 2:00 p.m. on weekdays and 1:00 for Saturday and Sunday games. The reason given by the Cubs was that the times seemed to work well for pro football. The new start time didn't prevent an April 10 snow out of Opening Day 1959, the first such Cubs opener cancellation in memory. Assumedly even Everett Lee, who first saw the Cubs play in 1903 and threw out the first pitch on April 11, didn't remember losing a game to snowfall.

The biggest news around Wrigley Field in April 1959 was the last-minute aversion of a possible vendor strike. Union local 236 asked Cubs management for a guarantee of five dollars per vendor in case of games called by rain as well as a hike in commissions. The Cubs agreed on the guarantee but balked at the commission raise. The two sides came to an agreement before Opening Day.

GOT BALLS?

June 30, 1959, saw perhaps the oddest play ever at Wrigley Field—one in which two balls were in play at once. Stan Musial walked in the fourth inning. The Cubs argued that ball four, which sailed by catcher Sammy Taylor, actually had grazed Musial's bat. Taylor didn't chase the ball, and the alert Musial headed for second.

Plate umpire Vic Delmore absent-mindedly handed pitcher Bob Anderson a new ball, while third baseman Al Dark retrieved the original ball from the Cubs batboy. Clearly, the original ball was still in play, despite Delmore's error. Dark threw this ball toward second, while Anderson fired *his* ball toward second at the same time. Anderson heaved his ball right over second baseman Tony Taylor's head, but Dark's toss bounced in to Ernie Banks, who tagged out Musial between second and third.

Players and managers from both clubs ran onto the field and began arguing. The whole episode succeeded in "promoting perhaps the most hilarious moments ever witnessed in the staid north side park," in the words of the *Tribune*'s Ed Prell. "Not even Bill Veeck of the White Sox could have conjured up such a zany episode." The umpiring crew eventually ruled Musial out, with the resulting St. Louis protest rendered unnecessary as the Cardinals went on to win 4–1. Umpire Delmore was fired over the winter.

THE LONGEST

On August 14, the Cubs blew out the visiting Giants 20–9. The nine-inning contest took three hours and fifty minutes to complete, a new National

League record. Pitchers from both teams walked a total of nineteen hitters. Giants starter Jack Sanford was ejected for arguing balls and strikes just three hitters into the first. Eight homers were hit, and the clubs combined to leave twenty-one men on base. The Giants actually led 7–6 after three innings, but the Cubs scored four in the fourth, two in the sixth, six in the seventh, and two in the eighth. They scored in seven of their eight frames. A crowd of 17,963 witnessed the carnage.

I GOT A NEW CLUBHOUSE, AND YOU CAN'T COME IN

Prior to 1960, the Cubs clubhouse was located on the mezzanine level on the third-base side. In 1960, however, the team finally moved into a new structure in the left-field corner. The new clubhouse came complete with a lounge, a trainer's room, and a separate manager's office. The visitors' clubhouse was also expanded and spiffed up.

The new dressing room was constructed in the corner because it was, according to Salty Saltwell, the only space available. The old upstairs cubbyhole is now used as the ballpark's security headquarters. "That was still inadequate," Saltwell said of the left-field corner clubhouse, which served the team until 1983. "With the clubs now, [it's] not only the twenty-five players on the active roster; [you have] your training rooms, your weight rooms, a whole new situation."

The Cubs made other changes as well. During the winter, the club had rebuilt more than a quarter of the lower grandstand, laying new concrete foundations and seat slabs. The foul screen behind home plate was replaced with a new screen laid at a sharper angle. A new fan entrance, with new ticket booths and façade, was built at Clark and Addison. Finally, the club repainted the scoreboard and re-sodded the playing surface. The cost of the assorted repairs was noted at four hundred thousand dollars.

. . . TO THE RIDICULOUS

On Opening Day, April 22, 1960, the weather was the best that anyone could remember for a Cubs opener, reaching eighty degrees. Eighty-three-year-old retired fireman John Miller and his wife threw out first pitches. Pat Pieper began his fifty-seventh year as the Cubs' field announcer. (He really did make his public address statements from the field, sitting near the backstop, close enough to hear the umpire officially announce new players into the game.) Although the Cubs lost to the Giants, 10–8, Dick Dozer of the *Tribune* reported that the bleachers were the real center of activity as "a young lady did an impromptu—and complete—striptease."

The next day, the Giants destroyed the Cubs 18–2 in front of, in Dozer's words, "an unbelieving assemblage of 24,703." He continued, "Spectator shenanigans have been at a new high in the balmy weather the last two days . . . One damsel was escorted from her box seat near first base due to over-imbibing. Youths have been climbing the new backstop screen to wrestle baseballs thru the mesh during the game's progress, and Saturday, hundreds of youngsters trampled over the field to hamper a TV crew attempting to make a film."

At least *someone* was having fun. On April 24, George Altman of the Cubs walked on just three balls. Umpire Ken Burkhart forgot the count after calling a balk on Giants pitcher Billy O'Dell.

"COME ON, MOOSE!"

The Cubs traded for hard-throwing right-handed pitcher Don Cardwell on May 13, 1960, obtaining him from the Phillies, with Ed Bouchee, for Cal Neeman and Tony Taylor. Cardwell started the second game of a Sunday doubleheader, May 15, at Wrigley Field, against St. Louis. An unexpected throng of 33,543 showed up.

After walking Alex Grammas in the first, Cardwell mowed the Cardinals down one by one. In the eighth, Jerry Kindall made a terrific play at second base against Daryl Spencer, then Cardwell fanned pinch hitter Stan Musial to retire the side. The ninth began at 5:45 p.m. with the Cubs up 4–0 and the shadows breaking across the field. Carl Sawatski lined hard to George Altman in right as the fans roared. Pinch hitter George Crowe flied to Richie Ashburn for the second out. Cardwell went to 3-and-2 on Cardinals leadoff man Joe Cunningham as the fans screamed in spasms of excitement. Cunningham rapped the next pitch to short left field. Slow-footed outfielder Walt "Moose" Moryn moved forward in pursuit, running toward the infield through the shadows. "Come on, Moose!" exhorted telecaster Jack Brick-house. Moryn picked the ball off his shoe tops and ran in holding the spheroid aloft, a huge smile creasing his face. Hundreds of fans broke out onto the field to mob Cardwell.

Radio color man Lou Boudreau could barely get to Cardwell, but he did eventually carry on a short postgame interview as thousands of fans milled around the field, chanting and cheering. It was, as Jimmy Enright wrote in *Chicago Cubs*, "Cubs' fans' biggest on-the-field celebration since Gabby Hartnett's famous homer in 1938." Andy Frain, according to Edgar Munzel in *The Sporting News*, claimed that it was the wildest celebration ever seen at Wrigley Field. Munzel continued, "It looked as if Cardwell actually was in danger of injury as the fans tried to get near their newfound hero."

Eventually, Cardwell finished the interview with Boudreau and made it to the clubhouse.

Videotape exists for the last two innings of this game; it is probably the oldest visual document of a regular-season no-hitter. At the time, WGN-TV used just three cameras to cover games: one behind the plate at field level; one in the vacant center-field bleachers looking toward the plate (a WGN innovation); and one in the first row of the upper deck on the third-base side. The next year, the Cubs added a fourth camera, behind the plate in the upper deck, for their game coverage.

RAYMOND ON THE FIELD

Longtime Cubs fan Ray Kush, a nephew of 1940s Cubs pitcher Emil Kush, was thirteen years old in 1960 and happened to be at the ballpark that magical day. "Because of the doubleheader, it was a big crowd. During the second games of doubleheaders, a lot of fans would leave early. But because of the no-hitter, many more stayed. The shadows were falling, and it was about 6:00 when the Cubs made the last out. It was so exciting, my friend Bucky and I just followed a lot of other fans right onto the field.

"Did we go through the door, or just jump over the wall? I think we went over the wall. It was just a few seconds and the whole infield was full." Kush became part of the milling mob that nearly squashed Cardwell and Boudreau.

"I'd never do something like that now," Kush remarked.

BEATEN SENSELESS

Cardwell's achievement aside, the Cubs were bad again in 1960. On August 1, Jerome Holtzman of the *Sun-Times* took aim at Phil Wrigley as Chicago's NL entry staggered along in last: "One of the intriguing aspects of the Cubs is the myth which P. K. Wrigley has successfully created about himself. In this myth, P. K. pictures himself as a 'hands-off' owner . . . merely a figurehead with his subordinates making all the important decisions. . . . But this is simply not true. It's Wrigley, himself, who sits at the head of the table and makes the final decisions. . . . That the Cubs are dying is not news, but they are disintegrating like a tree. They are dead at the top."

Four days later, Cincinnati Reds infielder Billy Martin took exception to a high and inside pitch and punched Cubs pitcher Jim Brewer in the face. The blow broke the orbital bone near Brewer's right eye. The Cubs won 5–3 anyway to move within 20^1/$_2$ games of first place. Grady Hatton, a thirty-seven-year-old journeyman who hadn't been in the majors since 1956, was at that time the Cubs' second baseman.

WHERE'S THE FIRE?

During the sixth inning of an otherwise sleepy 6–5 Cubs loss to the Giants on May 28, 1961, a portable hot dog cart blew up in the box seats down the right-field line. Ballpark personnel could not put out the blaze as the kerosene-powered cart shot flames twenty feet into the air.

Eventually, the men from Engine 78, the firehouse just down the block on Waveland Avenue, sprang into action. They dropped a hose over the right-field stands, entered the park, and quickly extinguished the fire.

ICE BALL

Opening Day 1962 at Wrigley Field was Friday, April 13. It was indeed an omen, as the team was about to suffer through its worst season to date. The Cubs entered the season full of optimism. But they dropped three straight at Houston to the brand-new Colt .45s, then returned home to find only 9,750 fans waiting at freshly painted Wrigley Field on a bitterly cold day. Before the Cubs and Cardinals took the field, longtime traveling secretary Bob Lewis, who had retired after thirty-three years of service, tossed the first ice ball.

It was frigid enough that St. Louis manager Johnny Keane built a fire under the stands so his pitchers could stay warm. To make everyone on the premises even more miserable, the contest went on for four hours and forty minutes, and the Cubs lost 9–5. Rookie outfielder Lou Brock led off the Cubs first by drilling a home run over the right-field wall onto Sheffield Avenue. Later that season, Brock would homer into the Polo Grounds' center-field bleachers, some 460 feet away, becoming only the second player ever to do so. For the year, he hit .263 with nine homers. Management was disappointed.

TELSTAR

The most important event of 1962 at Wrigley Field occurred July 24, when the first intercontinental broadcast, carried around the world via the Telstar broadcast satellite, brought a short piece of the Cubs–Phillies game to an estimated 200 million viewers.

WGN's Ward Quaal, a critical figure in early television broadcasting in Chicago, had offered the U.S. Information Agency some representative programming for the Telstar, and by luck a game happened to be on the schedule the very day of the international broadcast. As millions watched, most of them with no idea of what was happening, longtime Cubs telecaster Jack Brickhouse described Philadelphia infielder Tony Taylor's fly out to George Altman and then Johnny Callison's single to right. The entire segment at Wrigley Field lasted just over ninety seconds. "Our translators are at this moment going out of their minds trying to figure out how to say 'runs, hits, and errors' in Italian and Swedish," Brickhouse joked to the teeming millions during the short telecast.

The complex setup was explained by WGN's Carl Meyers in the next day's *Tribune*.

> The voices of Brickhouse and others were picked up from the WGN booth high in the Wrigley Field stands. The pictures were picked up from the four regular camera positions on the field and overlooking it. The signals then were sent by wire and coaxial cable to the big remote control truck situated under the stands.
>
> From the truck, by wire and coaxial cable, the TV signals were sent to the Illinois Bell Telephone company headquarters downtown, and then, in turn, to WNBQ [now WMAQ] in the Merchandise Mart; the New York network headquarters, where all segments of the three-network pool pickup were assembled for transmission over land lines or micro-wave relay to Andover, Me.; and then to Telstar, 3,000 miles up in the air.

On December 22, 1962, the surf-music instrumental "Telstar," written by studio genius Joe Meek and recorded by the Tornadoes, became the first song by a British group ever to hit number one on the *Billboard* charts—a full thirteen months before the Beatles.

I WANNA STAY HOME

The Cubs were awarded the privilege of hosting 1962's second All-Star Game. The contest was held July 30, less than a week after the Telstar broadcast. The All-Star Game, the first in Wrigley since 1947, was viewed as a big enough deal that for the first time in a decade (and the last to date) the center-field bleachers were opened.

One has to wonder about the wisdom of scotching a safety rule in order to jam more cheeks into the bleachers for an exhibition game, especially one featuring the game's best and most valuable players. But the AL and NL player representatives approved it; more people in the park meant more proceeds. Tickets were eight dollars and six dollars for the best box seats.

Barry Gifford, a writer who grew up going to Cubs games, recalls waiting in line for All-Star tickets in his memoir, *The Neighborhood of Baseball*: "Steve [Friedman] and I were determined to have our regular bleacher seats for the game and so joined an already considerable bleachers box office queue at four o'clock the morning of the game. Fans had set up card tables, playing by lantern light; some were wrapped up in sleeping bags; others were crouched down against the wall passing wine or whiskey bottles. The ticket sale began about ten."

A crowd of 38,359 fans jammed Wrigley Field for the contest. The bleachers were filled by 11:00 a.m., two hours before game time. Friedman, now a successful scriptwriter, and Gifford both got seats. The jammed press bus received a motorcycle escort from the journalists' hotel to Wrigley. Andy Frain hired 350 ushers, who reported at 7:00 a.m. for training. A Chicago police battalion was also on hand.

Arch Ward's widow, Helen, threw out the first ball, while all sorts of dignitaries, including Joe Cronin, Will Harridge, Stan Hack, Ray Schalk, Bill Nicholson, and Cal Hubbard, stood around looking dignified. Cubs Ernie Banks, Billy Williams, and George Altman all appeared in the game. In the eighth inning, Banks tripled off the center-field wall and scored on Williams's groundout. The National League still lost 9–4.

In a column later published in *The Jerome Holtzman Baseball Reader*, Holtzman notes that, when asked by the *Daily News*' Jack Kuenster if he was going to attend the game, Phil Wrigley demurred. The curious Cubs owner commented that he'd rather a fan have the tickets, and that he'd get a better view of the game if he stayed home and watched it on television. This comment, of course, led to derision. Bill Veeck, who had operated the crosstown White Sox until the previous season, gloated, "He's telling the fans to stay home and watch the game on television!"

"Staying home to watch the game on television" was a particularly apt choice of words. Cub fans all over the city were doing the same thing. In 1962, the Cubs were 59–103, their poorest record in history, and dropped to ninth place—their lowest standing ever thanks to the two new expansion franchises that had entered the NL that season. The club's overall attendance fell to 609,802, the lowest of any club in the majors and their worst since 1943.

THE DAILY PLANET

At this time, the Lake View neighborhood, especially that surrounding Wrigley Field, was deteriorating. Years of poor play had taken the excitement out of games at Wrigley, and in the latter part of the 1950s, management had stopped repainting and sprucing up the park.

When he went there—and he did, contrary to popular belief—P. K. Wrigley tried to blend in with the crowds, sitting in grandstand seats rather than drawing attention to himself in his field box. Said Claude Brooks, secretary of the Wrigley Company in 1977, "He always tried to go incognito because he wanted to be in the position of the fan. He said you would never find out how the fans were treated if you went and sat in the owner's box."

Wrigley risked this although he had plenty of reason to hide. The Cubs were at perhaps their lowest ebb. With a ridiculous managerial system (the "College of Coaches," instituted in 1961), a club of mediocrities, a fan base shrunk by poor management, and the strong play of the White Sox, the Cubs didn't seem to have a hope. Wrigley said at the time, "When the bulldozer breaks down, it's time to change the driver." As Jerome Holtzman wrote later, "What he didn't realize, or refused to acknowledge, was that it was the bulldozer that required repair."

Crowds in the low thousands were common. As George Castle has pointed out, Wrigley was losing money a lot of the time just by opening up his gates for the few thousand who might trickle in. Did P. K. Wrigley care? Of course he did. He had a competitive streak just like anyone else, as well as a cast-iron ego. But did he care enough to risk his ego, get rid of the deadwood, hire bright new people, and risk hearing "no" from his subordinates? No. Wrigley was an innovator, an inventor, a tinkerer. He certainly wasn't afraid to try new things—the College of Coaches is evidence of that—but any new ideas he would try were his own. He didn't want to be forced into adopting anything—by public opinion, by the press, by changing social conditions, or by the National League—so he wouldn't do something he didn't want to unless it became absolutely necessary.

Integration? Not his idea. Night baseball wasn't his idea. Selling the team wasn't his idea. Dumping Leo Durocher, during the clubhouse wars of the early 1970s, wasn't his idea. Nothing changed at Wrigley Field until Wrigley *said* it would change. Phil Wrigley appears to have been afraid of several things—the media, the public, letting things get out of his hands. Hence he maintained an organization full of yes-men afraid to tell him when his ideas were lousy. And by the 1960s, they were. He may have known how to sell gum and sell the ballpark experience, but his knowledge of baseball was simply inadequate.

Some have attributed his lack of innovation in hiring real baseball people to a generous streak, a paternalistic desire to provide security for his employees. Charlie Grimm said in 1977, "The reason he worked out that ten-coach system was just to give the men involved security. He confided that to me one time." While that kindness helped feed the families of Wrigley's baseball men, it didn't help the Cubs win.

OFF THE BASES

The Cubs hired the first black coach in big league history on May 30, 1962. Buck O'Neil, famous for many years for his goodwill, his great storytelling, and his pioneering work in scouting blacks for the majors, joined the Chicago staff, but with little on-field responsibility. O'Neil was *not* part of the College of Coaches managerial rotation. Despite his talents, O'Neil felt GM John Holland and longtime Cubs fixture Charlie Grimm would look for any excuse to keep him under a bushel for as long as possible.

George Castle, in *The Million-to-One Team*, quoted O'Neil: "I got all these players, but they weren't playing them at the same time. I told Mr. Holland we'd have a better ball club if we played the blacks. Then he showed me a basket of letters from fans saying, 'What are you trying to do, make the Cubs into the Kansas City Monarchs?' We weren't appealing to the black fans anyway, playing on the North Side of Chicago."

In his biography *I Was Right on Time*, O'Neil recalls a game in Houston when two coaches in the Cubs' rotation were ejected. Grimm, sitting in the press box, called down and had pitching coach Freddie Martin take over the third-base box rather than O'Neil. If Holland and Grimm allowed their personal viewpoints, or those of a few prejudiced fans, to dictate on-field policy, then the Cubs organization was craven and ignorant at best and racist at worst. And Phil Wrigley has to bear the responsibility for that. But Wrigley did agree to hire O'Neil, which says something about his willingness to "buck" tradition.

What Cubs fans wanted then was a winning team, just as they want one now. They took to Ernie Banks. They took to Billy Williams, and Fergie Jenkins, and Bill Madlock. And to Sammy Sosa.

COLONEL WHITLOW, IN THE OUTFIELD, WITH THE FUNGO BAT

To deal with the lack of spirit on the club, Phil Wrigley, a military and college man, decided that the Cubs needed an athletic director. Apparently, nobody told P. K. that this was a terrible idea, so former Air Force Colonel Robert Whitlow came on board. The 6'5", 230-pound Whitlow, who had no experience in organized baseball, came aboard to supervise the Cubs' field operations, training, conditioning, and the like. Bringing a crusty military man into the College of Coaches was foolhardy, especially when Whitlow took the field during workouts, toting a fungo bat and wearing uniform number one.

Opening Day, April 9, 1963, found Whitlow doing field drills with the players before the game. Some 18,556 fans braved temperatures below forty and winds from center field at seventeen miles an hour. And at this time, the dugouts at Wrigley were unheated. Chicago's Easter Seals child of 1963, eight-year-old Linda Cody, tossed out the first ball. During the game, the band playing in the stands broke into a rousing chorus of "Jingle Bells," much to the chilled fans' satisfaction. The Dodgers won 3–2, but perhaps the biggest story of the day was that while Arthur Allyn, owner of the White Sox, was on hand, P. K. Wrigley—as usual—was not. Whitlow was forced into some rather tepid explanations for Wrigley's absence.

THE WOOD AND THE WIRE

The first tangible evidence of Whitlow's effect on Wrigley Field was a wire fence, painted green, measuring eight feet high and sixty-four feet wide. Ivy was planted so that it would grow up the fence. This fence was installed June 18, 1963, atop the outfield wall in center field, spanning the closed-off bleachers. With the wire fence in place, the height now needed to hit a home run into the center-field bleachers was nineteen and a half feet.

According to Whitlow, Cubs players requested the new fence. Cubs head coach Bob Kennedy said that the fence was "news" to him, effectively distancing himself from Whitlow's decision. Meanwhile, GM John Holland, according to the *Tribune*, claimed that both Chicago and opposing players wanted an even better hitting background. "We've changed the color of the vacant seats several times in the last several years trying for compatibility. We just hope this new dash of ivy does it." The fence would soon come down.

THREE-HEADED HYDRA

The fence was just one sign of the tension between Whitlow, Kennedy, and Holland. By Opening Day 1964, it was no secret that dissension in the organization had reached a boiling point. The *Sun-Times'* Jack Griffin spent some of his Opening Day with a photographer in tow, interviewing fans about their feelings concerning the front office. One fan, Allan Jones, noted, "I don't think we should have an athletic director. You got three guys telling everyone what to do. So who's going to listen to whom?"

WRIGLEY AND O'MALLEY

By the early 1960s, the Cubs weren't drawing fans, and other NL owners were noticing. Dodgers owner Walter O'Malley claimed, at the 1962 winter meetings, that he lost money every time he brought his team to Chicago and that something should be done about that park without lights. While O'Malley might have commanded his limousine driver to stop so that he could pick up a penny he saw on the street, his colleagues were hardly less money-conscious and began to pressure Wrigley to add lights to his park.

At that point, the stubborn and civic-minded Wrigley asked the local Lake View Citizens Council (LVCC) to come up with a petition against the idea of night baseball. Once the group collected five thousand signatures against the installation of lights, Wrigley could then point to community opposition to the idea. There would be no lights at Wrigley Field on his watch.

BOWLING FOR STRIKES

Some Cubs remained in the neighborhood even after their playing days. During May 1963, former Cubs pitcher Russ "The Mad Monk" Meyer was hired as a manager of the Belmont Bowl at 1637 W. Belmont, four blocks west and four blocks south of Wrigley Field. The alley was owned by Joseph Stone Sr. and Jr., who together ran a nearby Bulko gas station.

HUBBS FANS BID KID ADIEU

Chicago Cubs second baseman Kenny Hubbs was killed while piloting his small plane on February 13, 1964, outside of Provo, Utah. Hubbs' performance helped the rebuilding Cubs improve twenty-three games in 1963 to finish 82–80, their best record since 1946. While Hubbs wasn't much of a hitter, his death dispirited the club, ruined the defense, and shot Chicago into another tailspin from which it didn't recover until 1967.

At the home opener on April 18, a day that reached eighty degrees, the *Tribune*'s Robert Markus reported on the pregame ceremony honoring Hubbs: "While the competing Cubs and Phillies stood at attention, heads bowed, along the third and first base lines, the Opening Day crowd of 18,868 rose for a minute of silent prayer. The storm clouds overhead gave an extra aspect of gloom to the proceedings. As the announcer intoned, 'Amen,' a sudden gust of wind raised a whirlpool of dust over the second base area where Kenny Hubbs performed so brilliantly for the Cubs. Then it was gone . . . just as Hubbs is gone."

CAN-CAN

Prior to the opening of the 1964 season, Wrigley Field did *not* get its usual coat of fresh paint. It did get its customary new sod, laid in early April. (By this time, Bobby Dorr had died and Pete Marcantonio was the new head of groundskeeping.) Wrigley *was* graced, however, by brand-new restrooms behind home plate. The facilities that were above average in 1947 were distinctly below by 1964, when senior circuit clubs in Milwaukee, Los Angeles, San Francisco, New York, and Houston were playing in newer parks.

The changes to the restrooms included new tiles on the walls; fluorescent lighting much brighter than the old bulb system; seven private stalls in the men's room and presumably more in the ladies'; wall-to-wall plumbing; and a stainless-steel circular washstand (a technology still in operation at Wrigley) operated by a treadle that allowed several people to wash their hands at the same time.

In the *American*, Bill Gleason remarked, "You have to say this for P. K. Wrigley. When he does something he does it in a big way . . . He has installed the major leagues' most modern comfort stations. Long after the score of the Cubs' '64 home opener has been mercifully forgotten, many fans will remember their first visit to the lavish new facilities that are located under the stands behind home plate."

Dick Hackenberg of the *Sun-Times* opined that "the new men's rooms are the last word in relief stations. A new hand-washing gadget seems too readily convertible to a shower bath, but nobody was complaining. The women's rooms, too, are the acme of perfection, but this will have to come to you as pure hearsay from an unimpeachable source."

SKOKIE SWIFT

The Chicago Transit Authority debuted a new train line on April 20, 1964. The Skokie Swift ran from the Dempster Street bus and train depot in Skokie nonstop to the Howard Street station at the border of Chicago and Evanston. Over the years, thousands of Cubs fans from Skokie, Morton Grove, Lincolnwood, and other suburbs have taken the Skokie Swift to the Howard line, which then transported them to Wrigley Field. Fares at the time for the Swift were forty-five cents for adults and twenty-nine cents for kids and students. Transfers were free.

ERNIE'S DAY

The Cubs gave Ernie Banks his day on Sunday, August 15, 1964, before a 6–4 loss to the Pittsburgh Pirates. Some 23,003 fans came to pay tribute to Ernie, one of the most popular players ever to appear in Chicago. Mayor Richard M. Daley decreed that August 15 was Ernie Banks Day. Two thousand youngsters from local little and pony leagues, dressed in their uniforms, took the field during the ceremony.

The Cubs gave their first baseman a diamond ring, while local fans chipped in to present Banks and his wife, Eloyce, with a car. Local sportswriters bought savings bonds for each of Banks's three children, and Ernie's teammates gave him a sterling silver tray. Cubs radio announcer Jack Quinlan presented Banks with a transoceanic transistor radio, while TV voice Jack Brickhouse acted as emcee. The *Tribune* noted, "Phil Wrigley, president of the Cubs, who conceived Banks day, was not present."

OUT OF COMMISSION

With new stadia—some of which could accommodate more than one sport—constructed or planned for construction in many major U.S. cities, Mayor Richard M. Daley decided to see about getting one of these new multipurpose parks built for Chicago's sports teams. Daley formed a commission in 1964 to examine the topic. P. K. Wrigley and White Sox president Arthur Allyn, as well as several distinguished local citizens, were members of the group.

But no such stadium would be forthcoming. After Allyn quit the group, wishing to keep the Sox in their own park, and Wrigley bowed out citing a conflict of interest, the commission folded.

(I WISH IT COULD BE) 1965 AGAIN

Fans coming to Wrigley Field for Opening Day 1965 saw Al Jourgensen, a forty-one-year Cub employee, throw out first ball. Jourgensen had worked as an usher, a grounds crew member, an office boy, a press box man, and, from 1946 on, a scoreboard operator.

Those fans in the first ten rows of the box seats were in new self-rising plastic chairs, replacing the less comfortable, barely-bolted-in chairs from previous years. It does seem amazing now that it would take the Cubs such a long time to provide the fans in the most expensive seats with quality chairs in which to sit.

The day before the game, grounds superintendent Pete Marcantonio and his twenty-man crew were scrambling around trying to get everything in top shape. "This is the toughest time we've ever had getting everything done," Marcantonio told Bob Smith of the *Daily News*. It had been a chilly spring, and the sod hadn't taken; therefore, green vegetable dye was hurriedly sprayed on the new, already browning grass. There was no batting practice, as the tarp remained on the field in threatening and chilly conditions. The gloom lent extra poignancy to a short pregame memorial to broadcaster Jack Quinlan, a rising star who had been killed in a spring-training auto crash in

Arizona. Vince Lloyd, formerly the number-two man on Cubs TV broad-casts with Jack Brickhouse, was shifted to the radio booth to fill the vacancy and began his long and successful tenure as the "Voice of the Cubs," team-ing with the equally popular Lou Boudreau.

The game, between the Cubs and Cardinals, was a cracker, going eleven full innings before being called a 10–10 tie. The Cardinals plated five runs in the first, but the Cubs came back and eventually knotted things up with three runs in the last of the ninth on a two-out Ernie Banks home run off former Cub Barney Schultz. Each team scored once in the eleventh before everyone decided to hang it up for the day. The 19,751 cold but enthusiastic fans saw St. Louis center fielder Curt Flood make one of the greatest catches in the history of Wrigley Field, leaping the wall in left-center to snare a line drive by Len Gabrielson. "Never seen anything like it! *Never* seen anything like it!" screamed Cardinals radio man Harry Caray.

WHAT COULD BE MORE SIMPLE THAN THE CUBS?

Columnist Armand Schneider, in the April 12, 1965, *Daily News*, heralded Wrigley Field as the favorite playground of the "night shift," both ridiculing and romanticizing the pathetic state of the club and its dwindling fan base.

> The Cubs and the people who work at night deserve each other. During the daylight hours, they live in a perpetual stupor, clinging to each other like lost brethren. Each comes out of winter hibernation into the sunshine.
>
> The Cubs are the comedy act for the night people, who sleep through such intellectual pastimes as the "Beverly Hillbillies" and "McHale's Navy" and "Peyton Place."
>
> There is no other place to sit for the night people but in the bleachers . . . To sleep while the sun radiates its warmth into the open bleachers is almost sinful.
>
> If the guy is really a swinger he sits in that little nook in the upper portion of the right-center-field bleachers where the gamblers hang out. It's like a poor man's Las Vegas. Every pitch means a bet.
>
> The White Sox are Chicago's sports equivalent of such deep-thinking stuff as Vietnam and the Berlin Wall and tax reform. Everyone takes the Sox too much to heart. It's the simple life a guy yearns for after a hard night's work, and what can be more simple than the Cubs?

This photo, from the March 29, 1914, *Tribune,* shows the construction of Weeghman Park from the new seats in right-center field. (Courtesy of Raymond D. Kush)

Sunday Tribune, 3/29/14

Record-Herald, 4/23/14

This testimonial ad, printed in the April 23, 1914, Chicago *Record-Herald,* describes in dramatic terms the Wittbold Company's work in landscaping Weeghman Park. (Courtesy of Raymond D. Kush)

Record-Herald, 4/23/14

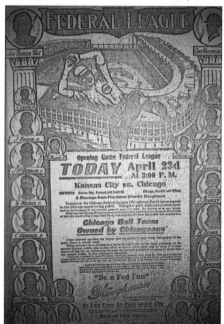

Charley Weeghman took out notices in all the Chicago dailies touting the opening of his new ballpark. This is from the April 23, 1914, *Record-Herald.* (Courtesy of Raymond D. Kush)

Chifeds manager Joe Tinker stands before a huge flower garland at Weeghman Park's Opening Day ceremonies, April 23, 1914. (Courtesy of Raymond D. Kush)

The *Chicago Herald* printed this picture of Charles Weeghman (in profile, sixth from left) purchasing the Chicago Cubs on January 20, 1916. (Courtesy of Raymond D. Kush)

This photo of the "new look" Wrigley Field ran in the April 7, 1923, *Tribune.* Newly completed renovations had expanded park capacity from nineteen thousand to around thirty-one thousand. (Courtesy of Raymond D. Kush)

Members of the Wrigley Field grounds crew line up for action down the right-field line in 1927. (Courtesy of Raymond D. Kush)

Cubs Park, 1927

Cubs vs. Giants, 1937

This 1937 shot captures Wrigley Field in the beginning of its eventual renovation. Note that the old scoreboard has been moved from center field to the left-field corner and that construction has begun on the shortened outfield wall. (Courtesy of Raymond D. Kush)

Rick Reuschel of the Cubs delivers the first pitch of the 1977 baseball season to Lee Mazzilli of the Mets. Note the red outfield wall doors (painted green in the early 1980s) and the Cubs flag on the left-field foul pole. (Courtesy of Raymond D. Kush)

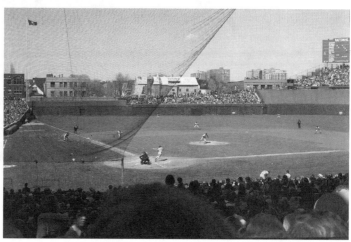

Opening Day, 1977

Wrigley Field on August 29, 1983. Beer advertisements hang from the scoreboard, and the tarpaulin, usually lying over the center-field bleachers to provide a good background for batters, has been rolled up. (Courtesy of Raymond D. Kush)

Legendary Cubs broadcaster Harry Caray fiddles around in the booth on September 15, 1984. The radio and TV booths were moved upstairs in 1990; the old booths are now luxury suites. (Courtesy of Raymond D. Kush)

The Cubs have just won Game Two of the 1984 National League Championship Series on October 3, 1984. Pitcher Lee Smith, catcher Jody Davis, and third baseman Ron Cey meet for congratulations. Members of the grounds crew rush to the tarpaulin, and a security man in a white pith helmet moves to safeguard the field. (Courtesy of Raymond D. Kush)

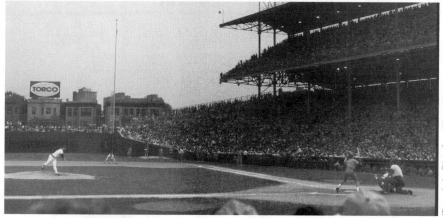

On August 8, 1988, Rick Sutcliffe of the Cubs delivered the first pitch of Wrigley Field's first night game to Phil Bradley of the Phillies. Bradley would homer in this at-bat. The game was eventually washed out by rain, and the first *official* night game would have to wait until the next day. (Courtesy of Raymond D. Kush)

NBC sent a crew to nationally televise the August 9, 1988, game. For this first official night game at Wrigley Field, announcers Joe Garagiola (left) and Vin Scully are sitting in a specially constructed box in the upper deck. (Courtesy of Raymond D. Kush)

CHICAGO FEDERAL LEAGUE TEAM—1914

Photo—Burke & Atwell

Top row, left to right—Walsh, Stanley, Wilson, McGuire, Tinker, Jackson, Watson, Kading, Flack, McDonough, Lang
Middle row, left to right—Fritz, Beck, Kavanaugh, Brennan, Black, Wickland.
Front row, left to right—Zeider, Farrell, Fisk, Block, Zwilling, Prendergast.

The 1914 Chicago Federal League franchise, the club for which Weeghman Park (later Wrigley Field) was built. (Courtesy of Stuart Shea)

A typical Cubs scene of the 1970s: full bleachers and a largely empty grandstand. (Courtesy of George Castle)

The lights are on! Wrigley Field, for the first time, sports its new lighting system for a charity benefit on July 25, 1988. (Photo by Sandy Bertog, courtesy of George Castle)

A shirtless Bill Veeck (left) speaks with George Castle in the Wrigley Field bleachers in 1981. (Photo by Sandy Bertog, courtesy of George Castle)

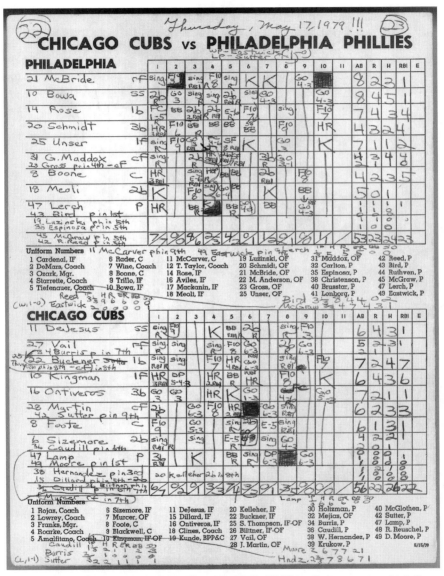

George Castle's scorecard of the May 17, 1979, Phillies–Cubs game, which the Phils won 23–22 at Wrigley Field.

CHAPTER 7

Bears, Bruisers, and Boxers: Wrigley Field's Non-Baseball History

KEEP IT IN A COOL DRY PLACE

At ninety years old, Wrigley Field needs its rest. With its centennial in sight, the green cathedral at Clark and Addison needs the peace and quiet of an off day during the baseball season as well as the off-season from October through April. Just like anyone (or anything) else of advanced age, the place needs no more agitation than the occasional groundskeeper's implement, the rumbling of the "el" into the Addison Street station, and the good old reliable Chicago wind. Would anyone in their right mind take their '53 Corvette on an everyday chore, navigating the Wal-Mart parking lot, when front-and-center placement in the Fourth of July parade is more apropos? Does one simply throw open the doors to a historic building and put more wear and tear on it?

Say what you want about the corporate owners, but the boys at Tribune Tower have carefully kept Wrigley Field for its original intended purpose: as a baseball park. The edifice is so legendary, so popular, one of Chicago's top five tourist attractions, that a truly greedy proprietor would abuse the property. A three-ring circus would reside in the ivy-covered confines as paying customers flocked in practically year-round, amazed at the simple fact they're in *Wrigley Field*.

But other than the occasional Cubs-oriented corporate event and the annual Chicago Public League baseball championship game (which alternates between Wrigley and U.S. Cellular Field, depending on which team is in town), Wrigley in its dotage stands empty, by design, on days when major league baseball is not scheduled.

"It's now an integrity-of-the-field issue," says John McDonough, the Cubs' vice president of marketing and broadcasting, and frequent business-side spokesman. "Right now, Wrigley Field being a national treasure, with the majority of our games being sold out and the field being kept in pristine shape, we seldom open it up to public events."

DEEP BACKGROUND

Anyone born since the days of the Nixon administration might think that Wrigley Field has always been exclusively a Cubs' summer playpen, echoing with an assortment of distinctive names and nicknames: Harry, Sammy, Kid K, Hawk, Billy Buck, Ryno, Captain Ron, Red Baron, The Bull, Popeye, even Tuffy. But their relative youth prevents them from imagining the ballpark with other faces and names, often mud-splattered or even bloody: Bronko, Super Crunch, The Kansas Comet, Gorgeous George, Goose, The Galloping Ghost, Strangler, Nature Boy, and a host of others.

From the early 1920s until 1970, there was an entirely different world at Wrigley Field besides the seventy-seven- or eighty-one-game Cubs schedule. It was pro football in both its infancy and maturity, linked together at both ends of a fifty-year run by the iron will of George Halas. It was wrestling and boxing, just as physical without the pads and helmets, staged under lights even before Andy MacPhail's grandpa, Larry MacPhail, introduced night baseball to the majors in Cincinnati. It was pro soccer, the last regularly scheduled non-baseball event at the ballpark. And it was women's ball, providing an outlet for professional competition previously denied to half the population. And there was more: circuses, rodeos, ski jumping, the Harlem Globetrotters, political rallies—everything, seemingly, except the flooding of the field for hockey or figure skating.

The other face of Wrigley Field was that of a hard-working, multipurpose ballpark that could be put to use even after dark. Wrigley shone at night with the help of portable lights set up on the field and rooftop floodlights, even as Cubs owner Phil Wrigley continued his eccentric, unexplainable ban on night baseball, which cost him hundreds of thousands in paid admissions each year. In another age, the Cubs played Saturday and Sunday afternoon games against the Milwaukee Braves, and, in between, on Saturday night, workers set up a portable court and lights for the Harlem Globetrotters to take on a college all-star team.

Soldier Field, along with the bygone Comiskey Park and Chicago Stadium, have long-standing reputations for staging every conceivable sports, entertainment, and political event. But if often-overlooked history is considered, Wrigley Field takes a back seat to none of the city's other arenas as host to a wide variety of activities.

THE PERSISTENCE OF MEMORY

The ballpark's bucolic atmosphere for baseball evokes almost one-of-a-kind loyalty from Cubs fans. Yet those who saw Wrigley Field in its other incarnations have similar affection. "I thought they should have played there [in 2002]," radio sports talk-show host Mike North said of the Chicago Bears, temporarily exiled to the University of Illinois at Champaign's Memorial Stadium. The move to Champaign came because Soldier Field was being reconstructed in a project that tore down historic buildings and diverted millions to a pro franchise already swimming in money while the Cubs continue to fight for the right to spend their *own* money improving Wrigley Field.

"It was magical," McDonough said of the summer day in 1981 when the North American Soccer League's Chicago Sting pulled thirty-five thousand into Wrigley Field. (At the time, McDonough served as the soccer team's marketing man.) "The games we played at Wrigley Field, it was like you were playing on hallowed ground," he added. "It was *loud*. When we played at Soldier Field and had fifteen thousand or eighteen thousand, it was like playing in front of a studio audience."

But no one ever could accuse Wrigley Field, famed for its intimacy, of being too spacious for its own good. No matter what the event, attendees came away not only with memories of the action on the field, but also the experience of a few hours in one of the country's most beautiful stadiums.

THE BEAR NECESSITIES

The Cubs are synonymous with Wrigley Field, but for many years, the Bears weren't far behind. They spent five memorable decades as the baseball team's top tenant. More championships, in fact, were won by the Bears than their landlords (who are still waiting for number one) on Wrigley's turf. And the Bears of the day wouldn't have chosen anywhere else to play.

"It was Chicago football," said Mike Ditka, Bears tight end from 1961–66, later coach, and ranking second only to Halas in all-time Bears stature. "The field conditions weren't very good. It was hard. The first-base side end zone almost always was frozen. But in those days, we just played. No one made a lot of money."

"It was a great place to play," said Gale Sayers, the Kansas Comet who possessed perhaps the greatest moves of a running back in modern times. "It was a real home-field advantage because the fans were so close to the playing field in every direction."

The fans lucky enough to gain entry to a packed Wrigley Field probably never felt so cold at a sports event, yet they've never been emotionally warmer, with the crowd noise ringing in their ears even decades later. "The roar of the crowd would reverberate against the lower- and upper-deck roofs and bounce around, magnifying itself," fan Richard Youhn told Richard Whittingham, who penned several Bears history books. "There were times in the big games when the stands literally shook with the noise."

The Bears consistently drew large, raucous crowds in the 330 games they played at Wrigley Field from 1920 to 1970. Counting games hosted by the Cardinals and others by early pro football entrants like the Decatur Staleys and the Chicago Tigers, the Confines still hold the record for most National Football League games in one stadium.

IT AIN'T LEGIT

Football came on the scene early at Wrigley Field, but the sport was not the first non-baseball event. From the first day it opened its gates as Weeghman Park in 1914, Wrigley Field was rented out when its baseball hosts were out of town. And why not? Large outdoor and indoor venues simply did not exist in great quantities in the early years of the twentieth century. The great football palaces and multipurpose indoor stadiums would not rise until after World War I, during the flush years of the 1920s—the first true boom in spectator sports.

Charley Weeghman had his fireworks and "first-class hippodrome acts." On June 26, 1920, with William Wrigley in charge, the High School of Commerce in New York dueled Chicago's Lane Tech in a baseball matchup. The game, witnessed by future bleacher elder "Papa" Carl Leone, featured a Superman in Commerce flannels: Junior first baseman Lou Gehrig, whose homer previewed an unparalleled career to come.

Youth teams and military squads played baseball at Wrigley Field. Future basketball coaching legend Ray Meyer recalled playing a mid-1920s game at the Confines. Meyer, a second baseman, squared off against a team featuring local pitcher Phil Cavaretta, who would carve his own reputation into Wrigley Field in future decades.

But it was the fledgling football teams of post–World War I Chicago who helped add to the coffers of Wrigley and team president William Veeck Sr. Professional football teams had relatively few choices among playing fields as the 1920s dawned. College ball was the more popular game, and fields at Northwestern and the University of Chicago were not available. Soldier Field had not yet been built. In 1919, a semipro team out of Hammond, Indiana, played three games in Wrigley Field. A year later, what would develop into the National Football League was formed, full of barnstorming-style franchises, many playing in small markets. Chicago had two clubs, the South

Side–based Cardinals, and the Tigers, who played several 1920 games at Wrigley Field.

BEARS, NOT CUBS, AND NOT STALE

But early pro teams often folded or packed up to move to another city at the drop of a hat. One such émigré was the Decatur Staleys, founded in downstate Illinois in 1920 by George Halas, a former University of Illinois star and briefly a New York Yankees right fielder. No longer fully sponsored by agribusiness mainstay A. E. Staley, the team sought a better future in Halas's hometown.

With his choice of home fields limited, Halas, who settled his young family in the booming North Side, cut a deal with Veeck. The club would pay 15 percent of its gross receipts to Bill Wrigley as rent. On any take over ten thousand dollars, the percentage rate would rise to 20 percent. The footballers would keep all revenue from concessions, while the Cubs raked in the gross from program sales. Halas recalled that these negotiations took all of seventy-five seconds.

Decades later, the deal evolved into one in which the Bears paid P. K. Wrigley a base fee for rental plus a percentage of the gate. The Cubs retained 100 percent of the receipts from concessions. In those later years, "It was a handshake deal between Mr. [Philip K.] Wrigley and George Halas," said E. R. ("Salty") Saltwell, for many years Wrigley Field's park operations director.

The Staleys had played as a visitor against the Tigers twice in 1920, then battled the Akron Pros to a scoreless tie before ten thousand. All seats were fifty cents. Finally, renamed the Cubs to curry favor with local fans, the eleven played their first regular-season game as the home team against the Rochester Jeffersons on October 16, 1921, at Wrigley Field. The 2:30 p.m. kickoff in mid-fifties temperatures featured tickets at a buck apiece. Player-coach Halas started at right end, with co-owner Dutch Sternaman at left halfback. Some eight thousand showed up at the then-fourteen-thousand-seat field, on which the gridiron ran east-west before it was soon shifted to its familiar north-south layout.

The team officially became the Bears in 1922 as Halas, figuring football players were bigger than their baseball counterparts, sought a new nickname. He and Sternaman made enough money to keep going back to Clark and Addison; the Bears turned a twenty-thousand-dollar profit in 1924. But interest did not really take off until Halas's masterstroke of signing University of Illinois gridiron legend Red Grange right off campus as the 1925 college season ended.

Grange's debut was scheduled for Thanksgiving 1925 in a Cubs Park that would soon undergo several waves of seating expansion. The previous Monday, crowds mobbed the Spalding Sporting Goods Store on State Street downtown in a rush for tickets. In three hours, all twenty thousand ducats had been sold, so Halas and Sternaman printed additional tickets. Eventually, thirty-six thousand attended the Grange debut, which ended in a scoreless tie against the crosstown Cardinals, with fans ringing the playing field. Three days later, twenty-eight thousand showed up in a heavy snowfall to watch the Bears play the Columbus Tigers before the team departed on a nationwide barnstorming tour to showcase Grange.

CONFLICTS OF INTEREST

Despite such successes, the Bears could not count on employing Wrigley Field for all home games. Early-season contests conflicted with the end of the baseball season, which starting in 1929 periodically stretched into October for the World Series. On September 21, 1930, the Bears had to play their home opener at Mills Stadium on the North Side. They also had to play games on the home fields of DePaul and Loyola universities, which in that era fielded football teams. On October 1, 1933, the Bears hosted at Soldier Field for the first time, entertaining the Boston Redskins. The late September/early October conflicts with the Cubs would plague the Bears for the rest of their tenure in Wrigley Field.

Contrast that attitude, when baseball was *the* game, with the attitude now that everyone must step aside for the Great King NFL. Baseball teams are shoved out of previous commitments to make way for football games. Broadcasts of regular-season stretch-run baseball games are shifted from station to station to make room for play-by-play of *exhibition* football games.

ARENA FOOTBALL, 1932

Poor weather forced the shift of the 1932 NFL title game away from Wrigley Field, resulting in the league's first indoor championship contest. In a snow-and-ice-encrusted Wrigley Field, the Bears posted a 9–0 victory over the rival Green Bay Packers on December 11, 1932, in a critical late-season matchup before just five thousand chilled fans. With the Great Depression nearing its nadir, Halas could not take a chance on losing the gate to the below-zero weather for the title game one week later against the Portsmouth Spartans. Papa Bear moved the game to still-sparkling Chicago Stadium, effecting several rule changes to accommodate an eighty-yard field. More than eleven thousand fans watched, protected from the elements, as the Bears won 9–0.

During the same period, the Bears' tenancy at Wrigley was supplemented by the South Side–based Cardinals, whose management decided on a change of venue for seven games at Wrigley Field during the 1930s, moving from the Big Red's usual home at Normal Park on the South Side. Eventually, the Cardinals settled in for a twenty-year run at Comiskey Park, playing their final Chicago season at Soldier Field in 1959. Halas, desiring the Chicago market for himself, helped engineer the Cards' move to St. Louis.

Also providing a challenge to Bobby Dorr's ground crew were the Loyola and DePaul University football teams, both of whom played some of their home games at Wrigley. But the Bears were the off-season face of the ballpark. Through brushes with insolvency in 1932 and all the other challenges of guiding the Bears through this antediluvian NFL era, Halas stayed put at Clark and Addison.

SYMBIOSIS

The first NFL title game at Clark and Addison took place on December 17, 1933, when the Bears beat the New York Giants 23–21 before twenty-six thousand. But big crowds were not always assured even for championship play. The December 12, 1937, title game, which the Bears dropped to the Washington Redskins 28–21, drew only 15,870. And on December 21, 1941, just 13,341 (the smallest crowd ever for an NFL title game) showed up in forty-seven-degree weather as the Bears thumped the Giants 37–9. Pearl Harbor had hammered the American psyche just two weeks previously. Season tickets for six regular season games in 1941 were $13.20, while six games of reserved grandstand seats were $10.80.

"Red" Mottlow began attending Bears games during his grammar school years on the West Side in the mid-1930s. "We went because Halas was giving tickets away," Mottlow said. "He had a deal with the *Chicago Times*. You had to apply for the tickets. We sat in the upper deck behind first base. There'd be 25,000, 28,000. When Sid Luckman came, the place started filling up."

It would take the further nurturing of the Luckman-led Bears dynasty and the postwar boom to ensure consistent overflow crowds for the "Halasmen," as newspapers dubbed the Bears. A new, hot rivalry with the Cardinals for the NFL title in 1947–48 certainly boosted Halas's coffers. A record throng of 48,632 appeared at Wrigley for the season finale on December 14, 1947, to watch the Big Red eliminate the Bears from title contention with a 30–21 victory.

To accommodate the increased crowds, Halas changed the layout of Wrigley Field after the Cubs' season ended. Beginning in October 1948, he erected temporary stands, costing $150,000, in front of the right-field bleachers to boost capacity and make the ballpark more intimate for football. Firemen from Engine 78, just down the street, often helped construct the temporary bleachers. In the spring, the football seats were disassembled and stored under the permanent bleachers.

Meanwhile, Halas crammed even more fans into the railed-off box seats. At the time, the Cubs used eight twenty-one-inch-wide seats in each box. Halas removed those chairs in favor of ten fifteen-inch-wide seats in an era when obesity apparently wasn't the epidemic it is now. The Bears crowds started to evolve into an exclusive club. Most of the seats were blocked off for season-ticket holders. Those not fortunate enough to gain entry had to use the theater of the mind (often a requirement during the Jack Brickhouse–Irv Kupcinet radio broadcasts of the 1960s) to envision Wrigley Field laid out for the Bears. While the Cubs had televised every home game since 1947, the NFL maintained a tight blackout on home telecasts to guarantee a better gate.

CHAMPIONSHIP!

Even the legendary Bears–New York Giants championship game at Wrigley on December 29, 1963, televised by NBC-TV with Brickhouse—broadcasting his only professional-team title in Chicago during his long career—and Chris Schenkel at the mikes, was blacked out locally. Bears fans were forced to either listen to WGN radio, with Jack Quinlan reporting, or head out of town to pick up the game from NBC affiliates in Rockford, Milwaukee, or South Bend. Closer to home, others paid four dollars or six dollars to watch big-screen theater telecasts at McCormick Place (almost 15,000 attendees), the International Amphitheatre (8,500), or the decrepit Chicago Coliseum (3,150).

The luckiest fellow at Wrigley Field may have been "Salty" Saltwell, director of park operations. While fans and media shivered in the open air, Saltwell viewed a special closed-circuit version of the blacked-out telecast in his warm and toasty Wrigley Field office. The CBS technicians had been nice enough to string a line from their truck to Saltwell's TV set. Scores of thousands of fellow Chicagoans would have loved to have joined him.

The neighborhood played a big part in the game. As usual, fans lined up to use the bathrooms at the Engine 78 fire station during halftime. And during the game, the firehouse basement served as a darkroom for wire service photographers, who could develop their pictures in relative peace and quiet, then wire them to their bureaus. In return for the firemen's generosity, the photogs brought in catered food and had the firehouse's broken-down pool table repaired.

Fans without tickets to the Bears' 14–10 comeback win had to be largely

content with next-day accounts of games, such as the prose the great syndi-
cated columnist Red Smith penned on the 1963 title game: "Under unplayable conditions mercenary monsters played a game for children, and when
it was over some of this city's sanest, solidest citizens bared their skulls and
flung hats and ear-lapped caps to the bitter breeze, defying every lurking
pneumococci. No germ could daunt them, no bacillus still their cheers, for
the Bears won the ballgame 14–10, and after 17 long years, George Halas
once again bestrode the world he helped create."

Stuck-at-home fans saw only snippets of Wrigley Field action when Chicago TV stations began filming highlights of games in the 1960s for Sunday-
night newscasts. Channel 7, then known as WBKB, believed it had an audience lure by advertising "red-hot color film" of that day's Bears game for
their late-Sunday sports wrap-up, anchored by quarterback Rudy Bukich.
But for the fortunate group who donned Bears pads or finagled their way
into Wrigley Field, the experience jumps out clearly even a generation-plus
later. There will never be another football stadium quite like it.

THREE DEAD RATS, OR THE SCENT
OF A FOOTBALL STADIUM

Wrigley Field as the Bears' den was a state of mind and much more. The
atmosphere racked the senses: sights and sounds for most, but for others,
the smells. The ballpark was cramped for the twenty-five men of the Cubs,
so figure just how cozy it was for an NFL team. The old clubhouse down
the left-field line was too small for the boys of summer; former trainer Gary
Nicholson recalled how his Cubs sat "butt to butt" by their locker stalls and
had to shower in shifts in the overheated quarters. Imagine stuffing twenty
more athletes—bigger, beefier, and generally meaner than baseball players—into an already inadequate space.

"It was tight. There were two johns for everyone," said former linebacker Doug Buffone, who later teamed with Mike North to host a popular
afternoon sports-talk show in Chicago. "[Dick] Butkus and I lockered next
to each other. He said, 'There's this horrible smell.' He thinks it's my tennis
shoes. I said, 'You're nuts.' But I take them home, put them in the washing
machine. I come back and the smell continues. Dick said, 'Maybe it's you.'
Then we got an idea. We poked a broom at the false ceiling above us. Three
dead rats fell out."

No Bears of the last days of Halas as coach, though, were going to be
mousy about such inconveniences. After all, this was pro football, even if
the facilities were substandard. Plush, palatial megastadia were still decades
away. The Bears' brethren in a score of other cities had equally tight quarters.

"It was awful," Gale Sayers said of the locker room. "But we were football players. We each had a stall, and we had to wait to get taped, the [trainer's] room was so small. But we did our work outside the locker room. I was playing professional football. No one seemed to complain about it."

"We were really close [in the locker room]," said Mike Ditka, then the Bears' star tight end. "Even the meeting room was close. We were piled on top of each other."

Postgame scenes were a maze of sweaty, battered bodies and equipment. The football writers, who had barely enough room to maneuver, were fortunate that TV mini-cams hadn't yet been invented. Mottlow, the first radio reporter to tote a tape recorder into the locker room, was barred by Bears publicity officials from entering. He was forced to wait at the top of the stairs and catch players as they departed.

Mottlow, a member of what was considered nontraditional media in the late 1960s, was assigned a seat in the first-base-side corner of the old baseball press box hanging from the upper deck behind home plate. He was placed right near the hot dog and hamburger grill. According to Mottlow, Halas usually used these seats to accommodate guests. Sportswriters and broadcasters were seated in a smaller, auxiliary press box behind third base, perpendicular to the fifty yard line. After the Bears departed Wrigley Field in 1970, Cubs general managers from John Holland to Jim Frey continued to use the auxiliary press box. They did so until 1989, when the entire underbelly of the upper deck was converted to private luxury boxes.

TINY STEPS

The cozy confines of Wrigley Field extended to the playing field. The north-south configuration allowed just enough room to squeeze in the hundred-yard length plus end zones. There was no slack at either end; one end zone was bordered by the left-field bleacher wall, the other by the visiting team's baseball dugout on the first base line and its attendant brick wall. A player running full speed through the end zones in either direction took a big risk.

"I ran into the dugout, I never ran into the wall. I was too smart for that," Ditka said.

"Many a time I'd see that brick wall coming up fast," Sayers said. "I ran into the wall and it knocked the wind out of me. If I could, I'd dive over the right-field side into the stands."

The sidelines on both sides of the field also were pinched. Another brick wall, this time fronting the left-field box seats, awaited players running full throttle. "The sidelines on the Bears' side were just six to eight yards deep," Sayers said. "Someone had to stop you if you were going out of bounds."

Still another hazard was the Bears' band, stationed in the left-field corner. "Guys were always running into the band," Mike North recalled.

Man-made obstacles played right into Butkus' raw-meat style at middle linebacker. "I remember Butkus ran [Lions running back] Altie Taylor into the tarp once," North said.

Despite suffering a career-destroying knee injury when tackled by the San Francisco 49ers' Kermit Alexander on November 10, 1968, at Wrigley Field, Sayers called the ballpark's turf "a beautiful place to play." The Saltwell-supervised grounds crew had, as usual, sodded over the baseball infield immediately after the season had ended. "It wasn't a challenge," Saltwell said. "Bobby Dorr, Pete Marcantonio, and Roy Bogren all made the changes. They just did it. It didn't take long." Sayers's famed cuts, though, might kick up a loose piece of sod or two when he scampered over the baseball infield.

Doug Buffone, though, recalls that the crew couldn't entirely shave down the infield. "There was still an incline where the mound was, and there was dirt in spots," he said.

Nothing, though, could improve the field on a rainy December 12, 1965, as the Bears and San Francisco 49ers slogged through the muck. "Everyone was slipping but me," Sayers said. He couldn't have slipped; that memorable day, Sayers barely even touched *terra firma*. He danced, darted, and dashed to an NFL record-tying six touchdowns. The 49ers grasped at empty air as Sayers cut and jiggled on the punt return that provided his share of the record. He could have easily scored a seventh touchdown in the 62–20 Bears blowout, but Halas elected to take Sayers out, both to avoid piling on the losers and avoid a risk of injury.

"I was being paid to do my job," said Sayers, still modest nearly four decades later. "I did not know that scoring six touchdowns was tying a record or a seventh would have broken the record. I didn't have a big ego."

GEORGE OF THE JUNGLE

Halas presented Sayers with the game ball that memorable Sunday. He was in an especially good mood. More often, Halas, slowed by bad hips, stalked after officials on the sidelines, creating a memorable sideshow for the forty-five thousand faithful. If NFL Films ever recorded Halas's histrionics, they'd still have to bleep him even amid the liberalized language of new-millennium TV. "He used to call them 'cocksuckers,'" Buffone said of Halas's invective against the referees. The old man also regularly used the same epithet against Roger LeClerc whenever the kicker missed a field goal or extra point. "He could talk to you like a gentleman or he could talk to you like a coal miner," Buffone added.

"I wish I had a tape recorder my first and second year in the league," Sayers said. "He was unbelievable. I don't know whether the commissioner

[Pete Rozelle] told the officials to leave him be. He founded the NFL, so let him rant and rave. No question he'd be ejected now if he did that on the sidelines. He's 71, 72, let him rant and rave."

Ditka may have learned coach-player body English from Halas. Buffone recalls that Papa Bear once *kicked* receiver Johnny Morris. But nobody complained in those days. These were "Halasmen."

PARANOID ANDROID

The old coach also put on a show during practices, which were also held in Wrigley Field. Halas staged the first battle against the rooftops, believing that spies from other teams had stationed themselves across the street to steal the Bears' plays. Gigantic defensive end Doug Atkins, one of the most colorful Bears of all time, who regularly brought several mean-looking dogs to practice, had fun with the old man.

"Doug used to drive Coach Halas nuts," Ditka said. "He'd point [to the rooftops], and there'd be nobody there. Guys would run up there and there'd be nobody there. Sure there were spies. Halas used to spy, and people would spy on us."

"I remember he stopped practice one day," Buffone said of a suspected spy being spotted. "He didn't find anyone. He was really paranoid."

Mottlow got to know Halas at these practice sessions. The media crush was nowhere near the level of the three platoons of reporters that currently track Bears practices in Lake Forest. Mottlow remained the only reporter with a tape recorder at this juncture of the 1960s. "I'd go out twice a week to talk to Halas," Mottlow recalled. "He was kind of suspicious of me at the beginning, kind of cautious. But once I started going out on a regular basis, he was respectful of me."

AUDIENCE PARTICIPATION

Halas continued holding ballpark practices until the December weather made the field unusable. Ditka remembers going to a lakefront park—he doesn't recall which one—to practice in such situations while Halas watched from the comfort of his limousine. (Sayers narrows that down to a park by Northwestern Memorial Hospital.) Lavish practice facilities were still a pipe-dream.

Ditka will never forget one practice session from 1963. The team was working out in Wrigley Field on a Friday for the upcoming Sunday game in Pittsburgh. Slowly and shockingly, players received word that President John F. Kennedy had been assassinated.

The Bears' 14–10 title victory over the New York Giants on an icy, nine-degree field buoyed spirits during the dark wrap-up to 1963. Halas's players, used to *very* modest paychecks, welcomed their championship payoff. Each Bear received a winner's share of $5,899, a year's salary for many average workers in '63. The frozen fans were overjoyed by the title.

But the Bears faithful didn't require championships to get motivated, verbally or physically. They let the players know immediately what they thought of their performances. It was only after the final gun had sounded that the players had to put on some of their best moves. "The fans were so close to the playing field in every direction," Sayers said. "Sometimes when you lost, you had things thrown at you. Beer bottles, flasks. [Security guards] didn't check 'em that much."

Once outside the park, the fans were forgiving. The Bears regularly had to run a gauntlet of autograph seekers to reach their parking lot by Engine 78's firehouse across Waveland Avenue. North used to stake out the place waiting for Sayers. "He's the one player I could never get an autograph from," he said. "Gale always walked out with a guy named Doc. He always told me he had a cold [and thus couldn't sign]."

HANGING ROOM ONLY

Comfort was not the byword for Bears fans in this pre-luxury suite era. Fans used hooks to snare hanging-room-only perches on the ramps behind the grandstand. Several other fans perched atop the fence behind the left-field bleachers, waiting to snare field goals and extra-point kicks. One used a fishnet attached to the end of a ten-foot pole to gain the advantage. Footballs not intercepted this way became property of ball hawks on Waveland Avenue.

Mike North did not add to Halas's coffers as a kid. In true knothole-gang tradition, he and his buddies developed a system for sneaking into Wrigley Field for games.

> We used to go through the double doors by the player entrance on Waveland Avenue. We'd stand on the right side and wait for the Burny Brothers bakery truck when it made a delivery. We'd walk alongside the truck as it pulled in.
>
> The other way was a guy would have a ticket. He'd put the stub in a cup and throw the cup over the wall. We'd get in with the stub, one at a time. We'd keep passing the stub back outside the ballpark. We'd keep telling the Andy Frain guy that we had forgotten stuff from outside the park and had to use the stub to get back in.

Connections with the top were rewarded—sometimes. *Daily Southtown* sportswriter Tim Cronin recalled how his father ate in a restaurant by the

Bears' old downtown offices on Jackson Boulevard. The elder Cronin thus got to know Halas's secretary. The end result was use of Halas's seats behind the baseball visitor's dugout for one game each during the last three seasons at Wrigley Field (1968–70).

North's father knew the husband of Halas's secretary. Thus he was able to score a job as a vendor in 1966. But North had to start at the bottom of the seniority scale. He was given the job of peddling Borden's Frosty Malt, a Wrigley Field staple on a ninety-degree baseball day but a hard sell in the winter winds. "I had wanted hot chocolate," North said. "It was zero out. I made *one* sale that day. Another time, I got seat cushions. I sold four. I lasted one year vending Bears games."

HALAS AND WRIGLEY

Wrigley Field was the strongest of the ties that bound George Halas with the Wrigley family. Having played in the majors briefly with the Yankees before he played one down of pro football, Halas always loved baseball. He reportedly made an overture in the 1940s to buy the Cubs from Phil Wrigley, who hung on to the team and ballpark in honor of his father. In response, the younger Wrigley supposedly told Halas that not only would he receive first right of refusal on any purchase, but also the last right of refusal. But, of course, Wrigley never sold, helping preserve the ballpark while at the same time condemning the Cubs to decades of on-field mediocrity.

Halas also had ties to the eventual Cubs owners, the Tribune Company. He was a longtime chum of Don Maxwell, the powerful *Chicago Tribune* editor. Thus, beat writers for *Tribune*-run newspapers who aggravated Halas did so at the danger of losing their plum assignments working the Bears. Many decades later, the Bears–*Tribune* link was still strong. Andy McKenna, the first president of the Cubs under Tribune Company ownership, teamed with insurance magnate Pat Ryan to buy 20 percent of the Bears. Then-Bears president Mike McCaskey was seen on one mid-1980s afternoon being escorted around Wrigley Field after a Cubs game by top Tribune Company honchos.

GONNA GET ALONG WITHOUT YOU NOW

But the longtime association between the Bears and Wrigley began to strain as the National Football League emerged as the leader among pro sports in the 1960s. At this time, maximizing of revenue became paramount. Halas had long endured built-in schedule conflicts due to the overlap of baseball and football seasons in late September. Since the contract between Wrigley and Halas stated that the Cubs always had priority over scheduling, the Bears had to periodically move early-season home games to other stadiums, a difficult task in Chicago. Later, Halas simply elected to play his first three games on the road, which some felt put the Bears at a competitive disadvantage.

The NFL schedule expanded from twelve to fourteen games in 1961. The following season, the National League schedule inflated from 154 to 162 games. Consequently, the Bears started a week earlier, in mid-September, while the Cubs sometimes played into the first week of October. The schedule conflicts started to become untenable, especially when the NFL began requiring teams to play at least one of their first three regular-season games at home in the late 1960s.

In that decade, Halas was part of the committee planning a new Chicago stadium. But in the interim, he had to make some tough adjustments. Unable to find an alternative field, he had to play his 1968 season opener at Wrigley, on September 15, without his temporary stands. (At that point, the Cubs still had five home games remaining in the season and couldn't allow the temporary bleachers to be erected in right field.)

Without temporary seats, the Bears lost five thousand customers for the game, angering many longtime season ticket holders relocated or squeezed out in the throng of 41,321. Making matters worse was a disappointing 38–28 loss to the Redskins (Sonny Jurgensen flung four touchdown passes) that put a crimp in optimistic preseason forecasts about the Bears.

Two years later, in 1970, the Bears were scheduled to play their second game at home on September 27. Management this time was unwilling to sacrifice attendance to play in Wrigley Field; the baseball season still had almost a week to run. The Bears made a deal to use Northwestern's Dyche Stadium but ran into months worth of community opposition. Evanstonians in the residential area surrounding Dyche figured that NFL fans were far less genteel than college football rooters and would run roughshod over their property.

The Bears, though, won in the end, capturing a sloppy 20–16 victory over the Philadelphia Eagles at Dyche before fifty-four thousand fans, a bigger gate than any at Wrigley Field. By then the NFL had a rule requiring teams to play in stadiums with a capacity of at least fifty thousand. Halas had goosed all the seats he could out of Wrigley Field. The Bears finished out the 1970 season at Clark and Addison, playing their final home game on December 13. Fittingly, the Bears thumped the Packers in the finale, smearing backup quarterback Frank Patrick in a 35–17 romp.

The Bears announced a move to Soldier Field for the 1971 season. The shift certainly wasn't Halas's first choice. "We got along with them just fine," Salty Saltwell said of the Bears.

The Bears' first season opener at Soldier Field came against the Pittsburgh Steelers on September 19, 1971. The temporary right-field stands went downtown with the team, closing up the cavernous field at the north end. But while the Bears gained seating capacity and schedule flexibility, they had lost a large part of their special experience. Such feelings have not been dulled with the passage of time.

"I was sad [to move to Soldier Field]," said Doug Buffone. "That field, to me, was too big. I never liked Soldier Field. I felt bad about moving. At Wrigley Field, there was only one thing to do—play football. We didn't win a lot of those games, but we beat the hell out of everybody."

But the Bears were not the only team to satisfy the fans' bloodlust at Clark and Addison. Wrigley Field's rough-hewn side also featured the slamming of bodies on the ring in the early days of pro wrestling as well as gloves on flesh under portable lights in an era when boxing was bigger than pro football.

LORDS OF THE RING

Bygone Comiskey Park and Chicago Stadium have lasting images as hosts of boxing matches. Joe Louis and Floyd Patterson fought heavyweight championship bouts at Comiskey, while the Stadium was beamed all over the country through nationally televised weekly boxing matches in the early and middle 1950s. But Wrigley Field has seen its share of ring events too, despite the lack of glamorous heavyweight title fights. Under portable lights, the ballpark hosted a series of matches. The largest number took place under the regime of Cubs general manager Jim Gallagher, the busiest ballpark executive in renting out Wrigley Field to non-baseball happenings.

Gallagher was still a sportswriter in 1934 when the *Chicago Tribune* staged a combination wrestling/boxing charity extravaganza on September 20. The event was another brainchild of *Tribune* sports editor Arch Ward, who in the previous two years had conceived the baseball and college football all-star games. Jim Londos and Ed "Strangler" Lewis grappled for the heavyweight wrestling championship of the world in the headline event in a ring set up on the infield, flanked by portable lights. Seats near the ring were placed on boards over the infield, while other on-field seats north and east of the ring were elevated. Also on the card was a preliminary wrestling match between Don George and Jim McMillen, refereed by former heavyweight boxing champ Jack Dempsey. A quartet of boxing matches also preceded the main event, headlined by Chicagoans King Levinsky and Leo Rodak.

Broadcast by the famed Quin Ryan on WGN radio, the big night exceeded all expectations. The gloom of the Depression did not prevent the crowd from paying between $1.20 and $6.00 for seats. A throng of 35,265 showed up despite threatening skies. Some ten thousand fans, according to published accounts, rushed the gates near the starting time, momentarily causing a crowd-control problem.

Fifty-two out-of-town newspapers, the majority from the Midwest but also including New York, Los Angeles, Detroit, and Montreal, were represented. Celeb referee Dempsey was joined by fellow boxing stars Barney Ross, Jim Jeffries, and Jess Willard. Political heavyweights Pat Nash and Jacob Arvey scored prime seats. Gross receipts for the evening were a handsome $96,302. Londos, the most colorful wrestler of the day, took home fifty thousand dollars after pinning Lewis after forty-nine minutes, twenty-seven seconds of choreographed theatrics.

Tribune writer Howard Barry penned a colorful account of Londos' triumph: "A few minutes after 10 o'clock Londos straightened up, his bronzed torso shining with perspiration beneath the white lights which beat down upon the ring. For a moment he stood motionless like the reincarnation of some great athlete of ancient Athens, the north wind whipping his coal black hair around his eyes. Those eyes were flaming like twin fires, for this was the instant of final triumph. The last and the greatest of his challengers lay prostrate at his feet, beaten after 49 minutes of superlative wrestling."

The success of the Londos–Lewis event persuaded other promoters to cut deals with Gallagher, a hearty sort who soon took over as Cubs general manager. Boxing and wrestling matches provided a nighttime diversion during and after World War II at Wrigley Field. "People wanted to schedule events at Wrigley Field at night," Gallagher said in 1988. "The world was full of entrepreneurs and promoters then."

"Ballparks years ago were the vogue for boxing," legendary Chicago pugilist promoter Ben Bentley recalled. "Boxing was flourishing, and they needed all those seats. It was the number-two spectator sport then. There was nothing like seeing a big fight live and outdoors."

Or covering it. The *Tribune*'s Frank Mastro covered many of the boxing and wrestling matches. "The ring was all lit up," Mastro said in 1988. "The lighting was no problem. Wrigley Field had a very nice atmosphere on a summer night." Sometimes, though, a ringside writer had to be just as quick as the ring combatants. "I'll never forget the night 'Gorgeous George' was wrestling," Mastro said. "He dove out of the ring and broke my typewriter. Smashed it to smithereens."

On August 9, 1943, 12,653 showed up under the portable lights, paying a gross $45,959.63 to watch heavyweight Lee Savold knock out Lou Nova in the second round. All that money for five minutes of fighting. "He slipped under the lead and drove Nova to the ropes with several explosive blows to the stomach," wrote Mastro in the *Tribune*. "These caused Lou to double up in pain, but a left hook to the chin sent him to the canvas and ended the fight."

But Savold's next appearance at Wrigley Field wasn't as fortunate. On August 7, 1944, he dropped a ten-round decision to Joe Baksi. A paying crowd of 7,635 generated gross receipts of $36,746.50. An additional five thousand servicemen and women were guests of the promoters.

Not long afterward, the Raging Bull himself made his Wrigley Field boxing debut. Jake LaMotta, an up-and-coming middleweight, advanced upward in class to take on light heavyweight Bob Satterfield on September 12, 1946. LaMotta earned thirteen thousand dollars by knocking out Satterfield in the seventh round before 9,950. He had to uphold the honor of the LaMotta family that night. Younger brother Joey, fighting on the same card, dropped a ten-rounder to Anton Raadick.

The number of ring events at Wrigley, though, declined sharply in the 1950s, replaced one memorable August night by the sounds of sneakers on hardwood.

SWEET GEORGIA BROWN

The Harlem Globetrotters truly lived up to their name. Not only did they entertain millions with their basketball savvy and on-court improvised humor, they also traveled to all corners of the world to perform. The 'Trotters played at Berlin's Olympic stadium. They set up in a bullring in Spain. They'd even show fancy passing, the only ball-handling skill feasible off a court, in an open field.

Abe Saperstein's traveling crew could light up the night when they took the court, accompanied by their anthem, "Sweet Georgia Brown." They lit up Wrigley Field on Saturday night, August 21, 1954, when they played NBA star George Mikan's U.S. Stars on a portable court bounded on one side by the pitcher's mound and the other by second base. Also on the bill was game matching college basketball sensation Bevo Francis, playing with the Boston Whirlwinds, against the House of David traveling team. Portable lights were set up around the court.

"The lights weren't very good, but I loved being in Wrigley Field," said lifelong Cubs fan Ray Meyer, then only a decade into his legendary tenure as DePaul coach. Meyer was traveling with Mikan, once his Blue Demons mainstay, on a nationwide tour with the 'Trotters. Although the Wrigley Field court had some dead spots, it sure beat playing at the Rose Bowl. "They put the floor over the grass, and it was like an ice-skating rink," Meyer recalled.

The 'Trotters' roster featured the entertaining Goose Tatum, who was presented a Cadillac before the game by his Chicago fans, along with Walter Dukes and pioneering National Basketball Association African American Nat (Sweetwater) Clifton. Other Saperstein players were Leon Hillard, Ermer Robinson, Josh Grider, J. C. Gipson, Clarence Wilson, and Sam Wheeler. The U.S. Stars fielded NBA notables Paul Arizin and Ray Felix, future Knicks coach Red Holzman (then a player with the Milwaukee Hawks), future NBA coach Gene Shue, and Red Klotz, famed for his role with the 'Trotters' number-one foil, the Washington Generals.

While eighty thousand jammed Soldier Field to watch Liberace and "Dragnet" star Jack Webb at the twenty-fifth annual Chicagoland Music Festival that evening, 14,124 turned out at Wrigley Field, paying admission of two and three dollars for grandstand, one dollar for bleachers. "The far left-field stands were dark; you could hardly see," was the recollection of late *Tribune* columnist David Condon, who covered the basketball games. "You'd only see people out in the bleachers when they lit up a cigar or cigarette." Mikan recalled the night as a "real festive affair. We had a lot of fun. They set it up well." Saperstein, as a native Chicagoan, was especially pleased to play in the bucolic stadium of his hometown. "It was something Abe wanted to do," Clifton said decades later after working as a Chicago cabdriver. Surprise! The 'Trotters won 57–51. Tatum scored twenty-three points. "Goose, in my opinion, was one of the finest of all the comedians on court," Clifton recalled.

White Sox fan Condon couldn't help but take a few shots at the Wrigley Field landlord in his game story in the paper the next morning. "It was a rare treat for the 14,124 fans to see someone on the home team [Tatum accepting his car] coming into home plate at Wrigley Field, and their ovation showed they liked it," he wrote.

After the 'Trotters finished, Francis displayed the touch that had led him to smash all collegiate scoring records the previous two seasons at Rio Grande College in Ohio. Francis was aided by playmaker Bobby Davies. Bill Spivey starred for the bearded House of David team.

The whole basketball crew slept fast. They played another doubleheader the next afternoon at southwest side Raceway Park, at 130th and Ashland. Had the Wrigley Field event been rained out, the 'Trotters and Company would have played at Clark and Addison on Sunday night, August 22.

The event kept the ballpark ground crew busy. The Cubs played the Braves on Saturday afternoon. The basketball event was pushed back to 8:30 p.m. in case of a long game. Then the field had to be re-converted to baseball for the Sunday game with the Braves. Rookie Ernie Banks slugged two homers in a 12–6 Cubs loss as Hank Sauer, "The Mayor of Wrigley Field," was honored with a special day. Mary Joseph, president of Sauer's fan club, presented the slugger with a year's supply of sauerkraut while fans in the right-field bleachers, among the throng of 30,093, gave Honker his customary shower of packages of chewing tobacco.

The 'Trotters weren't the first all-black sports ensemble to perform at Wrigley Field. Although Comiskey Park, much closer to Chicago's Black Belt, had been the customary city home of Negro League baseball, Satchel Paige brought an all-star team into Wrigley Field to play the Dizzy Dean All-Stars early in the 1942 season. The game drew twenty-nine thousand, but a rematch scheduled for July 4, 1942, at the Friendly Confines was canceled by baseball commissioner Kenesaw Mountain Landis, no real friend of associations between the races at any level of baseball.

And the four basketball teams on display in 1954 weren't the last ones to take the field at 1060 West Addison in short pants.

DER STING'S BUZZ

Like any other Chicago pro sports team without a stadium to call its own, the fledgling Sting soccer club of the North American Soccer League was not enamored of playing at cavernous Soldier Field. But owner Lee Stern, a native North Sider, did not have much of a choice when he wanted to play at night. But for a five-year period starting in 1978, Stern picked the obvious locale to host his weekend afternoon home games. The decision to use Wrigley Field for part of the home schedule paid off in some of the biggest crowds the Sting ever drew—throngs that exceeded what the floundering Cubs attracted in the same season.

Two former Sting employees are now Wrigley Field front-office stalwarts. Arlene Gill, a secretary to several Cubs officials in the late 1960s and early 1970s, moved on to the Sting when Stern founded it in 1974. Later, Gill returned to Wrigley Field to work as Dallas Green's top office assistant in 1981, holding that post for Green's five general-manager successors through the present day. Meanwhile, John McDonough launched his sports marketing career with the Sting before moving to the Cubs in 1983.

The playing atmosphere at Wrigley Field for pro soccer was "very warm," according to Gill, and she meant more than the summer sunshine under which a host of players from all over the world performed. With head coach Willy Roy and stars Karl-Heinz Granitza and Arno Steffenhagen, the Sting definitely had a Germanic flavor, hence the nickname "Der Sting."

"Soccer fans in general are just more animated, more vocal [than baseball fans]," McDonough said. "I couldn't get over the passion they'd have, and how they vocalized their displeasure."

The Sting played thirty-nine games, including two play-off contests and one exhibition game, in five seasons at Clark and Addison on an east-west field predominately in the all-grass outfield. Cubs fans always knew when the Sting had played there; remnants of the boundary lines for the soccer field could be seen in the outfield during baseball games.

The first Sting game at Wrigley Field was played on April 29, 1978. Crowds were initially quite modest; a July 9 Sunday contest, starting at 2:15 p.m., drew just 4,604. Management tried to tap into the budding youth soccer organizations by staging a pregame Public League–Catholic League high-school all-star contest. Soldier Field had hardly been any better for crowds; the top lakefront throng had been 5,756 for the home opener on April 16. But on Sunday, July 23, the Sting brought the gate up to a season-high 9,345 at Wrigley Field. The following Saturday, July 29, a gathering of 6,127 watched the Sting make the NASL play-offs with a 3–1 victory over the Memphis Rogues.

Attendance slowly grew from that point. Some games were near-disasters at the turnstiles, such as the 1981 Mother's Day gathering of just 1,861 fans who braved a torrential downpour that actually caused the game to be stopped at one point. But the team had some interesting upward attendance spikes at Wrigley Field, rivaling and then surpassing the weekend crowds for the sagging Cubs teams of the day.

On July 6, 1980, 26,468 showed up to witness a 2–1 loss to the Tampa Bay Rowdies. The peak came on June 28, 1981, when baseball fans, looking for spectator sports during the midsummer players strike, were part of a Wrigley Field–best crowd of 35,501 to watch the top gate attraction, the New York Cosmos. The Sting did not disappoint, beating the Cosmos 6–5 in a shootout. The gate was the second-largest Wrigley Field crowd of the year, ranking just behind the Cubs' home opener.

"It was very loud," McDonough remembered from his on-field vantage point. "We had fifteen thousand walk-up fans that day. To see thirty-five thousand for a soccer game at Wrigley Field was unique. It was magical. You just couldn't believe it. It was one of the thrilling sporting events that year to beat the Cosmos." The Cosmos game had some carryover into the 1981 NASL postseason. Sting play-off games at Wrigley Field drew 24,080 on August 30 and 24,658 on September 5.

The Sting split the 1980, 1981, and 1982 seasons between Wrigley Field and Comiskey Park. The team played exclusively in Soldier Field in 1983. Their Wrigley Field tenure ended with three home games in 1984, the final played on September 3. Between the Cubs' drive for the National League East title, Walter Payton's assault on the all-time NFL rushing record, and the Sting's gradual move to indoor soccer, the '84 wrap-up at the Friendly Confines did not draw the rave notices of the previous three years.

The record of Wrigley Field as a multipurpose arena, however, includes even more than football, basketball, boxing, wrestling, and soccer. Almost every conceivable outdoor event was staged in the ballpark when the final tally was made.

GIVE ME THAT OLD-TIME GIRLS BASEBALL

Jim Gallagher was not bashful about renting out Wrigley Field for a variety of events. But in the mid-1940s, he had to turn over the ballpark to the girls. Boss's orders. *A League of Their Own* was partially filmed at Wrigley Field in

1991, and this time the producers did not stretch historical accuracy. In 1943, the first year of the All-American Girls Professional Baseball League, a brainchild of Philip K. Wrigley, several exhibition games were played, at least one under portable lights on July 1, 1943. The women's game was played only one week after the Cubs and Cardinals squeezed in two and one-quarter hours of baseball without lights in Wrigley Field's first-ever "twilight game" starting at 6:00 p.m.

The women ballplayers were a far better sight than another event that caused consternation for Gallagher's grounds crew. Amazingly, even rodeos were staged in Wrigley Field, with rough riders taking the field in 1946, 1947, and 1952. The latter event, featuring bronco riding and steer wrestling, took place at night. "They kept the animals under the bleachers until they were ready to go," recalled Ray "Cotton" Bogren, then part of the crew. "After the rodeo, we had to do a lot of sodding. The animals had 'gone' all over the infield. It was rough."

Perhaps the oddest sports-oriented event was a ski-jumping exhibition in January 1944. The skiers raced from the upper deck behind home plate down a track and landed in the outfield. "The damndest thing I ever saw," was Gallagher's recollection. No doubt many in the crowd of six thousand, starving for wartime distractions, agreed.

Wrigley was not finicky about the political stance of those who came with cold cash to rent out the ballpark. Although no doubt a rock-ribbed Republican, the gum magnate permitted presidential candidate Henry Wallace's Progressive Party to stage a night rally during the 1948 campaign. Wrigley also believed in freedom of religion for all paying customers. The Jehovah's Witnesses staged their convention three consecutive years at Wrigley Field during the 1940s. "They paid us a good chunk of money and left the park cleaner than it was since it was built," Gallagher proclaimed.

JUST BASEBALL, FOLKS

The tide of Wrigley Field as a multipurpose venue began to ebb once Gallagher and several other Cubs executives were swept out in a Phil Wrigley-mandated housecleaning after the 1956 season. New general manager John Holland was as hidebound a traditionalist as they come. He would go to great lengths to avoid rocking the boat and upsetting P. K. Wrigley, to whom he showed perpetual fealty. The Bears continued to play on autumn Sundays due to the long relationship between Wrigley and Halas, but non-baseball night events ground to a halt.

Other than the Bears, it was baseball, much of it bad. And there was little to pull fans into the park. Promotions were rarely scheduled in the final two decades of Philip K. Wrigley's ownership, while the White Sox's formerly moribund attendance skyrocketed in the 1950s when the South Siders rose from their thirty-year sleep. Attendance at Comiskey rose even higher when former Cubs employee Bill Veeck Jr. took over the team in 1959 and showed what good promotion could do.

When Bill Wrigley, P. K.'s son, took over as owner in 1977, the reins were loosened ever so slightly. The Cubs began gingerly exploring the heretofore foreign concepts of promotional giveaways and low-level marketing. The first-ever old-timers game took place in midseason 1977 prior to a Cubs–Mets affair. And the Sting began its run on weekend afternoons.

But the worm turned again when the Tribune Company took over as owner. The September 3, 1984, Sting game would prove to be a milestone of a different kind: the last regularly scheduled non-Major League Baseball, paid-admission event at Wrigley Field. Only the very occasional high school championship baseball game or Randy Hundley fantasy camp utilized the existing diamond.

The non-baseball events besides the Bears games are largely forgotten, having receded far into history. Nevertheless, they were as much a part of. Wrigley Field as Hartnett, Banks, Williams, Santo, Jenkins, Sosa, and Wood—to say nothing of Vic Roznovsky, Leo Burke, Moe Morhardt, Gene Hiser, Rolando Roomes, Jeff Kunkel, and Dave Gumpert.

CHAPTER 8

New Wine in Old Bottles: Wrigley Field, 1966–83

IT'S NOT A REGULAR DAY

On April 19, 1966, the Cubs played their home opener against the Giants. One important change in the old yard was the installation of a new left-field foul pole. The previous pole had actually stood a few feet behind the left-field wall, causing some confusion on home-run calls. The new pole also had a Cubs flag atop it, like the one in right field.

A rather bitter spring had caused some problems in the outfield. The new sod didn't take; the *Tribune* reported that a team painter "was spraying new sod in the outfield a bright green, and a ground crew member explained, 'They like it pretty for the color TV nowadays.'" Painted grass aside, Pete Marcantonio had his field in decent enough shape despite consistent rains. New Cubs manager Leo Durocher got to Wrigley on time for his first game in pinstripes despite being involved in a small auto wreck en route to the park.

After Louis Sudler sang the national anthem, backed by Henry Brandon's band, former Cub batboy Al Bluhm, who had been going to Cub openers for fifty years, threw out the first ball. Due to the rain, only 15,396 fans were on hand to see the Cubs lose 11–10. Pinch hitter Ty Cline whiffed with the bases loaded in the bottom of the ninth to end the game.

Many more losses would follow in 1966. Despite the presence of Ron Santo, Ernie Banks, and Billy Williams, the Cubs were a second-division club. After his squad—full of well-past-their-prime players such as George Altman, Billy Faul, Wes Covington, Billy Hoeft, Harvey Kuenn, and Ernie Broglio—failed out of the gate, Durocher saw the writing on the ivy-covered wall: the team he inherited was a loser. By the end of the campaign, despite the ballyhooed arrival of the Lip, the Cubs were 59–103, tying the team mark for the most losses in history. Chicago was last, even behind the Mets who, up to that season, had never finished ahead of anyone.

Just as alarmingly, attendance fell to 635,891, the club's second lowest total since the war year of 1943. Only the Washington Senators kept the Cubs from being the game's poorest-drawing attraction in 1966. But following their pathetic 1966 performance under Durocher, things *had* to get better; they couldn't get much worse.

GAMBLING, PART II

And as the Cubs sank further into irrelevance, who bothered to show up? Gamblers. William Furlong wrote an article in the July 1966 *Harper's* about the investors in Wrigley's right-center-field bleachers: "Just inside the bleacher entrance to Wrigley Field in Chicago is a sign that warns: 'No gambling.' On the ramp leading up to the bleacher mezzanine is another sign that warns: 'No gambling.' At the top of a ramp, patrolling the aisle of the mezzanine, is a cop whose presence warns: 'No gambling.' In the right-center-field bleachers are Stace and Sambo, Jonesy and Zsa-Zsa, Dynamite and The Preacher—all there to sit in the sun and enjoy the National Pastime: gambling on baseball."

Furlong notes in his article that undercover cops had made dozens of arrests in order to shut down ballpark gambling, which was illegal. But the wagerers had "finger signals as abstruse as the bidding at Sotheby's" to exchange information, which helped them throw off law enforcement. With the Cubs in the dumps and Chicago's baseball fans going to see the White Sox instead, gamblers were some of the only folks around, at least until the Cubs improved and people began showing up to actually watch baseball.

SECRET VICTORY

September 21, 1966, wasn't particularly memorable for the Cubs. They did beat the visiting Reds 9–3, with Billy Williams and Adolfo Phillips homering, but this was one of those days where P. K. Wrigley lost money just by opening the gates. On that overcast Wednesday afternoon, just 530 fans visited Wrigley Field. It was the smallest crowd in the majors that year, and there hasn't been one as small since.

But from small things, big things come. A cadre of ten left-field fans, some of the forty or so hardy bleacherites in attendance that day, decided that they were a gang. The next year, a lady named "Ma" Barker brought a bed sheet with a hole cut in it to the park. The bed sheet read, "Hit a Bleacher Bum." Cub hitters were supposed to knock home runs right at the bleacher fan whose head stuck through the hole. Thus was born a lasting term.

RESURGENCE

What was amazing about the Cubs' late-sixties rise to National League power was its suddenness. To his credit, Leo Durocher spent much of the second half of the '66 campaign playing the youngsters. Several rookies, including pitchers Fergie Jenkins (swiped from the Phillies in an early-season deal), Bill Hands, and Kenny Holtzman, catcher Randy Hundley, and outfielders Adolfo Phillips and Byron Browne, showed sparks of talent, especially late in the season. While Browne's loopy swing, poor fielding, and bum shoulder soon landed him back in Triple-A, the others stuck around. Most of these players were not developed by the Cubs' moribund farm system, but rather liberated from other teams in trade.

A big change in April 1967 was the resumption of the preseason City Series, which had petered out after 1957 (although the teams had played some midseason exhibitions in the intervening years). The Cubs and Sox met for two games, one at Wrigley and one at Comiskey, on April 8–9.

On April 11, 1967, a sparse Wrigley Field Opening Day crowd saw twice-wounded Vietnam veteran Ronald Centers toss out the first pitch prior to a 4–2 Cubs victory over Philadelphia. (This brought to an end the custom of fans throwing out the first ball on Opening Day.) With the temperatures in the low forties, many of the sportswriters were more interested in the shapely dancers from Billy Minsky's chorus line, in town for a show, who were taking in the game from the box seats behind home plate.

For the first time, the Cubs had a full-time organist, Jack Kearney, seated behind a brand-new keyboard in his perch in the football press box on the third-base side. Kearney entertained the fans with various tunes and assisted in the playing of "The Star-Spangled Banner," which rang out before the game in honor of the war heroes. At the time, the national anthem was *not* regularly played at Wrigley Field, as management believed that the airing of the song at all eighty-one games would cheapen the experience. By 1969, however, it was played before every game in Chicago, and is now *de rigueur* at every park. (In 1966, the White Sox had sponsored a fan vote to decide which patriotic song should be played before their games. "The Star-Spangled Banner" won easily over "God Bless America" and "America the Beautiful.")

Shortly after Opening Day 1967, a new public address system was installed, and the Cubs were new as well. Bolstered by the sudden development of Jenkins, Hands, and Holtzman into top-flight starters, the Cubs rose from the ashes to contend in the NL. They were tied for first place as late as July 24, eventually finishing third, fourteen games out—the franchise's best finish in more than twenty years. Just as important, at least to P. K. Wrigley's pocketbook, the fans came back to Wrigley Field. Attendance rose to 977,226 for 1967, the highest total in a decade. This was the last season to date (excepting the strike year of 1981) that Cubs attendance was lower than a million. During the season, the Cubs began a seven-year, $3 million initiative to improve the park.

BACKGROUND NOISE

In 1967, the Cubs again addressed the hitting background issue, this time in a "Mod, Mod World" fashion. Before the Dodgers invaded Wrigley Field on May 19, the Cubs laid a huge bright-green sheet of Astroturf on the vacant center-field seating sections. This, for once, was a design concept that would remain in vogue. The hitting background was suitably improved by the uniformity of the Astroturf, and the look was attractive in a 1960s sort of way. At the same time, the floor of the Cubs' dugout was also decorated with a green Astroturf carpet.

THE CUBS? IN FIRST?

On July 2, the Cubs beat the Reds 4–1 at Wrigley Field for their thirteenth win in fourteen games (twelve of those fourteen coming in a triumphant home stand). Some fans streamed onto the playing field in joy. "From now on, I'm going to demand combat pay before I work in Wrigley Field," one usher told a reporter from the *American*.

Fans had begun to gather at the windows at 8:15 a.m. The gates had to be closed at 12:45 when all standing-room tickets had been sold. Ten thousand fans were turned away—the biggest group to unsuccessfully seek Cubs tickets in many years. For the first time in recent memory, dozens of fans parked themselves on rooftops and fire escapes past the left-field and right-field walls, soaking up the sun—and some winning baseball. Durocher said later, "Did you see those rooftops across the street? I can't remember seeing people over there since the early 1930s."

Following the game, most of the 40,464 paid remained in the park in order to see the results of the Cardinals' game at New York posted on the scoreboard. When the 5–4 Mets win was announced, the crowd went crazy—the Cubs had moved into first place by a half-game. The wild fans wouldn't vacate the park until the flags above the scoreboard were changed to reflect the Cubs' first-place standing. A parade of fans descended upon the local taverns and celebrated.

"Who ever heard of an entire city wanting to sleep inside a baseball stadium after the game was over?" asked Brent Musburger in the July 3 *American*. He went on to discuss the reaction of the players: "The players, tho, guzzled beer, ate Ron Santo's pizza, dealt cards, and raved endlessly about the fans, many of whom were still milling about outside the dressing room, chanting 'We're No. 1 . . . We're No. 1 . . .' or 'We Want Leo.' [Cubs reliever] Dick Radatz . . . put a Nazi helmet with 'Hell's Angels' lettered across the top, stepped outside the dressing room door, and held up both hands in the politician's familiar 'V' for victory sign. The crowd threw Radatz kisses in return."

This was the only time all year Chicago was alone in the lead, as they went on the road the next day and, beginning July 4, dropped seven in a row. But on July 22, the Cubs—down 5–4 in the last of the ninth to the Giants—came up with two runs to win, moving again into a tie for the top spot in front of 29,079 manic rooters. During the game, a bleacher fan was ejected from the park for lowering a bucket down in the direction of Willie Mays. Who knows what the fan wanted Mays to send up?

Jack Brickhouse yelled on WGN-TV after Randy Hundley's single scored the winning run, "Watch Wrigley Field go out of its mind! Andy Frain ushers [are] in the outfield to keep the fans from jumping over the fence! Some of those fans want to jump *right out of the stands*!"

Insane last-minute finishes, which became a staple of the club during the latter part of the 1960s and early 1970s, helped build tremendous excitement among the club's reconstructed fan base—and led to endless anxiety attacks. But from 1967 until the mid-seventies, the fans couldn't get enough of their resurgent Cubs. On July 24, some fans arrived at the park as early as 4:00 a.m. in order to get tickets to see the Cubs play a doubleheader with the Giants. When the sun came up a few hours later, approximately one hundred fans had already lined up by the bleacher gate. Eventually, a throng of 34,922 filled the park for the doubleheader split. The Cubs would not reach first place again.

David Claerbaut, in his book *Durocher's Cubs*, quoted young Cubs lefty Rich Nye about the crowds that came back to Wrigley in 1967. "The players parked their cars near the firehouse across the street from the left-field wall," recalled Nye, "and walked across Waveland to the bleacher entrance. By 9:00 people were lined up for bleacher seats, and you couldn't get through without being besieged by autograph seekers."

SAVE ME A PLACE

Cubs ticket manager Jack Maloney (whose son Frank is the currently the Cubs' ticket manager) was all smiles. He told Bob Billings in the *Daily News* on July 1, "If they keep it up, we're a cinch for a million. I had figured on about 800,000, but this could really percolate . . . When you've got a good team it isn't hard to get a million in here. That's without night games. It proves that you don't need night baseball to draw fans. It's the team that counts."

THE HORRIBLE YEAR

The year 1968 was one of the worst in modern American history. Racial tension, already at a boiling point, exploded with the April 4 assassination of Dr. Martin Luther King Jr. and got worse later that spring when Bobby Kennedy was shot down after capturing the California Democratic presidential primary on June 5. In the middle of all this was baseball in Chicago. After the Cubs–Sox exhibition game set for April 7 was wiped out by President Johnson's declaration of a national day of mourning for Dr. King, the Cubs opened with a win and a loss in Cincinnati.

The 1968 home opener came on Saturday, April 13, a nationally televised affair against St. Louis. Despite intermittent rain, 33,875 fans crammed into Wrigley, the biggest Opening Day crowd in many years. Another two Vietnam vets, David Shields and Michael Widhalm, convalescing at Great Lakes Naval Hospital from their war wounds, tossed out first pitches. (At various times, including in 1966 and 1967, the navy held a "recruit day" at Wrigley Field, where one hundred or so cadets took their induction oaths and officially joined the armed forces. These events would continue on and off into the 1970s.)

Despite Ron Santo's two hundredth homer, the Cubs blew a 4–0 lead and lost 8–5, setting the tone for much of the season. Santo, now a voluble and highly entertaining radio color man for the Cubs, is thought of as a veritable "Mr. Cub" in his retirement. When he played, however, Santo never had from the fans the unbridled love that Ernie Banks or Billy Williams received.

While "Captain Ron" had his boosters, including some fans who named Wrigley "Santo's Village" in homage to local amusement park Santa's Village, and those who called for "Pizza Power" (Santo's frozen pizzas were sold at the park), some detractors accused him of not hitting in the clutch, not playing hard, and other such folderol.

One man who *was* popular? Leo Durocher. The *Tribune* remarked that during Opening Day pregame ceremonies, "Durocher got such a deafening, standing ovation that the public address man, WGN's Roy Leonard, had to delay the introduction of the rest of the Cubs for a few moments."

With Santo and Hundley, among others, struggling, the Cubs lost twelve of thirteen at one point, setting a senior circuit record in June by going forty-eight innings without scoring. On June 28, after losing to the Cardinals, the Cubs stood at 31–41, in ninth place. From that point, the team woke up. On July 6 and 7, they swept back-to-back doubleheaders from the Pirates, ending the first half of the year in a flash and sending the Bucs to a ten-game losing skid. In the second twin bill, both wins came in the bottom of the ninth, with reliever Phil "The Vulture" Regan notching the victories. From July 5 through the end of the year, the Cubs' 49–33 record was the best in the league. They won their last five games to finish third.

CLOSE TO THE MADDING CROWD

While the Cubs slumped for much of 1968 and were never really in the race, North Side fans were, after many lean years, excited to have a competitive team to watch. Perhaps the real sign that the Cubs had reclaimed the fans' hearts came July 28, with the dull, ninth-place Dodgers in town for a Sunday doubleheader. The Cubs battered Los Angeles 8–3 and 1–0 before 42,261 screaming fans, who spent six hours chanting, yelling, cheering, and drinking. "Try to argue with the 42,261 fans who jammed Wrigley Field yesterday and the thousands that were turned away that the Cubs are not on the move," wrote George Langford the next day in the *Tribune*. "The largest baseball crowd to overrun Wrigley Field in 20 years came out because of the Cubs, a fifth-place team almost in fourth, a half game out of third and 2¹/₂ lengths from second place."

For the first time in many years, traffic around Wrigley Field was a problem. Buses running toward the park from both Addison and Clark were well behind schedule because of the cars. The *Tribune* reported that the fans "stood four deep on the ramps, perched on railings, and sat in the aisles. And several thousand were turned away at the gates." The 22,140 grandstand seats that went on sale at 10:30 a.m. for the twin bill sold out in less than one hour. The Cubs had increased capacity after 1967 by selling more standing-room seats, and this policy would pay off.

AUGUST SPAWNED A MONSTER

When the league-leading Cardinals came into town on August 12 for a four-game set, the fans packed Wrigley Field even though Chicago was fourteen games out of first place. The Cubs won the first two games but lost the final two. Over the four-game set, 121,740 fans packed Wrigley Field—an average of more than 30,300 per contest, and a record at the time for a four-game set at the park. For a weekday series in 1968, that was a remarkable number.

Fergie Jenkins, in his first autobiography, *Like Nobody Else*, relates an anecdote about the Cardinals' reaction to the crowds: "Before the third game of the series, Cardinal left fielder Lou Brock brought a towel with the words 'We're No. 1' written on it to the outfield to flash at the bleachers. Center fielder Curt Flood pulled the towel off Brock's shirt and waved it at the fans, particularly the Bleacher Bums, who had been on Brock and Flood the entire series. The fans went wild, showering Brock and Flood with beer cans, flashlight batteries, milk cartons, and whatever else they could get their hands on."

Success had created something exciting yet more than a little threatening.

SPITTING IN THE WIND

Less than a week later came one of the biggest controversies at Wrigley Field in many years. In the first game of an August 18 doubleheader against the Reds, plate umpire Chris Pelekoudas, upset at what he felt was a proliferation of spitballs and other illegal pitches being thrown, took matters into his own hands. Pelekoudas decided that if Phil Regan—often accused of tossing the spitter—were to appear, he would go after the hard-throwing sidearmer. Regan did pitch, and Pelekoudas ruled that the pitcher threw three illegal deliveries.

He allowed two batters (Pete Rose and Alex Johnson), who had made outs, to come to bat again. Rose singled after his swinging strike three was disallowed. Pelekoudas made the calls even though he found no evidence of any foreign substance on the ball or on Regan's uniform, despite a long search. "This man defied us," Pelekoudas said later. "I wanted to make him suffer."

The fans didn't react happily, hurling debris at the umpires. That the Cubs eventually lost both games of the doubleheader, to make it six straight defeats, just made the fans hotter. National League President Bill Giles flew into Chicago for an investigation and upbraided Pelekoudas for making a call without physical evidence. General manager John Holland, according to George Vass in the August 19 *Daily News*, was "alarmed" by the angry reaction of the crowd during Pelekoudas's show. Now that the Cubs were serious about winning, their fans were plenty serious too.

By the end of the 1968 season, in which the Cubs again finished third, 1,043,409 fans had crammed into Wrigley Field. The team hadn't drawn so many since 1950. But even over a million, the Cubs' attendance still ranked just fifth among ten NL teams; they were outdrawn by, among others, ninth-place New York and last-place Houston.

YOU GOTTA BE KIDDING

According to E. M. Swift in a 1980 *Sports Illustrated* article, P. K. Wrigley was in the late 1960s considering looking into installing artificial turf at Wrigley

Field. At the time, the only big league park that had the plastic was the Houston Astrodome. "When we have the money we'll probably install synthetic grass," Wrigley said. "There's no doubt it would pay for itself in a few years."

By 1970, new parks in Cincinnati and Pittsburgh used the fake stuff, and several existing parks had converted. Luckily, Wrigley resisted the temptation to go modern. If Wrigley put off the decision for financial reasons, he probably wasn't disappointed when the White Sox went ahead and installed it for their 1969 campaign. In their typical half-hearted, stumbling, late-1960's manner, the Sox didn't even put the turf on the whole field—instead simply installing it on the infield while leaving the outfield grass as it was.

That experiment ended in 1975, and plastic hasn't shown up on a Chicago baseball field since.

NINETEENTH HOLE?

Golfer Ray Floyd has been a lifelong Cubs fan and in the late 1960s even worked out regularly with the team. The Cubs gave Floyd a locker in the clubhouse and even assigned him a uniform—number six.

"IT'S *NINE-TEEN-SIXTY-NINE* . . ."

After another third-place finish in 1968, the Cubs jumped off the mat in 1969 and led the newly created NL East for 155 days. Unfortunately, they were the *first* 155 days rather than the *last*. The story of the ill-fated 1969 squad has been told over and again. Suffice it to say that any Cubs fan old enough to remember the season still cringes, as do many of the pennant race's participants. Ron Santo, for example, still cannot discuss the club's collapse down the stretch without becoming emotional.

The season began on April 8, 1969, with the Phillies in town. With both leagues split into two divisions with the addition of expansion teams (the NL's in Montreal and San Diego), many pundits and fans believed that this was the Cubs' year. Pennant fever began to manifest itself at 8:00 a.m., when fans began lining up outside Wrigley Field's ticket windows in hopes of obtaining one of the five thousand bleacher seats and twenty-two thousand general admission tickets that regularly went on sale the day of each game.

The next day's *Tribune* reported that "sale of bleacher tickets was cut off long before game time. Standing room tickets were sold in the outer precincts and standees packed the walking area behind the lower deck stands." The overall crowd of 40,796 was reported to be the largest ever at a Wrigley Field opening, although some games in the 1920s likely attracted more.

The Cubs decided to "go Hollywood" for their 1969 Opening Day ceremonies; instead of having a wounded Vietnam vet throw out the first ball, showbiz veteran Jimmy Durante came out and told a joke or two. Then veteran sportswriter Edgar Munzel of the *Sun-Times* tossed the first pitch. Loyola Academy High School provided the band, and the crowd observed a moment of silence for former president Dwight Eisenhower, who had died on March 28. The biggest noticeable change in Wrigley Field, at least to the writers, was the new green carpeting inside the Cubs' small dugout. But part of the upper deck had also been rebuilt as part of a four-year project that began in 1968.

On the field, the Cubs played their typical game of the era, getting out to a big early lead, blowing it in the late innings, then putting on a wild finish. (Jack Griffin of the *Sun-Times* said, concerning the Cubs' penchant for late-inning wins, that the explanation must be mass hypnosis. "Dick Selma or [relief pitcher] Hank Aguirre waves a forefinger above his head, and Leo Durocher says a magic word, and the organ grinder plays a special tune. And everybody goes home in blind hysteria.") Ernie Banks hit two homers in the first three innings, driving in five runs. As Ray Sons of the *Sun-Times* wrote nine years later, "The roar of adulation almost lifted the roof off the grandstand and Ernie raised his batting helmet with both hands in delighted response."

In the ninth, up 5–2, the Cubs blew the lead. Rookie infielder Don Money's three-run homer off a tiring Fergie Jenkins knotted the score. In the eleventh, the Phils went up 6–5 on a double by Money (who knocked in five runs in the game). In the Cub half, Randy Hundley singled off Barry Lersch with one out. Left-handed-hitting "Wonderful" Willie Smith came up to bat for Jim Hickman, and when he launched a 1–0 fastball into the right-field bleachers, the crowd exploded. Fans danced in the aisles, and the entire Cub bench mobbed Smith as he crossed the plate.

From this point, it was "ignition on" for the Cubs; they won eleven of their first twelve. By May 16 the Cubs were 24–11 and up by six in the National League East division.

DEM BUMS

With success, and more fans in the park, came a new series of challenges, most relating to crowd control. The left-field bleachers had become the territory of the "Bleacher Bums," an assemblage of (mostly) young, male, politically conservative fans who wore yellow hard hats, drank beer in copious amounts, chanted slogans, insulted opponents, and deified their Cubs.

Pitcher Dick Selma, a somewhat goofy type nicknamed "Moon Man" after being acquired from the Padres in April, quickly became a Bleacher

Bum favorite and would lead cheers from the Cubs' bullpen down the third base line. The big cheer was this:

> Every time I go to town, the boys all kick my dog around.
> Makes no difference if he is a hound; ya better stop kicking my dog around.

The Bums, who usually loaded up before the game at Ray's Bleachers Bar at Sheffield and Waveland, would also engage in inspirational cheers for their Cubs, calling for a double play from Santo, Kessinger, Beckert, and Banks: "14, 11, 18, 10: come on, infield, do it again!" Some of the Bums' fun was harmless—most of the chants, clapping, cheers, throwing-back of opponents' home runs, and good-natured razzing usually didn't bother anyone that much. But they could be insensitive to other fans in the bleachers who wanted to watch the game, insulting and sometimes assaulting supporters of other teams. The Bums found out the names of players' girlfriends and loudly screamed insults about them. At times, the Confederate flag flew in the bleachers—ostensibly honoring Southern Cubs like Jim Hickman and Randy Hundley—and the Bums would adopt the Black Power chants of the day ("Abeebee! Ungowa! *Cub* Power!"). The more the beer flowed, the more obnoxious the Bums got.

Not everybody bought the Bums' act. Mudcat Grant, when he was with the Cardinals that season, simply said, "You oughta put a cage over 'em."

Griffin quoted a St. Louis fan sitting at Ray's Bleachers in late June: "Those people frighten me. First day in, one of our guys is signing autographs for them in left field. Being a nice fellow. There is no being a nice fellow with those people. While he is signing autographs somebody pelts him on the head with a large rubber ball. Right on the head."

Ray and Marge Meyer, who bought Ray's in 1962, had great memories of the Bums. Marge told Bob Ibach and Ned Colletti in 1983, "So much of their lives revolved around what the Cubs did. Not only did they go to the games, but they hoped to have breakfast with a player . . . or maybe a nightcap at the bar." And did we mention irreverent? During the playing of the "Star Spangled Banner," it was commonplace for Bleacher Bums to alter the words of the last verse in honor of a Cubs reserve outfielder: "Oh, say does that *Al Spangler* banner yet wave . . ." Ron Santo tried to curry favor with the fans by running toward the left-field corner clubhouse after games and leaping into the air, clicking his heels. The Cubs' opponents thought it was bush league, but the fans ate it up.

WE COULD BE HEROES

Cubs players of the era remain heroes to Chicagoans as much as players from teams of the era that actually won, like the 1968 Tigers, 1970 Orioles, or 1971 Pirates, do in their respective cities. In fact, the Cubs' very inability to win, both in 1969 and in the following few years, has helped bond them to what nobody who actually *lives* in Chicago refers to as "the second city."

George Castle wrote, "The majority of the players kept their off-season homes in Chicago; they were part of the community. You could drink with the Cubs at Ray's Bleachers behind the center-field scoreboard or watch their off-season basketball team perform. That's why their failure to get to the World Series is so painful."

In 1969, Cubs fans turned out in all-time numbers, with their total of 1,674,993 ranking fourth highest in baseball despite playing in a small park. This was the Cubs' best attendance ever until 1984. Averaging 22,333 per home date (there were six doubleheaders), the Cubs posted a 49–32 home record. The 1969 season was also the first since 1945 that the Cubs were over .500 on the road.

BILLY WILLIAMS DAY

The Cubs gave their All-Star outfielder a day on Sunday, June 29, 1969, with the Cardinals in town for a double dip. A crowd of 41,060 attended, with ten thousand more turned away at the gates. During the season, fans could buy twenty-five-cent Billy Williams buttons at Wrigley Field, with proceeds going to a college scholarship fund established in Williams's name. In addition to setting up the scholarship fund, the Cubs also gave Billy and his family a new car. Williams also received a fishing boat and an outboard motor from his Cubs teammates. He was given a Weimaraner puppy, a pool table, a washer and dryer, and a watch as well. Local baseball scribes pitched in to give Williams a new deep-sea fishing pole as well as a check for the scholarship fund.

Billy then went out and drove in Ernie Banks with the winning run in the bottom of the eighth of game one, and then in game two, he went 4-for-5 with a double, two triples, and three RBI. Sweeping the twin bill 3–1 and 12–1, the Cubs moved eight games in front of the second-place Mets.

THE NEW KOUFAX

Since coming to the Cubs in 1966, lefty Kenny Holtzman had been touted as a "new Koufax." On August 19, 1969, he finally did one thing Koufax did four times: throw a no-hitter. Without anything but a fastball, Holtzman shut down the eventual NL West champ Atlanta Braves 4–0 in front of an overflow crowd of 41,033. When Glenn Beckert threw out Hank Aaron for the last out, hundreds of fans—mostly young men—jumped out of the stands and jubilantly ran onto the field.

Ushers and policemen couldn't stop the fans from swarming the Cubs, and Holtzman was nearly choked in the mayhem. After the on-field melee, the players gathered in the cramped clubhouse and celebrated. Backup catcher Gene Oliver not so subtly hinted that Holtzman should charge the press for interviews, and a local car dealership phoned in to give the lefty a new automobile.

STEP UP TO THE MIKE

The late Martin "Red" Mottlow was the first radio reporter to regularly cover games at Wrigley Field. He had a 5:45 p.m. sportscast at the downtown studios of top-forty station WCFL, but he never did his reports remote from the ballpark. "I had all kinds of ways to get downtown [by car]," Mottlow noted. "If the game ended at 4:15, 4:30 p.m., I was fine. I'd go to the clubhouse and get tape and leave. But if I left after 5:00 p.m., I was sweating it. Most of the time I made it."

Cubs players were not used to mike-wielding interviewers in 1969. Player representative Phil Regan tried to bar any interview that ran more than ninety seconds. A tough ex-navy man, Mottlow protested and eventually won through sheer persistence. Mottlow was the only radio reporter in the ballpark for most of Holtzman's no-hitter. Others, including Brad Palmer, then with WBBM radio and today on WLS-TV, sped to Wrigley when the game reached the eighth.

Usually, few broadcast types came to the park; rarely did TV crews conduct postgame interviews. As a result, Mottlow could navigate the crowded, cramped Cubs clubhouse down the left-field line. Manager Leo Durocher didn't always give Mottlow an interview; the Cubs skipper had his own radio show, "Durocher in the Dugout," on WGN. Mottlow recalled, however, that one day, WMAQ-TV sportscaster Johnny Erp came up with a brilliant way to "get" Durocher. Prior to a game, Erp pretended to speak off-the-cuff to Durocher down the left-field line near the Cubs bullpen. But Erp was also carrying a hidden microphone. In addition, a WMAQ crew filmed the conversation with a zoom-lens camera set up near the dugout. (When Durocher found out that he had been interviewed without his knowledge, he raised holy hell.)

AND AN ASSIST TO THE CREW

Following the game, Braves hitters and even the sportswriters credited the Cubs grounds crew for the no-hitter. Edgar Munzel of the *Sun-Times* noted that "the long grass of the infield also played a part in foiling the Braves in several instances." Grounds chief Pete Marcantonio insisted, however, that the grass was no longer on August 19 than it had been at any other point during the season. Marcantonio did note the new sod on the infield but also said that the grass had recently been cut to its normal height of two inches.

Two days later, on August 21, the Cubs had their largest crowd of the season—42,364, a Ladies Day assemblage. For the three-game Braves series, the Cubs drew 119,089 fans.

CRUMBLE

From this high point, the season quickly devolved. After winning a suspended game and a regular game at Cincinnati on September 2, the Cubs were five ahead of the Mets. But the club almost immediately collapsed. A three-game weekend home series on September 5, 6, and 7 against the Pirates proved to be the turning point. On Friday and Saturday, the Pirates destroyed the Cubs 9–2 and 13–4, knocking Holtzman and Jenkins silly. Chicago had now lost three straight. Saturday was Boy Scout Day, with three thousand scouts among a surprisingly small crowd of 27,791. Meanwhile, the Mets had won two of three from Philadelphia and were suddenly just 3 1/2 games behind.

Sunday afternoon's contest looked like it would be the kind of game that the Cubs had been winning all season. Down 4–2 in the seventh, the Cubs scored a run, then went ahead 5–4 on Jim Hickman's dramatic two-run eighth inning homer off former Cub reliever Chuck Hartenstein. (Hickman had already clouted two walk-off homers earlier in the season, one against the Pirates.) In the ninth, closer Regan got Matty Alou and Gene Alley, then went 2–2 on Willie Stargell. The next pitch, in Regan's words, was "a sinker that didn't sink." Boom. Onto Sheffield Avenue, over the right-field wall, as 28,698 fans (again, an oddly small crowd—on a Sunday, people were probably watching the Bears) sat stunned. In the eleventh, Don Kessinger's error on an Al Oliver grounder scored the lead run, and Richie Hebner knocked in another with a single.

The 7–5 defeat, and the Mets' 9–3 win over the Phillies, cut the lead to 2¹/₂. The Cubs then went on the road for nine games, going 2–7, and by the time they came back home, the race was over. Most of the exhausted regulars simply lost it in September, and manager Leo Durocher seemed powerless to deal with the stress of the situation. The Cubs of 1969 are fated forever to be the Little Team That Should Have.

MCWRIGLEY?

Chicago-born restaurateur Ray Kroc, the mastermind who turned McDonald's from a Des Plaines, Illinois, hamburger house into a multibillion-dollar international business, tried mightily to buy the Chicago Cubs during the late sixties and early seventies. Kroc asked his friend George Halas, owner of the Bears, to serve as an intermediary to the sale. Unfortunately for Kroc, Phil Wrigley chose not to divest himself of the team. According to Halas, Mrs. [Helen] Wrigley liked the Cubs so much that she asked her husband not to sell them. It's more likely, however, that P. K. retained the Cubs because of the promise he had made to his dying dad to keep ownership of the club.

Rebuffed in his attempt to buy the Cubs, Kroc went on to purchase the San Diego Padres in early 1974, later dressing them up in the McDonalds-influenced brown, yellow, and orange uniforms that made 1980s outfielder Carmelo Martinez resemble a messy Quarter Pounder.

LIFE IN THOSE DISTANT TIMES

In those times, a day at Wrigley Field began for many fans with a ride on the el, or perhaps the number thirty-six bus on west Addison Street. Lake View was still a working-class neighborhood, and few fans stuck around after the game to soak up the area. By the early 1970s, local residents with vacant-lot or paved-driveway property had begun to hawk somewhat-safe parking spaces for increasingly high prices. The game of finding adequate street parking in the neighborhood was still fair—the city had yet to close off chunks of Lake View parking, as would be the case in the years ahead.

Tickets to Cubs games in 1970 were a bargain. All reserved seats, whether lower or upper deck boxes, cost $3.50. Grandstand seats were $1.75 for adults and just $1.00 for kids under fourteen, while bleacher tickets cost just $1.00 for all. Given the sunshine, the camaraderie, and the closeness to the action, the bleacher seat ticket for Cubs games at Wrigley Field was, for many years, the greatest deal in professional sports.

In 1971, it cost just forty cents for a hot dog, fifty-five cents for a cup of beer, and a quarter for a soft drink. The spicy, shriveled smokie links ran forty-five cents, while cheese sandwiches cost a quarter. It wasn't sushi or garlic fries, but it was all Cubs fans had back then.

The Cubs had a long-standing practice of selling all 3,250 bleacher seats, as well as all lower- and upper-deck grandstand tickets, *only on the day of the game*. In 1967, there were 19,160 such grandstand seats, but by 1970 the number had grown to 19,182. P. K. Wrigley believed that fans should have the walk-up option, and all grandstand and bleacher seats were day-of-game sales only while he continued to own the club. A smaller number of grandstand tickets, and all bleacher seats, remained day of game until 1987.

HOUSE THAT WE USED TO LIVE IN

By the 1960s, Lake View was really two separate neighborhoods—east of the ballpark and west. East of Wrigley, from Broadway to Lake Michigan, was troubled by gangs. The low-priced real estate, however, was bringing an increasingly young, upscale, singles crowd into what would soon be called "New Town." The area featured plenty of trendy bars and restaurants. A gay scene, which remains in the community, also began to grow.

Meanwhile, the western portion of Lake View, as well as the area immediately south of Wrigley, became home to an increasing number of recent immigrants. As the young residents of Lake View moved away, others came in to find an established shopping district and well-built residences. To the west of Wrigley were apartments on the main streets and houses on the side streets.

By the latter half of the 1960s, the Lincoln–Belmont area had turned largely Latino as the vacancies in well-built apartments and houses were snapped up by recent immigrants aspiring to a middle-class life. Latinos also lived south of Wrigley Field on Sheffield; Dominic Pacyga and Ellen Skerrett, in *Chicago: City of Neighborhoods*, note that "in 1974, there were 2,000 Spanish-speaking people living in the area around Wrigley Field between Halsted and Racine."

The two sides of Lake View were very different, and the schism was reflected in the neighborhood's key group, the Lake View Citizens Council. The politics of the group near the lake were liberal, while the blue-collar enclave west of Wrigley ran more conservative. In 1968, a group of lakefront activists began the Independent Precinct Organization, which today combines with the Independent Voters of Illinois to offer nonpartisan (but often left-leaning) endorsements of candidates for local elections.

The U.S. Census Bureau estimated that in 1950 there were approximately 125,000 residents in Lake View in an estimated forty-five thousand housing units. By 1970, there were fewer residents (around 120,000) but far more housing units—somewhere near fifty-five thousand. Koreans and Japanese, who had begun arriving in Lake View in the 1930s and 1940s, saw their numbers expand in the 1960s as well. While the Korean population has largely moved slightly north and west, myriad Japanese noodle shops remain on Clark Street to cater to the food lovers around Wrigley Field.

NEW FAVORITE

The Cubs, as usual, buffed up the park for 1970. As part of the continuing work to reinforce the structure of the nearly sixty-year-old stadium, workers installed seventy-five hundred new seats and re-laid concrete over the stadium foundation and walkways. For the April 14 home opener against visiting Philadelphia, the Cubs asked Lou Boudreau, WGN radio color man and recent Hall of Fame inductee, to throw out the first ball to Gabby Hartnett. Milton Berle stopped by and received a Cubs jacket from Ernie Banks and Ron Santo. The Cavaliers Drum and Bugle Corps performed on the field from 1:00 to 1:30, and Louis Sudler sang "The Star-Spangled Banner" after a local Boy Scout recited the Pledge of Allegiance.

SELMA

Pitcher Dick Selma, unofficial leader of the Bleacher Bums cheering section in 1969, had been dealt to the Phillies that winter. On Opening Day 1970, he led cheers before the game in his Phillies uniform and a yellow hard hat. During the game, he came in to pitch and was hit hard.

During batting practice, fans threw coins at him. According to E. M. Swift, Selma scooped up the coins and, after the game, went to Ray's Bleachers outside the bleacher entrance at Waveland and Sheffield, threw the coins on the bar, and bought drinks for everyone. This may have been Selma's first "legal" time enjoying a cold one at Ray's; Durocher had labeled the tavern off limits for Cubs players soon after arriving in Chicago in 1966.

THE 1960S HIT WRIGLEY—IN 1970

Despite the patriotic festivities, the 1970 home opener was one of the most violent and unpleasant days ever seen at Clark and Addison. The violence that had buffeted America during the late 1960s had missed Wrigley Field, viewed at the time as a bastion of conservative American values: baseball, short hair, and beer. Rock music, political upheaval, and non-alcoholic drugs hadn't yet penetrated the most old-fashioned of Chicago's public arenas.

But it did this day. Young fans, many of them drunk or stoned schoolskippers and others old enough to know better, began piling up early in the morning by the left-field and center-field bleacher entrances. Things began to get rowdy, some fans were pushed out of line, and one fan suffered a broken leg. More than one ticket-seeker fainted in the crush of humanity and had to be passed, end over end, to the outer rim of the crowd.

"Intermittent fisticuffs among fans in deep left field occupied the attention of the Cub bullpen during the game," reported Cooper Rollow in the April 15 *Tribune*. Chicago eventually won the game 5–4. Dick Dozer, also in the *Tribune*, noted that "isolated fistfights had erupted continually during the game, taxing the Andy Frain fully staffed ushering crew and officers of the Burns Agency." (The Cubs had brought two hundred ushers and thirty Burns men to the park for the contest, according to John Holland.)

Bands of teenagers roamed the bleachers and upper deck, buying beer from willing vendors and, in some cases, terrorizing fans. As Ron Grousl, lead spokesmen for the Bleacher Bums, said later, "They try to look like Bums, but they're just bums." When the game ended, the Cubs were forced to rush off the field through a cordon of Andy Frain ushers. Fans from the right-field bleachers, some of whom were in Chicago to protest against the Vietnam War, jumped over the bleacher wall and swarmed on to the field. Three fans knocked down second baseman Glenn Beckert. One teenage usher was kicked in the face repeatedly by members of the mob.

Chicago police, at that time, refused to enter any private premises to restore order unless asked in. As a result, they didn't come into the park to fix things until the worst had already transpired. Told that the Chicago police had fifty officers on hand at the park, Salty Saltwell told the *Tribune*, "The only trouble is that they were all out directing traffic when we needed them."

Rick Talley wrote an angry editorial in the Chicago *Today* on April 15.

> It's a certain type of spectator . . . the lout, or clod, or exhibitionist, or whatever you want to call him, who thinks that for the price of a ticket, he's free to (1) get drunk, (2) throw things, (3) pour beer on people, (4) leap over walls onto the playing field, (5) knock down ushers, (6) snatch a ballplayer's hat, or glove, or tear his shirt, and (7) see a picture of himself in the next day's newspaper . . . We've got thousands of people—mostly young people—who are more concerned with performing, rather than watching the performers in Wrigley Field.

Talley's book *The Cubs of '69* included a story of a fan who approached Cubs outfielder Jim Hickman after Opening Day 1970 to invite him to a pot party in the Lake View neighborhood. (Steady, Cubs fans; Hickman declined, though not all the players on the club might have.)

A TISKET, A TASKET, AN UGLY WIRE BASKET

The Cubs were beside themselves. What could they do to control drunks and protesters? And how could this have happened? This was not the kind of friendly thrill-of-victory field swarming familiar to Cubs fans from 1938, 1960, or even 1969. Years later Salty Saltwell recalled,

> The Chicago Police Department said they should have forewarned us [of the anti-war protest group. The protestors] were out-of-towners, not locals, that were gathering for the demonstration. [A police official] told us that they

were sports fans, and logic would have said if the Cubs were playing, they
would have shown up there.

St. Louis had a problem in controlling the crowds at Busch Stadium.
My counterpart, Joe McShane, with the Cardinals, heard about it. He called
me [and told about the basket in front of the Busch Stadium wall]. He said,
"C'mon down here, I'll show you what we did."

The concept of a fence was proposed. Initially the wire fence was to jut
straight up from the top of the outfield wall, but such a fence would block
fans' view of the outfield. Back to the drawing board. On May 5, the Cubs
installed a new organ on the press-box concourse and brought in new loud-
speakers as well. The equipment had to be hauled in by helicopter and de-
posited on the roof. The next day, according to the *Tribune*, "Finishing
touches were applied to a new oblique screen which is angled 42 inches out
over the playing surface to help control littering and keep exuberant patrons
from leaning onto the field." The new wire fencing would add "into the basket" to the Wrigley lexicon every time a fly ball landed there, rather than
bouncing off the top part of the wall as in older days. And few people
seemed to be bothered by the new fence. Bleacher Bum Don Alger, for example, told Bill Jauss in the May 7 *Daily News*, "It's a great idea. Now those
idiots won't be jumping down on the field." A foot-high plastic barrier was
also erected atop the brick outfield wall. However, this blocked the view of
the field, and public outcry led to the barrier being removed almost immediately. It would be just the screen from then on.

OTHER STEPS

In addition to installing the wire fence, the Cubs took several other measures
to improve security at the Friendly Confines. Edgar Munzel laid them out in
the May 16, 1970, issue of *The Sporting News*:

◆ The Cubs installed a video monitoring system, with zoom-lensed video
cameras shooting pictures of several locales in the ballpark at once.
◆ Beer sales by vendors in the bleachers were forthwith prohibited. Fans
would have to leave their seats and go to the concession stand at the back
of the bleachers to purchase their intoxicants.
◆ Standing room tickets were no longer sold for bleacher seats.
◆ Bleacher gates were to open at 9:00 a.m., rather than the previous time of
8:00.
◆ After a request for help by the Cubs, Chicago police agreed to be stationed inside the park for weekend games and on holidays.

GM John Holland told Munzel, "The most effective thing will be the introduction of these video cameras. They will enable us to pinpoint where

the disturbances are and also the troublemakers involved. Our security men will be equipped with walkie-talkies so that they can move in within a matter of seconds."

There was talk in 1970 that the Cubs were also using their new security equipment to zero in on gamblers in the right-field bleachers, who would flash signs to their wagering counterparts in the left-field bleachers. While Saltwell himself did train his binoculars on the wagering, the actual investigation was a Chicago police department matter and did not lead to wholesale arrests.

In addition to working on keeping fans off the field, Salty Saltwell and Cubs financial man Bill Heymans also toured other ballparks during these years in order to see how they were set up for hosting a World Series. These studies were undertaken during the Durocher era, when a Cubs postseason trip seemed possible.

500

One of the great moments in Chicago sports history came on May 12, 1970. In front of just 5,264 fans at misty Wrigley Field, Ernie Banks hit his five hundredth home run. Banks had entered the season with 497 dingers and connected early in the year at Wrigley for the next two. In the bottom of the second inning on May 12, Ernie took a 1–1 pitch from Atlanta's Pat Jarvis and lined it just over the left-field wall. The ball was gone almost before anyone could grasp the significance of what was happening.

The ball bounced in and out of the half-filled bleachers to left fielder Rico Carty, who threw it toward the Cubs bench. Banks received a standing ovation from the fans as well as from the assembled press corps, and the game was held up for a short ceremony. Trailing 3–2 in the last of the ninth, the Cubs rallied. Billy Williams connected off Hoyt Wilhelm to knot things up, and in the eleventh, Ron Santo's seeing-eye single scored the winner in the 4–3 triumph.

PROBLEM DRINKER

If things weren't rough enough for the Cubs, they suffered another PR hit when the *Daily News* broke the story on May 6 that the team had been selling 3.2 beer ever since they had first been allowed to do so back in 1933 "as a crowd control measure." While White Sox fans had long been enjoying 3.8-caliber Meister Brau on the South Side, North Side supporters had to be content with "near beer." P. K. Wrigley told John Holland, "I don't care who knows it," when the news came out, although city commissioner of sales Jane Byrne (later a Chicago mayor) felt that the public was being bilked.

Ron Grousl of the Bleacher Bums had the last word about the 3.2 controversy. "I heard rumors to that effect," he commented at the time. "But it doesn't make any difference to me. I drink mine at Ray's Bleachers across from the park before the game."

ANY DAY IS A GOOD DAY TO DIE

On May 5, 1970, a group of aggrieved Native Americans began camping out kitty-corner from Wrigley Field's left-field corner, on the northwest corner of Waveland and Seminary just west of the fire station. The group, led by a man named Chosa, was protesting housing conditions for local poor Native Americans. Around that time, Mrs. Carol Warrington (a Native American) and her family were evicted from 3700 N. Seminary for refusing to pay rent on a building they said was substandard. When the city investigated, inspectors found rats infesting the place, as well as several other code violations.

The group of Native Americans remained at the corner of Waveland and Seminary—in the 2000s, quite the high-rent area—until June 1970, setting up teepees and other shelters. On some nights, while campfires crackled, as many as fifty people stopped by, including, on at least one occasion, Ernie Banks and Billy Williams. Eventually, the police came in and evicted the protesters, who offered no opposition despite earlier threats to resist with violence if necessary. "Any day is a good day to die," Chosa had told reporters.

COTTON FIELDS

One of the Wrigley Field grounds crew's legends, if members of the grounds crew can *be* legends, is Ray "Cotton" Bogren, who was said to have begun his association with the Cubs in 1925. A few years after his hiring, Bogren moved to Bobby Dorr's grounds crew and in 1957 was named Dorr's assistant. By 1970, Bogren, who knew the ballpark inside out, became grounds superintendent. He was responsible for trimming the outfield wall's vines before every home stand. The Kentucky bluegrass on the field was mown every third day in the spring, as well as every fifth or sixth day during the summer. The mound and plate were clay; the infield was three parts loam to one part bank sand.

By the time Bogren was in charge, the Cubs employed a twenty-two-man crew. In addition, local kids were let into the park for free in exchange for raising the seats up after games so that the aisles could be cleaned. The practice, which had begun in the 1920s, lasted through the 1980s, with Bogren often giving out fifty free passes a game. One such kid in the 1980s was future Cubs pitcher Kevin Foster, a native of suburban Evanston.

The vines continue to fascinate fans. After the 1979 season the Cubs put up twenty-five hundred Wrigley Field wall ivy plants for sale at $1.50 each. This was a first-time enterprise, and they all sold.

By the 1980s, Bogren had been assigned to work in the scoreboard, following in the steps of other longtime Cubs employees like Al Jourgensen. At the time that Bogren worked the scoreboard, there was no bathroom available inside, and the operators were not allowed to descend the ladder and use the bleacher fans' facilities. E. M. Swift, in an interview done for his 1980 *Sports Illustrated* article, asked Bogren—with no little decorum—how anyone could get through a game without having a facility. Where did he relieve himself? "Right there," Bogren told Swift, pointing at an old copper funnel. "Same one that's been there since 1937. Shows you how good copper is."

CHANGE OF THE GUARD

By the early 1970s, life was different even at Wrigley Field, bastion of the traditional. Player–owner labor squabbles, which first began to surface in 1969, blew up in 1972 with the first Major League Baseball Players Association strike. The labor action canceled the first few days of the regular season and left a bitter taste in the mouths of many. Such bitterness would intensify in the next thirty years.

Fans still lined up early in sleeping bags to get tickets—Elmwood Park cabbie Randy Bratu was first in line in 1969, 1970, and 1971—but things were changing. The rowdiness of the era was increasingly manifested on Opening Day, which has always been a spectacle rather than a game. There have always been people who wanted to be at the park on Opening Day because it was an event. Many spectators at Wrigley's Opening Day have come for nothing but the beer. But somehow things changed in the early 1970s. Perhaps the anger of the era—anger of young people at a system that had gone wrong—manifested itself in bad behavior even though traditions like baseball had little to do (at least at a surface level) with Vietnam, civil rights, drug laws, or urban poverty.

Opening Day 1971 was chilly, and 41,121 were in the park to see Billy Williams hit an eleventh-inning homer to win the game 2–1. Some thirty-six hundred fans bought one-dollar bleacher tickets and sat in the forty-degree temperatures, braving twenty-five-mile-per-hour winds, with another several hundred refused entry. "It was a mad scene," said an Andy Frain usher named Dave Noren. "But it was nothing like last year." John McHugh of the

Chicago *Today* reported that "the pile of debris at the gates was ample testimony to the mad scramble to get in the bleachers. Blankets, knit caps, gloves, clothing, playing cards, [and] shoes were among the items left behind." At least one usher was assaulted and had his uniform torn.

IN EVERY DREAM HOME A HEARTACHE

The Cubs continued to contend into the early 1970s, but they never won a division crown. Much has been written about why they didn't win, with some analysts blaming the Cubs' eighty-one-game day schedule for wearing the club down in the stretch. Plenty of players from the era take each side of the argument; some believe that the Cubs were at a disadvantage playing all their home games in the heat, while others feel that other clubs had problems adjusting to the sunshine and heat when they came to Chicago. Many factors involved—both measurable and immeasurable—in determining why teams win and lose make it difficult to come up with a clear statement as to whether playing day games helped or hurt the Cubs.

Looking at the difference between the Cubs' home and road winning percentages from 1940 through 1988, when the team put in lights, it's clear that when the Cubs were bad, they had a very high differential between their home and road winning percentages. In some years, they won fewer than 30 percent of their games in road parks, even while posting records above .500 in Wrigley Field.

The only time in that nearly fifty-year span that the Cubs were consistently good was from 1967 through 1972. In those years, the differential went way down. That is to say, their home and road winning percentages were more comparable, largely because since they had talented players, they were a good club on the road as well as in Wrigley Field.

PIZZA POWER

The first serious seeds of dissent in the Durocher administration came in August 1971 with the Cubs struggling to stay in contention. On Monday, August 23, the Cubs had a fractious pregame clubhouse meeting in which Durocher invited his players to speak their minds and then ripped the ones who did. The well-known clubhouse lawyers of the team were Milt Pappas and Joe Pepitone, and they both got in their shots before Durocher took the floor and ripped new orifices for them and several other Cubs, including Ron Santo.

Santo, an emotional man, had apparently wanted a "day" of his own. Durocher used Santo's vulnerability to make him look bad during the meeting, claiming that the only reason that the Cubs were staging such a day later in the week was that Santo had begged GM John Holland for it. This was the last straw for Santo, who nearly came to blows with the sixty-six-year-old manager, and the whole situation forced a showdown with Holland.

The clubhouse blowup got into the papers and also forced Wrigley's hand. Later in the season, P. K. took out ads in all Chicago papers supporting Durocher, telling those who wanted to get rid of him that they had best "give up." Wrigley also threatened to deal any players not happy under Leo. If this was Wrigley's true intention, he would have had to trade at least half the club.

Santo's day came that Saturday, August 28, with the Braves in town. The Cubs gave their third baseman a new car and a speedboat, and presented his wife, Linda, with a mink coat. Santo's teammates gifted him with an engraved shotgun, which he did not use on his manager. Unfortunately for the Cubs, Atlanta won 4–3 and kept the Cubs in their fatal spiral. They eventually finished third, fourteen games back.

AN UGLY SEASON

Baseball suffered its first strike in 1972. On April 11, the scheduled Opening Day, several dozen fans picketed in front of empty Wrigley Field to protest the absence of baseball. While the Players Association and the owners argued over benefits, salaries, and other contractual details, the Cubs tried to stay in shape. Prohibited by the National League from working out in Wrigley Field, several Cubs players let the press know on April 9 that they'd love to come over and work out with the White Sox at Comiskey Park. The Pale Hose had defied American League president Joe Cronin's order to lock the doors to players. Unfortunately, the potentially fascinating scene of the Cubs and Sox working out together never came to pass. The strike was settled shortly afterward, and the Cubs opened at Wrigley on April 15 against Philadelphia.

This appears to be the time that the Opening Day follies of earlier years disappeared for good. There was no Opening Day glitz or hoo-hah in 1972; resentment over the strike meant that only 17,566 fans bothered to show up for Chicago's 4–2 loss to Steve Carlton and the Phillies. The newspapers were full of quotes from angry fans wishing ill to the players, and perhaps for the first time, people really began to question whether the fun had gone out of baseball. John Husar of the *Tribune* quoted Bill Duncan, a bartender at Ray's. "I'm really bitter about this, myself. I lost money by not working this week. Those players lost money, too, but they can afford it." It's not clear from Husar's article whether Duncan ever got on his knees and thanked the players for performing their jobs well enough that people actually came to Ray's and paid his salary.

Attendance, at 1,299,163, was down around three hundred thousand fans from 1971's total. The strike was certainly to blame, but the Cubs did not play well despite their second-place finish. The rapidly aging club was on the way down. To make matters even worse, the 1972 season was the debut year of the Cubs' new 1970s-style uniforms. The home jerseys were double-knit pullovers with big blue built-in polyester belts, while the club's road uniforms resembled ill-fitting beer-league softball suits.

HANG THREE STARS

Society for American Baseball Research member Stew Thornley was at a Cub–Pirates game at Wrigley Field on June 25, 1972, and witnessed a three-pitch inning from Cubs rookie hurler Burt Hooton, with all three pitches resulting in fine plays: "It was the top of the fourth. Roberto Clemente hit a line drive that Ron Santo jumped and grabbed. On the next pitch, Willie Stargell grounded one up the middle. Don Kessinger went to his left, gloved it, and threw out Stargell at first. Al Oliver then hit a slow roller to second. Glenn Beckert charged, barehanded it, and threw Oliver out at first."

NO-HITTERS

The last two no-hit games thrown at Wrigley Field came in 1972. On April 16, just the second day of the season, Burt Hooton tossed a 4–0 no-hitter at the Phillies in front of just 9,583 cold, wet fans, walking seven and fanning seven as he baffled hitters with his goofy knuckle-curve. Hooton's gem was just one of two Cub wins in their first eleven games, setting the tone for a bad season in which Leo Durocher was forced out on July 24. The Cubs were never in contention.

On September 2, with the Cubs in second place but well behind the NL East champion Pirates, veteran Milt Pappas fired an 8–0 no-hitter against the visiting Padres. Pappas set down the first twenty-six hitters before walking pinch hitter Larry Stahl on a 3–2 delivery that sailed a few inches low of the strike zone. After yelling angrily at plate umpire Bruce Froemming, Pappas then retired former Cub Garry Jestadt on a pop-up to second to complete his no-no in front of 12,979.

INTO THE WOODS

As the Cubs stars of the late 1960s got old or were traded, the team sank into a nearly uninterrupted ten-year span of mediocrity. Changing managers every couple of seasons, trading undeveloped future stars, and bringing in a parade of aging big names to prop up a poor talent base, the Cubs finished below .500 every year from 1973 through 1983, with the exception of 1977 (81–81).

The Cubs continued to make some changes to the ballpark, although the maintenance schedule was nowhere near that of the 1950s. Prior to the 1972 season, the club reported spending five hundred thousand dollars on turning more seats in the right-field grandstand toward the field, continuing the project begun in 1952. In making this change, Cubs management razed the large aisle in back of the right-field boxes and added another thousand seats to the right-field grandstand section, filling a section in the deep right-field corner of the lower deck that had remained empty for many years.

April 6, 1973, was Opening Day. Jazz chanteuse Sarah Vaughn sang the national anthem. With temperatures reaching sixty-five degrees and no clouds in the sky, 40,273 fans stuffed Wrigley and saw the Cubs emerge with a 3–2 win by plating two runs in the bottom of the ninth. Pinch runner Tony LaRussa scored his only Cub run on Rick Monday's bases-loaded walk that won the game.

This wasn't to be a good Cubs year, though; they finished 77–84 and attendance began to suffer. From 1974–76, attendance dipped sharply, barely clearing a million fans each season. In each of these three seasons, the Cubs had lower attendance at Wrigley than at any time since 1967.

LEFT FIELD SUCKS

While the left-field Bleacher Bums had gotten the attention in the late 1960s and early 1970s, many claim that the *real* fans—the longtime sufferers—have always been in right field. That's where, for example, author Barry Gifford and screenwriter "Big Steve" Friedman yelled at their favorite Cubs during the 1960s. (Of course, right field was also home to a significant crowd of gamblers, who sat in the back rows near the concession stand.) Friedman, a well-known loudmouth of the time, claimed that Ron Santo once tried to run him over outside the Cubs parking lot.

In the 1970s and 1980s, old-timers like Caleb "Chet" Chestnut, Papa Carl Leone, and Marvin Rich passed on baseball traditions to younger fans. Chestnut, an African American born in 1896, puffed a pipe while dispensing baseball knowledge. Rich, a relative youngster born in 1930, consistently sat in the first row of the right-field bleachers. As George Castle wrote in August 1980, "On Opening Day 1978, [Leone] . . . tied ropes to posts next to the bleacher benches, next to the top of the stairway in right field, to prevent portions of the near-riotous mob of 45,000 from stepping over the people in his [sic] section." The next year, Leone reported to Wrigley Field at 3:30 a.m.

for a Cubs–Reds doubleheader that was scheduled to begin just eight and a half hours later.

Fans in the bleachers have always had a good-natured rivalry that involves a fairly consistent stream of insults going back and forth; not a game goes by without a group of fans from left field yelling "Right field sucks!" and their counterparts in the sun field answering in turn. This custom appears to have begun in the 1980s and usually occurs at least once per game—more if it's especially hot outside, which leads to increased consumption of alcohol.

Many of the well-known right-field denizens of those days are gone. Chestnut passed away early in the 1977 season. Papa Carl Leone, whose daughter was married at one time to a member of the Dave Clark Five, a 1960s British rock band, died in 1986. Marvin Rich left the earth midway through the 1989 season and did not see the team's first-place finish. The right-field faithful, however, still claim to be the *real* bleacher fans.

COLD TEAM, COLD FANS

For 1974, the Cubs spent $385,000 remodeling seats in the upper deck. They also rid themselves of veteran players to go with younger, cheaper talent. This rebuilding phase, meant to keep costs down, was sold to the fans as the first step in returning to contention.

Some concession prices went up at Wrigley Field. Twelve-ounce bottles of beer went from fifty-five to sixty cents, the first price increase since 1971. Both popcorn and scorecards were raised from fifteen to twenty cents (although you did get a free pencil with your scorecard). The only true souvenir items sold at Wrigley at the time were pennants, t-shirts, sweatshirts, and caps, and for all of them except pennants the Cubs raised prices by a quarter.

On Opening Day, April 9, Sarah Vaughn again sang the anthem, rearranging her concert schedule in order to do so. She appeared with an all-service color guard. Prior to the game, the two-hundred-member Dundee High School band performed, and the Proviso East state basketball team (led by Joe Ponsetto, later a star for DePaul University) tossed out ceremonial first pitches.

Bill Bonham shut out the Phillies 2–0 in forty-degree temperatures in front of 30,601 fans, who saw the highlight of the season. For the first time since 1966, the Cubs fell to the basement, finishing 66–96.

SICK MUSTARD

The Cubs were snowed out for their first home game of 1975; this was one of the few snow-cancelled openers in club history. When the club finally got things going on April 10, after two snow days, the Pirates clubbed four homers in an 8–4 win. With snow piled up outside the ballpark, just 19,239 fans braved temperatures in the thirties to see the game. David Condon, in the *Tribune*, noted that "the outfield grass was as jaundiced as sick mustard . . . Vendors found icebergs in the hot coffee."

Jim Enright, longtime Chicago sportswriter, took over public address duties; veteran field announcer Pat Pieper, who had done the job for fifty-nine years, had passed away October 22, 1974, at age eighty-eight. For the last few years, Pieper had worked from the press box after spending most of his career making announcements from the field.

IF A TREE FALLS . . . DOES TARZAN HEAR IT?

On September 15, 1975, the Pirates officially eliminated the Cubs from the NL race with a 9–1 win in the second game of a doubleheader. The big story of the day, however, involved popular Cubs center fielder Joe Wallis, nicknamed "Tarzan" by fans and teammates. When Wallis pinch-hit in the first game of the doubleheader, the loudspeaker blared out a Tarzan yell that, in the words of Cubs traveling secretary Blake Cullen, sounded like "a sick cow." This public address system stunt horrified the player. "What's going on?" he said after the game. "That's embarrassing. I don't even *like* the name 'Tarzan.'"

This is the first recorded Wrigley Field instance of the tape-recorded antics so commonplace now during games at most parks. The next day, September 16, the Pirates plastered the Cubs 22–0, posting the biggest margin in a shutout since 1883. Infielder Rennie Stennett of the Bucs went 7-for-7, becoming the first player ever to do so in a nine-inning contest. However, only 4,932 fans were on hand to see this "spectacle."

A SALT OUT OF WATER

Perhaps Salty Saltwell's least enjoyable memories as a Cubs executive are those of his one season as general manager in 1976. The hiring of Saltwell for a position he was utterly unprepared for is one of the low points of modern Cubs history—through no fault of Salty's. Aging and out-of-touch Phil Wrigley scarcely could network throughout the game, so he simply went one notch down the executive depth chart after longtime GM John Holland was eased out of the job and became a "consultant." Wrigley rarely saw the value of bringing in new people to the baseball side of the organization to bring about change. As former Cubs pitcher Jim Brosnan said, "Wrigley was perfectly willing to hire his old athletes instead of bright, hardworking people."

Holland assistant Blake Cullen was thought to be a favorite for the job; others in the front office felt Cullen was a cinch. Saltwell's appointment was a surprise to almost everyone. Derided by the media as simply a "peanut vendor," Saltwell went back to supervising ballpark and business-side operations after the '76 season.

By his estimation, Saltwell held thirteen different titles in his Cubs tenure, which continued all the way through the 1990 season, when he retired. Although Dallas Green staged a big housecleaning of Wrigley-ownership-era personnel in 1982, Saltwell was retained for his knowledge of the ballpark, earning a vice president's title. He now lives in Park Ridge, Illinois, and regularly attends spring training in Mesa, Arizona.

THE BICENTENNIAL MINUTE

During 1976, baseball wrapped itself in the red, white, and blue to celebrate America's two hundredth birthday. The Cubs put special patches on their uniforms, and for Opening Day, April 13, Cap Anson's daughter came by to throw out the first ball. Not to say that the Cubs were out of touch with popular culture, but their selection to sing the National Anthem was James Darren, a former teen idol whose day in the spotlight had come fifteen years before. The Cubs at this point were resistant to change. George Castle notes in *The Million-to-One Team* that Cubs Bill Bonham, Pete LaCock, and Bob Locker, who did yoga exercises to stretch out before home games, were told to take their weird hippie business off the field and to a small room near the clubhouse.

Optimistic forecasts had thirty thousand turning out for the game, but good weather led to a huge walk-up crowd. By game time, 44,818 fans had passed through the turnstiles, the largest paid total to see a game at Wrigley since 1948. It's still hard to figure why so many came to the park that day, but they did go home happy as the Cubs beat the Mets 5–4 with a run in the last of the ninth. Unfortunately, the Cubs were never a factor in the NL East race; they were already nine games back by mid-May and finished the year twenty-six out. Attendance barely cleared a million; after the big gathering on Opening Day, the Cubs didn't have a crowd of more than 28,287 the rest of the season.

That crowd gathered a few days later, on April 17, when Mike Schmidt of the Phillies hit four homers in a ten-inning 18–16 Philadelphia win. The Cubs jumped out quickly and led 12–1 after three innings, but the bullpen faltered and the Phils finally caught up. Amazingly enough, Schmidt's first homer of the game did not come until the fifth; he then connected in both the seventh and eighth innings as the Phillies tied the game. Schmidt's fourth homer, in the tenth, was a two-run job that proved the winning margin. His box score: 6 4 5 8.

KONG

Just three days earlier, another opponent had hit a memorable Wrigley Field home run. Dave Kingman was one of the most powerful hitters ever to play at Wrigley Field. In his three years as a Cub (1978–80), he hit ninety-four homers, including a league-leading forty-eight in 1979, but made plenty of enemies with his prickly personality and let in a lot of runs with a mediocre glove.

On April 14, 1976, as a member of the Mets, he hit perhaps the longest long four-bagger ever seen at the ivy-covered grounds. In the visitors' half of the sixth, Kingman rode a 1–1 Tom Dettore fastball over the left-field wall. The ball kept carrying. As Eddie Gold wrote in the 1979 *Baseball Research Journal*: "The usual gang of kids was waiting outside with gloves poised. But the ball sailed over their heads. They turned and started running north on Kenmore Avenue. The ball struck the porch of the third house from the Waveland Avenue corner and was caught on the rebound by Richard Keiber."

Monumental home runs have been clubbed at Wrigley over the years by sluggers such as Roberto Clemente, Ryan Klesko, Bill Nicholson, Ransom Jackson, Glenallen Hill, Sammy Sosa, Hank Aaron, Jim Hickman, Willie Stargell, and Hank Sauer, but Kingman's may be the biggest shot ever. Some will argue for Sosa's mammoth blast against Milwaukee in June 2003.

OUTLIVING MY USEFULNESS

Philip K. Wrigley died on April 12, 1977, at age eighty-two. His death, which came just five days after Opening Day, was not unexpected; the tireless worker had not been into his office in nearly half a year. "Everything has changed," Wrigley said shortly before passing on. "I have outlived my usefulness."

It was truly the end of an era. Wrigley was nearly the last of his kind; of the remaining big league owners, only Calvin Griffith of the Twins could be compared to him, and Griffith wasn't in Wrigley's league as a sportsman or in his concern for the comfort of the fans. Wrigley, who spent much of his time in the seventies trying to hold down salaries and costs, had seen the game get away from him with the advent of free agency and the influence of national television. He remained opposed to lights for the park until the end and still believed in baseball as a great way to market a healthy lifestyle—which included, of course, plenty of chewing gum.

Transfer of the Cubs went to Wrigley's only son, Bill, who had taken over the gum operations in 1961. Bill didn't get all of the estate, though. To ease tax burdens on his son, P. K. Wrigley had willed that his devoted wife, Helen, receive half the estate as well. Helen Wrigley, however, passed away only two months after her devoted husband.

A LITTLE LONELY

When news of Wrigley's death reached the public, the flags at the Wrigley Building and at Wrigley Field were immediately lowered to half-mast. Cubs outfielder Jose Cardenal, with the team in Philadelphia, sat in his hotel room and cried. "I don't know why more players didn't take the time [to know him]," Cardenal said. "Too many of them thought about him only on the first and the 15th of the month, when the checks came with his name on them. But Mr. Wrigley's door was always open. He loved when a player came to talk to him. I think he was a little lonely."

OLD-TIMERS' DAY

On Saturday, June 25, 1977, the Chicago Cubs held "A Day of Fame," an event billed by the team as "the first old-timers' game played within the friendly confines of Wrigley Field." With the surprising Cubs, riding the pitching arm of Bruce Sutter, seven games in front in the National League East with a 43–22 record, a huge crowd was guaranteed for the three-inning exhibition and, to follow, the "real" game against the Mets.

On a warm and sunny day, 33,130 fans came to the ballpark. The Cubs old-timers whipped a group of Hall of Famers 5–1. Ernie Banks got the loudest ovation, but former Cub hurler Moe Drabowsky made the funniest entrance, running from the Cubs dugout and sliding into home plate. Charlie Grimm was the Cubs' manager. The Cubs pitchers included Drabowsky, Dick Ellsworth, Don Elston, Rich Nye, John Klippstein, Dutch Leonard, Phil Regan (ejected by umpire Tom Gorman for protesting a ball call), Dick Drott, Bill Hands, and Larry French. The position players included Paul Popovich, Ron Santo, Jerry Kindall, Moose Moryn, Clyde McCullough, Bob Will, Gene Baker, and Andy Pafko. Banks, as well as Billy Herman and Fred Lindstrom, played for the Hall of Fame club.

Retired *Tribune* sportswriter Ed Prell, asked back to cover the event, noted that "The old-timers' 'clubhouse' was the Ambassador West [Hotel], and the group arrived at Wrigley Field in an open-air bus, slightly remindful of the era when visiting teams came to the ballpark in horse-drawn hacks."

Following the warm and fuzzy ceremonies, the Cubs went out and fell behind to the visiting Mets. Down 4–1 in the ninth, the Cubs rallied. With Ernie Banks sitting with Chicago mayor Michael Bilandic in the left-field bleachers, Steve Swisher singled. With one out, Ivan DeJesus doubled Swisher to third. Larry Biittner then doubled to right for two runs. Bill Buckner then hit a fly ball to left center. The wind whipped the ball around, and as Banks, Bilandic, and the other bleacher fans screamed, Mets outfielders Steve Henderson and Lee Mazzilli collided. The resulting double scored Biittner. Two walks later, Manny Trillo hit a bases-loaded roller to third. Doug Flynn bobbled the ball, and by the time he threw to first, Trillo was safe, pinch runner Mick Kelleher scored, and the Cubs won 5–4.

ANOTHER SUBWAY RIDE

On July 27, with both the Cubs and Sox in first place, the city saw another "subway doubleheader." The Cubs split an afternoon twin bill with the Reds, drawing 42,342 sun-baked fans to Wrigley Field, while the White Sox pulled in 39,177 to a night game that they lost to Detroit. The combined 81,519 turnstile clicks set a record at the time for the biggest one-day baseball crowd in Chicago.

JULY 28, 1977

The next day, the Cubs vanquished the Reds 16–15 in an insane thirteen-inning contest that some possibly hyperbolic members of the Chicago press called "the most exciting game ever played." With 32,155 fans on hand for the four-hour, fifty-minute struggle, the Cubs and Reds pulled out all the stops. Cincinnati scored six runs in the top of the first, but the Cubs themselves scored four in the bottom of the frame. The two teams combined to hit five homers in that first inning.

In the last of the ninth, down 13–12, Chicago tied the game on Steve Ontiveros's RBI single. After the Reds scored in the twelfth, Cubs catcher George Mitterwald hit his second homer of the game into the right-field bleachers to knot things again. Then, in the last of the thirteenth, pitcher Rick Reuschel (on in relief after defeating the Reds two days before) singled to center, went to third on Ontiveros's single, and scored on another hit by infielder Davey Rosello.

By the time the game ended, the Cubs had used twenty-one players and the Reds sixteen. Reuschel scored the winning run just after 6:00 p.m., and

Chicago players ran to the center of the diamond and celebrated. As Tom Fitzpatrick wrote in the next day's *Sun-Times*, "The fans stood on their feet and kept cheering at the top of their hoarse voices and pounding their hands together. As the Cubs trotted through the dusk of the early evening, the fans remained, chanting in unison: 'We're No. 1. We're No. 1.'"

This was the high point of the 1977 season, which ended unhappily for the Cubs. The team was clearly playing over its head, and when star reliever Bruce Sutter went down with a shoulder injury, the Cubs collapsed. Sutter t-shirts became big business around Wrigley Field in 1977. Unfortunately for the young right-hander, he wasn't cut in on the action. At Sutter's request, the Players Association filed suit to stop two women from selling shirts reading, "Only the Lord saves more than Sutter."

YOGURT WAR

The following season featured one of the wildest openings on record. George Castle recalled the day in the *Times* of Northwest Indiana in 1996: "No Cubs opener has featured day-of-game sales since April 14, 1978, when 4,000 showed up at dawn for bleacher seats. Fearing a riot from the impatient throng, ballpark officials opened the bleacher gates at 8 a.m., 5^1/$_2$ hours before the first pitch . . . Fans kept storming ticket windows until 45,777 squeezed into Wrigley Field. That meant 8,000 were either standing, lap-sitting, or blocking aisles. Fearing a repeat, Cubs management banned [Opening Day] day-of-game sales from then on."

By all accounts, it was a mad day at Wrigley. Joe Goddard noted in the *Sun-Times* that "many had slept overnight at the gates. One youth entered the park with yogurt all over his jacket, the spoils of a food war with his friends."

Thousands of fans were already lined up for tickets at Clark and Addison by 7:00 a.m. Ray's Bleachers, across from the bleacher gates at Waveland and Sheffield, opened for business at the same time and was jammed two hours later. By then, all bleacher seats were filled. Once the grandstand gates opened, two turnstiles actually broke down in the crush, which delayed entry for some fans and held up the official ticket count. During the game, Pirates infielder Jim Fregosi was almost hit by a chain thrown from the seats by a fan. The game was wild, too. Larry Biittner's ninth-inning homer off Jim Bibby gave the Cubs a 5–4 win. Later, in the clubhouse, Cubs manager Herman Franks and a local radio reporter engaged in a postgame shouting match.

That year, the Cubs changed the lights above the scoreboard indicating wins and losses. The blue light above the board would signal victory, while a white light indicated a loss. This feature remains one of the most charismatic parts of the park, especially for those souls riding the late-night ele-vated trains. Following the season, the Cubs built new concession stands as well. The old areas had become obsolete. It would take several years for any-thing to be done about the equally outmoded menu.

"AYYYYYY"

The ABC-TV series *Happy Days* was staggeringly popular in the 1970s, and even the event-phobic Cubs got on board. On August 17, 1979, a team of actors and producers from the show came to Wrigley Field to take on a con-tingent of Chicago media figures in a pregame softball contest. After just two innings, the game was washed out by rain but was completed two days later. In a seven-inning contest, the *Happy Days* team (featuring Henry Win-kler, Ron Howard, Anson Williams, Tom Bosley, Marion Ross, Donny Most, Erin Moran, Scott Baio, and Garry Marshall) and the Chicago media club (managed by Lou Boudreau) tied 4–4.

Prior to the August 17 exhibition, Bosley—who attended Lake View High School, just four blocks north of Wrigley—received a "Sword of Hope" for his work in raising money for cancer research.

TOO SHORT FOR DRINKING

Opening Day 1980 came on April 17. The Cubs won 4–1 in front of 33,313 fans, less than capacity, even though the park had been sold out long before. George Halas threw out the first pitch. While many people like short games, this one—which took only an hour and fifty-eight minutes—may have been a bit too brief. Beer-drinking fans, according to the *Sun-Times*, were "barely left time for the foam to subside in their cups."

At least one fan, Sigmund Walsch, had a great time in what people have come to see as one of the world's largest outdoor saloons. "We really got primed," he told the paper. "I took the day off from my job, and we're gonna break the record of 17 [beers] in one game—all 12 of us. There's no doubt about it. This is the greatest day of the year."

ALL THOSE YEARS AGO

On June 14, 1980, the Cubs held a thirty-fifth anniversary celebration of the team's last appearance in the World Series. Teams of ex-Cubs and ex-Tigers took the field for an exhibition, which the Tigers won 4–1. Before the game, Ernie Banks lost to Eddie Mathews in a home-run hitting contest.

That same day, left fielder Dave Kingman showed up at Wrigley after an unexcused absence the previous game. Cubs GM Bob Kennedy fined Kingman $1,250, and in a pregame clubhouse meeting, several Cubs aired out their wayward teammate.

TAXMAN

Bill Wrigley had a big problem. Estate taxes from his 1981 inheritance of the Cubs and of Wrigley Field, following the deaths of his parents, threatened to cost $40 million. Most of the taxes were paid after a long negotiation with the federal government, but Wrigley needed more money to pay the rest of the bill. He spent three years after his parents' passing trying to settle the estate with the IRS and during that time came to realize that he couldn't hold on to the team much longer, especially with attendance down, the club performing badly, and little talent available from a decimated farm system.

CASH ON THE BARRELHEAD

The front page of the June 17, 1981, *Chicago Tribune* trumpeted the big news: the Tribune Company itself had purchased the Cubs. The Wrigley family made no public offers of the team, instead choosing the Tribune Company as the first and only suitor. Many other people could have entered the bidding in an open sale; Athletics boss Charlie O. Finley stated immediately that he would have loved to know that the team was on the block.

Costs of the sale, which was announced by Tribune Company President and CEO Stanton Cook, totaled $20.5 million. That amount covered the baseball team's assets and most of its liabilities, as well as Wrigley Field itself, but not the land on which the stadium stood. (In 1980, the Cubs claimed their worth at $2.2 million.) A few months after the sale, the Cubs exercised their option to buy the land itself.

Bill Wrigley controlled 81 percent of the team's stock, which made approval of the sale by the Cubs' board of directors a mere formality. But the news was good for the club's minority shareholders, who would get around $2,050 per share from the Tribune Company. The Tribune Company chose to buy the club's assets, rather than the corporation itself, for the tax advantages. Writing off player salaries against company earnings would allow the Trib to save around $1 million a year for a five-year period.

Alice Bright, an attorney who helped administer the Wrigley estate, noted that there was nothing that Bill Wrigley could have done to settle the tax bill and keep the team under his control. "It was a great family tradition, and it's rather sad that taxes can break it up."

CHANGE IS NOW

While Cubs fans were shocked by the news, they weren't necessarily saddened. It had been four years since P. K. Wrigley's death, and with the Cubs continuing to wallow in mediocrity, public sympathy favored the sale of the team to *anyone*. Bill Wrigley never was able to find a footing as the head of the organization. Fair or not, the public perception was that Bill Wrigley wouldn't spend the money to create a contender. The truth is that years of farm neglect and poor personnel decisions had rendered the Cubs unable to compete. The competitive streak of the mid-1960s was due largely to a series of fortuitous trades that brought in young talent.

What would happen to the *Tribune*'s ability to cover the Cubs? Sports editor George Langford said, "We will cover the baseball news as diligently as possible and critique the management and ownership when appropriate." By and large, the newspaper has done a good job in a tough position. There have been times, however, when the paper has soft-pedaled legitimate criticism.

WE'RE GONNA TAKE THIS CABLE NOW AND STICK IT DOWN YOUR THROAT

At the time of the sale, most everyone—including the *Tribune* itself—believed that the company wanted the baseball club as a large part of its plans for the rapidly growing cable TV field. Unfortunately, the Tribune Company's own success got in the way of these grand plans. The company's own over-the-air super station, WGN, had gone on basic cable systems all over the country just a short time before and was pulling in huge ratings and advertising dollars by telecasting more than 140 Cubs games per season.

After the team's WGN contract ran out at the conclusion of the 1983 season, the Tribune Company chose to keep games on the super station rather than move them to the still uncertain cable arena. In fact, the Cubs didn't televise a single game on cable until 1993, when the Tribune Company's local cable news channel, CLTV, began showing blacked-out Wednesday night contests to Chicago-area viewers.

RUMORS OF WAR

Some Wrigleyville residents were happy that the big boys had bought into the neighborhood. A *Tribune* story the day after the sale painted a picture of happy fans celebrating the sale at the Bleachers Bar on Sheffield (soon to be renamed Murphy's): "The fans who sit in the bleachers at Wrigley Field often are the same people who have a hot dog and a beer before the game at the Bleachers Bar. These people, the fans said, would go to the games no matter who owned the team."

With Tribune ownership, however, came fears that lights would be installed at Clark and Addison. Most observers believed that the new owners would try to strap light towers to the ballpark as soon as humanly possible. With this in mind, the Lake View Citizens' Council in July 1981 named Christy Cressey chairperson of a committee opposing lights at Wrigley Field. Andy McKenna, a paper company executive appointed chairman of the board of the club when the Tribune Company took over, promised neighborhood activists that year that there would be no lights installed at Wrigley Field for at least three years. This wasn't nearly good enough for many in the community.

Another local, Charlotte Newfeld, became active around this time and remained a strong presence in Wrigley matters for most of the next two decades. "They can play night ball," she told the *Tribune* in 1982, "but not in our neighborhood." Newfeld and the C.U.B.S. organization (Citizens United for Baseball in the Sunshine) made quite a splash in the 1980s. With the Cubs refusing to make a long-term commitment to keeping the park light free, C.U.B.S.' yellow t-shirts with "No Lights!" in bright red letters began to make increasingly frequent appearances in the bleachers.

Even celebrities began to sport them. Bass guitarist Mike Mills of the Georgia rock band R.E.M., a longtime baseball fan, donned one of the shirts for an album signing at a Rose Records location just a few blocks from Wrigley in June 1984.

BACK IN BLACK

Frank Maloney, the Cubs' current director of ticket operations, joined the organization in 1981. He noted, in a 2002 interview conducted by Shamus Toomey, "When I started here, I wasn't sure that this neighborhood wasn't going to become a slum. We were located between [upscale] Lincoln Park and [lower-middle-class] Uptown, and there's a major difference between the areas on a socio-economic level. I came in and thought: 'Which way is it going?'" Maloney is right that the Lake View neighborhood was between two vastly different areas. But at no point was the area around Wrigley ever truly dangerous; some people tend to think all areas in which "minorities" live are potentially hostile.

By the 1980s, the real estate market in Lake View had already hit bottom and was bouncing back. According to Michael Miner in the April 12, 1985,

Chicago *Reader*, "A Sheffield Avenue three-flat that cost $18,000 in 1971 was appraised last year at $175,000." Reality aside, however, the Cubs found that there was a lot of room for improvement in the *perception* of the neighborhood. All the organization needed was a spark.

BUILDING A NEW TRADITION?

Shortly after buying the club, Tribune Company hired Dallas Green, fresh from building the Phillies into a world championship club, as the Cubs' new general manager. Perhaps a little too eager to put his stamp on the club, the blustery and hard-bitten Green cut all organizational ties to the 1969 Cubs as part of his "Building a New Tradition" campaign, which also included painting the slogan on the walls of the bleacher entrance.

In a move that won him enmity from fans and the media, Green exiled the most famous Cub of all, Ernie Banks. Since retiring in 1972, Banks had been associated with the club in various capacities, mostly in the group ticket sales department where he could schmooze with high-volume customers. At least Green didn't stop the club from retiring Banks's number fourteen and putting a flag up on the left-field foul pole honoring him. This ceremony was held August 22, 1982.

The new general manager, dubbed "Dallas Sha Na Na" by columnist Mike Royko for his ducktail haircut, didn't seem to understand the hold that past Cubs greats have on their fans. Even five-year-olds today know who Ernie Banks is, but nobody around town clamors for Dallas Green—who actually did a lot to help the club—to return to town and throw out a ceremonial first pitch.

LEE ELIA'S F***ING ASS

In 1982 and 1983, the brassy Green seemed to make little progress. Under Green's handpicked skipper, Lee Elia, the Cubs were 73–89 in '82 and got off to a poor start the next season. Following a 4–3 loss to the visiting Dodgers on April 29 that marked the Cubs' fourteenth defeat in their first nineteen contests, Lee Elia had had enough—enough of the press, enough of bad baseball, and enough of Cubs fans, whom he saw as lazy, backstabbing, violent-tempered ignoramuses.

> 'They're really, really behind you around here.' *My f***ing ass!* What the f*** am I supposed to do? Go out there and let my f***ing players get destroyed every day? And be *quiet* about it? For the f***ing nickel-dime people that show up here? They ought to go out and get a f***ing *job* and find out what

it's *like* to go out and earn a f***ing living. Eighty-five percent of the f***ing world's working; the other 15 [percent] come out here. It's a f***ing *play-ground* for the c***suckers! . . . Rip the motherf***ers! Rip them c***in' c***suckers like the f***ing players. Got guys bustin their f***in' ass and them f***in' people boo. And *that's* the *Cubs*? My f***in' *ass!* . . . They talk about the great support the players get around here. I haven't seen it *this* f***in' year! . . . The changes that have happened in the Cub organization are *multifold!* [sic] All right, they don't show because we're 5–14. And unfortunately, that's the criteria [sic] of them dumb 3,000 f***ing fans who come out to watch day baseball. The other 85 [percent] are earning a living!

Unfortunately, the tape recorders were rolling, and the nationally publicized incident made the Cubs even more of a mockery. It also effectively ended Elia's career in Chicago. He was mercifully relieved of his job on August 22, with the Cubs at a sad 55–69. Elia would serve several major league teams as a coach over the following two decades.

Meanwhile, the 15 percent would soon multiply.

CHAPTER 9

Blinded by the Light: Wrigley Field, 1984 to the Present

DIG WE MUST!

Players, and some front office figures, spent years crying for improvements in the size and utility of the home dugout, but only after P. K. Wrigley passed away did the Cubs make changes. For decades, both Cubs and visiting players would have to walk down the foul lines to their clubhouses in order to use the restroom during games. The clubhouses were not accessible from the dugouts. The showers in the old dressing rooms were small, rats ran wild, and the facilities hardly could hold the players, much less the press.

Both the home and visiting dugouts at Wrigley Field were greatly enlarged in 1978, when Bill Wrigley took over as owner. The younger Wrigley gave the thumbs-up for some minor reconstruction and modest improvements in the Cubs' substandard facilities. "We'd always been criticized for having such small dugouts," recalled Salty Saltwell in 2003. "The dugouts *were* inadequate. That had been under discussion for several years prior to Mr. Wrigley's passing. His primary concern had been fan comfort, then to do what's necessary as far as players were concerned."

When Saltwell was asked what had been on the drawing board for improvements when the Tribune Company took over in 1981, he confirmed that additional corporate funds were made available above and beyond club cash flow to improve Wrigley Field. The real improvement, which involved building a new clubhouse for the Cubs under the third-base grandstand, wasn't completed until just before the 1984 campaign. Saltwell explained that the clubhouse behind the dugout was constructed by excavating downward. "It had to be dug out, literally."

General manager Dallas Green prompted that project. "It was one of the first things Dallas wanted to do," Saltwell recalled. Funds were not available for such an expensive project under the Wrigleys, but as a former player, Green clearly believed that it was important to have a classy dressing room, and the Tribune Company coughed up. (By 2000, the company had spent approximately $35 million refurbishing the franchise's greatest asset— Wrigley Field itself.)

The new dressing room was one of the first real indications that the Cubs were serious about doing things better. The old clubhouse was ridiculous; the new one, not bad by 1984 big league standards. "We've put in a beautiful new clubhouse for our team," Green said at the time. "I considered doing the same thing for the visitors, but then I said, 'Nah, let 'em suffer.'"

MESSAGE IN A BOTTLE

Unfortunately, the "New Tradition" was experiencing some hiccups. Not only did the manager curse out the fans, but the team also sullied the scoreboard with electronics and beer ads. Shortly after Opening Day 1983, the Tribune Company chose to add an electronic message board to the bottom of the legendary scoreboard. This was done, supposedly, to give statistical information for players and announce pitching changes, but the board was really there to convey between-inning advertisements.

To make things worse, signs advertising two brands of beer were hooked to each side of the new electronic board. These signs, and the message board, blocked the view of the last rows of the high center-field bleachers. Prior to the 1986 season, the beer signs were removed, but the message board stayed.

JUMP

The 1984 season did not begin smoothly. Two spring training fights between teammates and a late March trade kept the Cubs up in the air, but it soon became clear that this was to be a special Cubs season.

The Cardinals lost seven in a row in April and were never a factor in the race. Former contenders Pittsburgh, Philadelphia, and Montreal had collapsed. Meanwhile, the Cubs started hot, as did the formerly moribund New York Mets.

THE SANDBERG GAME

Second baseman Ryne Sandberg, in his third season with Chicago, was quickly establishing himself as an all-star. No game did more to cement his reputation—and that of the rising Cubs—than the nationally televised June 23, 1984, tilt against visiting St. Louis.

It was all Cardinals from the start. A six-run second inning knocked out Cubs lefty Steve Trout, and Willie McGee had tripled, homered, and singled by the sixth inning. But ahead 7–1 in the fifth, the Cardinals' pitching weakened. During a five-run Cubs rally in the sixth, Sandberg hit his third single of the day (and drove in his third and fourth runs). With St. Louis ahead 9–8 in the bottom of the ninth, former Cub Bruce Sutter tried to finish the game out. Sutter had been on the mound since the seventh—yes, closers were used in that way twenty years ago—and Sandberg took him deep to lead off the ninth. The Cubs almost won it later that inning, but Sutter induced Gary Woods to ground out to force extra innings.

In the tenth, McGee doubled in two runs to complete the cycle. He went four for six on the day and drove in six runs, yet he was upstaged. In the Cubs tenth, Cardinals up 11–9 and Sutter still on the hill, Bob Dernier worked a walk with two out. Sandberg then came up and drilled a Sutter splitter over the left-field wall to tie things *again*. Last-ditch game-tying home runs in consecutive innings off the best closer in the game—a hysterical crowd of 38,079 howled; NBC broadcaster Bob Costas couldn't believe it. Harry Caray, in the Cubs radio booth, yelled, "Sandberg did it *again!*" Five for six, two homers, seven RBI.

In the last of the eleventh, Leon Durham walked, stole second, and went to third on a bad throw by St. Louis catcher Darrell Porter. After Jeff Lahti walked the bases loaded intentionally, scrub infielder Dave Owen lifted a short single to right center that plated Durham with the winning run.

TWO MILLION

As the Cubs won, the fans came back to Wrigley Field. In 1984, the Cubs broke two million for the first time, drawing a record 2,107,655 at home to finish second in the league in attendance. In 1983, only 1,479,717 fans had clicked the turnstiles, just the seventh best rate in the NL.

The 1984 season kick-started a renaissance; only once since then (in 1986) have the Cubs drawn fewer than two million fans over a full season. It is now expected that they will draw two million every year, just as it was expected in the late 1960s that they would draw *one* million every year.

The club also reaped benefits on TV. Broadcaster Harry Caray, who had come over from the White Sox in 1982, was an immensely popular figure with his good-time, beer-drinking persona, and Cubs games on super station WGN were among the most popular shows on cable.

THOSE PEOPLE STANDING 'ROUND WILL
SCREW YOU IN THE GROUND

With the Cubs breezing toward the National League East division title, the muckety-mucks running the game from New York sat bolt upright, aghast at the possibilities. What if the Cubs made the World Series? And had to play in the *daytime*?

Major League Baseball and NBC, its rights-holding TV network, fretted that games played during the day (and on weekdays, no less) would engender millions of dollars in lost advertising revenue. At no time did these people admit that the novelty of the Cubs, playing day games in the postseason, might actually *increase* viewership.

When the networks coerced baseball into introducing night games to the World Series in 1971, traditionalists moaned. Kids won't be able to watch the games, they said. Primetime television, they believed, would lead to more control of the game by advertisers. While the sky hasn't fallen, it is clear in retrospect that those concerns were well founded. The holy order of the television contract forced baseball to abandon its tradition of daytime postseason play, making the game just another nighttime television show rather than something truly special. In addition, evening postseason contests, which sometimes last until near midnight, lead to more media criticism.

During the fourteen-year span (1971–84), the landscape had shifted so much that the Cubs, in their old-fashioned brick ballpark with no lights, suddenly threatened the existing order. So Commissioner Bowie Kuhn said to hell with tradition and to hell with fairness and showed that television really *did* run the game. Kuhn ruled that should the Cubs win the best-of-five 1984 National League play-offs, they would lose their rightful home-field advantage in the World Series. To protect NBC's advertising revenues, Major League Baseball would force the Cubs to play the middle three contests at home rather than the first two and last two.

Manager Jim Frey of the Cubs had it exactly right when told that the games would be rescheduled. "When baseball and TV signed the contract, didn't they know that the Cubs were in baseball and this might happen?" he said. "Did they just find out in the last week that we're in the league?" But the Cubs made the controversy moot. After winning the first two play-off games at home, 13–0 and 4–2, before capacity throngs of 36,282, they went to San Diego and dropped three heartbreakers. Oddly enough, in 1985, the NLCS was expanded to seven games. Just one year later, the Cubs would have had four home games instead of just two.

NIGHT TIME IS THE RIGHT TIME

Even with the Cubs losing the National League play-offs, the lights issue would be addressed. New baseball commissioner Peter Ueberroth made not-so-veiled threats against the Cubs, directing them in no uncertain terms to install lights under penalty of having any future Series games transferred to other parks—just so that television could have its precious night games.

On December 18, 1984, Ueberroth said that unless the Cubs installed lights, any future postseason games involving the team would be played at a neutral location, such as Comiskey Park or—horrors—St. Louis' Busch Stadium. "It's not just a question of lights in Wrigley Field. It's a question of *if* Wrigley Field. If Wrigley Field, in my opinion, doesn't have lights . . . at some time in the future, it won't *be* a field sometime in the future," Ueberroth told the National Press club a few months later.

Local media responded with appropriate venom toward the blow-dried commissioner, but the Tribune Company now had the excuse that it needed. Dallas Green had always wanted lights installed anyway, and the inexorable march toward artificial illumination began in earnest. The day after Ueberroth's threat, the Cubs filed suit in Cook County Circuit Court to keep the city from enforcing city and state laws banning night ball at Wrigley Field.

GIVE ME LIGHTS, PRECIOUS LIGHTS

In June 1983, according to George Castle, Musco (an Iowa-based stadium lighting company) and ABC wanted to stage a night game at Wrigley Field during the season as part of the network's "Monday Night Baseball" package. The Cubs may not even have been part of the talks, because according to Andy McKenna, the team had no plans at the time—at least for public consumption—to install lights. Dallas Green, of course, felt that playing eighty-one home games in the sun was a disadvantage.

ABC Sports senior vice president Jim Spence was the point man for the project, which was most likely proposed to the network by Musco President Joe Crookham. Eventually the plan foundered on the rocks because the Cubs weren't even scheduled to be at home on June 6, the date planned for the event. Had anyone bothered to check a schedule before going ahead?

STOP THE BUM

Bob Wood's 1986 book *Dodger Dogs to Fenway Franks*, the first to address the now-common activity of touring major league ballparks, had an especially interesting review of Wrigley Field. In his book, Wood talks his way onto a rooftop on Waveland Avenue, past the right-field wall. At this time, building residents and their friends sat on the rooftops, which were not yet the province of private clubs. Wood notes: "[My rooftop seatmate's boyfriend] was the lawyer who during the '84 play-offs had brought suit against the owner of the building. Capitalism flourishes even in Wrigleyville. The owner had barred his tenants from the roof for the Padres games. Instead he planned to rent it out for high-priced parties . . . [The lawyer] went to court and got an injunction to stop the bum. She also, gratefully, explained how through the entire trial the bleacherites across the street would turn around in unison and chant, 'Landlord sucks,' followed by a round of applause."

TELL IT TO THE JUDGE ON SUNDAY

The "No Lights in Wrigley" movement was galvanized by the arrogance and aggression of Major League Baseball. Neighborhood opposition to the Cubs, and to baseball itself, grew sharply. And this wasn't unfair. Part of what made Wrigley Field special was its lack of lights and its old-time feel, reminders of the pre-television days of baseball. And the Lake View neighborhood had a right to make sure its business tenants worked within the letter and spirit of local laws.

But some members of the anti-lights faction wanted simply to make life as difficult for the Tribune Company as possible; some didn't even care if the Cubs were forced to leave Wrigley Field. Most of the anti-lights protesters and activists *weren't* like this, but the loudest and most uncompromising of them tended to tarnish the movement.

There is nothing that should have, prima facie, held the Cubs to a different standard than the White Sox. The South Siders, in fact, had been playing night ball in their residential neighborhood for more than forty years. Chicago judge Richard Curry didn't seem to consider this when, on March 25, 1985, he rejected the Cubs' lawsuit to reverse the ban on night ball at Wrigley. He opined that lights would destroy a residential community to make sports team owners richer in an act "repugnant to common decency."

Did Curry not recall that residents of Armour Square and Bridgeport, near Comiskey Park, were subject to this "repugnant" practice forty to fifty times per season? Clearly a Cubs fan and a traditionalist, Curry used all sorts of baseball imagery in his ruling, but none of it explained why this misery was acceptable to South Side fans but not to North Siders.

The Cubs immediately appealed Curry's decision.

CASHING IN

Several smart locals began buying up property around Wrigley Field in the late 1970s. Two of the most well-known speculators were George "Gus" Loukas, who as of 2002 owned nearly twenty buildings around the park, including popular hangouts the Cubby Bear and the Sports Corner. The other was the late Jim Murphy, a former policeman who bought Ray's Bleachers in 1980.

Once the Cubs started winning and more and more people came to the area, the race was on to rehab old apartments and turn them into condos, to tear down old structures and rebuild, and to open up new bars, stores, and restaurants. Unfortunately, given a chance to make a killing, some people will do anything. A series of "mysterious" fires gutted a bunch of old buildings in the area during the early 1980s, providing insurance money to the owners for rebuilding. "We'd get two or three fires a day," noted fireman Marc Patricelli of Engine Company 78 in an article published in the July 2002 *Cubs Quarterly*.

In the mid-1980s, young people flocked to the area to see rock shows at the Metro (a nightclub formerly known as Stages) as well as at the Cubby Bear, the Wild Hare, and Exedus. Both local and national acts performed at these clubs, and with popular acts in town, parking was scarce.

Sometime during the decade, according to Forty-Fourth Ward alderman Bernie Hansen, local real estate agents began referring to the Wrigley Field area as "Wrigleyville." But Michael Miner in the April 12, 1985, *Reader* claimed that developers coined the term back in the 1970s. Whatever its genesis, the name has stuck.

THE BEST OF SUMMER

Once again, the Cubs, their ballpark, and their fans were media darlings. The peculiar habits of Wrigley's bleacher denizens—tossing back enemy home runs, tossing back beers, and tossing around bets with fellow fans— became a draw in their own right. Bill Veeck, after divesting himself of the White Sox, became a semi-regular presence at Wrigley Field, enjoying his dotage shirtless in the bleachers with a frosty beverage. His words on the bleachers, spoken to *Chicago* magazine in 1984, came to represent what many people still believe about Wrigley Field: "The scent of suntan oil, broiled hot dogs, and spilled beer create a wondrous feeling of euphoria—a feeling that neither crowds, hard benches, long ticket lines, nor the endless trek to distant toilets can diminish. The bleachers aren't just concrete and steel, cheap seats, and concession stands; they're a state of mind, a way of life, the best of summer."

With announcer Harry Caray's move from the South Side to the North in 1982, the Cubs and their fans were the beneficiaries of Caray's bottom-of-the-seventh tradition of singing "Take Me Out to the Ballgame." The boozy, high-spirited sing-along became another special ritual of Wrigley Field. Bob Wood puts it this way: "Harry sings, everybody else joins in. They stand, in the box seats, upper and lower, in the crowded bleachers, on the rooftops across the street, and on Waveland below. All sing from the heart, for they truly don't care 'if they ever get back.' "

DISPLACEMENT

The underside of the influx of money into Lake View was the displacement of locals. By the late 1980s, everyone in the area knew that gentrification was changing things. Grant Pick, in the September 1987 *Chicago Reporter*, wrote: "The seemingly steady foothold that minorities cling to in Lake View appears threatened, however, by the upward mobility sweeping the neighborhood. The last five years have seen more than $350 million in new commercial and residential development in this part of the 44th Ward. The price of real estate is zooming; residents' incomes have doubled. Displacement is occurring."

Some folks no longer able to afford Lake View moved a few blocks north to Uptown, which remains a struggling community. Others went west, or even to the suburbs. Latinos displaced from some urban communities have made large inroads into Schiller Park, Berwyn, Evanston, and even Schaumburg.

Just south of Wrigley Field, New Town plays host to a constant turnover of young, mostly white, post-collegiates looking for an "authentic" city experience. Such youngsters, with skin ready for tanning, money to spend, and copious appetites for alcohol, became instant Wrigley Field converts. Each class of young affluent twentysomethings seems to convert to Cubbie fandom upon hitting the big city for the first time after graduation.

HELL BENT ON COMPROMISE

With the team pushing for lights in the park, and much of the neighborhood against it, war broke out. In June 1985, the Illinois House of Representatives and Senate both voted to prohibit night ball at Wrigley Field. The Cubs immediately started rattling sabers at the people of Lake View, threatening to junk the stadium if need be. Dallas Green and the Tribune Company, not burdened by sentimental feelings for Wrigley tradition, spoke of their frustration in not being able to play some night games at home as every other team was able to do. Vague threats of moving to an acceptable suburban location began emanating from the mouths of Cubs' lawyers, officials, and lobbyists.

To the credit of the mayor's office, the idea of the Cubs moving to the suburbs didn't play well downtown. Harold Washington, Chicago's first African American mayor, said in June 1985 that he would keep Chicago's borders guarded "like Horatio at the bridge" to ensure the team didn't move. Despite a tendency toward excess verbiage, Washington was a very intelligent, common-sense man. He understood that some sort of compromise would have to be worked out, so he, the Tribune, neighborhood groups, and lawmakers set about brokering an agreement between the Cubs and Lake View's anti-lights faction.

The Cubs' long campaign of lobbying state and local politicians led to the team's announcement, in early 1987, that a limit of eighteen night games a season would be acceptable. The house and senate soon voted to exempt postseason games from the anti-lights bill, and by November 1987, Washington endorsed the installation of lights with the eighteen-game limit.

On November 25, 1987, Harold Washington passed away. The city's new mayor, Eugene Sawyer, also endorsed the plan, but without Washington's coalition-building ability and strong hand, the issue became a political super ball that bounced all over the Chicago City Council.

MONEY—IT'S A HIT . . .

What had turned the tide? Money, as always. Baseball found a way to grease the road to installing lights. The Cubs had recently applied to Major League Baseball to host the 1990 All-Star Game, perhaps hoping that the public relations windfall from bringing extra money into the city would push politicians toward agreeing to light up Wrigley Field. Baseball commissioner A. Bartlett Giamatti informed Mayor Sawyer on February 24, 1988, that the Cubs wouldn't get the All-Star Game unless the Chicago City Council approved the lights resolution—and quick.

The next day, two weeks after a *Tribune* editorial blistered "political bums" working against the lights proposal, the city council voted 29–19 on February 25 to endorse the agreement. The council approved the installation of lights at Wrigley Field and, not coincidentally, made it possible for city hotels, restaurants, cabbies, and taverns to receive somewhere around $40 million in revenues for the 1990 All-Star Game and its attendant festivities. On February 26, the Cubs signed an agreement to stay at Wrigley Field through 2002—given the stipulation that the neighborhood was not voted "dry." If the sale of alcohol was banned in Lake View, the Cubs had an escape clause to leave the park.

The night game plan, eventually accepted by all sides, provided that the Cubs could play eight night contests in 1988, then eighteen under the lights each season for a fourteen-year period from 1989 through 2002. This gave the Cubs the opportunity to make more money off their gate and their television broadcasts, and allowed for night postseason games to be played if necessary.

FAMILY SECTION

Bristling at suggestions that they wanted to install lights just to draw older, better-paid customers and sell more beer, the Cubs tossed the locals a bone prior to the 1986 season by converting the three rows of bleacher seats along the catwalks down the left-field and right-field lines to no-alcohol "family" sections. A few years later, citing low attendance in the section, the Cubs reconverted the catwalk bleachers in right field to a "group section." But the no-alcohol family section in left field remains open, albeit at prices higher than any other non-box seats in the park.

FACING ANDRE

Free agent outfielder Andre Dawson, nearly locked out of baseball by owner collusion, signed a ridiculously cheap five-hundred-thousand-dollar contract with the Cubs in spring 1987. The hustling Dawson became an immediate favorite with right-field bleacher fans in Wrigley, and he showed his gratitude by hitting forty-nine home runs to capture National League MVP honors.

Perhaps the most memorable moment of the Cubs' poor 1987 season, however, was scary rather than triumphant. On July 7, Dawson clubbed a homer in the first inning against the Padres' Eric Show; it was his twenty-fourth homer of the year, and his seventh against San Diego. When Dawson batted in the third, Show beaned him in the right side of the face. Dawson, who habitually leaned into the plate, went down, bleeding from a wound that would require a trip to the hospital for twenty-two stitches.

Several seconds later, as many in the crowd of 26,615 murmured angrily, Cubs pitcher Rick Sutcliffe charged out of the dugout to attack Show. Both benches emptied, and a real fight—not the milling-about kind often seen in baseball—broke out while trainers examined Dawson. By the time Dawson came to, the fight had abated. But then, Dawson lurched to his feet and tried to charge Show, who was quickly led off the field by umpire Charlie Williams as the crowd roared.

Following the incident, a seemingly contrite Show, who had problems with some players because of his well-publicized right-wing views, released a statement in which he disclaimed any desire to hit, or even throw at, Dawson (or any other hitter). The Cubs didn't think much of the apology. Padres manager Larry Bowa, a former Cub, simply said, "The Cubs don't know Eric Show too well. Knowing Show, he tried to pitch inside. He did not try to hit the guy."

The Cubs won 7–5.

SHINE A LITTLE LOVE

The process of designing the lighting system and constructing the light towers had started long before the politicians hammered out their compromise. The goal was to build a structure that would work effectively while disturbing the neighborhood as little as possible. On the evening of April 6, 1988, several trucks transported the structural steel of the light towers to the players' parking lot at Wrigley Field. The next morning, a helicopter lifted, to the upper deck roofs, the first in a series of girders that would hold the six lighting structures (three would go on each side of the roof). Cleveland's Osborn Engineering Company built the structural system.

The first three towers were installed (on the third base side) in a project completed April 26. A helicopter crew worked from 8:30 a.m. to 4:00 p.m. for several weeks to lift the pieces. The first-base towers were installed by June 21, and the wiring finished a month later. The lights themselves, which had been stored in a nearby warehouse, were lowered into place—again by helicopter—after each light tower was completed. It took thirty minutes to bolt in the first series of light banks, according to former Cubs publicist Bob Ibach, but by the end of the process, workers were installing the banks in four minutes.

According to the January 1989 edition of *Consulting/Specifying Engineer*, 546 floodlights were used in the six light towers. The lamps, which had an average life of three thousand hours, could last for up to five hundred games. At the time, General Electric, which provided the lighting system, estimated that it would cost $518.40 per night game to keep the grounds illuminated. The magazine went on to note that "minimizing light trespass into the surrounding neighborhood was a prime objective in the design process. The narrow NEMA 2 beam spread of the floodlights allows precise aiming and control of light output. A matte-black metal band around the outer edge of the reflector surface minimizes stray light."

The Cubs added other lighting to the park as well. Eight lights were attached to the top of the scoreboard, in order to illuminate it, and lights were installed all around the park, both in the stands and under them, to make sure that fans could find concession areas, restrooms, and exits. The team also fitted the parking lots and the outside of the stadium with lights. According to the Cubs, the entire project cost $5 million.

TRIAL RUN

The first night game was set for August 8, 1988. A month earl· .r, the wiring for the system had been completed, and a test showed th·· all the lights worked. On July 25, 1988, the Cubs held a charity "Cubs Care" home-run-hitting contest at Wrigley Field, under the lights, in front of three thousand fans. The occasion was meant to raise money for the club's official charity as well as to test the lighting fixtures and troubleshoot them one final time before the lights were turned on "for real." That evening, Mickey & the Memories, a popular 1950s- and 1960s-styled band, played on a stage in right field as fans filed into the park. Some attendees sat in the bleachers, while others crowded the box seats. Billy Williams and Ernie Banks signed autographs, and the two then teamed with Andre Dawson and Ryne Sandberg for a home-run hitting contest.

LIGHTS ON

August 8, 1988, was hot and humid. Ninety-one-year-old Cubs fan Harry Grossman flipped a switch at 6:06 p.m., and the lighting slowly took effect. A throng of 565 reporters was on hand, making this the most widely covered regular-season baseball game in history.

During the bottom of the first inning, Ryne Sandberg stepped into the batter's box only to be greeted by the bouncing breasts of Morganna, the "kissing bandit" who made a habit in the 1970s and 1980s of running onto various athletic fields to plant wet ones on pro athletes. Unfortunately for Morganna, Cubs security led her off the field before she could plaster the beloved Ryno.

Despite the excitement of the evening, the fans would be sent home without a result. During the fourth inning, with the Cubs leading the visiting Phillies 3–1, it began to rain hard. More than a dozen fans jumped out of the stands to slide on the wet tarpaulin; one fan careened so quickly that he crashed into the brick wall behind third base and had to be carted off on a stretcher. Cubs pitchers Greg Maddux and Les Lancaster slid on the tarp as well, but without injury. After two hours of rain, the game was called at 10:15 p.m.

The first *official* night game was played the next evening, August 9, when the Cubs whipped the New York Mets 6–4 in front of 36,399. Acquiescing to some legitimate neighborhood concerns, the Cubs cut off beer sales at 9:20 p.m. and stopped organ playing half an hour later to keep things a bit quieter. "I've never been to a night game before," eighty-six-year-old bleacher regular Carmella Hartigan told United Press International. "But you know, times change and you can't be a stick in the mud."

THE WORLD DID NOT END

And despite lights in Wrigley Field, the world did not crumble. In fact, the eighteen night games a year at the ballpark were real events—special in their scarcity. While the Tribune Company increased the number of night contests for 2004, their desire to squeeze more profits out of the team should be viewed with skepticism. If the team plays more night contests, such games will no longer be special. The Washington compromise was a smart move and did not need to be changed.

LUXURY TAX: PAY SEVENTY-FIVE DOLLARS

Flush with success from the lighting plan, the Cubs went to stage two of their modernization campaign in 1989, spending $14 million to install luxury boxes, build a new press box, establish a permanent upper-deck concession stand, and construct a balcony in the upper deck. The luxury boxes were the top priority. The team installed sixty-seven high-rent seating areas above the lower-deck stands, ranging from foul line to foul line, in what had been the press box. Each luxury suite was, at the time, rentable for between forty-five and sixty-five thousand dollars a season depending on its size and location.

Local corporations such as Beatrice, Baxter Healthcare, and First Chicago Corporation signed up quickly to rent out luxury suites. Along with providing prime seating for the game (windows protected viewers from severe weather), the luxury boxes came with meals, beverages, and a dizzying array of freshly prepared desserts.

The architectural firm of Hellmuth, Obata, and Kassabaum (HOK), which two years later made a big splash by designing Camden Yards in Baltimore, planned the Cubs' renovation. Turner Construction of Chicago did the building. Meanwhile, the press, ejected from their perch above the lower deck, moved upstairs. The Cubs tore out a chunk of high-level upper-deck grandstand seats behind home plate and built a new press box that could hold 130 media members—fifty more than the old one. For those used to the old, cramped press box, the new restrooms, larger dining area, and upgraded facilities were a welcome change.

In essence, the Cubs traded up, losing upper-deck seating but gaining a new section of far more profitable luxury seats. To ameliorate the loss of the upper-deck grandstand seats, the Cubs added around four hundred new seats behind the last row of the previously existing upper-deck boxes—and thus came out ahead.

Another part of the rebuilding involved concessions. First, the Cubs built a permanent concession stand under the new press box; in previous years, upper-deck fans could buy concessions only from carts near the restrooms. In addition, the Cubs constructed a balcony, facing southwest, behind the home-plate section of the upper deck. The balcony offers a great view of the city. Groups have rented the space for pregame parties.

When, in the 1980s, Tribune Company types discussed the Cubs' "need to be competitive," they were talking in code about night games and luxury seating. Having accomplished both of these goals in less than a year, the Cubs quickly turned on the profit faucet.

ZIMMERED

The Cubs bounced up again in 1989. Nobody expected the Don Zimmer–led team to do much of anything, but fine seasons from Sandberg, Andre Dawson, rookie outfielders Jerome Walton and Dwight Smith, first baseman Mark Grace, and a surprising pitching staff sparked the team. The silliness began on Opening Day, April 4. As 33,361 fans shivered at Wrigley Field, the Cubs took a 5–4 lead into the ninth. Newly acquired closer Mitch "Wild Thing" Williams allowed singles to Bob Dernier, Tommy Herr, and Von Hayes, loading the bases. No problem. Williams simply fanned Mike Schmidt, Chris James, and Mark Ryal to send the crowd into an uproar.

LONG WALK TO FOREVER

The new press area, though larger and better equipped, was not without its detractors. Located at the top of the upper deck, the press box had no elevator. This meant that writers, broadcasters, technicians, and radio/TV reporters had to walk up a long series of ramps to get to the box.

The press box pros who often walk from the clubhouse and field to the press box two or three times a day to do their jobs, complained—justifiably—of exhaustion. It's a long walk from field level to the top of the upper deck, even in a park as small as Wrigley Field. On April 8, 1989, just two days after the conclusion of the season-opening series at Wrigley Field, veteran *Trenton Times* writer "Bus" Saidt—who had covered the Phillies during the series—passed away back east. He was sixty-eight. At the time, there was speculation that the long walk had put extra stress on Saidt. The writer's passing was enough to spur the Baseball Writers Association of America into action; sources reported that the BBWAA formally protested the lack of an elevator to then-Cubs President Don Grenesko.

Despite the protest, the Cubs did not build an elevator to the press box, with Grenesko claiming that doing so would damage Wrigley Field's façade. The press would, literally, have to take a hike. Some members of the press, of course, are exempt. By the 1990s, Harry Caray was getting a ride up the ramps in a motorized cart, and at times, Ron Santo, suffering from diabetes-related leg problems, took advantage of the free ride as well.

In 1996, the Cubs finally installed an elevator near the left-field line. Post-game cleaning crews and kitchen suppliers use the elevator to save time, and some members of the working press (especially older ones and those coming from the Cubs clubhouse down the third-base line) take it after the game as well.

SING CHILD

Rookie outfielder Dwight Smith was not only a good player but also a fine singer. He belted out the national anthem on July 21, becoming the first Cub player to perform "The Star-Spangled Banner" since infielder Carmen Fanzone took the field with his trumpet on June 18, 1972.

COMEBACK KIDS

Injuries to key players and some inconsistent play dropped the Cubs as low as fourth by mid-May, and the team didn't claim first place for good until early August. This writer's wedding was held August 5, 1989, the day the Cubs moved into a tie for first with a 4–2 win at Pittsburgh. The August 29 game indicated that it really might be the Cubs' year. Houston, always a Cub nemesis, came into Wrigley Field and blew Mike Bielecki and Dean Wilkins off the hill with two runs in the second, two more in the fourth, and five in the fifth. Trailing 9–0, the Cubs looked done.

In the sixth, the Cubs scored a pair and then tallied three more in the seventh on a two-run homer by Lloyd McClendon and a pinch single by Dwight Smith. Houston trooped out Brian Meyer, Danny Darwin, and Juan Agosto, but none could stop the Cubs. In the eighth, down 9–5, the Cubs rallied to tie on RBI singles by Sandberg, McClendon, and Grace, and a sacrifice fly by Smith.

With the crowd going bonkers, and fans all over the city tuning in to watch the improbable comeback, the Chicago bullpen held the Astros in check over the last five innings. In the last of the tenth, Walton walked, McClendon singled him to third, and Smith drove in his third run in four innings by lashing a single to right. The 10–9 win, the Cubs' first comeback from being nine runs down since 1930, was probably the team's most dramatic victory since the 1984 "Sandberg Game." The Cubs began to pull away and ended the season with a six-game advantage over the New York Mets.

GARDENING AT NIGHT

With the 1989 division title came the first postseason night games at Wrigley Field. The Cubs and San Francisco Giants would square off in a best-of-seven National League Championship Series. On Wednesday, October 4, a sellout crowd of 39,195 filled the venerable park at Clark and Addison for Game One. Unfortunately, Will Clark had four hits, including two homers (one a grand slam), and six RBI as the Giants stormed Greg Maddux and the Cubs 11–3.

The next day, the Cubs blew former teammate Rick Reuschel out of the box by scoring six runs in the first inning en route to a 9–5 win. Again, fans jammed Wrigley Field to its capacity. Unfortunately for the Cubs, the Giants took the next three contests at Candlestick Park and captured the National League pennant in just five games.

A PROMOTIONAL FEE HAS BEEN PAID BY

The Cubs, during the Wrigley era, had only one consistent promotion: Ladies Day. While other teams had bat day, cap day, or other such giveaways, the Cubs held fast to a non-promotion stance. The Cubs did hire a full-time director of promotions, Marea Mannion, in 1977, but only nine "special days" were held that year, and the giveaway concept was shelved. Once the Tribune Company bought the team, however, everything changed. For the first time, the Cubs built a marketing department, realizing that with the team in the dumps, other measures were necessary to bring in the fans and their dollars. In 1982, veteran baseball front-office man Jeff Odenwald was hired. He soon became director of marketing.

In 1984, the Cubs began an aggressive campaign of "special dates," giving fans such items as calendars, batting helmets, sports bags, tote bags, caps, toiletry kits, ponchos, floppy hats, big sunglasses, mesh shirts, thermoses, sun visors, backpacks, baseball cards, and scarves. Of courses, all the items were decorated with the logos of whatever company paid to have the items manufactured. Since that time, the Cubs have festooned fans with giveaway items ranging from the traditional pennants, autographed balls, baseball cards, t-shirts, and plastic cups to newer-style novelties like magnetic schedules, collectable dolls, growth charts, sports water bottles, and lapel pins. In addition, Cub fans have been allowed on Wrigley Field's surface once a year for camera day, and kids participate in on-field pregame baseball clinics.

Some early 1980s promotions, such as father–son (or daughter) games and Farmer's Day, didn't catch on, but Ted Giannoulas, the San Diego Chicken, made several well-received appearances at Wrigley in the 1980s. While Giannoulas was not the first team mascot, his wacky antics made overstuffed animals *de rigueur* at most parks—although Wrigley Field, thank goodness, has never sported one.

Current kitschy promotions, such as "70s Night," have become very popular (the sight of broadcaster Steve Stone in a slightly era-challenged navy blue "Austin Powers" costume and full wig was alone worth the admission), featuring musicians such as Sister Sledge and K.C. and the Sunshine Band. In addition, major companies like Rawlings, American Girl, Topps, and Mattel eagerly line up to present their imprinted tchotchkes to Cubs fans. In marketing terms, the Cubs have held their own with the extremely competent White Sox organization.

Sometimes, the organization's giveaways work too well. The phenomenon of collectable dolls, for instance, has proved troubling. When the team gives away Beanie Babies®, Precious Moments®, or Cherished Teddies® dolls decorated with Cub themes, many of the "fans" who wait to be among the first five thousand or ten thousand to get the collectables simply leave the park once they've presented their tickets and secured their dolls. Is this really a fan demographic that the Cubs want to court?

TICKETS, TAKE OUT A LOAN FOR YOUR TICKETS

By this time, it had been years since bleacher seats cost a dollar. Between 1970 to 1990, Wrigley's ticket prices rose astronomically. In 1970, all box seats were $3.50 each. Grandstand ducats were $1.75 for adults and $1.00 for kids, while all bleachers were also a buck. On the morning of every home game in 1970, 22,432 unreserved seats went on sale.

By 1973, prices had gone up a quarter on all seats but the bleachers, which were still a dollar. But in 1976, all box seats went to $4.50. A new category of seats, reserved grandstand (the first dozen or so rows of the seats behind the boxes) were $3.50, and regular grandstands were $2.50 for adults and half that for kids. Bleachers went up to $1.25 as well.

Between 1977 and 1980, box seat tickets increased in price every year, at a rate of 50 cents each. Spending $6.50 per box and $5.00 per reserved grandstand seat didn't seem like much of a bargain for such a lousy ball club; even the bleachers had risen in price to $2.00 by 1980. By that time, only seventeen thousand seats were sold on the day of the game.

The floodgates really opened when the Tribune Company bought the club. In 1983, bleachers cost three dollars, and the team created new categories for box seats and made the best ones much more expensive. "Club boxes" and "field boxes" were now eight dollars a shot. Only general admission and bleacher seats (around thirteen thousand tickets overall) were available for sale on the day of the game. It had become far more profitable to count on season ticket sales of all possible seats than to leave them open for walk-ups.

By 1987, the movement toward reserving everything in advance became official—there was no more "general admission" seating at Wrigley. *All* chairs were reserved, even the four-dollar bleachers and the seats in the farthest corners of the lower deck. Those corner seats, like all other lower grandstand reserved tickets, cost $6.00; the cheapest place in the park was the upper deck, where the under-fourteens could sit for $3.50. For the first time, a ticket price cleared ten bucks in 1987; boxes were $10.50.

In less than twenty years, the club's entire ticketing policy had been overturned. Wrigley's vision of seats available for anyone wanting to walk up had been replaced by ticketing procedures made possible by computing systems. The most expensive tickets in the park had risen in price more than three times; the bleachers were now four times their 1970 price.

The Cubs rolled out new ticket prices for 1990, apparently believing that their Eastern Division title justified the cost. Of course, the new luxury boxes were creating enough money to help pay their own construction cost, but why not have some of the other fans shoulder the burden as well? Field boxes rose in cost to thirteen dollars, then to fifteen dollars the following year, while bleachers went to six dollars by 1991. Almost imperceptibly, lower-middle-class fans had been priced right out of the park. Even though the Cubs didn't spend much money on free agents, their ticket prices continued to go through the roof.

In addition, by the mid-1990s, the Cubs apparently had enough customers for their full-season ticket packages that they discontinued the weekend/night package, good for around forty to forty-five games a year, that had allowed middle-class fans the chance for season tickets as well.

FOR THOSE WHO THINK YOUNG

The usual gentrification and squeezing out of lower-income residents continued as the 1980s turned into the 1990s, and new generations of young people came into Wrigleyville never knowing about the area's history. All they knew was that this was a fun neighborhood to hang around. And Wrigleyville *is* fun, especially if you're young; the neighborhood is built for youth. Population totals between 1980 and 2000 stabilized around ninety-five thousand, with a few more residences built each year. It is a far younger area, on average, than it has ever been—as late as 1970, 15 percent of Lake View residents were over sixty-five; now, it's around half of that, while nearly 70 percent of the neighborhood's population is currently between twenty and forty-four. In 1980, more than half of the population was in the twenty–to–forty-four bracket for the first time since 1930.

MUCH-NEEDED REPAIRS

With the All-Star Game coming to Wrigley in 1990, baseball impressed upon the Cubs the need to upgrade the visitors' clubhouses, which had not been significantly improved since the 1930s. This project was completed prior to the 1990 season at a cost of $6 million. Bruce Levine wrote in the *Sun-Times* that the new quarters included "state of the art clothing stalls and carpeting. Moreover, mirrored pillars give the appearance of more room." It was still a small clubhouse, though.

The long walkway from the dugout, upstairs over the concourse, remained, but the Cubs in the 1980s installed canvas around both sides of the walkway to protect visiting players from the barbs of Cubs fans. The move was also undertaken to keep fans from climbing up the wall to access the visiting clubhouse; some equipment had disappeared from the visitors' quarters.

At the same time, the Cubs re-roofed Wrigley Field and installed new gutters at a cost of eight hundred thousand dollars. The organization also installed a new phone system, built new washrooms in the left- and right-field corners, opened a new restaurant, "The Sheffield Grill," under the right-field lower deck, and remodeled the Stadium Club, where the club held promotions and press conferences.

ALL STARS, NO PEOPLE

The 1990 All-Star Game was held at Wrigley Field on Tuesday, July 10. Most fans had no chance to get tickets. Of the 38,710 seats in Wrigley Field, fewer than 8,000 were made available to the general public. Around 18,000 went to Cubs season-ticket holders (who weren't even guaranteed their regular-season seats), and another 12,000 were allotted for purchase by Major League Baseball, which had club officials, sponsors, and celebrities to stroke.

Of course, if you were Michael Jordan, you could call the Cubs a week before the game and secure a couple of tickets. Joel Bierig, in the July 10, 1990, *Sun-Times*, noted that plenty of celebs were taken care of. Recently elected Mayor Richard Daley received fifty tickets; Governor Jim Thompson was on hand, and football coach Mike Ditka got seats too. Former broadcaster Jack Brickhouse and wife Pat had tickets, as did DePaul University basketball coach Joey Meyer.

Eventually, 39,071 fans jammed the park to see the game. Following a long rain delay, the American League won 2–0 on a two-run double by Texas' Julio Franco. Countless others sat on rooftops.

DAWSON'S FREAK

Many players can't stand umpire "Country" Joe West, finding him combative, arrogant, arbitrary, and often wrong in his calls. Andre Dawson, who didn't often take on umpires, had heard just about enough of West the night of July 23, 1991. With the Cubs already out of the pennant race, Dawson's frustration boiled over when he was called out on strikes in the seventh inning. Dawson questioned the call longer than most umpires like, and West simply waved the star outfielder away.

This enraged Dawson, who overreacted by bumping West, then tossing his bat. West ejected him. West quickly thumbed Cubs manager Jim Essian as well. Dawson, shoved into the dugout by teammate George Bell and umpire Eric Gregg, began to toss bats out from the bat rack onto the field.

The crowd of 34,458 went nuts. West began counting the bats, noting the amount that Dawson would be fined, and the outfielder angrily decided to throw out more and more bats until fifteen of them sat near the third base coaching box. In support of Dawson, bleacher fans began tossing items onto the field: full and empty beer cups, scorecards, hats, and anything else at hand. The Dawson–West match, and the fan display, delayed the game for around fifteen minutes.

In the bottom of the eighth, frustrated Reds reliever Rob Dibble allowed two runs to stretch the Cub lead to 7–4. When Doug Dascenzo bunted against him, Dibble—in West's opinion—threw the ball directly at Dascenzo, running toward first. Dibble, ejected for intentionally attempting to injure another player, claimed innocence. Both players were suspended. Dawson, perhaps judged to have been egged on by West, was bounced for only one game.

THE WALK OF FAME

The Cubs lack an official Hall of Fame, but they did open a "Walk of Fame" in 1992. Each honoree had his name etched in a stone placed into the sidewalk near Wrigley's Clark and Addison entrance. The inaugural class included Ernie Banks, Fergie Jenkins, Ron Santo, and Billy Williams. Eventually, the Walk of Fame (whose members were elected by fans) also included players Cap Anson, Glenn Beckert, Bill Buckner, Phil Cavaretta, Andre Dawson, Stan Hack, Gabby Hartnett, Rogers Hornsby, Don Kessinger, Andy Pafko, Rick Reuschel, Ryne Sandberg, Hank Sauer, Sammy Sosa, Rick Sutcliffe, and Hack Wilson, broadcasters Lou Boudreau, Jack Brickhouse, and Harry Caray, public address announcer Pat Pieper, and even longtime clubhouse man Yosh Kawano.

After ten years, however, the Walk had not really captured the fans' imagination, and the stones were beginning to deteriorate. Therefore the Cubs took out the stones and instead commissioned a series of twenty-five banners to be hung under the Wrigley Field grandstands in the concourse. The banners went on display for the first time on April 5, 2002.

POSTER DAY

Cubs late-inning reliever Randy Myers came into the game in the ninth inning on Saturday, August 14, 1993, with a 2–0 lead. It was "Randy Myers Poster Day" at Wrigley Field, with twenty thousand of the brawny lefty's likeness in the satisfied hands of Cubs fans. Myers, though, didn't have it. As 39,645 fans watched, Robby Thompson doubled to lead off the frame. After Barry Bonds walked, Willie McGee moved the runners up. Todd Benzinger then singled in the tying runs.

Slowly, then in a huge torrent, Randy Myers posters began to rain down from the bleachers, the upper deck, and even the box seats. It reminded observers of a Mark Grace poster day a few years before, when the popular first baseman saw tens of thousands of likenesses heaved back at him after he hit into a game-ending double play.

THERE'S A MEETIN' HERE TONIGHT

The 1994 season was miserable for the Cubs, who lost their first twelve home games. After a particularly painful defeat on April 29, manager Tom Trebelhorn decided to try some public relations strategy. Trebelhorn had promised to hold a "town meeting" for fans in front of the firehouse near the left-field corner, and he kept his vow. After talking to the press, showering, and changing, Trebelhorn emerged from the ballpark and walked up to a bench outside the firehouse and tried to answer questions from the throng of perhaps two hundred fans.

The angry crowd, which included a fair number of inebriated souls, simply yelled at first, but Trebelhorn eventually gained control. "OK, what do you want to know?" he shouted to the throng. Trebelhorn was unusually frank with the fans about his hitters, one of whom, he said, was a "dumb****" for not moving a man over. He was cheered by the fans at the end of the thirty-minute meeting and went inside the firehouse for broiled chicken.

Few associated with the team, however, were happy with Trebelhorn's meeting. Players don't much like being aired out in public by their manager, and Trebelhorn lost the respect of the team and the confidence of the front office. The Cubs hired Jim Riggleman to manage in 1995. Asked if he'd be holding any town meetings, an annoyed Riggleman just shook his head from side to side.

RANDY INDEED

Randy Myers didn't care if you threw his poster around. Just don't get in his face. On September 28, 1995, with the Cubs fighting a losing battle for a wild-card play-off spot, Myers allowed a two-run pinch homer to Houston's James Mouton in the eighth inning. The homer gave the Astros a 9–7 lead. As the ball sailed over the left-field wall, James Murray, a twenty-seven-year-old bond trader, leapt over the brick fence down the first-base line and rushed toward the mound. With the smallest crowd of the season (14,075) on hand, security had been thinned out for the game.

Myers saw Murray coming. A survivalist, hunter, and a student of martial arts, Myers dropped Murray with a hard forearm, then pinned him to the ground until security officers took the intruder to the Town Hall police station.

WHEELS

In 1994, four wheelchair-bound Cubs fans filed suit in federal court against the Cubs, claiming that they had inadequate access to their seats in Wrigley Field. The suit was settled January 3, 1996. To bring Wrigley Field into compliance with the Americans with Disabilities Act, the Cubs agreed to double the reserved seating for the disabled from forty-four to eighty-eight. The club also installed an elevator from the entrance level to the terrace and built more wheelchair-accessible restrooms and concession stands. In addition, the Cubs reimbursed the Legal Clinic for the Disabled's costs from the suit.

BUSH LEAGUE

In 1997, the Cubs made a dramatic improvement in the park's beauty. They replaced the tarp covering the center-field bleachers with juniper bushes. While the original Astroturf covering of the closed-off section was appropriate in the 1960s and 1970s, newer times called for a change. The addition of plants was clearly in harmony with P. K. Wrigley's attempts to plant Chinese elms near the scoreboard. With the new bushes, the park had yet another beautiful layer of green.

Reports that another kind of green—marijuana—had surreptitiously been planted in the juniper section remained nothing but smoke.

GOODBYE HARRY

Legendary broadcaster Harry Caray died on February 18, 1998. His age was given as eighty-four. Caray's passing led to mourning in Chicago and all over the baseball world. He had been with the Cubs since 1982 and before that had spent thirty-seven years broadcasting the Cardinals, Athletics, and White Sox. A native of St. Louis, he gained his greatest national fame with the Cubs, describing the action on WGN as cable television made the Cubs available all over the nation and even into Central America.

What was especially strange was that Chip Caray, Harry's grandson (son of Skip, excellent broadcaster of the Atlanta Braves), was slated to join the Cubs' broadcast team in 1998 and call games with his granddad. Harry Caray is memorialized at Wrigley by a statue outside the right-field corner.

CELEBRITIES AT THE GATE

Everything at Wrigley Field changed when Harry Caray died. With the beloved broadcaster gone, the homespun tradition of him leading the communal "Take Me Out to the Ballgame" sing-along after the top of the seventh inning was gone as well. But the bigger-than-life broadcaster's passing left a Harry-sized gap that the franchise's marketing forces decided to fill. Starting in 1998, the seventh inning break featured "guest conductors" leading the crowd in singing. These guests are usually gleaned from the rolls of whatever celebrity happens to be in town plugging a book, a TV show on WGN's WB network, or a new CD.

As a result, such renowned baseball figures as N'Sync, Cuba Gooding Jr., Jane Seymour, and Mel Gibson—and these aren't even the most embarrassing ones—have taken turns in the television booth trying to remember the words to "Take Me Out to the Ballgame," a song some of them had never heard. This cynical "new tradition" puts up a wall between the fan and the game. Harry Caray, at least, could claim to talk like a fan, think like a fan, and sing like a fan. Singing with him was a pleasant, locally generated tradition (from his 1970s days in the White Sox booth) that had real meaning. On the other hand, the new "celebrity conductors" are generally not locals and often know *nothing* about baseball—a fact often made embarrassingly clear during their television interviews during the bottom of the seventh.

To make things worse, the Cubs have adopted the dangerous idea of allowing celebrities from other, lesser sports to claim airtime on their broadcasts by serving as "guest conductors." What in the world can Dick Vitale, Kordell Stewart, Digger Phelps, or Denis Savard (to name just a few) add to a baseball game? What is gained by reminding Cubs fans that their team has competition for the entertainment dollar? It simply looks desperate to prop up some athlete from another sport, as if it legitimizes baseball by having the buffoonish Mike Ditka stop by Wrigley Field on his way home from the golf course.

Asking any old celebrity (Dan Patrick? Jesse Ventura? *George Will?*) to visit the booth is the kind of decision that marketing people may love but one that indicates a disregard for the audience and for baseball itself. And it cheapens what once was a nice part of the Wrigley experience.

Just let it go.

GOODBYE JACK

Jack Brickhouse, the Cubs telecaster from 1947 through 1981 (and also the White Sox' from 1947 through 1967), passed away in Chicago on August 6, 1998, at age eighty-three. While he lacked the high national profile that Harry Caray enjoyed during the 1980s, Brickhouse was *the* voice for a generation of Cubs fans. He called himself a "gee-whiz" broadcaster, and Brickhouse's genial, avuncular manner provided the soundtrack to many a Chicago area summer. His memorable "Hey, Hey!" home run call, a trademark, is now preserved in red-painted letters on Wrigley Field's yellow foul poles.

BALL HAWKS INDEED

When Sammy Sosa and Mark McGwire spent the 1998 season threatening Roger Maris's single-season home run record of sixty-one, it brought the Wrigley Field ball hawks—and the greed inherent in souvenir collecting— into the spotlight. For many years, groups of men have gathered outside of Wrigley Field on Waveland and Sheffield Avenues to await home-run balls flying from the park, both during batting practice and games. Names like Dave Davison, Moe Mullins, and Rich Buhrke are legendary among the Cubs' ball hawk contingent; these grown men have spent decades going after baseballs.

On September 13, 1998, Sosa hit his sixty-second homer in the ninth inning of the Cubs' eventual 11–10, ten-inning victory over the visiting Brewers. The sixty-second tater tied McGwire for the league lead. The Cardinals' slugger eventually won the title with seventy.

A huge crowd roved around on Waveland Avenue, past the left-field wall, during the game. Mothers with babies in strollers stood around while would-be souvenir hunters jockeyed for position. When Sosa hit his homer, hell broke loose. Strollers were shoved aside, kids elbowed, and bystanders knocked down as the more aggressive collectors, ball hawks, and glory hounds piled up to get the ball. Moe Mullins claimed he had the ball but that it was pried from his hands. Many locals supported Mullins's claim.

The fateful home run ball wound up in the mitts of Brendan Cunningham, a suburban mortgage broker who was not a regular at the park. Cunningham, clutching his prize, took off down Kenmore Avenue, being followed by members of the press, other fans, and angry allies of Mullins, and he finally needed a police escort to get back home. Cunningham immediately announced plans to sell the ball. Mullins, injured in the pileup, sued Cunningham. The whole ugly business dragged on until both parties agreed to simply give the ball to Sosa.

THE FLOWERS OF PROGRESS

One problem facing Lake View (and the Cubs) is that many new residents are resentful of the fallout from Wrigley Field's presence. Property values are higher than they've ever been in the area, and this increase in value comes largely because of the ballpark and its inherent attractiveness. But the noise, traffic, and overly emphasized problem of drunken fans urinating in yards make a lot of locals angry.

Clearly, this is a real problem for the Cubs. Anything that goes on in the ballpark or its immediate surroundings is indeed their responsibility; the team must shoulder a big chunk of the blame for postgame shenanigans from fans who have been overserved. Not all of the problems in the neighborhood, however, come from baseball patrons—not even *most* of them. Every Friday and Saturday night, fun seekers travel from around the city and the surrounding suburbs to Wrigleyville, most of them not to see a game but to eat, drink, dance, listen to music, shop, or just hang around.

Nobody is suggesting that Murphy's, Cubby Bear, Cabaret Metro, Exedus II, Gingerman, Yak-zies, or any other popular local establishments that serve alcohol be forced to close down their nighttime business because the occasional patron loses his dinner on someone's lawn. To be frank, people who move into Wrigleyville and complain about crowds and noise are like people who move near airports and whine about all those planes. Their anger would be more palatable if they hadn't chosen to live there, and it would be easier to work up sympathy if the aggrieved citizens' property values weren't still soaring through the roof.

There is, to be sure, an anti-Cubs faction in Lake View, largely due to lingering anger over the issue of lights. Many community leaders who fought the installation of lights in the 1980s still feel betrayed by the Tribune Company. And this resentment, which is not totally illegitimate, has played itself out in some increasingly strange ways.

TEAR THE ROOF OFF

As far back as Wrigley Field has existed, fans have gathered on rooftops (illegally, in earlier years) to watch Cubs games—usually on lawn chairs with a sandwich and a beer. In the 1990s, it became big business. Some very innovative building owners began to charge increasingly large sums for fans to sit on the roofs of condos and apartments on Waveland and Sheffield. These entrepreneurs actually built tiered stands, with stadium seating and bleachers, on the rooftops, then installed barbecue grills, obtained liquor licenses, and set up shop. Prices for a seat can run into the three figures.

The Cubs did not like this, feeling that their product was being stolen. While the Cubs have certainly benefited from the neighborhood feel of the park for many, many years, and it's arguable that the neighborhood deserves some ancillary profit, the team does have a right to protect its financial interest in every possible legal way. After negotiating with the building owners, attempting to collect a rights fee from them, and threatening lawsuits, the Cubs in 2002 took what they felt was a provocative but necessary step: they put windscreens over the back fences in the bleachers.

Perhaps it was an overreach. Nobody liked the green vinyl windscreens, which were an eyesore to those inside and outside of the ballpark. Of course, the rooftop owners fumed. Some of them, ridiculously, claimed that their rights—their rights, apparently, to *steal a product and resell it*—were infringed on by the Cubs' decision. But the city, believe it or not, listened to the rooftop owners.

Why would they do this? Politics as usual. The Tribune Company and autocratic mayor Richard J. Daley have had a long-running feud, resulting in Daley's continuing rejection of any expansion plans to Wrigley Field that the Cubs dream up. Taking the side of the rooftop owners, despite the ridiculousness of their claims, was just one more piece of Daley's anti-Tribune strategy.

LANDMARK

A new hot potato is the attempt by some neighborhood activists, aided and abetted by the city, to have Wrigley Field declared a national landmark. Granting landmark status would mean that the Cubs would have to go through an appeal process—which would, as likely not, be denied anyway—in order to alter most aspects of the ballpark.

This process has put both the Cubs and their opponents in some strange contortions to explain their views on the park's value. The Cubs, on one hand, have been forced to run down their own facility in public—while continuing to market Wrigley Field's enduring beauty—in order to make the case that renovations are needed. On the other side, neighborhood opponents to park changes are in the weird position of claiming that the park is just perfect as it is, while at the same time arguing that Wrigley is a nuisance to the area and that the Cubs aren't good neighbors.

In 2001–02, the Cubs kept busy fighting efforts to make Wrigley a historic landmark. Cubs executive vice president of business operations Mark McGuire said in a Fran Spellman *Sun-Times* article, "Upon close scrutiny, there are areas of Wrigley Field that are neither historic nor very special." McGuire and the Cubs want to alter certain areas of the ballpark, but the city noted that they didn't want the Cubs to change the ivy, the scoreboard, the marquee outside the main entrance at Clark and Addison, or the shape of the park. The city doesn't seem to care about washrooms or concession stands. Since the Cubs have no interest in altering the ivy, the scoreboard, or the marquee, the real question is what will happen to unspecified areas such as the bleachers, the areas underneath the stands, the grandstand seating, and the outside walls.

STRIP MALL

It was determined in 2001, after much legal wrangling, that the city actually owns the strip of land just west of the left-field corner on which the player parking lot currently stands. The fact that the city owns this land, and not the Cubs, makes it difficult for the franchise to consider building on it. In 1982, the Cubs paid $150,000 to the Chicago, Milwaukee, St. Paul, and Pacific Railroad, which was going bankrupt, for the piece of ground. But in August 2001, the city announced that it did not ever belong to the railroad and therefore should not have been sold. It was, in fact, a part of Seminary Street. Worse yet for the Cubs, the city asked the Cubs to pay back rent on it. The Cubs have already been paying property taxes.

YOU CAN'T DO THAT

On June 18, 2001, the team announced plans for three significant alterations to Wrigley Field:

◆ To convert the parking lot/car wash between Clark Street and Wrigley into a multilevel complex with team offices, stores, and parking.
◆ To build a new stadium club and restaurant below the box seats and install new high-priced seating at field level near home plate.
◆ To build new bleachers above and out from the current seats.

Some were opposed to all three plans, but the real stink arose over the Tribune Company's desire to install extra bleachers. The proposal involved propping up the new bleachers over the sidewalks on Waveland and

Sheffield with poles. The new construction would create twenty-six hundred new bleacher seats, which would have—not so coincidentally—blocked the view of many pricey rooftop seats across the street. Initial resistance to the plan focused on the construction of the poles to hold up the new bleachers. Some opponents said that the new seats would create places for homeless people to stay; others said that more bleacher fans meant more urination in their front yards; others simply felt that the new seats would be ugly. Still others simply didn't want the Cubs to get their way about *anything*.

Alderman Bernie Hansen was an initial supporter of the plan. He said the Cubs' ideas rated an "A −," telling the Associated Press, "The calls I've been getting have been very much in favor of it. There will always be the naysayers . . . but they really don't speak for the majority of the community." Soon, however, Hansen began hearing noise from locals. Some folks, including owners of the rooftop buildings, circulated petitions invoking the Urine Card and accusing the Cubs of wishing to destroy the neighborhood, an argument that makes *no* sense. Meanwhile, the club put together its own hand-picked "citizen's group" to attempt to counteract the publicity from the vocal and well-connected rooftop owners. Hansen and the mayor's office were simply obstructionist.

In early 2002, the Cubs sheared off five hundred seats from the original bleacher expansion plan, vowed to plant ivy on the outside of the new walls and on the poles and set up a neighborhood watch program. That still wasn't enough, and the battle raged on. And it was all quite ridiculous. While Soldier Field, a national landmark, was torn apart—over the objections of many Chicagoans—in order to accommodate the Chicago Bears' desire to increase their revenues through new luxury seating, and the White Sox bullied the city and state into building them a new park in 1990, the Cubs can't even get city approval to make changes to their *own park* with their *own money*.

Unfortunately, there is no black-and-white solution; there are no good guys in this crowd. Who should an objective observer pull for: The baseball club run by an exalted, union-busting corporation used to getting its own way? Neighborhood loudmouths fueled by delusions of grandeur and their own naked greed? Or a city government more interested in goring an ox than serving the public interest?

SOME FANS

Not all the commotion was off the field. During the 1980s and 1990s, a hand-ful of veteran fans, including "Bleacher Preacher" Jerry Pritikin, Ronnie "Woo Woo" Wickers, The Duchess, and Carmella Hartigan, among others, carved out their places in Cubs lore. But Carmella and Ronnie are special.

Ms. Hartigan, who died at age one hundred on December 21, 2002, was a favorite of many. Born the same day as Charles Lindbergh, February 4, 1902, she threw out a ceremonial first pitch in 1998 and collected her reward—a kiss from Sammy Sosa. She was always being interviewed, talked to, and given babies to hold and kiss. She fell in front of the Waveland Avenue firehouse in 2001 and broke her hip. Taken to the hospital in the fire department ambulance, she underwent hip replacement surgery. From that point, she wasn't often in her seat, although her place in the back row of the bleachers was as good as reserved; Ms. Hartigan was at the park nearly every day when healthy.

Ronnie Wickers, on the other hand, you don't have to look for. An African American man in his forties or early fifties, he wanders around Wrigley Field in a Cubs uniform, constantly yelling "Cubs! Woo! Cubs! Woo!" until nobody around him can stand it. He's always in the park—usually someone buys him a ticket—and there is no shortage of people who will buy him a beer. Like him or loathe him, Ronnie is as much a part of Wrigley Field as anyone.

HIGHER AND HIGHER

Baseball's "new economics"—in other words, paying players what they're worth—meant that ticket prices had to rise. But at Wrigley, they've gone to unconscionable levels in the last few seasons. In 1994, the Cubs had a policy whereby tickets for weekday games in April, May, and September would cost less than those for contests during the warmer summer months. Club and field boxes were nineteen dollars for the summer games, fifteen dollars in the spring and fall. Bleachers, now up to ten dollars in the summer, were "just" six dollars during the earlier and later months.

During 1994, major league baseball owners—in an attempt to curb salaries—provoked a strike that crippled the sport and forced the cancellation of the World Series. When the 1995 season opened after a delay, the Cubs kept ticket prices right where they were. In a welcome show of good faith intended to help bring fans back to the park, the Cubs held ticket prices at pre-strike levels through 1996 as well. Possibly as a result, attendance at Wrigley Field came back to pre-strike levels more quickly than in many other ballparks despite the club's on-field ineptitude.

But in 1997, with the team coming off a 76–86 season, ticket prices exploded with a vengeance. Prime tickets were now twenty-one dollars for the best boxes, fourteen dollars for lower deck reserved, and twelve dollars for bleachers. Budget tickets were fifteen, eight, and six dollars, respectively, and there were only seventeen budget-price games that year.

Sammy Sosa enjoyed a great season in 1998, and the Cubs made the play-offs. For 1999, management jacked up ticket prices again. Club and field boxes now cost twenty-five dollars each for prime games, and terrace reserved seats were sixteen dollars. Bleacher seats now cost fifteen dollars, and family section tickets were twenty bucks apiece. Even standing room seats were eight dollars for the sixty-three prime games.

After slumping in 1999, the Cubs couldn't justify raising prices for 2000, but they did the following season. For 2001, club boxes leapt to thirty dollars, the field boxes twenty-eight dollars, and the bleachers an amazing twenty bucks for prime games, with prices for those seats approximately half that for the seventeen bargain games, now called "value dates." The cheapest seats were now in the upper-deck grandstand, costing ten dollars for adults and six dollars for kids, and less on value dates.

In 2002, the Cubs raised prices again after an 88–74 finish. Infield club boxes were now thirty-six dollars each during prime games. No box seat in the park costs less than twenty-six dollars. Bleachers went up to twenty-four dollars for prime games and twelve dollars for value dates, and for the first time, there were no special discounts for kids—breaking a tradition the Cubs started back in the 1930s.

The parade of insanity continued in 2003 as the Cubs now split their games into three plans—prime (nineteen games), regular (fifty-four games), and value (eight games). This way, they could retain their former "prime" game costs for *regular* games while lifting prices even higher for selected contests. And there were fewer "value" games than in years past. The *cheapest* box seats in the park—upper-deck boxes—now cost a whopping thirty-two dollars on prime dates, while bleachers were a spectacular thirty dollars on prime dates, jacked up to twelve dollars even on so-called "value" dates. The only tickets available at Wrigley Field, at *any* time, for under ten dollars were upper-deck grandstand (six bucks) and senior citizen tickets (five bucks) on the eight value days.

Exactly how high can ticket prices go? Now that a terrace reserved seat, at twenty dollars, costs approximately three times the hourly minimum wage, it's clear that the Cubs are counting on a high-income fan base to stick with them through the years.

WAR AND REMEMBRANCE

The Cubs–Cardinals rivalry is one of the best in baseball, spanning decades and inspiring fans of both clubs to travel with their team to the enemy city. The friendly war has spawned hundreds of great stories, loads of good times on both sides, and at least one book. Saturday, June 22, 2002, however, was memorable for another reason. Cardinals pitcher Darryl Kile didn't show up at Wrigley Field that day. None of his teammates had seen him, and calls to his cell phone went unanswered. Finally, hoping that they'd find nothing, law enforcement officials and hotel workers forced open the door to his room at the Westin Hotel and saw Kile's body. He had died from an undiagnosed heart problem.

News of the passing quickly filtered back to Wrigley Field. His teammates, stunned and saddened, met among themselves. The Cubs were informed. Commissioner Bud Selig gave the clubs the okay not to play. Just after 2:20, the time of the first pitch, Cubs catcher Joe Girardi—one of the most respected men in baseball—informed the fans that there would be no game. As his Cubs teammates stood behind him, Girardi walked up to a hastily connected microphone and said, "We regret to inform you that because of a tragedy in the Cardinals family, the commissioner has canceled the game today. Thank you.

"Be respectful. You will find out eventually what has happened. I ask you to please say a prayer for the St. Louis Cardinals family," Girardi concluded, choking back a sob.

The fans, few of whom knew the story, were shocked. Some booed. A few applauded. Most, however, simply filed out of the park. Word quickly spread through the stands, and many fans left Wrigley in tears. The following evening, the Cubs and Cardinals played an ESPN game. Distracted and saddened, the Cardinals lost 8–3 in front of 37,647. There were no between-innings commercials and no music played besides an unaccompanied version of "Take Me Out to the Ballgame."

The left-field foul pole flag, sporting Ernie Banks's number fourteen, was taken down, replaced instead by a Cubs flag at half-mast. Down the right-field line, Billy Williams's number twenty-six flag was supplanted by a Cardinals flag. The National League team flags surrounding Old Glory on the center-field scoreboard were absent.

On the small electronic board in center field, Kile's number fifty-seven was shown all game long and remained bright even after the game was over and the stadium's lighting system turned off.

SABOTAGE?

During a Cubs home stand in June 2002, a section of the ivy on the right-center-field wall began to wilt and die, eventually turning an ugly shade of brown. Early speculation had a White Sox fan pouring some sort of bleach on the ivy to kill it—the Sox had just been in town for an interleague series—but no hard evidence could link anyone to the death of the ivy. By the middle of the 2003 season, the patch had returned to its beautiful dark green.

SNOW DAY 2003

After their 2003 home opener was canceled due to snow on April 7, the Cubs hosted the Expos the next day in thirty-two-degree temperatures. The announced crowd of 29,138 was perhaps half that. Prior to the game, Ted Butterman's Cubs quintet, fixtures at Wrigley Field for many years, played Dixieland jazz. Steve Stone, returning to the WGN television booth following a two-year absence, emceed the pregame ceremonies. With the outfield soggy and snow resting in the outfield basket and in the still-bare ivy branches, seventy-two-year-old Ernie Banks, eternally youthful in spirit if not in body, hobbled to the mound along with Sammy Sosa to throw out simultaneous ceremonial first pitches. Wayne Messmer sang the Canadian and American national anthems, with some misguided yobbos booing "O Canada" (in response to some north-of-the-borderites doing the same to "The Star-Spangled Banner" at a recent hockey game). The Cubs won 6–1.

The Cubs made an interesting change to the bleachers in 2003. The very top of the center-field seating section, under the scoreboard, was turned into a standing-room area. Seats from the last rows were removed to give fans some room to walk or look out the back fence toward the northeast. Probably the most important part of the top of the bleacher section, however, was the newly installed beer stand.

In addition, the Cubs installed two large electronic message boards into the left- and right-field upper decks. These boards give out-of-town scores (for those fans apparently unable to remember to look for them on the center-field scoreboard), show animated pictures of the American flag during "The Star-Spangled Banner," and run ads for a popular retail outlet between innings.

Inappropriate and unnecessary? Sure. Profitable? Of course.

BROKER THAN BROKEN

What the Cubs really needed, going into 2003, was a shot of solid, positive publicity. The hiring of manager Dusty Baker gave the organization a shot in the arm. Unfortunately, greed and sloppiness took it away. In a bruising story published April 10, 2003, Greg Couch of the *Sun-Times* (the *Tribune*'s chief rival) made clear what many had believed for several months: the Cubs had been running their own brokering operation. Wrigley Field Premium, a short distance from the ballpark, sells tickets provided by the Cubs—never made available to the public—at highly inflated prices. Through extraordinarily sloppy administration, the Cubs laid a trail back to their own front door. While the Cubs claim that Premium is a separate business, the company's president was found to be . . . Cubs executive vice president of business Mark McGuire.

With Premium selling some tickets for a July 2003 Cubs–Yankees series for as much as fifteen-hundred dollars apiece, some bright spark in the organization should have realized that the press would jump on the story. The Cubs' defense is that brokers buy up tickets and resell them at outrageous rates all the time, so the club should be able to do it, too. That argument *seems* logical, but just because some creeps insert themselves as unnecessary middlemen in the process doesn't make it right, and the Cubs—as purveyors of the product—should hold themselves to a higher standard. Everyone knows that ticket brokers are a pox. Isn't it better that the club itself isn't?

RUN DUSTY RUN

The hiring of Dusty Baker as Cubs manager for 2003 injected some optimism into the Cubs' fan base, and the team, built around an impressive starting rotation including Kerry Wood and rookies Mark Prior and Carlos Zambrano, carried high expectations. Chicago moved into first place on April 15 and remained on top until late June.

From that point, the Cubs sank, staggering into the All-Star break on a 6–13 skein, and by July 26 were in third, $5^1/2$ games behind Houston and St. Louis. A July 22 deal with Pittsburgh, however, had brought over outfielder Kenny Lofton and third baseman Aramis Ramirez, and the newcomers began hitting. A string of ten wins in fourteen games brought the Cubs into first again on August 15, and, despite a short slump, the Cubs reached September within striking distance of the top.

HOUSE OF CARDS

The St. Louis Cardinals, tied with Houston for the NL Central lead and $2^1/2$ games up on the Cubs, entered Wrigley Field for a five-game series starting on Labor Day, September 1. Following a seemingly interminable four-hour, seventeen-minute rain delay, Mark Prior shut down the Cardinals 7–0 as the Cubs blew out Woody Williams with six runs in the fifth.

The next day, the Cubs played a day/night doubleheader, winning the fifteen-inning first game 4–2, in four hours and forty-seven minutes, on a Sammy Sosa home run. The Cards won the nightcap 2–0, keeping Chicago in third, $1^1/2$ games out. (The second game turned on a Moises Alou line drive with runners on base that umpire Justin Klemm ruled foul; with the crowd of 39,290 in an uproar, Alou and Cubs reliever Antonio Alfonseca were ejected for arguing.)

With the season hanging in the balance on September 3, the Cubs fell behind the Cardinals 6–0. But as the fans roared, Chicago struck back for three in the sixth, then three more in the seventh after the Cards had gotten a run back. Down 7–6 in the eighth, the Cubs tied it on Mark Grudzielanek's triple and went ahead for good on Alou's RBI single. The 8–7 win knocked the Cards from first, bringing the Cubs within one game of Houston's division lead.

On September 4, the five-game set closed with the Cubs again coming back from 2–0 and 5–3 deficits to win 7–6, pulling to just a half-game behind the Astros. From that high point, the Cubs swept a series at Milwaukee, then after losing two of three to the Expos in Puerto Rico, came back home and took five of six from the Reds and Mets. By September 17, the second-place Cubs were 82–70, still a half-game behind Houston.

A four-game series at Pittsburgh brought Chicago into a tie with Houston, and after taking two of three at Cincinnati, the Cubs returned home on September 26 still knotted. That day the first game of the Cubs' season-ending series with the Pirates was rained out, but Houston's shocking 12–5 loss to visiting Milwaukee put the idle Chicagoans ahead by a half-game.

DOUBLE WHAMMY

With the Astros now in second, the Cubs controlled their own destiny. On a murky Saturday, September 27, 2003, 40,121 frenzied fans jammed Wrigley Field for a makeup doubleheader. Mark Prior, who in just a few months had become perhaps the NL's marquee pitcher, defeated the Pirates 4–2 with Joe Borowski gaining his thirty-third save. Meanwhile, in Houston, the Astros were again losing to Milwaukee.

Game two saw the Cubs jump out immediately to a 1–0 lead in the first on Sosa's fortieth homer. In the last of the second, Chicago routed Ryan Vogelsong from the mound, scoring five times to put the game away early. As the crowd grew ever more celebratory, the Astros succumbed 5–2 to the Brewers, giving the Cubs a clinch for a tie. An hour or so later, when the Cubs took the title outright with their 7–2 win, the shy sun suddenly came out and illuminated the fans and the celebrating Cubs in brilliant late September light.

The celebration went long into the night in Wrigleyville; the team had clinched its first division title since 1989. Fans poured from the park and into the streets, joining the many thousands who had been in local bars or just milling around the intersection of Clark and Addison. Television crews gathered to film the spectacle as the police were forced to shut down automobile traffic for blocks around. It was quite a party.

The following afternoon, on the season's last day, the Cubs in a pregame ceremony retired Ron Santo's uniform number 10, running a flag up the left-field pole to make it official. Santo, who would undergo a cancer operation in October as well as a procedure to amputate a second leg later over the winter, said that if he ever was elected to the Hall of Fame, the honor couldn't possibly mean as much as this.

CURSES! FOILED AGAIN!

After defeating the Atlanta Braves in a dramatic five-game division series, the Cubs then took on the surprising Florida Marlins in the NLCS. Chicago had home-field advantage but dropped Game One 9–8 in eleven innings after blowing a 4–0 first-inning lead. From that point, the Cubs blew through the Marlins, winning Game Two 12–3 behind Prior and traveling to Florida and taking Games Three and Four by 5–4 and 8–3 margins.

Chicago could have won it in Florida, but the Marlins stayed alive with Josh Beckett's 4–0 shutout. But Cubs fans weren't worried—they had Prior and Wood on tap for the final two tilts at Wrigley. For Game Six, on October 14, the Cubs stuffed 39,577 into Wrigley Field. (One fan was Ronnie "Woo Woo" Wickers—how did he get in?) Scoring once in the first, sixth, and seventh, Chicago had a 3–0 lead. With one out in the eighth and Juan Pierre on second, disaster struck. Luis Castillo lofted a fly ball to left field that veered toward the wall. Wrigley Field's unique design, which allows for very little foul territory down the foul lines, worked against the club in this instance; Moises Alou ran toward the wall, leapt for the ball, but couldn't get it; several fans had instinctively reached for the ball. Alou angrily argued fan interference, but the umpires didn't buy it.

And the roof fell in. Castillo walked, and Juan Pierre went to third on the rattled Prior's wild ball four. Pudge Rodriguez singled in a run to make it 3–1. The Cubs bullpen began heating up and restless fans worried. Alex Cabrera then momentarily calmed the fans by hitting a chopper to short. But Alex Gonzalez muffed the ball, loading the bases, and Derrek Lee's double to left on the first pitch off a tiring Prior tied the game.

Reliever Kyle Farnsworth didn't help. Two intentional walks and a sac fly later, the Marlins were up 4–3, then Mike Mordecai ripped a three-run double to left-center. By the time the twelve-batter inning had ended, the Cubs were down 8–3—and that's how the game ended.

Anger centered on a fan, Steve Bartman, who had reached for the foul ball. By the ninth inning, Bartman was forced to vacate his seat because of threats to his safety. Over the next few days, the *Sun-Times* irresponsibly published his name, place of employment, phone number, and even his address, which furthered the frenzy of blame.

The Cubs themselves issued the following statement: "Games are decided by what happens on the playing field—not in the stands. It is inaccurate and unfair to suggest that an individual fan is responsible for the events that transpired in Game 6."

The following night, almost as an anticlimax, the Cubs blew another lead and lost to the Marlins 9–6, ending their season. Feeling cursed indeed, Chicago players and fans went home for the winter licking their freshly salted wounds.

COURT OF PRIVATE OPINION

With the players off the front pages, the Cubs had a busy off-field schedule. First came some legal business. In November 2002, a local group (including several rival ticket brokers) filed a class-action suit to force the Cubs to stop reselling tickets through their Premium Tickets agency. The suit, which sought refunds for all customers who bought tickets through Premium from April 2002 through mid-May 2003, claimed that the team was engaging in fraudulent business practice by filtering tickets to a shell corporation, then selling them at higher prices.

The trial ended in August 2003, but it wasn't until November 24 that Judge Sophia Hall ruled in favor of the Cubs, finding that nothing in Illinois law prevented the Cubs from the practice of selling tickets at higher prices through the subsidiary corporation. In the judge's words, the plaintiffs needed to, but did not, "prove that the business relationship between them violates any law or violates custom or practice." Hall recommended that since the current laws concerning such relationships between parent and subsidiary businesses are obsolete, that state legislature consider making such transactions illegal. As of spring 2004, however, the issue appears to have died on the ivy vine.

What hasn't fallen off the radar screen are the extra Cub profits. And using a shell corporation to filter tickets to the public is a nifty way to get around baseball's revenue-sharing program. Now that it's unnecessary for the Tribune Company to pretend that Premium Tickets, Inc. is a separate entity, its offices can sit proudly in the same building where the Cubs' concessionaires meet before each game.

SAVE US FROM THE BALL AND CHAIN

It was obvious that the Cubs couldn't make changes to the ballpark until the city council had weighed in on the landmark status issue. On January 27, 2004, as expected, a city council committee granted Wrigley Field limited landmark status. The areas deemed unchangeable by the city include the park's four outside walls, the roof, the marquee sign at Clark and Addison, the large center-field scoreboard, the grandstands, the brick wall and ivy surrounding the playing field, and the bleachers. The ruling would seem to have scotched the team's hoped-for bleacher expansion, but it does allow for a chance to build some sort of restaurant either behind home plate (at ground level) or in the center-field bleachers. Alderman Tom Tunney of the 44th Ward said that the designation did not either prohibit or allow bleacher expansion, but rather that any such expansion would be taken up by the city council.

Hand in hand with the landmark issue was the question of whether the Cubs could add night games for 2004 and beyond. After the Cubs and the mayor's office dickered around with plans for several months, the two sides announced on March 6 that Wrigley Field, until 2004 bound to eighteen night games, would begin a plan to phase in additional evening contests. Twelve additional night games—making for a yearly total of thirty—will gradually be added to the schedule by 2006 or 2007.

Key to getting the deal done was the insistence by the city that the Cubs contribute to a fund set up to address neighborhood concerns concerning sanitation, parking, and traffic congestion. One piece of the deal included money set aside to fund a study of a possible Addison Street off-ramp for Lake Shore Drive. Only after the deal was completed did it become known that the Cubs would be contributing only slightly more than eighty-three thousand dollars a year toward the fund. From this came some grumbling that Alderman Tunney and the mayor had been a bit too generous, giving the team what it wanted while getting little in return.

For 2004, the Cubs added four night games to the schedule.

YOU ARE MY FRIEND

Next on the team's docket were the owners of rooftop clubs. Having failed at negotiations, threats, and legal action, the Cubs decided to take a page from Mayor Daley's book and—as Hizzoner has done of late with increasing success—convert their enemies into friends. "Keep your friends close and your enemies closer," the saying goes.

On March 20, the Cubs announced that they had reached an agreement with twelve rooftop clubs (whose owners had formed the Wrigleyville Rooftop Owners Association) to share revenues for 2004 and, presumably, the near future. The treaty provided for twelve rooftop businesses to remain in operation with the Cubs' blessing, agreeing to pay 17 percent of their gross revenues to the team. In return, the Cubs dropped all attempts to interfere with the rooftops' operations. Unknown is how the Cubs and the rooftop organizations will work together, but the former enemies now cozily share a bed. In the words of Andy MacPhail, "We're pleased to have added a new partner. We've always stated that a negotiated settlement is preferable to litigation."

One rooftop business, however, Skybox—which sits on a three-story building down the left-field line—held out, with attorney Chris Gair stating that the company would "never pay anything" to the Cubs. Other rooftop business owners, such as George Loukas, who had already agreed to pony up, were incensed at the possibility that Skybox could successfully hold out.

As the season began, the Cubs hired engineers to devise ways to block the building's view of the field. Alderman Tunney criticized the Cubs for this, and the two sides seemed headed for another court battle. On April 8, however, U.S. District Judge James Holderman called the Cubs and Skybox into his chambers and brokered a closed-door agreement that brought the errant rooftoppers into the fold.

This agreement certainly benefits the Cubs, who now receive significant additional dollars. The rooftop owners can now operate their businesses with complete freedom, and fans who want to sit on an apartment building roof to watch a baseball game can continue to do so. The Cubs' proposed bleacher expansion plan, created as much to block out the rooftop owners as to generate revenue, is probably off the table due to this newfound "partnership."

Between the Premium Ticket setup and the rooftop deals, the Cubs have created new revenue streams, generating increased operating capital by eliminating or converting former rivals. What they've also done is to convey, in brutally naked terms, that baseball at Wrigley Field is now almost exclusively for the moneyed class.

TIX TOX

The wave of 2003 excitement led to another sold-out Cubs Convention during January 2004, and tickets for the year's home schedule went fast. By Opening Day, almost every seat had already been sold for the season. Of course, many of those seats were never made available to the public in the first place, having been "sold" by the Cubs to their own ticket brokerage, then resold to them at a higher rate.

Ticket prices ballooned by 17.5 percent, the third-highest increase in the game for the 2004 campaign. Bleacher seats (which are no longer reserved) topped out at an amazing thirty-five dollars for "prime" dates, during which all boxes reached thirty-six dollars. Senior citizens were now allowed half-price terrace reserved tickets for all Wednesday games, but all children above the age of two were required to have a ticket.

The 2004 *Team Marketing Report*'s "Fan Cost Index" numbers rate the Cubs with the second-highest ticket prices in the game, just behind the Boston Red Sox, playing in ancient Fenway Park.

Back in the 1970s and 1980s days of new construction of fifty-thousand-seat stadia, one could have argued that the scarcity of seats at Wrigley excused such high prices. But now, five parks in the majors—Comiskey Park, Fenway, Joe Robbie Stadium, PNC Park, and Kauffman Stadium—have capacities either smaller than Wrigley or around one thousand fans larger, with several others boasting capacities just over forty thousand. The trend toward building smaller parks makes the scarcity factor a less valid justification for Wrigley Field's skyrocketing prices, leaving the far more basic calculation of supply and demand.

To cram in even more customers for 2004, the Cubs decided to cut down their already bite-sized foul territory behind home plate and install four new rows of seats. This required tearing down the brick wall behind the plate, in place since the late 1930s, and building out into foul territory. As required by landmark status guidelines, the construction company used the old bricks in rebuilding the wall, preserving an important piece of the park's history. The 213 new behind-the-plate chairs were sold in a preseason lottery, with some seats held back for visiting celebrities and friends of the Tribune Company.

The park's changes weren't limited to new seats, though. Building on the "success" of the upper-deck message boards installed in 2003, the team replaced the traditional auxiliary scoreboards on the left- and right-field-line upper-deck facings with computerized boards. These new digital readouts do not list the game's current line scores (runs, hits, and errors), showing only the score and the count (in new, smaller type) while displaying rotating advertisements at all times.

In addition, the center-field message board was extended the full length of the scoreboard, allowing for the same advertising shown on the auxiliary boards. With these changes, Wrigley Field has abandoned some of its previous claims to tradition and beauty.

THREE TRUE OUTCOMES

The history of Wrigley Field and the history of Lake View are tied to one another. Both have prospered from a unique, symbiotic relationship. Their common interests are peace, prosperity, and mutual respect.

It's important to the neighborhood, to the city, and to Major League Baseball to balance these interests and try to keep everyone as happy as possible. History suggests that in this current crisis, there are three possible outcomes.

◆ *The neighborhood wins*. What if the more radical Lake View activists succeed, and the Cubs don't get their parking lot, office building, or bleacher restaurant? Would the Cubs move?

While it's unlikely they would pack their bags, the Cubs do have little room to add more seats if not allowed to build their sub-level stadium club, and if they are given an excuse to claim they can't compete, they may use it. Of course, even if the Cubs do get their expansions, nothing guarantees they won't claim poverty in the future anyway, but it's far more likely that they'll move if they are pushed.

Should the Cubs move to the west or northwest, the effect on Lake View—which has become a tourist spot due to Wrigley Field—would be devastating. Jobs would disappear, neighborhood income would be lost, and businesses would be forced to close. For many residents, the quality of life in Lake View would suffer.

Sure, life without the Cubs would be quieter. Without all those people around, nobody would have to worry about businesses making any money.

◆ *The Cubs win*. What would happen if the Cubs get their way, either through the courts or through increased lobbying, and simply crush community concerns?

Even with a very attractive lighting system atop the park, only eighteen night games, and increased security around the park and in the neighborhood, a lot of local residents resented the way in which the Cubs brought night baseball to Wrigley in the 1980s. And that was before the increased night games scheduled for 2004.

Not all of the wounds have healed. Another case of Lake View residents feeling screwed would increasingly poison Wrigley Field in its own neighborhood. The feeling lingers among many residents that the new alderman, Tom Tunney, "gave away the store" to the Cubs in recent night game negotiations.

If things get more fractious, is it inconceivable that a few activists would picket, protest the games, or even commit acts of violence against the park? Some folks living near Wrigley might simply choose out of frustration to leave the neighborhood, and a glut of new residences could easily depress property values. Enough people already feel that Lake View is full of the rootless rich, happy to flip their city properties and leave at the first provocation.

There is also a valid question of how the neighborhood will handle more customers. Admitting forty thousand fans to the park is one thing, but inviting more of them to sit on rooftops increases foot and auto traffic and necessitates increased crowd control, police, and city services. Are the Cubs prepared to share these expenses and the increased responsibility?

◆ *Compromise.* If all sides can meet without rancor and air their concerns with a city government interested in fixing problems rather than playing politics, something could be worked out. Of course, if either side refuses to give an inch, no good can ensue. The Cubs have already compromised their initial ballpark expansion plans, but surely they built wiggle room into their original proposals.

It's also important that at least *some* negotiation take place in public, rather than behind closed doors. There is indeed a need to cool down the tone of the debate, but doing all the negotiating in private makes citizens feel that they're not part of the proceedings. After all, while Andy MacPhail works in Wrigleyville, he doesn't live there; neither does Mayor Daley. The residents of the neighborhood—not just the moneyed rooftop owners or the loudest yellers—deserve to be heard. The Cubs, in turn, deserve to be treated with the respect accorded any other neighborhood business that employs hundreds of people.

No party with any authority to husband Wrigley Field's future is objective enough to do so by itself. That being said, here are a few suggestions from a hardly dispassionate observer. These suggestions are intended only to help visualize peaceful solutions to any tensions that rise.

◆ *Roll back night games.* Eighteen night contests a year is quite enough, thank you. The residents of the neighborhood do have rights, one of which is to have some peace and quiet. There is nothing in the Bible, Gideon's or baseball's, that says the game has to be played at night.

The cries and claims of baseball people that day games force them to lose money are hooey. Just because you can make *more* money televising games at night doesn't mean that you are *losing* money by televising them in the daytime. Why should the world rotate only to help advertisers, television executives, and other suits make as much money as they want? WGN-TV and Fox Sports Net collect plenty of money telecasting Cubs games during the day. If they didn't, the games wouldn't be on. It's that simple.

◆ *Give the Cubs their restaurant and office building—and have the team pay the going rate for it.* The team wants to build a dining facility either behind the plate or in the center-field juniper bushes section. That doesn't seem like a terrible invasion of space. In addition, the Cubs want new offices, shops, and employee parking on the lot between the Park and Clark Street, just south of Waveland.

More power to them if they want that, and the city should make sure the Cubs pay just as the Bears and White Sox did—that is, very little. The Cubs have been treated unfairly at times, especially since the Bears, Sox, and even the Bulls and Black Hawks' stadium plans were treated with kid gloves by city and state government. City Hall has done little to speed this debate.

◆ *Build a tripartite committee to address legitimate concerns.* The Cubs, the city, and the neighborhood should each have a representative on the board, with one arbitrator available to make sure the committee adheres to sound decision making. To his lasting credit, Mayor Daley has proposed using arbitration for all further Cubs–city business.

◆ *Everybody calm down.* The Cubs don't seem to know how to do much but complain. Impartial observers might note that the Cubs are the luckiest purveyors of a bad baseball franchise ever. They're lucky Charlie Weeghman built his park, lucky he bought the Cubs and transferred them to his park, lucky fans fill the park, and lucky the neighborhood has been good to work in.

Meanwhile, despite the prosperity the Cubs have brought to Lake View, neighborhood activists want to paint themselves as victims of hordes of drunken suburbanites urinating on their collective lawn. Sure, plenty of fans are boorish morons. Plenty of *Americans* are boorish morons, including some residents of Lake View. Once the citizens of Wrigleyville decide to turn back 120 years of tradition and shut down their bars, restaurants, and clubs, then the claim that Wrigley Field and its patrons threaten the neighborhood's peace and quiet can be taken seriously.

Finally, Mayor Richard Daley should not have let this go on. Nobody really should have to suffer because of his petty dispute with the Tribune Company.

◆ *Be aware.* Cubs fans—those who have filled Wrigley for years, paying ridiculous parking prices, ticket prices, and beer prices, buying scalped tickets for even more money, attending Cubs conventions, and watching games on TV and listening to them on radio—have the power to influence club policy. They're where the buck stops.

AND IN THE END

When all is said and done, Wrigley Field remains an oasis of purity, its supporters say, in the increasingly polluted world of sports. In fact, Wrigley's essence—the ivy, clean lines, scoreboard, grass field, bullpen mounds, hitting background in center field, intimate seating, neighborhood high-rises, gorgeous blue lake looming east of the park, and local trains rumbling by—

might as well have escaped from a fairy tale, for the way it captures a childhood vision of a day at the ballpark.

But the reality is quite different. Wrigley Field is, in economic terms, a thoroughly modern ballpark, trading on nostalgia while making plenty of room for current business practices. Wrigley Field may not have advertising all over the outfield walls, but there is no shortage of commercial signage at the park. In addition, the Cubs do as much—if not more—concession business than larger, newer parks. There is no column for the added value of fairy tales in the Tribune Company's spreadsheets.

The team has shifted from serving a truly democratic customer base to serving a high-income, largely white clientele, with only a few refunded tickets and high-end boxes available for general admission on the day of the game. This strategy is a conscious repudiation of a ticketing philosophy the Cubs had held for more than sixty years. Were William and P. K. Wrigley, who owned the team from 1920 through 1977, still alive, they'd probably be aghast to see their philosophies, which helped build a fanatical customer base, discarded like gum wrappers.

It is also no longer heaven to play at Wrigley Field, especially if you're on the opposing team. A 2003 *Sports Illustrated* poll of more than five hundred major league players named Wrigley Field the game's worst playing surface and Wrigley Field's visitors clubhouse the second worst in the majors.

So, given that there are plenty of reasons to be cynical, why are even the most hard-bitten baseball bugs in love with Wrigley Field? Why do sober adults dissolve into childlike paroxysms of ecstasy when entering the park? Why do we feel that such a place stands for the past?

One reason that fans aren't generally outraged by changes to Wrigley Field is that the park has been open longer than any of them have been alive. Most of the important changes to Wrigley, the ones that made the park look like it does today, don't threaten fans' emotional ownership of the park because they occurred more than sixty years ago. There may not be anyone alive who remembers when the park had only one deck in the early and middle 1920s. Few, if any, fans can recall what the park looked like before the ivy was planted. Most fans don't even remember the place before the luxury boxes or television monitors were installed. It's already been more than fifteen years since lights were lifted onto the upper-deck roof.

Gradual, rather than radical, change has been the rule for the park, which was constructed in 1914. The left-side and right-side upper decks were added, separately, in 1927 and 1928. The ivy and the large center-field scoreboard followed in 1937. Seats were added, removed, reconfigured, moved, and curved in toward the field over the years, then replaced with plastic chairs, and eventually fitted with cup holders bearing advertising slogans.

The basket was added to the outfield wall in 1970. The left- and right-field catwalks were converted for seating in the 1980s. A press box was added to the upper deck in 1989, with luxury boxes constructed in the old press box space. The process of latching the light towers to the park was completed in 1988.

All these changes outline the fact that Wrigley Field is really old. But in a tribute to its beauty, only when Wrigley Field is empty do you notice its age. The field, still beautiful, looks very large compared to the stands surrounding it. Most modern stadia are so large and broad that they dwarf their fields. When you look out at the flat, green-painted planks that make up the bleachers, noting their uneven, sloping pattern, you see the very lack of uniformity that helps make Wrigley Field special.

And it is not a prefabricated uneven design, like those at Minute Maid Park or the Ballpark in Arlington or Comerica Park. Wrigley Field is asymmetrical *by necessity*. Somehow, Wrigley's design is, and feels, much more real and sincere than the artificially irregular fields of the current "retro" parks.

The seats at Wrigley Field also reflect the park's age. Over the years, the Cubs have replaced rows and sections of seats at various times, slowly substituting newer, contoured plastic chairs in a forest green for the earlier metal seats. There are still some seats down the foul lines in a brighter, somewhat sicklier shade of green. Individual seats are often replaced with ones just a bit off in color, giving a feel as charming as it is ragtag.

During the 1980s, the Cubs found new ways to install more seats, putting in extra rows behind what had been the back of both the lower-deck boxes and the lower-deck grandstands. In a few sections of the boxes, extra seats have even been added in the aisles. This retrofitting gets more people in the park, albeit in a rather inoffensive way that subtracts little from Wrigley's aesthetics.

The concrete under the seats is blotchy and dirty, a victim of years of spilled beer and crushed peanut shells. Sections of the concrete are occasionally repainted or even relaid, and the joins always show. The backs of some seats are scratched. The concrete ramps show their ages. The ugly concrete facings on the outside of the stadium betray no hint of the beauty inside.

While the park is old, however, and looks it, that is part of its charm. Nobody comes to Wrigley Field for uniformity or predictability. But back in P. K. Wrigley's day, he *was* selling uniformity, a sporting version of Wrigley's Gum: a happy, clean day at the ballpark, with an expectation of good service, clean sightlines, and tasty concessions. The park was, at that time, much nicer than any other—it was new, clean, attractively laid out, freshly painted, and well constructed. But now, so few places are anything like Wrigley Field that a very *lack* of uniformity is its top drawing card. And every time the Cubs try to make the place hipper, more 2000s, they risk losing bigger and bigger chunks of what they have.

This is not to say that repairs can't be made, or that the park should be static. Indeed, much of Wrigley Field's current beauty is a result of changes made in the 1930s, 1950s, and even 1980s. The park has consistently been altered. But someone who understands the history of the park and has *a personal stake* in the long term, rather than where the next dollar is coming from, must manage those changes. You don't leave history to a marketer.

Andy MacPhail, the Cubs' current CEO, said when he was hired in 1994 that he didn't come on board to be party to the destruction of Wrigley Field. There's no reason not to believe him; baseball is in MacPhail's blood. Just like Bill Veeck and P. K. Wrigley, MacPhail is from a great baseball lineage. He loves and knows the game, and taking over the Cubs was a once-in-a-lifetime opportunity.

But it is critical to realize that management's explanations for altering the park, raising prices, and such are not necessarily to be taken at face value. The club's definition of "improvement" is arguable. While there always will be tension between the baseball people running the Cubs and the corporate types at the Tribune Company, most everyone involved in Cubs ownership knows what they have in Wrigley Field: an attraction greater than the baseball played inside of it. And if the Cubs establish the dynasty that their young talent would augur, there is plenty more money to be made at Wrigley Field in the coming years. Taking the high road—learning from history, remembering to take care of the fans and the neighborhood, and truly protecting the product sold within its walls—will ensure that Wrigley remains the palace of baseball.

It's only by looking closely at the park and its history that one can see the nature of the changes at Wrigley Field and how those changes have served to build an image of constancy and steadfastness against the encroachment of modernity. It's taken a lot of money and a lot of time to make Wrigley look so unpretentious—or, to paraphrase Dolly Parton, "I had to get mighty rich to sound this poor."

And rich the Cubs' owners and players have become from Wrigley Field. Bleacher seats—literally slats without seat backs—have ballooned in price from two dollars to more than thirty dollars in just two decades as the gap between rich and poor in America has widened considerably. Corporate luxury boxes, constructed directly in the sight lines of seats in the rear of the lower grandstand, block the view of fly balls. Season ticket plans have been gradually rewritten to be affordable only to the wealthiest of patrons. Endless in-stadium promotions having little, if anything, to do with baseball serve the club's bottom line but distract fans from the game.

And the Cubs' financial aspirations have rubbed off on the neighborhood. The advent of cable television has made Wrigley Field a destination spot for visitors from all over the world. Ticket resale agencies—including the one owned by the Cubs themselves—have sprung up around the neighborhood. In addition, dozens of young and middle-aged men wander the streets hustling tickets—some real, some fake—for each day's game at highly inflated prices.

The rooftops of surrounding apartment buildings, used long ago by residents to catch some sun while watching the game from a distant perch, have now become private clubs where the rich few pay high prices to sit in specially constructed bleachers. The proprietors of these clubs have garnered enough favor with local politicians that they became players in negotiations concerning expansions to Wrigley Field itself—and are now business partners with the club.

Some neighborhood residents and community groups, whose property values have risen because of the development and the housing scarcity resulting from Wrigley Field's popularity, complain about their gift horse, looking for concessions from the Cubs rather than thanking their lucky stars that they live in such a desirable area.

Lake View once was working class, a neighborhood of small houses, three-flats, and factories, a few bars, and a big ballpark that people came to when they had free time. When the Cubs were good, the fans came; when they weren't, the fans didn't come nearly so often. At times, the area was seedy.

But even when the club wasn't good, the park was at least clean, safe, and family-oriented, so generations of Cubs fans were raised on the idea of fun at the ballpark rather than on the expectation of watching a winning team. It was an inexpensive place to spend an afternoon and watch baseball, and the combination of sunshine, baseball, green grass, and fun was unmatched, even at Comiskey on the South Side.

But now Wrigley Field is an industry unto itself. It is no longer inexpensive. Baseball is often the last thing on the mind of many of the park's patrons. In fact, the Cubs seem to thrill in making baseball a momentary distraction.

The Cubs' increasingly wealthy fan base has made the Tribune Company barrels of money. With all that capital, though, the Cubs have been unable to put together a consistently winning club. And yet the fans still come to revel in Wrigley's atmosphere. It's a living wonderland for baseball fans, one so grand—surely greater than the team it houses—that it has become shrouded in myth and legend.

Most of Wrigley Field's patrons seem to like feeling that they've stepped into baseball's past. The truth, however, is that if the sport is to again recapture the imagination of America, the particular charm of Wrigley Field will have to be baseball's future. It is uncertain, however, whether the Cubs, the city of Chicago, and the residents of Lake View can hold together the fragile magic of Wrigley Field long enough to save the game.

Bibliography

BOOKS

Angle, Paul. *The Memoir of a Modest Man*. Chicago: Rand McNally, 1975.

Asinof, Eliot. *Eight Men Out*. New York: Holt, Reinhart, and Winston, 1963.

Banks, Ernie, with Jim Enright. *Mr. Cub*. Chicago: Follett, 1971.

Benson, Michael. *Ballparks of North America*. Jefferson, NC: McFarland & Company, 1989.

Brown, Warren. *The Chicago Cubs*. New York: G.P. Putnam's Sons, 1946.

Browne, Lois. *The Girls of Summer*. Toronto: HarperPerennial, 1993.

Castle, George. *The Million-to-One Team*. South Bend, IN: Diamond Communications, 2000.

Chieger, Bob. *The Cubbies*. New York: Atheneum, 1987.

Claerbaut, David. *Durocher's Cubs: The Greatest Team that Didn't Win*. Dallas: Taylor Publishing, 2000.

Clark, Steven Bedell. *The Lakeview Saga 1837–1985*. Chicago: Lake View Trust and Savings Bank, 1985.

Duis, Perry. *Challenging Chicago*. Urbana, IL: University of Illinois Press, 1998.

Enright, Jim. *Chicago Cubs*. New York: Collier Books, 1974.

Gershman, Michael. *Diamonds*. Boston: Houghton Mifflin, 1993.

Gifford, Barry. *The Neighborhood of Baseball*. San Francisco: Donald S. Ellis, 1981.

Gold, Eddie, and Art Ahrens. *Day by Day in Chicago Cubs History*. West Point, NY: Leisure Press, 1982.

Golenbock, Peter. *Wrigleyville*. New York: St. Martin's Press, 1996.

Green, Steven, and Mark Jacob. *Wrigley Field*. Chicago: Contemporary Books, 2003.

Hageman, Bill. *Baseball between the Wars*. Chicago: Contemporary Books, 2001.

Hartel, William. *A Day at the Park*. Rock Island, IL: Quality Sports Publications, 1994.

Holtzman, Jerome. *The Jerome Holtzman Baseball Reader*. Chicago: Triumph Books, 2003.

Ibach, Bob, and Ned Colletti. *Cub Fan Mania*. New York: Leisure Press, 1983.

Jenkins, Fergie, with George Vass. *Like Nobody Else*. Chicago: H. Regnery, 1973.

Johnson, Lloyd, and Miles Wolff. *The Encyclopedia of Minor League Baseball*. Durham, NC: Baseball America, Inc., 1997.

Kruse, Karen. *A Chicago Firehouse: Stories of Wrigleyville's Engine 78*. Chicago: Arcadia, 2001.

Langford, Jim. *The Game Is Never Over*. South Bend, IN: Icarus Press, 1980.

Longstreet, Steven. *Chicago, 1860–1919*. New York: McKay, 1973.

Lowry, Philip. *Green Cathedrals*. Reading, MA: Addison-Wesley Publishing, 1992.

Mayer, Harold, and Richard Wade. *Chicago: Growth of a Metropolis*. Chicago: University of Chicago Press, 1969.

Okkonen, Marc. *The Federal League 1914–15*. Garrett Park, MD: Society for American Baseball Research, 1989.

Pacyga, Dominic, and Ellen Skerrett. *Chicago: City of Neighborhoods*. Chicago: Loyola University Press, 1986.

Pietrusza, David. *Judge and Jury*. South Bend, IN: Diamond Communications, 1998.

Pietrusza, David. *Major Leagues*. Jefferson, NC: McFarland & Company, 1991.

Santo, Ron, with Randy Minkoff. *For Love of Ivy*. Chicago: Bonus Books, 1993.

Society for American Baseball Research. *1979 Baseball Research Journal*. Cooperstown, NY: Society for American Baseball Research, 1979.

Society for American Baseball Research. *1981 Baseball Research Journal*. Cooperstown, NY: Society for American Baseball Research, 1981.

Society for American Baseball Research. *The National Pastime, Spring 1985 Edition*. Cooperstown, NY: Society for American Baseball Research, 1985.

The Sporting News, *Take Me Out to the Ball Park*. St. Louis: The Sporting News, 1987.

Talley, Rick. *The Cubs of '69*. Chicago: Contemporary Books, 1989.

Theodore, John. *Baseball's Natural: The Story of Eddie Waitkus*. Carbondale, IL: Southern Illinois University Press, 2002.

Veeck, Bill. *Veeck—as in Wreck*. New York: Bantam Books, 1962.

Wheeler, Lonnie. *A Year in the Bleachers*. Chicago: Contemporary Books, 1988.

Wilbert, Warren. *A Cunning Kind of Play*. Jefferson, NC: McFarland & Company, 2002.

Wood, Bob. *Dodger Dogs to Fenway Franks*. New York: McGraw-Hill, 1988.

◆ NEWSPAPERS

Chicago American
Chicago Daily Journal
Chicago Daily News
Chicago Defender
Chicago Evening Post
Chicago Herald
Chicago Herald-American
Chicago Inter-Ocean
Chicago Reader
Chicago Reporter
Chicago Sun
Chicago Sun-Times
Chicago Today
Chicago Tribune
Good News Weekly
Lerner Newspapers
New York Times
St. Paul Pioneer-Press
The Sporting News
The Times of Northern Indiana

◆ MAGAZINES

Chicago History
Collier's
Consulting/Specifying Engineer
Cubs Magazine
Cubs Quarterly
Harper's Weekly
Leslie's Weekly
Literary Digest
The Saturday Evening Post
Sporting Life
Sports Illustrated

About the Author

This is Stuart Shea's third book, following *Rock & Roll's Most Wanted* and *1960s Most Wanted*, both published by Brassey's.

Shea recently served as an associate editor of Barnes & Noble's new *Baseball Encyclopedia*, as well as co-authoring (with Gary Gillette) two editions of *The USA Today Baseball Weekly Insider*. He also worked for several years as a baseball columnist for America Online and Total Sports. A full-time writer, editor, and researcher, Shea resides twenty-four blocks north of Wrigley Field.

His first game at Wrigley Field, in 1971, was life-changing in at least one way: once Shea realized he couldn't read the numbers on the center-field scoreboard, he had to start wearing glasses.